The NBA's Global Empire

ALSO BY JOSHUA K. WRIGHT
AND FROM MCFARLAND

"*Wake Up, Mr. West*": *Kanye West and the Double Consciousness of Black Celebrity* (2022)

Empire *and Black Images in Popular Culture* (2018)

The NBA's Global Empire

*How the League Became
an International Powerhouse*

Joshua K. Wright

McFarland & Company, Inc., Publishers
Jefferson, North Carolina

LIBRARY OF CONGRESS CATALOGING-IN-PUBLICATION DATA

Names: Wright, Joshua K., 1978– author.
Title: The NBA's global empire : how the league became an international powerhouse / Joshua K. Wright.
Description: Jefferson, North Carolina : McFarland & Company, Inc., Publishers, 2025. | Includes bibliographical references and index.
Identifiers: LCCN 2024062348 | ISBN 9781476695822 (paperback : acid free paper) ∞ ISBN 9781476654683 (ebook)
Subjects: LCSH: National Basketball Association—History. | Basketball—Economic aspects. | Basketball—Marketing. | Sports and globalization.
Classification: LCC GV885.515.N37 W75 2025 | DDC 796.323/6406—dc23/eng/20250102
LC record available at https://lccn.loc.gov/2024062348

ISBN (print) 978-1-4766-9582-2
ISBN (ebook) 978-1-4766-5468-3

© 2025 Joshua K. Wright. All rights reserved

No part of this book may be reproduced or transmitted in any form or by any means, electronic or mechanical, including photocopying or recording, or by any information storage and retrieval system, without permission in writing from the publisher.

Front cover images: (top, left to right) Los Angeles Lakers guard Kobe Bryant (Joseph A. Lee); Denver Nuggets center Nikola Jokić (All-Pro Reels); French EuroLeague ASVEL center/forward Victor Wembanyama (Thomas Savoja); bottom image by Sergey Nivens (Shutterstock)

Printed in the United States of America

McFarland & Company, Inc., Publishers
  Box 611, Jefferson, North Carolina 28640
    www.mcfarlandpub.com

This book is dedicated to Peanut

Table of Contents

Preface 1
Introduction 9

1
It Was All a Dream 19

2
Redemption Song 47

3
Views from the 6ix 73

4
The Joker 100

5
Hoops Diplomacy 131

6
The Air Up There 159

7
American Pastime 185

Epilogue 209
Chapter Notes 215
Bibliography 243
Index 263

Preface

While teaching an Introduction to Global Studies course at Trinity Washington University in 2021, I became increasingly interested in globalization's impact on sports. This curiosity affected the way I consumed my sports. I began counting the number of non–American players dominating Major League Baseball's annual Home Run Derby. Basketball is my favorite sport. As I watched games, I began counting the number of NBA players with names ending in "-vic" (usually denoting they were of European descent). I paid closer attention to ESPN basketball analyst Fran Fraschilla's breakdown of the international talent being considered for the upcoming NBA draft. Eventually, I came across a self-published book, *Basketball Beyond Borders: Globalization of the NBA* (2019), that Chris Milholen, a sports journalist, wrote when he was in college. While *Basketball Beyond Borders* is an in-depth look at the foreign-born players and contributors who have shaped the NBA, it reads more like a tertiary source, providing biographical sketches and contextual information on nearly every significant international player entering the NBA before 2019.

To my surprise, there has been only a limited amount of academic research devoted to the NBA and globalization. Multiple scholarly journal articles and dissertations and theses examine the NBA's business dealings with China. The NBA's expansion into Africa has been discussed a great deal by the African Press Organization. Despite many journal articles and dissertations about globalization and sports, few books exist. In 2023 New York University professor David Hollander published *How Basketball Can Save the World*. Hollander's chapter on globalization includes a draft of the United Nations General Assembly's 2023 resolution for World Basketball Day. Steven Secular's 2023 book, *The Digital NBA: How the World's Savviest League Brings the Court to Our Couch*, is an academic study devoted to the NBA's embrace of cable television, the Internet, digital streaming, and multilingual broadcasting to reach diverse global audiences.

Louis J. Kern's essay "'And One': Bruisers in the Paint and the Globalization of the NBA" in *Contact Spaces of American Culture: Globalizing Local Phenomena* (2012) argues that the NBA is a "contact space" for American and foreign-born athletes to engage in American cultural performances. International players are integrated into American society through this space provided by basketball. Likewise, the NBA's popularity helps to grow the sport of basketball around the world. Jack McCallum's *Dream Team* (2013) is the first and only book to explore the 1992 Olympic team composed of the NBA's premier players in depth. McCallum, an esteemed storyteller and columnist for *Sports Illustrated*, writes the book from a journalistic approach. He also produced *The Dream Team Tapes*, a podcast series produced by iHeartRadio between 2020 and 2021, which offers an oral history of the 1992 and 2008 Olympic teams. The podcast provides excerpts from interviews conducted with the Olympic team players, coaches, media members, and the administrative figures responsible for the NBA's involvement in the Olympics.

Unfortunately, there is a shortage of adequate sports biographies dedicated to foreign-born NBA stars. Thomas Pletzinger's *The Great Nowitzki* (2022) about Dirk Nowitzki and Todd Spehr's *The Mozart of Basketball* (2016) and Todd Spehr's *The Mozart of Basketball*, documenting the late Dražen Petrović, are among the early exceptions. Pletzinger, at times, delves into a deeper discussion that is more appropriate for academic audiences and individuals interested in more than basketball. The most recent biographies, Mike Singer's *Why So Serious? The Untold Story of NBA Champion Nikola Jokic* and Miran Fader's *Dream: The Life and Legacy of Hakeem Olajuwon*, were both published in late 2024 after I completed my manuscript.

Dream is Fader's second sports biography. The senior staff writer for *The Ringer* published *Giannis: The Improbable Rise of an NBA Champion*, profiling Giannis Antetokounmpo in 2022. Doug Smith's *We the North* focuses on the Toronto Raptors and NBA expansion into Canada. Smith explains the league's motives for establishing franchises north of the border in the early 1990s. While there is some discussion of the failed Vancouver Grizzlies expansion experiment, his chief objective is to detail the Raptors' journey from their founding in 1995 to their first NBA championship in 2019.

As I contemplated the possibility of writing a book on this topic, I kept asking myself these dominant questions: What does the NBA's ascension to a billion-dollar global empire teach us about the globalization of American sports and culture since the end of the Cold War and the dawn of the millennium? How beneficial is globalization for the NBA? Is it necessary for American sports leagues to thrive in the 21st century? Is globalization responsible for a decline in American-born NBA players and declining domestic popularity? The findings revealed that international expansion has brought the league prosperity and problems. Yet, the financial benefits and increased viewership outweigh the downside. Globalization keeps the NBA from being entirely outpaced by the National Football League (NFL) and keeps it ahead of Major League Baseball (MLB) in popularity. It has forced most American corporations, including the NBA, to embrace foreign markets and a foreign workforce.

I approach this study from the vantage point of a college professor who is also passionate about the NBA and sports. My methodological approach is primarily qualitative. However, I use quantitative analysis to explain issues such as television ratings, social media analytics, and the use of analytics to evaluate international players like Nikola Jokić. As a trained historian, not a sports journalist or sociologist, I connect past examples with contemporary ones to emphasize significant points and provide historical context. I rely on biographical sources, oral histories, and secondary data analysis throughout the book.

My research includes the previously mentioned readings; academic studies on globalization, basketball, and the NBA; biographies; past interviews with players, coaches, and other related figures; documentaries; newspaper and magazine articles; social media data; and analytical data. I was able to study historical and contemporary game footage on ESPN Classic, the NBA app, NBA Radio, NBA TV, and YouTube. While most of these games are domestic, some international games are sponsored by the International Basketball Federation (FIBA) and the Basketball Africa League (BAL). Throughout the book I explore issues of race, class, geopolitics, international business, and neocolonialism, which required me to review academic books, dissertations, news documentaries, and articles published in the domestic and foreign press.

I was fortunate to interview David Aldridge, a prominent NBA writer for *The Athletic* and recipient of the Curt Gowdy Award by the Naismith Basketball Hall of Fame. Aldridge was featured numerous times in the Emmy Award–winning 2020 docuseries *The Last Dance* and was even portrayed by comedian Chris Redd in a *Saturday Night Live* spoof of the docuseries. Excerpts from our conversation will appear throughout the text. I limited my focus to Africa, Asia, Canada, and Europe. Although the NBA had 33 players from Australia, including lottery picks Ben Simmons and Josh Giddey in 2022, I did not focus on Australasia due to a lack of significant research and sources. Although I avoided Latin America and the Caribbean for similar reasons, the NBA has included many Puerto Rican players dating back to Alfred "Butch" Lee, Jr., drafted in 1978.[1] There were five players of Caribbean descent on 2024 NBA rosters.[2]

This book is written in a manner to appeal to both academic and popular audiences. Academicians and secondary school teachers teaching courses on global studies and international affairs can use this book as a resource to discuss the globalization of American sports. Likewise, researchers studying the NBA, sports business, the globalization of sports, and the intersection of sports and popular culture should find this book helpful. However, I did not intend to limit this book to classrooms or scholarly research groups. It is also for basketball zealots and casual NBA fans who have grown up following the exploits of their favorite players and teams. It is for the millennials and Generation Zers in the U.S. and abroad addicted to NBA highlights on YouTube and the latest breaking NBA news on social media, the NBA app, and morning sports debate shows like ESPN's *First Take*. Hopefully, this study will not only help sports fans understand how and why the NBA has globalized, creating a successful international business model for other leagues to copy, but also help them think critically about the benefits and drawbacks of globalization.

The book consists of seven chapters, which document the evolution of globalization in the NBA and address its effects on the league. The final chapter compares the impact of globalization on the NBA with that of its chief competitors, the NFL and MLB.

Chapter 1: It Was All a Dream

The 1992 Dream Team set the stage for the globalization of the NBA at the Summer Olympic Games in Barcelona, Spain. The Dream Team was created following an embarrassing subpar finish at the 1988 Summer Olympics and the World Championships. Fearing it was falling behind the rest of the world in basketball, America replaced collegiate amateurs with the NBA's most accomplished players. The team's success and a shrewd marketing campaign by the sneaker giant Nike elevated its star, Michael Jordan, the league's best and most exciting player, to unfathomable heights that would eventually make him a billionaire. This chapter explores the origins of the Dream Team and Michael Jordan's rise to global superstardom. It also analyzes how the Dream Team and Jordan promoted not just the league and the game of basketball but, more importantly, capitalism and American exceptionalism worldwide at the dawn of the post–Cold War era.

Chapter 2: Redemption Song

The Dream Team's success in Barcelona was a gift and a curse for the NBA. It introduced the NBA's product and incredible talent pool to the world. Basketball rapidly became the world's second most popular sport, behind soccer. Consequently, the world caught up with the U.S. by the mid-2000s. While the Dream Team and its early successors overwhelmed all foreign competitors who played in awe of them, this was no longer the case by 2004. A poor bronze medal-winning performance in the 2004 Olympics led to the creation of a new USA Basketball program and the formation of the "Redeem Team" at the 2008 Summer Olympics in Beijing, China. This chapter explores how this team, led by America's most respected college coach, Mike Krzyzewski, succeeded in reestablishing the U.S. as a world leader in basketball and carrying out a larger objective—selling American patriotism in a post–9/11 world. The chapter also focuses on the ascension of the team's two headliners, Kobe Bryant and LeBron James, to global stardom.

Chapter 3: Views from the 6ix

In 1995, the NBA created two new teams in Canada: the Toronto Raptors and the Vancouver Grizzlies. They were the first additions since Canada's inaugural 1946–47 basketball season. The Grizzlies eventually relocated to Memphis after six losing seasons; however, the Raptors remained Canada's team and became one of the world's most popular sports franchises thanks to American-born players like Vince Carter; their crafty Nigerian general manager, Masai Ujiri; a devoted native and immigrant fanbase; and their connection to Drake, Canada's homegrown global hip-hop superstar. The Raptors' success culminated with a stunning defeat of the league's reigning dynasty, the Golden State Warriors, in the 2019 NBA Finals to capture Canada's first world championship. This chapter assesses the NBA's expansion into the northern border by examining the following questions: How did the Raptors teams of the 1990s inspire an entire generation of Canadian-born players who eventually made their mark in the NBA by the 2010s and 2020s? What do the NBA's mixed results in Canada mean for future international expansion in other parts of the world?

Chapter 4: The Joker

In the early 1980s, the NBA was on the verge of collapse. Globalization was an unlikely pipe dream at this point. Critics lambasted the league for being "too Black." The league's lifeline came with the introduction of "safe" and "unthreatening" Black stars Earvin "Magic" Johnson and Michael Jordan, and the Boston Celtics' newest leading man, Larry Bird. Bird unwittingly became the NBA's version of the Great White Hope. Bird's retirement in 1992, shortly after his Dream Team appearance, marked the beginning of the end for the American-born white superstar in the NBA. Over the next three decades, fewer American white players were drafted into the league. Globalization unintentionally became the cause and solution to the growing absence of white American players. Europe has produced the league's highest number of foreign-born players since the 1990s. In recent years, some current and retired Black players and Black media members have called out racial bias in the coverage and praise of certain white European players like Nikola Jokić, arguably the best player in the NBA. This chapter analyzes the evolution of the NBA's white European talent pool and the polarizing debate over racial bias.

Chapter 5: Hoops Diplomacy

The Harlem Globetrotters were America's earliest version of basketball diplomats. They used hoops to spread goodwill around the world in the 1950s. The Globetrotters were called on again in the 21st century to join an unlikely new sports ambassador to spread goodwill in arguably the most restrictive country on the planet: North Korea. The Globetrotters accompanied retired NBA "bad boy" Dennis Rodman for an exhibition for that country's dictator, Kim Jong Un. During the 1990s, Kim Jong Un became obsessed with Rodman's Chicago Bulls team.

Rodman's controversial attempts to broker peace with North Korea and convince Russia to free imprisoned WNBA star Brittney Griner in 2022 could be viewed as positive effects of the NBA's globalization. Likewise, the NBA's refusal to speak out against China's mistreatment of Hong Kong citizens in 2019 due to a significant financial commitment of China, its largest foreign partner, is a sign of globalization's adverse effects. The NBA's silence and complicity in human rights violations abroad for financial reasons contradicted the league's constant outspokenness on domestic civil rights issues involving Black Americans. This chapter will explore the NBA's role in diplomacy and geopolitics.

Chapter 6: The Air Up There

In 1984, Hakeem Olajuwon made history by becoming the first African-born player to be selected as the overall top pick in the NBA draft. The future Hall-of-Famer was chosen ahead of future legends Michael

Jordan and Charles Barkley. Olajuwon's success and other Africans like Manute Bol and Dikembe Mutombo paved the way for a future generation of African-born stars and role players making up NBA rosters in the millennium. Joel Embiid, the 2022–23 league Most Valuable Player (MVP), was born on the continent. Both two-time MVP Giannis Antetokounmpo and the 2023–24 Rookie of the Year, Victor Wembanyama, are the children of African fathers. The NBA is committed to Africa in ways that are not seen in Europe or Asia. In 2021, the NBA launched the Basketball Africa League (BAL), which is a joint effort between the NBA and the International Basketball Federation (FIBA) with sponsorship from American corporations Nike, Pepsi, and Jordan Brand. ESPN and NBA TV provide television coverage of BAL games. Is the NBA's relationship with Africa a positive effect of globalization or the sports equivalent of the neocolonialism that has been taking place in Africa in recent years? How much does Africa have to gain from this relationship? This chapter will analyze these questions while spotlighting significant African NBA players and the evolution of the NBA on the continent.

Chapter 7: American Pastime

The NBA may never become America's pastime. Major League Baseball (MLB) has held that title since the Civil War. The National Football League (NFL) surpassed baseball in domestic popularity in the 1970s. During the 21st century, the NFL has steadily outpaced the NBA and MLB in domestic viewership and ticket sales. Nevertheless, the NFL, despite recent efforts, lags far behind both leagues in terms of globalization. MLB has embraced globalization for decades. Asia and Latin America, especially the Dominican Republic, have become breeding grounds for professional baseball talent. More than 28 percent of MLB players in 2022 had been born outside the United States. This chapter compares the NBA's global influence with that of the NFL and MLB. How beneficial is globalization to the NBA's leading competitors?

Introduction

The streets of Denver, Colorado, were packed with tens of thousands of revelers cheering on their favorite basketball players as they rode atop fire trucks and buses during a festive parade. The Denver Nuggets had just defeated the Miami Heat in the 2022–23 NBA Finals to capture the franchise's first world championship. Drunken Denver players and their drunken head coach, Mike Malone, jumped on the microphone like rowdy college frat boys to hype up their adoring crowd and proclaim that another championship parade was ensured for the next summer. Caught up in the moment and clearly intoxicated, the team's superstar and leader, Nikola Jokić, could not refrain from dropping an F-bomb as he told the fans how much he was enjoying the parade. The horse-loving Serbian center and his Canadian sidekick, Jamal Murray, captured the sports world's attention during their two-month playoff run to the championship. Many sports fans consider Jokić the best basketball player in the world and one of the most transcendent players in NBA history.

Four days after the Nuggets' parade, another European was the talk of the town. Victor Wembanyama was in the Big Apple, taking his first ride on the New York City subway system and throwing out the first pitch at Yankee Stadium. While his pitch was only moderately better than 50 Cent's infamous attempt, none of the hundred reporters in attendance were there to critique his curveball.[1] Wembanyama, a 7'3½" 19-year-old center from France with an eight-foot wingspan, was in town for the NBA draft later that week at Brooklyn's Barclays Center. Wembanyama (or Wemby for short) became a viral sensation, the most-talked-about teenage athlete in the world, with two jaw-dropping performances in Las Vegas, Nevada, in October 2022. The biracial French phenom accumulated 73 points, nine three-pointers, 15 rebounds, and nine blocked shots in two exhibition games against G League Ignite, the marquee squad of the NBA's development league (the G League). In their first exhibition, he matched up against Ignite point guard Sterling "Scoot" Henderson, the third overall pick in the 2023 NBA draft.[2]

Victor Wembanyama grew up west of Paris in Le Chesnay. At 14, he left home to live in a dorm provided by Nanterre, a French basketball club. He began playing professionally a year later. Wembanyama's Las Vegas performances made him the lead story in sports media and received praise from many high-profile NBA stars. LeBron James called him an alien. "He's like the [NBA] 2K create-a-player, every point guard that wants to be 7-foot. Cheat-code-type vibes, man," said Stephen Curry.[3] NBA commissioner Adam Silver told reporters in Abu Dhabi, where he was visiting for an NBA preseason game between the Hawks and Bucks, that he expects this kid to change the game. Silver even warned teams against tanking their seasons to earn the number-one pick in the 2023 draft lottery to select him.[4]

Fans who wanted to see what all the fuss was about could livestream Wembanyama's games on the NBA app using their computers and smartphones. He was the world's eighth-most-searched basketball player on social media in 2022–23. ESPN's Brian Windhorst, who flew to Paris twice to profile the young phenom, described him as the most anticipated amateur prospect to enter the NBA since LeBron in 2003.[5] Windhorst called him a hybrid of Kevin Durant and Kareem Abdul-Jabbar. Durant is a skinny 6'10" forward with the dribbling skills of a small guard who can shoot from anywhere on the court. Jabbar, a 7'2" center, was the NBA's all-time scoring champion from 1984 until LeBron surpassed him in 2023. ESPN's Adrian Wojnarowski called Wembanyama the most anticipated prospect in the history of all American team sports. Some NBA executives told Wojnarowski they anticipated him becoming the league's best offensive and defensive player by his third year.

The week of the draft, every major American newspaper featured a story on Wembanyama. *NBC Nightly News* ended its June 20 episode with a segment dedicated to this intriguing Frenchman. Robin Roberts interviewed him for ABC's *Good Morning America* on the eve of the draft. When asked if he was ready for all the pressure and expectations, he confidently told Roberts that was nothing compared with the goals he had already set for himself. Windhorst continued to rave on ESPN about the kid's intentional efforts to master English and play professional ball in Europe to prepare himself for the NBA and American life. The San Antonio Spurs, a franchise known for winning with international talent, selected Wembanyama as the top pick in the draft on June 22, 2023.[6] Wembanyama, who sported a double-breasted forest green Louis Vuitton suit with rings on fingers of each hand, described the five-minute waiting period to hear his name called first by Commissioner Silver as the longest five minutes of his life. Overcome with emotion, he broke down in tears during an interview with ESPN's Monica McNutt and his siblings, Oscar

(16) and Eve (22). "Oh my God, I am a Spur." The oddest moment in all the Wembymania came two weeks later in Las Vegas when Wembanyama was in town for the NBA Summer League. Pop idol Britney Spears reached out to tap his shoulder when she saw him walking by. His security guard, unaware of who she was, slapped her hand away, causing Spears to inadvertently hit herself in the face. Spears initially threatened to press charges but dropped them after a police investigation determined she was unintentionally harmed.[7]

One of the biggest highlights of Wembanyama's stellar rookie season was a matchup with Jokić, arguably the league's best player, on April 2, 2024. Although the Nuggets won the game, Wemby stole the show with an impressive 23 points, 15 rebounds, eight assists, nine blocks, and one steal. When Wembanyama played his first regular-season game with the Spurs, he joined hundreds of foreign-born talents in the league. At the start of the 2022–23 season, there were 109 international players from 39 countries. Jokić was the reigning two-time league Most Valuable Player (MVP). Luka Dončić from Slovenia of the Dallas Mavericks was one of the favorites to win the MVP award that season. The eventual winner was Philadelphia 76ers center Joel Embiid from Cameroon. There was the Houston Rockets' emerging Turkish superstar, Alperen Şengün, entering his sophomore season. A 2023–24 ESPN preseason poll ranked five foreign-born players representing Africa, Canada, and Europe among the NBA's 10 best current players. The Milwaukee Bucks' Greek power forward, Giannis Antetokounmpo, the 2019 and 2020 league MVP, was voted the best player on the list.[8]

The 2023–24 season had a record 125 international players on opening-night rosters. Thirteen international players were involved in the 2024 NBA finals. Twenty-six foreign press outlets covered those finals.[9] The NBA's international appeal was reflected not only in its players and growing global fanbase but also in its governorship. Three of the league's 30-team governors were foreign-born. The Sacramento Kings were governed by the wealthy Maloof family, of Lebanese and Irish descent, until they sold the franchise to Vivek Yeshwant Ranadivé in 2013. Ranadivé is the founder and former CEO of real-time computing firm TIBCO and Teknekron Software Systems. Ranadivé, a native of Mumbai, India, is the first person of Indian descent to govern an NBA team.[10] Joseph Tsai, a Taiwanese-born Canadian businessman and the co-founder of the e-commerce company Alibaba, is the governor of the Brooklyn Nets.[11] He purchased the Nets from Russian billionaire Mikhail Prokhorov in 2019 for $2.35 billion, the highest price paid for an American sports team that year.[12] For clarification, the NBA began using the term *governor* in place of *owner* in 2019 because of the optics of having a league composed mostly of Black men calling White billionaires their owners.[13]

Larry Tanenbaum, a Canadian businessman and the chairman of Maple Leaf Sports & Entertainment, purchased the Toronto Raptors in 1998. Tanenbaum is the grandson of a Polish immigrant who settled in New York before moving to Toronto, Canada. Besides governing the Raptors, he oversees the Toronto Maple Leafs Hockey Club. Under the leadership of Tanenbaum and his president of basketball operations, Masai Ujiri (a Canadian citizen with Nigerian and Kenyan heritage), the Raptors won the 2019 NBA Finals. They are the only non–American team to capture an NBA title. The Raptors are currently coached by Serbian native Darko Rajaković, who caught the sports world's attention with an epic 2024 rant about NBA officiating following a loss to the Los Angeles Lakers.

Every June, the NBA hosts its annual draft for teams to select the top young amateur prospects. After Commissioner Silver finishes announcing the players taken in the lottery and first round, Mark Tatum takes over for the final hours of the internationally televised event. In 2014, Tatum was elected as the league's deputy commissioner. The Vietnamese native, ranked by *Forbes* as one of the 10 most influential minorities in sports, migrated to the United States when he was a young boy and grew up in Brooklyn. Silver was former NBA commissioner David Stern's top assistant for eight years before replacing him in 2014. The 55-year-old Tatum is a logical successor to Silver.

Defining Globalization

NBA players have become fashion icons, social activists, and diplomatic ambassadors worldwide. It has become a nightly social media pastime to watch NBA players "walk the runway" as they enter the arenas in their best, Instagram-ready pregame (out)fits. Many are sporting attire, unisex handbags, designer sneakers, and styles that originated overseas. For example, Belgian fashion designer Raf Simons created Kyle Kuzma's utterly ridiculous giant pink sweater. Images of Kuzma's sweater "broke the internet" in America and other parts of the world. The league's international appeal is a byproduct of globalization. What is globalization, and how is this connected to sports?

In recent years globalization has transformed everything about our way of life in America. Our technology, education, entertainment, employment, environment, and politics have all been impacted as our world becomes increasingly smaller. Most of us unconsciously experience it daily. The T-shirts and hoodies we buy from Walmart are often produced by poor young women and girls working in hot factories in Bangladesh and Vietnam. Pietra Rivoli's *The Travels of a T-Shirt in the Global*

Economy (2014) is required reading in my Introduction to Global Studies course. Rivoli takes readers on a T-shirt's journey from the cotton fields in Lubbock, Texas, to factories in Shanghai, China, to American department stores and receiving ports for "mitumbu" (Swahili term for bundles of used clothing) in Tanzania.[14] Are you a parent? The Nike or Adidas shoes that your kids wear were likely made in Asia. Mark Juergensmeyer explains globalization this way:

> Globalization permeates the air that you breathe. It affects your weather, as cycles of warming and cooling air react to global climate change. And globalization is part of the food that you eat. This is obvious if you have a taste for Chinese take-out or pad Thai noodles or Mexican burritos.... When I visit the McDonald's in Delhi, I find that none of the hamburgers are, in fact, beef burgers, reflecting the predominantly vegetarian eating customers of people in India. In Kyoto's McDonald's, you can get a Teriyaki McBurger; and in the McDonald's in Milan, the sophisticated Italians may choose pasta rather than fries.[15]

Globalization is the process of interaction and integration among companies, governments, people, and cultures around the world. I lead an undergraduate course called Global Hip-Hop that teaches students how this art form and culture, birthed in the South Bronx on August 11, 1973, now influences every part of the world. Likewise, hip-hop borrows from other global musical genres like Afrobeat and dancehall. Thomas Friedman, a columnist for the *New York Times*, says globalization began with the collapse of the Berlin Wall in 1989 and the dawn of a New World Order.[16] However, English sociologist Roland Robertson coined this term in a scholarly article as early as 1985. Robertson used sociological theory to explain this concept in his 1992 book *Globalization: Social Theory and Global Culture*. Robertson also authored the 2009 book *Globalization and Football*, a study of soccer's (futbol's) international growth and appeal. Before Robertson's book, Martin Albrow and Elizabeth King, sociologists from England, published *Globalization, Knowledge, and Society* in 1990. In a more recent study, *Globalization: A Very Short Introduction* (2020), Australian scholar Manfred Steger argues that globalization became a phenomenon between the end of the Cold War and 2000. According to Steger, 9/11 resulted from our global interconnectedness in terms of ideology and technology. "Some observers argue that the terrorist attack was the violent expression of anti-globalization; it was an act of revenge by people marginalized by the global economy," writes Lael Brainard.[17]

Interest in the globalization of sports grew in the 2000s. Alan Bairner argues in his 2003 article "Globalization and Sport: The Nation Strikes Back" that globalization of sports began as early as the 19th century. Bairner points to the diffusion of sports founded in Great Britain due to global migrations. As athletes left the island, they took their native games to their new destinations. Furthermore, the modern Olympics and the FIFA World Cup in soccer predate the years that sociologists and economists associate with globalization.[18] To revive France following the Franco-Prussian War (1870–71), French Aristocrat Baron Pierre de Coubertin adopted the sporting ethics of the American colleges and British schools he had visited during the 1880s.[19] He was inspired to revive the Olympic games of ancient Greece to accomplish his goal.[20] The first modern games were held in Athens in 1896.

On July 13, 1930, France defeated Mexico 4–1 in soccer's first World Cup in Montevideo, Uruguay. Today, the Olympics and FIFA World Cup both bring nations together from around the globe during times of war and peace. In 1950, the inaugural FIBA Basketball World Cup was held. This event is an international tournament between the senior men's national teams of the member countries belonging to FIBA. Currently, there are 32 teams in FIBA. The United States and Yugoslavia have won the most championships (five each). Many international NBA players represent their countries in the FIBA World Cup and the Olympics. Some players with dual citizenship, such as Joel Embiid, have opted to represent the U.S. in international play.

The NBA and Globalization

On March 11, 2020, the NBA became the first American sports league to shut down due to the coronavirus (Covid-19). The move was precipitated by a positive Covid test result for Rudy Gobert, the Utah Jazz's 7'1" center from France, who playfully breathed over all the microphones at a postgame press conference days earlier. The NBA's decision to suspend their season created a trickle-down effect in the world of sports at all levels of play. Before long, most people around the globe were self-isolating in their homes due to this new pandemic. The absence of live sports left a void in programming for ESPN, the world's most-watched cable sports network. Consequently, the network promoted the April 19, 2020, premiere of its new docuseries, *The Last Dance*, as if it was the NFL draft (an event overpromoted for two months). ESPN's 11 p.m. *SportsCenter* host Scott Van Pelt provided an hourlong post-show analysis. Van Pelt delivered the highlights from the series' premiere as if they were from an actual game. ESPN repeated this spectacle every Sunday evening for the next four weeks.

The Last Dance, a 10-part Emmy Award–winning docuseries coproduced by ESPN Films and Netflix, covered the final season (1997–98) of the Chicago Bulls dynasty. The film focused heavily on Bulls star Michael

Jordan, taking viewers on an exhilarating journey from Jordan's early years as a skinny kid (with hair) in North Carolina to his final season in Chicago. The debut episode started with the mesmerizing flow of the Notorious B.I.G. singing the hook to Puff Daddy's number-one *Billboard* hit "Been Around the World."

"*Been around the world and I I I. And we been player hated. I don't know, and I don't know why … bay-bee-bay-bee!*"[21]

By the late 1990s, the Chicago Bulls had become the world's most famous team and basketball's equivalent of the Beatles, with Jordan cast as John Lennon and Paul McCartney rolled into a 6'6" athletic frame and baggy shorts. Seventeen minutes into the episode, the film's location shifted from the Windy City to Paris, France. The Bulls arrived in the City of Love on October 15, 1997, for what the film's caption described as an international preseason exhibition tournament. As Jordan strolled through the streets of Paris wearing a black beret turned backward, throngs of media members and adoring fans followed behind as if he were the pied piper. "Some say he's bigger than the pope," stated one reporter. The front page of a local newspaper, *L'Equipe*, read "Jordan Attendu Comme Un Roi," which means enters like a king or royalty. After posing for team photos in front of the Eiffel Tower, Jordan (or MJ as fans affectionately call him) was off for an appearance on the *Nulle Part Ailleurs Show*. The live audience stood to their feet and applauded as Jordan, dressed immaculately in a light brown tailored suit, a blue shirt with a crisp white collar, tie, and his trademark gold hoop earring in his left ear, walked onto the stage.

Commissioner David Stern addressed the team in the locker room before their first game. The fans, many wearing Bulls jerseys, had been lining up outside the stadium since early that morning for a chance to see the NBA's top headliners in action. Once play began, Jordan was in regular-season form, hitting his fadeaway jump shots, gliding to the basket, hanging in the air, and slam-dunking in a fresh pair of "He Got Game" Air Jordan 13s.[22] No NBA team had lost a game in this tournament's history, and the five-time defending NBA champions did not plan to be the first. The Bulls easily swept through their competition. As the players walked off the court at the end of the championship game, one of the players from Greek professional basketball club Olympiacos Piraeus asked Jordan for the armband he was wearing. Jordan, who had just scored 27 points, politely obliged and continued walking to the locker room to celebrate another trophy presentation.

This international tournament was known as the McDonald's Open. It was a promotional event sponsored by the NBA and FIBA between 1987 and 1999. Commissioner Stern and Borislav "Bora" Stanković, FIBA's secretary general, organized the tournament to unite American and European basketball. The tournament, debuting in Milwaukee in 1987, attracted the NBA's best teams during the era. Defending NBA champions and finalists like the Bulls, Los Angeles Lakers, Houston Rockets, Phoenix Suns, and San Antonio Spurs competed. Jordan won the tournament's 1997 MVP award named in honor of the late Croatian-born NBA star Dražen Petrović. Petrović, Vlade Divac, Dino Radja, and Jordan's Chicago teammate Toni Kukoč were among the European-born NBA stars representing their home countries in the tournament.[23]

The McDonald's Open was not the NBA's first attempt to expand globally. The Washington Bullets lost to Maccabi Tel Aviv 98–97 on September 9, 1978. The game in Tel Aviv, Israel, was the NBA's first international game of the modern era.[24] The Bullets, winners of the 1978 NBA championship, took their talents abroad three more times in 1979, becoming the first professional American team to play in communist China. They defeated the Chinese National Team in the capital city of Beijing 96–85. Next, they beat the Shanghai team, led by 6'10" center Yao Zhiyuan (father of the 2002 overall number-one NBA draft pick Yao Ming), 113–80.[25] Their final victory, 133–123, came against the Philippine Basketball Association All-Stars. The game was played in the Philippines, and the country's first lady, Imelda Marcos, was in attendance.

In 1984, the New Jersey Nets and the Phoenix Suns represented NBA teams traveling abroad. However, these teams were less successful than the Bullets. The Nets lost to Maccabi Tel Aviv 104–97 on June 28. The Suns suffered a 113–97 defeat at the hands of the same team two days later. The Seattle Supersonics played exhibition games in Germany, Italy, and Switzerland in August 1984. The Sonics were undefeated for their entire road trip. Four years later, the Atlanta Hawks became the first NBA team to play in the Soviet Union (USSR). The Hawks struggled to beat the Soviet National Team in two exhibition games before losing a third game by nine points.[26] Today it is common for NBA teams to play preseason exhibition games internationally and for foreign teams to play in the U.S. While the NBA teams win most of these games, there are rare exceptions. On October 2, 2022, the Adelaide 36ers, the seventh-best team from Australia's 10-team National Basketball League (NBL), stunned the Phoenix Suns 134–124 in Phoenix. This game was the first time an NBA lost to an international team since the Oklahoma City Thunder lost to future NBA star Luka Dončić and Real Madrid 142–137 in 2016.[27]

During the 1970s and 1980s, coaches like Hubie Brown and Lenny Wilkens began holding clinics in Europe and Asia to introduce the NBA's brand of basketball to kids and young men abroad. Coach Don Nelson and his son, Donnie, were instrumental in mining Lithuania for talent in the mid-'80s. The Golden State Warriors, coached by the Nelsons, drafted Lithuanian Raimondas Šarūnas Marčiulionis in 1987. A group of NBA players, including future Hall-of-Famer Earl "the Pearl" Monroe, traveled to China in 1984 with other NBA All-Stars for exhibition games serving as diplomacy. Their trip helped plant the seeds for the league's current popularity in the country. China is now the NBA's largest global market. The league ran an academy there from 2016 to 2019. Several former NBA players have extended their careers by playing in China.

The NBA has had international ties since its birth. Canadian educator Dr. James Naismith introduced the sport of basketball in 1891. On November 1, 1946, the New York Knickerbockers played the Toronto Huskies in Toronto, Canada, in the inaugural game of the new Basketball Association of America (BAA). In 1949, the BAA merged with the National Basketball League, the first professional basketball league, dating back to 1898, to form the NBA. The 1946 Knicks-Huskies game is counted as the NBA's first official game because the league includes the BAA's three seasons in its history.[28]

The first two international players in the NBA also had Canadian ties. Hank Biasatti was a member of the Huskies team that played the Knicks. Biasatti was born in Italy but was raised in Windsor, Ontario. Another Canadian player, Gino Sovran, also played for the Huskies. The NBA had 84 international players from 38 countries and territories in its 2010–11 seasons compared with only three players in its 1993–94 season.[29] One of those international players that season was Dirk Nowitzki from Germany. Nowitzki steered his Dallas Mavericks to a shocking upset of the favored Miami Heat, featuring LeBron James and Dwyane Wade, in the 2011 NBA Finals. Three years later, the Heat suffered defeat in the finals against the Spurs, who were led by center Tim Duncan (from the Virgin Islands), point guard Tony Parker (from France), and shooting guard Manu Ginobili (from Italy). Each Spurs player has since been inducted into the Naismith Memorial Basketball Hall of Fame. Ginobili delivered his induction speech in English and his native tongue. Parker was one of three international players, including Nowitzki and Spain's Pau Gasol, inducted into a historic 2023 Hall of Fame class.[30]

Basketball Without Borders was formed in 2001. An academy system was established in 2016 to provide athletic and academic opportunities for prospective young players in Africa, Asia, Australia, and Latin America. The league began holding games abroad annually in the early 1990s. The Bahamas and Puerto Rico were among the earliest destinations. A series of preseason games have been held in Canada almost every year since 2012. An annual game has been played in Mexico City since 2014. Abu Dhabi has hosted two preseason games since 2022. Since 2020, the NBA has held two regular-season games in Paris.[31] The inaugural In-Season Tournament, renamed the Emirates NBA Cup, was held from November 3 to December 9, 2023. The NBA modeled this event after European soccer tournaments, which are extremely popular internationally. The league's 30 teams were divided into five groups within their conferences based on their win-loss records. After nearly four weeks of action, eight teams advanced to the single-game elimination knockout round (quarterfinals). The semifinals and championship games were held in Las Vegas. The last team standing won the new NBA Cup.[32]

The In-Season Tournament was intended to liven up the often-mundane action of early season games with a vibe akin to March Madness (NCAA basketball tournament). The games were highlighted by the special courts used instead of the traditional hardwood floors. The new court designs, fully painted in bold and vibrant colors, like purple and neon green, with an enlarged image of the NBA Cup at center court, garnered as much attention on social media as the players' performances. The Lakers defeated the Indiana Pacers in the championship game. The Bucks, led by Greece's Giannis Antetokounmpo, won the cup the next year. At the conclusion of the 2023–24 season, the league's best players spent their summer in Paris playing for Team USA or their native countries at the Olympics. This marked the 22nd anniversary of the Dream Team's Olympic debut in Barcelona, the moment responsible for the NBA's current global dynasty.

1

It Was All a Dream

It is a Thursday night, sometime in December, around 1:00 a.m. It is far too late for any sensible person with work in the morning to be up watching television. Yet there I was, listening to TNT's award-winning *Inside the NBA*. The TNT crew—Ernie (Johnson), Kenny (Smith), Charles (Barkley), and Shaq (Shaquille O'Neal)—were up to their usual shenanigans. Barkley, the brightest star of this foursome, sarcastically asked why they had to pretend to be excited breaking down the highlights of the lousy 30-point blowout that viewers had just painfully watched for the last two hours. Barkley is one of America's few celebrities who can irreverently say almost anything without repercussion. The rest of the world got its first taste of "Sir Charles" at the 1992 Summer Olympics in Barcelona, Spain. "I don't know anything about Angola, but Angola is in trouble," he told reporters during a press conference leading up to the Dream Team's first game against the lowly team from Angola.[1]

The Dream Team moniker has been overused over the years. It was applied to O.J. Simpson's star-studded defense team in his 1995 double-murder trial. Quarterback Vince Young used the moniker to describe his overrated 2011 Philadelphia Eagles roster. But there is only one true Dream Team, the U.S. men's basketball team at the 1992 Summer Olympics. Barkley was among the 11 NBA stars selected to fill out the 12-player roster. His Nostradamus–like prediction about Angola came to fruition. The U.S. won by a lopsided score of 116–48. The victory was marred by an ugly incident in the second half when Barkley received a technical foul for intentionally elbowing Angolan player Herlander Coimbra, who was less than twice his size. In his postgame press interviews, Barkley claimed that Coimbra had elbowed him three times before he retaliated. "People always say turn the other cheek. You turn the other cheek; I will hit that cheek, too," said Barkley.[2] A public butt whipping did not prevent Angolan players from asking their American idols to pose for pictures after the game. A few Angolans requested autographs before the game started. Despite being criticized by some journalists for playing the part of the "ugly American" in the Dream Team's debut, Barkley became a beloved figure in Barcelona. If a large crowd gathered on La Rambla, a tree-lined pedestrian street in the city, after hours, Barkley would surely be in plain sight. The Angola trouncing was a prelude to the Dream Team's legendary two-week odyssey to a gold medal and much more.

The Dream Team set the stage for the NBA's globalization. Fearing that it was falling behind the rest of the world in basketball, the U.S. decided to replace its collegiate amateurs with the NBA's most accomplished players on the Olympic roster. The Dream Team's success and a shrewd marketing campaign by the sneaker giant Nike elevated the team's marquee star, Michael Jordan, the league's best and most exciting player, to unfathomable heights that would eventually make him a billionaire. This chapter explores the origins of the Dream Team and Michael Jordan's rise to global superstardom. It also analyzes how the Dream Team and Jordan promoted not just the league and the game of basketball but also, more importantly, capitalism and American exceptionalism worldwide at the dawn of the post–Cold War era.

Olympic Hoops Before the Dream Team

Charles Barkley was only nine when the U.S. suffered its first Olympic loss. This improbable defeat occurred during the gold medal game at the 1972 games in Munich, Germany. Those games were overshadowed by a Palestinian terrorist group called Black September killing two Israeli Olympic team members and taking nine others hostage.[3] The U.S. played the Soviet Union (USSR) in the gold medal game just before midnight on September 7, three days after the Munich massacre. There were 6500 pro–Soviet fans packing the gymnasium to cheer on the USSR. By 1972, basketball had become a tool for the Soviets to prove their might. A win against the Americans equated to communism's striking a blow to capitalism.[4]

International basketball was limited to America's best collegiate players at the time. The U.S. trailed the USSR 26–21 at halftime. During the second half, both teams traded blows like two elite prizefighters in the ring. The U.S. was down 49–48 with 10 seconds remaining in the game when their power forward Tom McMillen blocked Soviet Sergei Belov's shot. Belov recovered the ball and accidentally threw it to American shooting guard Doug Collins.[5] Most NBA fans in their mid-30s to late 40s know Collins as a broadcaster for NBA games on TNT and, previously, NBC. After an eight-year career with the Philadelphia 76ers, who selected him with the overall top pick in the 1973 draft, Collins went on to coach

Michael Jordan in Chicago (1986–1989) and Washington, D.C. (2001–2003), and 1996 Olympian Grant Hill in Detroit (1995–1998). Collins was a student at Illinois State University when he played in Munich. As previously stated, Belov's errant pass was picked off by Collins, who was fouled on his way to the basket. His head was buried in the stanchion as he lay face down on the court. Collins said he felt like he had been knocked out in a fight. Once he gathered himself, Collins walked up to the foul line to knock down two free throws, giving the U.S. a one-point lead. Then all hell broke loose.[6]

As Collins took his second free throw, the scorer's table horn blew. FIBA rules prohibited coaches from calling time-outs after a second foul shot was taken. However, a coach could alert the scorer's table to their desire for a time-out by either pushing a button on the bench that set off a red light or walking up to the table to call a time-out. Since USSR coach Vladimir Kondrashin did not appear to signal a time-out, the Soviets prepared to inbound the ball from under their own basket after Collins finished shooting. Kondrashin angrily told the officials at the scorer's table that he had signaled for a time-out when Collins first walked up to the foul line. Unaware of this interaction, his players inbounded the ball and proceeded to play. Suddenly, FIBA secretary general R. William Jones, sitting nearby in the stands, told the officials to stop the game, place three seconds on the shot clock, and allow the USSR to replay the final seconds. The Soviets failed to score. The U.S. claimed its eighth consecutive gold medal.[7]

The American celebration on the court had barely begun when Bulgarian referee Artenik Arabajan told officials he had given the ball to Ivan Edeshko, the Soviet player inbounding the ball, before resetting the shot clock. U.S. coach Hank Iba objected to Arabajan's claim, but his protest was ignored. The USSR inbounded the ball for a third time. Edeshko passed the ball to Belov, who hit a turnaround layup as time expired to win the game.[8] Belov sprinted down the court rejoicing with his arms raised to the heavens. The U.S., believing that they had been robbed of the gold, immediately filed a protest. A five-person jury vote of 3–2 defeated their appeal. All three negative votes came from jury members affiliated with pro–Soviet communist countries. Coach Iba and his players refused to participate in the medal ceremony and declined their silver medals.[9]

The 1972 defeat during the middle of the Cold War was a catastrophic shock to the American athletes and their fans back home. American troops were still in Vietnam fighting a proxy war with the Soviet-backed Viet Cong. The youth of America were in the streets and on college campuses protesting this war. From a purely athletic standpoint, the Soviet loss was new territory for Americans. The U.S. men's team had won every gold medal in Olympic history. Basketball was first introduced at the

1936 Summer Olympics in Berlin, Germany. Those games were renowned for African American track star Jesse Owens disrupting host Adolf Hitler's plan to use the games for his racist Nazi propaganda.[10] While Owens was running and jumping to earn four gold medals, the U.S. basketball team defeated Canada 19–8 to clinch their first gold. The 1936 U.S. Olympic squad consisted of players from the Universal Pictures Amateur Athletic Union (AAU) of Hollywood, California, and the Phillips Globe Oilers AAU team from McPherson, Kansas.

Hitler's invasion of Poland three years after the Berlin Games, igniting World War II, postponed the next Olympics until 1948 in London's Wembley Stadium. International rule changes and the continued evolution of the game contributed to better play on the basketball court. The U.S. averaged 65.5 points per game, a 22-point increase from their output in Berlin. The 1948 roster consisted of both AAU and collegiate players, a new trend that would continue until the 1968 games. The friendly competition on the playing field did not lessen geopolitical rivalries between countries. Historian William J. Baker writes in *Sports in the Western World*, "No less than the Berlin Blockade, the Korean War, and the Cuban Missile Crisis, East-West athletic contests represented tests of will and strength of skill. The Soviet versus US basketball rivalry that emerged after the London games indicated this."[11] Beginning with the 1952 Olympics in Helsinki, Finland, basketball became an extension of the Cold War.

In 1958, a year after launching *Sputnik*, the USSR upset the U.S. in the World Championships in San Diego and then defeated the American Air Force team in a tournament in Santiago, Chile. The U.S. reclaimed supremacy two years later at the summer games in Rome, Italy. The 1960 Olympic roster, considered the greatest amateur team ever, was coached by University of California's Pete Newell and featured future NBA Hall-of-Famers Jerry Lucas, Oscar Robertson, and Jerry West. Robertson led the team in scoring with 17 points per game. The U.S. defeated their opponents by an average of 42.2 points. They blew out the Soviets 81–57 in the quarterfinals on their way to a 90–63 defeat of Brazil in the championship round.

Winning gold every four years became routine for the U.S. Yugoslavia won gold in 1980 after the Americans boycotted the games to protest the Soviet invasion of Afghanistan. It was only fitting that the U.S. reclaimed gold at the 1984 games held in Los Angeles, California. The mighty U.S. appeared unbeatable, but the world was slowly catching up, and then came the unthinkable. John Thompson, Jr., was selected to coach the 1988 Olympic squad that would play in Seoul, Korea. The late Thompson, affectionately known as "Big John" by former players and admirers, has a special place in my heart. He redefined college basketball and challenged stereotypes of Black masculinity and mental aptitude while coaching the Georgetown University Hoyas men's basketball team in my hometown of Washington, D.C., from 1972 to 1999. Thompson's Hoyas, known for their hardnosed defense, swagger, and majority Black rosters, became Black America's unofficial team. Thompson, the first Black coach to win a national championship, was one of Black America's favorite college coaches. His outspoken demeanor and unforgivable Blackness often rubbed white media members the wrong way. When he was chosen to coach the team, one reporter sarcastically questioned if any white players would be allowed on the team.[12]

Coach Thompson took the Hoyas to three Final Fours between 1982 and 1985. Unfortunately, his success in the collegiate game did not translate to international competition for multiple reasons. Thompson did not adjust well to the differences in the rules and style of play overseas. Although his roster included future NBA stars David Robinson, Danny Manning, Stacey Augmon, and "Thunder" Dan Majerle, these players were still collegiate amateurs. The international teams included professional grown men who played together year-round. At the time, the rules allowed foreign players who earned a salary to play on their national teams as if they were amateurs. Such laws did not apply to American athletes, so only collegiate and AAU players had been on past teams. "Those other teams were using pros playing against 18- and 19-year-olds. That's really unfair," said Barkley.[13]

The U.S. failed to reach the gold medal game for the first time. The USSR did not need assistance from the officials this time to beat the U.S. 82–76 in the semifinals or Yugoslavia in the final round of competition. A 78–49 defeat of Australia in the consolation game for the bronze medal did soften the blow to the American psyche. Nevertheless, the fact that the Soviets won the gold only added salt to their wounds. If America wanted to regain supremacy on the world stage, drastic changes were needed. Two men from different ends of the globe had a revolutionary solution.

The Meat Butcher and the Friar

Luka Dončić, Nikola Jokić, Victor Wembanyama—American sports fans might not know these names today if it were not for Borislav "Bora" Stanković and Dave Gavitt. We have these two men to thank for the 1992 Dream Team and the NBA's rise as a global superpower. Stanković, whom sports journalist Jack McCallum once dubbed "the butcher of meat," was a professional basketball player in Serbia and a member of the Yugoslav national basketball team between 1948 and 1953.[14] After his playing days concluded, he coached professional basketball clubs in Serbia (OKK Beograd) and Italy (Pallacanestro Cantu) for the next 13 years. In 1976, he became FIBA's second secretary general, a position he held until 2002. Stanković proposed the idea of having NBA players replace collegians in the Olympics. But as you will soon learn, this was challenging to accomplish.

Stanković believed that the international game would never reach its full potential if the best foreign players were not competing against the best American players. At the time, the rules prohibited American professional players from participating in sanctioned games against other pros abroad. In 1983, Stanković began lobbying FIBA's members to adjust the rules. Three years later, at the FIBA Congress in Madrid, Spain, his resolution lost 31–27, with both the U.S. and the USSR casting dissenting votes. It seems unfathomable now that the U.S. would vote to keep its pros out of the Olympics and other forms of international competition; however, the NBA's powers that be, namely Commissioner David Stern, saw little value in sending their best and brightest abroad to compete in little more than preseason exhibition games. Stern, a proud capitalist, could not envision how America could effectively use international competition to market and monetize the league.[15]

Few people were as crucial to the growth of basketball in the U.S. and abroad as Dave Gavitt. The Rhode Island native first made his mark in the 1970s, coaching his alma mater, the Providence College Friars, in five NCAA tournament appearances and a Final Four. In 1979, he spearheaded the creation of the Big East, an athletic conference originally consisting of seven private colleges and universities from the Northeast. The Big East dominated college basketball in the 1980s and early 1990s. Three of the league's teams—Georgetown, St. John's, and Villanova—reached the Final Four in 1985. The league's team played in NBA arenas like the fabled Madison Square Garden in New York City. The Big East turned star players like Patrick Ewing, Chris Mullin, and Dwayne "Pearl" Washington into household names. A fledgling 24-hour cable station named ESPN got its start by covering Big East games. Soon the titans of the sneaker industry, Nike and Adidas, were sponsoring college teams and paying coaches like Georgetown's John Thompson more than their annual university salary. In addition to his Big East duties, Gavitt became the chairman of the NCAA's Division I basketball committee. He oversaw the expansion of its national tournament to 64 teams, essentially creating what sports fans know as March Madness.[16]

Gavitt would have coached the U.S. Olympic team in 1980 if the country had not boycotted those games. In 1988, he was chosen to preside over USA Basketball, the governing organization representing the U.S. in

FIBA and the Olympic and Paralympic committees. Gavitt shared Stanković's vision for the future of basketball. A year after Gavitt's presidency began, Stanković's resolution finally passed 56–13 at the FIBA Congress. Although Stern was still skeptical about having NBA players involved, Gavitt was supportive. He introduced the idea of having a select team of the NBA's premier athletes participate in the upcoming summer games in Barcelona.[17]

Don't Wake Me; I'm Dreamin'

The 1990s is unequivocally my favorite decade. Pop culture played a vital role in defining that period of my life. I graduated from Saturday morning cartoons to TGI Fridays. I fell in love with hip-hop and R&B. Oh, how I looked forward to spending summers with my grandparents in Sumter, South Carolina. My granddaddy, Arthur, was an avid sports fan. I thought I could win his affection by becoming a sports fan, too. So, I began watching and playing sports as much as possible. I naturally gravitated toward basketball because I was too skinny for football, and my friends did not play baseball, soccer, or hockey. We did not know what lacrosse was at that time. I briefly flirted with skateboarding before basketball became my new obsession, and the NBA's stars became my superheroes. In my eyes, Michael Jordan was Superman, Batman, and Spider-Man all rolled into one magical human being who could fly. I begged my mom to buy me a pair of Air Jordan sneakers so I could be like Mike.

My parents, recognizing my growing interest in sports, enrolled me in basketball and tennis camps during the summers. My dad bought me a subscription to *Sports Illustrated for Kids*. By the time I reached high school, I had begun reading the magazine's version for adults. For readers born after 2010, there was a time before the internet, podcasts, and countless sports cable channels when you had to get your sports news from the weekly issues of *Sports Illustrated*. Consequently, the magazine carried great prestige in the early '90s. The cover of its February 18, 1991, issue first used the "Dream Team" moniker to describe the new Olympic team. From that point forward, the nickname stuck. Without the internet or social media, there was little buzz surrounding the team when the *Sports Illustrated* issue hit the magazine racks.[18]

Rod Thorn, a former NBA executive for the Chicago Bulls (who famously drafted Michael Jordan in 1984), was the chairman of the USA Basketball Men's National Team selection committee for the 1992, 1996, and 2000 Olympics. He had the responsibility of putting together the Dream Team. The first piece in Thorn's puzzle was the head coach. Big

John was not the right man for the job. The best college coaches were Dean Smith (University of North Carolina at Chapel Hill), the volatile Robert Montgomery "Bobby" Knight (Indiana University), Jerry Tarkanian (University of Nevada, Las Vegas), and a young Michael Krzyzewski (Duke University). Under normal circumstances, Mike Krzyzewski, best known as Coach K, would have been the most likely candidate. His Duke Blue Devils had just upset Tarkanian's UNLV Runnin' Rebels in the Final Four on their way to the first of back-to-back national championships. Krzyzewski was on the precipice of becoming college basketball's foremost coach for the next 30 years. But Thorn and the others on the selection committee believed an NBA coach was necessary to lead professionals.

The selection committee chose Chuck Daly to lead the Dream Team on Valentine's Day, 1991. Daly's coaching career began at the high school level. During the 1960s and 1970s, he held multiple collegiate coaching jobs. He took over the University of Pennsylvania's team in 1971 and led the Penn Quakers to a 25–3 record and the NCAA tournament in his second season. While Daly was coaching at Penn, he befriended Jack McCloskey, who coached at Penn from 1956 to 1966. McCloskey, nicknamed "Trader Jack," became the general manager of the floundering Detroit Pistons NBA team in 1979.[19] His first significant move was to hire his old Penn pal. Daly had minimal NBA coaching experience when he came to the Pistons in 1983. Before that, he unsuccessfully coached the Cleveland Cavaliers to a 9–32 record in the 1981–1982 season. He was fired at the end of the season and took a job broadcasting games for the Philadelphia 76ers. McCloskey's risky hire paid off in ways that few would have predicted. Daly's Pistons, led by cherubic point guard Isiah Thomas, made three straight appearances in the NBA Finals between 1988 and 1990. The Pistons won the title in 1989 and 1990, replacing the Boston Celtics and the Los Angeles Lakers as NBA royalty. They were the only team to keep Michael Jordan's Bulls in check before their decade of dominance began in 1991.[20]

Daly's Pistons became the villains of the NBA during their reign of terror. Their aggressive play on defense and unsportsmanlike behavior on the court earned them the nickname the Bad Boys. Piston players such as Bill Laimbeer, Rick Mahorn, and a young Dennis Rodman reveled in wearing the proverbial black hat. "Okay, we'll be the Oakland Raiders. We wanted your whole city to shake when we walked through the door. We wanted the fans to fear us because we were about to destroy their team," said Isiah Thomas.[21] The Pistons' rough play and "Jordan rules" nearly injured Michael Jordan and his Bulls running mate Scottie Pippen in their numerous playoff meetings between 1988 and 1990. Their brand of basketball lacked the beautiful choreography of the "Showtime" Los Angeles Lakers. Consequently, it was surprising that Daly was chosen over other leading candidates, Pat Riley and Don Nelson. Despite the Pistons' image, Daly's players in Detroit and the Olympians in Barcelona loved him. "He coached the Bad Boys. If you can coach those assholes, you can coach anybody," said Barkley.[22]

John Salley and his Pistons teammates referred to Daly as "Daddy Rich" because of his stylish demeanor.[23] "His hair was beautiful. His suits were immaculate. He wanted to win, but he wanted to look good," said Barkley.[24] With Daly in place as the coach, it was time to form a team. The number-one guy on Rod Thorn's wish list was #23 in Chicago red and black. But he knew Jordan would be the most challenging player to sign on. Michael Jordan was the most famous athlete in America. He already headlined the gold-medal-winning Olympic team in 1984. Everyone knew Jordan spent his summers playing nine holes on the golf course, not running up and down the court. But you could have a legitimate Dream Team only with him. Thorn worked backward by building the core of the team before reaching out to Jordan. He started by recruiting the NBA's biggest celebrity of the 1980s, Earvin "Magic" Johnson.

Few people can light up a room with their megawatt smile and charisma like Magic Johnson. Born in Lansing, Michigan, in 1959, this son of a school janitor and an assembly worker for General Motors was no stranger to hard work. As a teen, he rode through town with his father in a garbage truck, picking up trash. Johnson developed a tireless work ethic from watching his parents slave to make a living and care for him and his six siblings. He also learned the game of basketball from his parents, both of whom played in their youth. By the time Johnson was in the eighth grade, he was showing signs of future stardom, scoring 48 points in a game.[25]

Magic Johnson came of age during the later years of the Civil Rights Movement. Busing was an outcome of the movement. Black children would be bused into white neighborhoods to integrate schools, and white kids would be bused to Black schools. This noble plan often met violent resistance. The worst examples of violence were found in Boston, where a high school student was nearly stabbed to death. Johnson desired to play at the local Black high school, Sexton, but he was bused to Everett in a white neighborhood. Unlike many of his Black classmates, he was immediately well-received because of his athletic prowess and gregarious personality. When Johnson was a sophomore, his principal asked him to use his influence to quell brewing interracial tensions. It was also during his sophomore year he went from being called "June Bug" to "Magic." Fred Stabley, Jr., a journalist for the *Lansing State Journal*, covered one of his games. After Johnson scored 36 points, dished 16 assists, and grabbed 18 rebounds, Stabley dubbed him Magic.[26]

Johnson rejected offers to attend national powerhouses, such as UCLA and Indiana University, to play his college ball at nearby Michigan State University. As a sophomore, he led the MSU Spartans to a national championship and was named the Most Outstanding Player of the Final Four. His brilliant play and vibrant personality caught the attention of Dr. Jerry Buss, the new maverick owner of the Lakers. Buss selected the 19-year-old prodigy with the first overall pick in the 1979 NBA draft. Johnson reinvigorated a lackluster Lakers roster, leading them to the first of five championships during his rookie season. With Johnson at the point and the stoic Kareem Abdul-Jabbar at the center, the Lakers dominated the league in the 1980s. Johnson's no-look and around-the-back passes sparked a breathtaking offense known as "Showtime." With head coach Pat Riley on the sidelines donning expensive Giorgio Armani power suits, the gorgeous Lakers Girls cheerleading, and the star-studded Gucci row of celebrities, the Los Angeles Forum, home to the Lakers, was the coolest place on earth. Magic Johnson's star always shined the brightest. But another player, not as flashy and personable, rivaled him for league supremacy and popularity.[27] Johnson told Thorn he would play on the Dream Team only if his archrival joined him.

A Courtship of Rivals

Magic Johnson first met his match in 1978 at the World Invitational Tournament. There was a "White boy" on his team named Larry Joe Bird who had just dominated Jack Evans, the national College Player of the Year, in a scrimmage. Johnson had never seen a white player with Bird's skill set. A year later, Johnson and Bird were college basketball's most preeminent stars. Johnson's Spartans faced Bird's Indiana State Sycamores on March 26, 1979, in Salt Lake City, Utah, for the national championship. This game still stands as the most-watched college basketball in television history, with 40 million viewers.[28] The Spartans won 75–64. The 1979 Final Four was the start of a beautiful courtship of rivals that redefined basketball. The two men were described as "basketball savants who fused the substance of the sixties with the style of the seventies to create a new and exciting, yet selfless way to play the game in the eighties."[29]

Today, it is unfathomable to hear that the NBA Finals used to be on tape delay. In fact, television executives at CBS tried to air the sixth game of the 1977 finals between the Portland Trailblazers and Philadelphia 76ers at 10:30 a.m. PST to clear the afternoon for the Professional Golf Association's Kemper Open. The players refused to play, and the game was moved to 12:30 p.m. The postgame championship trophy presentation was not aired live due to coverage of the golf tournament. The draft, which is now a glossy six-hour product on ESPN and NBA TV, was not televised before 1980. The league had the lowest ratings of the three major American professional leagues by the late '70s. When the NBA signed its new TV deal with CBS before the 1982–83 season, the executives decided the best way to boost ratings and move the finals out of tape delay was to sell "Magic v. Bird." CBS aired regular weekend doubleheaders with the Boston Celtics, led by Larry Bird, in the early game, followed by the Lakers in the late game. The Lakers met the Celtics in the NBA Finals in 1984, 1985, and 1987. Bird won only their first meeting. The Lakers-Celtics rivalry of the '80s was a godsend for David Stern's overlooked league.[30] Bryant Gumbel, the host of HBO's *Real Sports*, called the 1979 NCAA championship game. He said the following of these two basketball giants: "One of my pet peeves is when people say Michael [Jordan] saved the NBA. Bullshit!!! Magic and Larry saved the NBA."[31]

By the time the Dream Team took the court in the summer of 1992, Johnson and Bird were seen more as symbolic selections than key contributors to the roster. Bird was suffering from a back injury that resulted from shoveling crushed rock to create a driveway at his mother's house. The injury occurred in 1985 and worsened over the years. He retired from the NBA on August 18, 1992, nine days after the Olympics closing ceremony. Johnson had abruptly retired on November 7, 1991, after contracting HIV. The fans voted him to start the 1992 All-Star Game in Orlando, Florida. Johnson proved he was worthy of the fans' support by recording 25 points and nine assists and winning the game's MVP trophy. His brilliant All-Star performance in February was enough to maintain his spot on the Olympic roster five months later.

With Magic Johnson and Larry Bird secured in the spring of 1991, recruiting other NBA stars to play was easier. Patrick Ewing (New York Knicks), Scottie Pippen (Chicago Bulls), Chris Mullin (Golden State Warriors), and David Robinson (San Antonio Spurs) agreed to play. Utah Jazz stars Karl Malone and John Stockton committed to play. Charles Barkley (Philadelphia 76ers) was the team's most controversial selection. Barkley was known for his outspoken demeanor and volatile temper. His famous "I am not a role model" Nike commercial was still two years away. But an incident at a Sixers game in March 1991 nearly cost him his spot on the team. During the fourth quarter of a game in New Jersey, Barkley accidentally spat on an eight-year-old girl named Lauren Rose. He meant to spit on an obnoxious adult fan who had been heckling throughout the game. He was suspended and fined $10,000 for the grotesque act. Sir Charles was no saint on or off the court. He had been involved in multiple bar brawls and was charged with carrying an unlicensed handgun.

Five years after the Barcelona games, Barkley spent a night in jail after throwing a 20-year-old construction worker named Jorge Lugo through a window. Lugo, who was only 5'2" and 110 pounds, was guilty of cursing and throwing a cup of ice at Barkley as he was hanging out at a bar in Orlando, Florida, with Clyde Drexler. Lugo was taken to Orlando Regional Medical Center and treated for minor cuts to his right arm.[32] During an episode of the *Let's Go* podcast in 2022, Barkley told co-hosts Jim Gray and Tom Brady that when the judge asked him if he had any regrets, he replied only that they were on "the first damn floor" when he tossed him out the window.[33] Commissioner Stern did not want him on the 1992 team, but Rod Thorn badly wanted him due to his supreme talent. Duke University forward Christian Laettner was the lone collegian on the team, beating out Louisiana State University 7'1" center Shaquille O'Neal. At the time, Laettner was considered one of the five greatest college players in history. He led Duke to back-to-back national championships in 1991 and 1992.

The final Dream Teamer chosen was Portland Trailblazers shooting guard Clyde Drexler. In the early '90s, Drexler was compared to Michael Jordan. Drexler even dared to say he was as good as MJ. Jordan permanently put that comparison to rest in the 1992 NBA Finals when the two squared off. Jordan's 35-point first-half performance, consisting of six three-pointers and his iconic shoulder shrug, set the tone for the Bulls' 4–2 series win. No disrespect to Drexler, but he had no business on the team in the first place. The final spot should have gone to Isiah Thomas. The exclusion of Thomas from the roster has been debatable for over 30 years. It resurfaced in the public's consciousness during the 2020 release of ESPN/Netflix's *The Last Dance* docuseries about Jordan and his Chicago Bulls. In the series, Thorn denied the rumors that Jordan kept Thomas off the team. The Detroit Pistons had been a thorn in Jordan's side for years. They eliminated the Bulls from the Eastern Conference playoffs for three consecutive years. When the Bulls finally got over the hump in the 1991 conference finals, the Pistons walked off the court before time expired and without shaking the Bulls' players' hands. Cameras caught Thomas leading the team off the court and ducking his head to avoid being noticed.

Russ Granik, USA Basketball vice president (1989–1996), blames the Pistons' walk-off after losing to the Bulls for Thomas being left off the roster, but it goes deeper than that. One reason for Thomas's exclusion was the polarizing Dennis Rodman-Larry Bird episode. After game five of the 1988 Eastern Conference finals, reporters asked Rodman, who had little media training and public speaking experience at the time, what he thought of Bird. Unlike the majority of mainstream America, Rodman was not that impressed with the Celtics' MVP. Thomas came to his teammate's defense when reporters asked him to respond to the comments. "I think Larry is a very, very good basketball player. He's an exceptional talent. But I have to agree with Rodman. If he were Black, he'd be just another good guy," said Thomas.[34] His attempt to explain his comments during a joint press conference with Bird only heightened the disdain for him.

Another reason for Isiah Thomas's exclusion was his contentious relationship with several Dream Team members. Jordan and Pippen despised him. Malone elbowed Thomas in the forehead so hard during a game on December 14, 1991, that it required him to receive 40 stitches. Thomas was left on the floor bleeding. Malone was ejected from the game, fined $10,000, and suspended the next game. Thomas and Johnson had been best friends until Thomas speculated that Johnson may have gotten HIV from closeted homosexual behavior.[35]

I would also argue that Thomas was left home because he represented an image of Blackness that the NBA and the Olympic committee did not want on a global platform. Apart from Barkley, all the Black Dream Teamers were noncontroversial and unoffensive. None of the players opened their mouths to speak out against the acquittal of the four white police officers who beat Black motorist Rodney King in 1991. The Los Angeles uprisings, in response to the acquittal, occurred three months before the Olympics. For all of Barkley's bluster, he was nonthreatening to white America. He voted Republican and married a White woman with whom he had a daughter. Barkley was not involved in civil rights protests or publicly taking stands on social issues like players from past generations, such as Bill Russell and Kareem Abdul-Jabbar. Jordan's Chicago Bulls teammate Craig Hodges, one of the only outspoken athletes at the time, was quietly blackballed from the league because he dared to speak out on racial issues during a visit to the White House after the Bulls won their first championship.

I am not saying that Thomas was marching against South African apartheid, speaking out about police brutality, or quoting Nation of Islam leader Louis Farrakhan in the 1990s. Still, the fact that he was unafraid to call out racial bias in the media was threatening at that time. His Pistons also represented a majority working-class Black city, left desolate by the 1967 racial uprisings, and engaged in a style of roughhouse play associated with the hood.[36] The Dream Team had to meet mainstream America's standards of middle-class respectability. They also had to promote American values for the entire world to see. While Barcelona provided the ideal platform, like the 1968 Mexico City games did for John Carlos and Tommie Smith, to make a public stance on American racial injustice, that was not the time.[37] Consequently, there was no room in the inn for Mr. Thomas. But this team was the perfect vehicle for the NBA to evangelize about the greatness of its Black Messiah.

Rare Air

The NBA would not be an international juggernaut if Michael Jeffrey Jordan had never picked up a basketball. He is the greatest basketball player in history and the most influential professional athlete of the 20th century. As a kid, I often found myself in the gym counting down the shot clock and taking the game-winning shot at the buzzer like Mike. Three, two, one, swishhhhh! I would jump in the air and kick out my little feet to imitate his game winner over Craig Ehlo in the 1989 playoffs. Jordan's mesmerizing moves caused fits of exuberance among spectators that would make one think they were at Sunday service catching the Holy Ghost. Watching him was like seeing The Beatles on the *Ed Sullivan Show* for the first time or the rush a teenage girl might get at a Taylor Swift or Beyoncé concert.

Jordan was a six-time NBA champion, six-time Finals MVP, five-time league MVP, 14-time All-Star, 10-time scoring champion, two-time Slam Dunk Contest champion, and 2009 inductee into the Naismith Hall of Fame. He was as successful off the court, transcending race and breaking barriers for future Black athletes. At the height of Jordan's playing career, his endorsements included Chevrolet, Coca-Cola, Gatorade, Hanes, McDonald's, Upper Deck, and Wheaties. In 2010, he purchased the Charlotte Hornets basketball franchise from Black Entertainment Television (BET) founder Robert L. Johnson. As the majority owner of the Bobcats from 2010 to 2023, he was the only Black majority owner in professional sports. In 2020, he became the majority owner of 23XI Racing in the NASCAR Cup Series. Jordan is currently one of only 18 Black billionaires worldwide.[38]

Michael Jordan was born on February 17, 1963. His father, James, served in the air force before accepting a job with General Electric as a forklift operator in Wallace, North Carolina. He eventually became a supervisor. Jordan's mother, Deloris, is a native of Rocky Point, North Carolina. She met James before he left for the military. Mrs. Jordan attended Tuskegee Institute, an HBCU in Alabama founded by Booker T. Washington. Washington, a former slave from Virginia, preached self-help and financial empowerment for Blacks. He did not believe that agitating and protesting for civil rights was the best way for Blacks to overcome and empower themselves.[39] After Tuskegee, Deloris returned to North Carolina and married James. The Jordans relocated to Brooklyn, New York, in 1962 but later settled in Wilmington, North Carolina.[40]

Mrs. Jordan moved up the corporate ladder at United Carolina Bank. She and Mr. Jordan provided a comfortable middle-class upbringing for their five children. Despite North Carolina's history as a former

1. It Was All a Dream

Confederate state and as a stronghold for the Ku Klux Klan, the Jordans stressed tolerance. They chose not to dwell on the racial tension engulfing the country. Michael Jordan's middle-class upbringing and his parents' decision not to make race a big issue may have contributed to his sociopolitical apathy in his adult years.[41] Jordan admitted to being racist toward all whites after a white classmate in primary school called him a nigger. His mom told him he could not go through life with a chip on his shoulder and viewing white people as enemies.

Like all the legendary superheroes in the DC and Marvel Comics universe, Michael Jordan has a fantastic origin story that has become a part of his lore. He grew up playing baseball and basketball. Baseball was his first love. Jordan was not the best athlete in the family. His older brother Larry beat him out on the playing field and garnered more attention and affection from their father. When Jordan was a scrawny 5'11" sophomore at Emsley A. Laney High School, he tried out for the boys varsity basketball team. Coach Clifton Herring selected the taller Harvest Leroy Smith instead of Jordan. In one of his pettiest gestures, Jordan invited Smith to his Hall of Fame induction ceremony to remind his coach that he had made a colossal mistake. Jordan went on to play for the junior varsity squad. After growing four inches over the summer, he was able to make the varsity the following season. But Jordan's tireless work ethic, not the growth spurt, earned him that roster spot. His parents told him he had to work harder to excel in sports and life. Jordan averaged 25 points in his junior and senior years. He was named to the 1981 McDonald's All-American team and recruited by Dean Smith to play for the University of North Carolina at Chapel Hill.[42]

Jordan capped his freshman season at UNC by sinking the game-winning shot in the 1982 NCAA championship game against Georgetown. He was college basketball's most exciting player in his junior year, known for his high-flying acrobatics and pretty slam dunks. On June 19, 1984, the Chicago Bulls selected Jordan with the third pick in the NBA draft. The acclaimed sportscaster Bob Costas got his start calling games for the Bulls. According to Costas, the Bulls teams that preceded Jordan's era could be politely described as mediocre. Most Chicago residents were fans of the Bears, Cubs, White Sox, and Blackhawks. The Bulls could barely sell out Chicago Stadium.[43] With Jordan in the backcourt, the Bulls gradually improved each year. The additions of Scottie Pippen and Horace Grant in 1987 transformed the Bulls from lovable losers to winners. Coach Phil Jackson used Zen Buddhism to help his players meditate and relax under pressure. The team won their first of six championships in eight seasons in June 1991. With Magic Johnson's sudden retirement, Jordan was now the face of the league. By the time the Dream Team headed off to Barcelona, he was the most celebrated athlete in the world.

What made Michael Jordan the quintessential ambassador for the Dream Team and America in the 1992 Olympics was much more than his championships, scoring titles, and dunks. Historians often define the 1980s as the age of Reagan and the conservative revolution. Ronald Reagan campaigned during the 1980 U.S. presidential election on a promise to lift the country out of Jimmy Carter's financial recession and "malaise" of the 1970s. Reagan promised to free the American hostages detained in the U.S. embassy in Tehran, Iran. He vowed to win the Cold War by defeating the Soviets' Evil Empire. And he promised to roll back the civil rights initiatives and liberalism "run amok" of the '60s that conservatives blamed for rotting traditional values of faith and family. As president, Reagan and his followers emphasized less government interference, rugged individualism, work ethic, capitalism, militarism associated with patriotism, and masculine heroism.

In her dissertation "'Clean Air': Representing Michael Jordan in the Reagan-Bush Era," Mary Genevieve McDonald says Jordan became the ideal icon and ambassador for Reagan's brand of conservatism. Jordan embodied conservative, Reaganite principles of hard work, discipline, competition, and individualism.[44] Before winning championships, he joked that while there was no *I* in *team*, there was an *I* in *win*. "On the basketball floor, Jordan represents the athlete personified, ego-centric and single-minded, hard on himself, on teammates, on opponents—fearless and unbending, never backing down, eager to put his signature on an opponent, looking for new worlds and teams to conquer," says David Halberstam.[45] A series of NBA home videos—*Michael Jordan's Playground* (1990), *Come Fly with Me* (1991), and *Air Time* (1993)—marketed toward kids glorified his inspirational Laney High School narrative. The videos depicted him lifting weights with his personal trainer, Tim Grover, as he strengthened his body to conquer Detroit's Evil Empire. Once Jordan defeated the Pistons and his other NBA opponents, he was ready to take his talents to Barcelona.

Off the court, Jordan manifested the traditional family values promoted by Reaganites. The home video *Air Time* concludes with him at home with his then-wife Juanita and their two young sons, Marcus and Jeffrey. Pictorials depicted the image of a happily married man and a loving father. His parents could often be found at his games. They attended his 1984 press conference when he signed his $6 million rookie contract. His dad was his best friend and protector from an increasingly obsessed press and paparazzi. Jordan was among a rare group of Black celebrities at the start of the 1990s—Michael Jackson, Whitney Houston, Bill Cosby, Oprah Winfrey, Prince, Eddie Murphy, and O.J. Simpson—able to transcend race. David Halberstam says:

As Jordan smiled, race simply fell away. Michael was no longer a Black man; he was just someone you wanted to be with, someone you wanted as your friend.... If Michael Jordan was not burdened by race, why should you be burdened by it either?[46]

The Boys of Summer

Training camp for the Dream Team commenced on June 22, 1992, in La Jolla, California. The dominant concern was how these 12 alpha males would mesh on the court. Could they control their egos long enough to play like a team and win the gold? "Everybody in the world has an ego; the only difference between us is we have a reason to have an ego," Barkley told the press.[47] Ahmad Rashad, host of NBC's Saturday morning NBA series for kids *NBA Inside Stuff* and Jordan's close friend, asked MJ and Ewing who would take the game-winning shot if they played a close game. They both answered, "Me!" The first practice was little more than a showcase of everyone's individual talent. "It was a very competitive practice, and I'm thinking, 'Aren't we on the same team?'" said Drexler.[48] None of the players wanted to be on the same team as their rivals. Jordan wanted to prove that he was better than Johnson. Barkley dunked on Malone to prove he was the better power forward. Ewing refused to play alongside Robinson. Perhaps this was not such a good idea!

The Dream Team faced their first real competition days later in a scrimmage against the nation's top college players, including Duke's Grant Hill and Bobby Hurley, Michigan's Chris Webber, Kentucky's Jamal Mashburn, and Memphis's Anfernee "Penny" Hardaway. Unlike during their first practice, the pros left their egos at the door. No one wanted to take a shot. The guys were overpassing. Hurley sliced and diced the Dream Team's defense. Webber, the cornerstone to Michigan's Fab Five, threw down rim-shattering dunks.[49] Before long, the Dream Team found themselves trailing by double figures. The college kids won 62–54. The scrimmage was played in a private gym. The scoreboard was quickly erased before the hundreds of media members were allowed inside to interview the players. Brian McIntyre, NBA public relations, said they could sense something strange in the air when they walked into the gym.

Was the Dream Team overrated? Were they destined to suffer the same dreadful fate as their predecessors in 1988? "He threw the game. Chuck [Daly] threw the game," said Mike Krzyzewski, one of Daly's assistant coaches for the Olympics. Daly played Jordan for a few minutes, frequently substituting players in and out, and made few adjustments to prevent the collegians from scoring. Jordan says this was Daly's strategy to help his players realize they could be beaten if they failed to follow his instructions or overlooked their opponents. When the teams met for a rematch the next day, normalcy was restored. The collegians struggled to score a basket. If you ask Barkley, he says they won the rematch by 100 points.

For the Dream Team to play in Barcelona, they had to qualify by winning the Tournament of the Americas in Portland, Oregon. This tournament, later known as the FIBA AmeriCup, consisted of the United States, Argentina, Brazil, Canada, Cuba, Mexico, Panama, Puerto Rico, Uruguay, and Venezuela. The top four finishers earned a trip to the Olympics, where the masses would first see the Dream Team in action. Johnson and Bird were named team captains. Their presence on the court together as teammates was a magical moment for the fans fortunate enough to get tickets to the tournament. The Dream Team debuted against Cuba on June 28. "The Cuban team spontaneously drops to its knees as if 12 popes had come by on Easter Sunday," says Jack McCallum, describing the scene at the start of the game.[50] The Americans were startled by the deference their opponents showed them. This behavior would become a trend throughout the tournament and later in Barcelona. The crowd gave Bird a standing ovation as he and Johnson led the way to a 77-point beatdown of the Cubans. The U.S. won all six tournament games by an average of 50 points.

The Dream Team landed in Monte Carlo, Monaco, on July 18, 1992, for their final leg of training camp. Monte Carlo was a hybrid of a training camp and a vacation for the players. "I don't worry about playing basketball. I just want to have fun. David Robinson, Patrick Ewing, Michael Jordan. This is like spring break in the ghetto," Barkley told the foreign press.[51] Pippen and Barkley could not wait for practice to end so they could hang out at the beach and admire all the beautiful topless women sunbathing and asking them for autographs. Jordan bonded with Coaches Daly and P.J. Carlesimo on the golf course every day. His teammates were amazed by his ability to play 36 holes of golf and stay up until 5:00 a.m. playing cards every day.

While in Monte Carlo, they won a sloppy exhibition game against the French national team. Prince Albert II of Monaco, sitting in the stands, was amazed by how the crowd was glued to the Americans. Unimpressed by the team's lackluster performance, Coach Daly called for a scrimmage between the players the next morning. He told them to play as if it were an actual NBA game with four quarters. Many basketball aficionados call this scrimmage the greatest basketball game ever played. If Daly had not recorded the game, there would be no evidence of its existence. Sneakerheads (shoe enthusiasts) like me recognize this scrimmage as the game that inspired the coveted Trophy Room Air Jordan 7 retros.[52] Daly divided the players into a blue team and a white team. The blue team consisted of Johnson, Mullin, Barkley, Robinson, and Laettner. The white team had Jordan, Pippen, Bird, Malone, and Ewing. The game was noted for excessive trash-talking between Johnson and Jordan. Remember, Johnson, along with Bird, was the face of the NBA until 1991. That summer, Jordan's Bulls defeated his Lakers 4–1 in the NBA Finals. Johnson retired for health reasons five months later. This scrimmage allowed him to prove to his peers that he was still the "Big Dog." Jordan led all scorers with 17 points. Despite trailing for much of the game, he led the white team to a comeback 40–36 victory. After the match ended, Jordan walked into the locker room, glanced in Johnson's direction, and cooly said, "There's a new sheriff in town!"[53]

Every player on the Dream Team says Monte Carlo was the climax of that summer. In the 1990s, players did not spend time with their rivals as they do today. This trip was their first opportunity to hang out with each other on and off the court, apart from the brief three-day All-Star weekend every February. The team celebrated Malone's 29th birthday while they were there. Unlikely friendships such as that of Bird and Ewing were formed. "I got a White guy from Indiana and a brotha from Jamaica," says Barkley about this odd couple. Now, they were finally a team and ready for world domination. They landed in Barcelona on July 24. As their plane landed, helicopters flew overhead. Hundreds of fans were lying on the ground outside their hotel. Barkley admits that this was the first time he was fully aware of the enormity of their presence at the games. There was no margin for error. Another silver or bronze medal would be considered the greatest upset in sports history. While all the players did their best to appear coy before the international press, Sir Charles was up to his old shenanigans. After a reporter asked him how he felt about the Soviet upset in 1972, he joked that he was too busy flunking his kindergarten entrance exam to stress over it. He then added the following quip:

> Why don't they just take their ass whopping and go home? We're going to have a little revenge in our hearts for '72 and '88. David [Robinson] can't say that because he's a Christian.[54]

During this press conference, Barkley made his infamous comments about their first opponent, Angola. The game was played on July 26. Marv Albert, who called the game for NBC's telecast, referred to it as the biggest mismatch in Olympic history after the U.S. went on a 46–1 scoring outburst. The score was 64–16 at halftime. The Dream Team's dominant performance was sullied in the second half when Barkley elbowed Angolan Herlander Coimbra. After the game, Barkley told reporters he did not believe in turning the other cheek. In fact, he would hit him on that cheek, too, if he stuck it out. His teammates were not supportive of his vile behavior.[55] Drexler said his actions made them look like the stereotypical ugly Americans. Johnson had to remind him that he was a reflection on the entire roster. From then on, Barkley was on his best behavior and became the most popular athlete in the Olympic Village and Barcelona.[56]

The Dream Team's second game was against Croatia on July 27. The game's underlying narrative was the matchup between Croatia's 23-year-old small forward Toni Kukoč and Jordan and Pippen. The Bulls teammates had circled this game on their calendars once the schedule was announced. While Jordan and Pippen were winning consecutive championships in Chicago, their team general manager, Jerry Krause, was publicly wooing the foreign phenom to become the organization's new face in the future.[57] Krause drafted Kukoč in 1990, but he remained in Europe until the 1993–94 season. Neither the hypercompetitive Jordan nor Pippen was thrilled with Krause's infatuation with the budding star. "That's like a father who has all his kids, and now he sees another kid that he loves more than his own.... We were playing against Krause in a Croatian uniform," says Jordan.[58] Consequently, they took their bitterness out on Kukoč the entire game. From the opening whistle, Pippen, one of the league's best defenders, refused to let him get the ball or score. Once Pippen finished with him, it was Jordan's turn. It got so bad that the other Croatian players asked Kukoč why he was being singled out. He was so naive that he thought all NBA players were typically that aggressive. The Dream Team cruised to a commanding 103–70 win. Kukoč scored a measly four points.[59]

America's sheer dominance at the onset of the Olympics resulted in criticism and detractors. When asked if the team was too great for its own good, David Stern asked if we should also ban the Kenyan runners from competing in marathons due to their excellence. Reporters also asked Johnson if he heard the rumors about other American Olympians being jealous of all the attention they were receiving. Remember that most Olympic athletes were amateurs who trained their entire lives to be seen on a global stage for one or two weeks every four years. Unbeknownst to most people, David Gavitt had to convince the players to waive a $75,000 stipend to play.[60] None of the other American Olympians were getting paid for their participation. The criticism did not deter fans from witnessing history and greatness on display. One young woman called watching the Dream Team the most exhilarating 15 seconds of her life. They defeated Germany 111–83, Brazil 127–83, Spain 122–81, Puerto Rico 115–77, and Lithuania 127–76.

The Dream Team met Croatia again in the gold medal game on August 8. This time Kukoč was ready, scoring 16 points and passing for nine assists. The performance proved to his naysayers that he was tough enough to play in the NBA. Michael Wilbon, co-host of ESPN's *Pardon*

My Interruption, scoffs at the suggestion that Kukoč was "soft" because he lived in a war-torn country unlike anything these American celebrities had ever experienced.[61] Kukoč was not enough to beat the Americans, who won the rematch 117–85. Some players fought back tears as they walked to the podium to receive their medals afterward. Malone says being up on that podium made him truly understand the significance of the national anthem and feel like he served his country. He got goose bumps every time he heard the song after that night. For Bird, hearing the anthem reminded him of his late father, who would stand in the house with his hand over his heart whenever the song played. Johnson and Barkley were overcome with uncontrollable joy.

The most noticeable player on the medal stand was Jordan, draped in a giant American flag. As a little kid watching this in Sumter, South Carolina, I thought MJ was America's ultimate hero. I was too young to know anything about patriotism other than reciting the Pledge of Allegiance every morning at Saint John Baptist de la Salle Catholic School. But I assumed that he must really love America, and since he was my hero, so did I. If Jordan wanted to publicly display his patriotism on a world stage, it certainly made sense considering the historical context. The Berlin Wall in Germany came down on November 9, 1989. The wall's collapse signaled the end of the Cold War after almost five decades. President Reagan's successor, George H.W. Bush, saw the world through a lens as if World War II had never happened. He idealistically believed in a world where nations worked together and avoided bloody rivalries for power. He called this concept a New World Order.[62]

This New World Order received its first test on August 1, 1990, when U.S. intelligence confirmed that Iraq had invaded its neighbor Kuwait. The U.S. government feared that if Kuwait fell to Iraqi dictator Saddam Hussein, the same fate would befall oil-rich Saudi Arabia. Hussein believed that no one in the West would care if he conquered Kuwait and other parts of the Middle East. But President Bush lived by a moral code, and in his eyes, Hussein violated that code by invading Kuwait without cause.[63] This invasion was more than a conflict between two Arab nations. It was about oil and the price of gasoline, the balance of power in the Middle East, America's role in defending her allies, and what the world could do to restrain Hussein. In keeping with the spirit of the New World Order, Bush acted multilaterally, gaining the support of the United Nations to form a coalition of 35 countries. On January 12, 1991, Bush announced that America was going to war with Iraq.

If you are over 35, you remember Whitney Houston's soul-stirring performance of the national anthem before Super Bowl XXV on January 27, 1991. Houston, originally scheduled to sing the anthem in 1987, was the world's best-selling female pop star, with six number-one songs and two number-one albums on the *Billboard* charts. Her performance, accompanied by a military flyover at Tampa Stadium in Tampa, Florida, was a microcosm of the patriotic spirit in the nation just 10 days into the Persian Gulf War. Under the exemplary leadership of generals Colin Powell and Norman Schwarzkopf, the U.S. won the war in only 42 days. This was the first time images of war were shown on live television, and news correspondents reported live from bunkers amid bombs being dropped over Baghdad. Saddam Hussein was allowed to remain in power, something that would come back to bite the U.S. a decade later.[64]

Although the war ended more than a year before the Olympics, that patriotic spirit was still heightened in America. Whitney Houston, a Black woman from New Jersey, became the embodiment of Americana when she sang the anthem. (Most people do not know that the NFL initially rejected Houston's version of the anthem when they heard a recording taped in rehearsal. They claimed her gospel-music-influenced rendition was inappropriate.) "She was able on that night in a very complex and scary situation to do what she did so often, which was to make everyone feel like things were going to be okay," says former *Billboard* editor Danyel Smith.[65] When white Americans heard Houston sing the anthem at the Super Bowl, they did not hear a "Black" woman. They heard a proud American woman. Similarly, when white Americans witnessed Jordan draped in that flag, they did not see a dark-skinned Black man with a bald head. They saw another embodiment of Americana. Years later, the public learned the genuine reasons for Jordan's patriotic display, which had nothing to do with his love for his country.[66]

Be Like Mike

At the start of Jordan's rookie season in 1984, his agent, David Falk, introduced him to sneaker companies looking for the next superstar to endorse their product. Until then, the marquee NBA players had modest endorsement deals worth $100,000 annually with Converse or Puma. Jordan wanted to sign with the German company Adidas because those were the sneakers he had worn in college. Furthermore, Adidas was the hip brand all the cool kids wore, thanks to the rap group Run-D.M.C. However, Adidas never invited him to their headquarters for an interview. Sonny Vaccaro, a sports marketing executive, convinced Falk that Jordan should sign with his employer, an upstart company named Nike.[67]

The Nike story begins with Phil Knight, a former student-athlete at the University of Oregon. Knight traveled to Kobe, Japan, in 1963 to meet with the producers running sneaker brand Tiger. While he was in Kobe, Knight invested $500 in the company. He returned to America with a large quantity of Tigers to sell out of his car's trunk at track meets. Knight's company, originally named Blue Ribbon Sports, earned $1 million in sales by 1969. In 1971, Knight and his partner, Bill Bowerman, developed Nike's first sneaker. Bowerman poured melted rubber in his wife's waffle iron to create the iconic waffle sole of Nike's running sneakers. The company's new name came about after Jeff Johnson, a young graphics designer, had a dream about Nike, the Greek winged goddess who symbolized victory. A year later, Carolyn Davidson, a student at Portland State University, designed the brand's trademark swoosh logo for $35.[68]

In the early 1980s, Nike trailed Reebok in sales and Adidas in swag. "Nike was considered to be a stepchild in the shoe game. Nike was this little company that could," says sportswriter Jemele Hill in the 2019 Air Jordan documentary *One Man and His Shoes*. Michael Jordan initially met with Nike executives at Tony Roma's restaurant in Santa Monica, California. He sat down with Sonny Vaccaro to discuss possibly joining the Nike family. It took multiple follow-ups with Jordan's parents to convince him to meet with Nike designer Peter Moore and other representatives from the company. Jordan appeared to be bored with Nike's presentation during their pitch meeting. One version of the story says that as soon as Jordan and Falk left the meeting, a huge smile appeared on Jordan's face. He loved Vaccaro's idea to construct an entire marketing campaign around him. Bird and Johnson were among a series of NBA players endorsing Converse. Jordan was guaranteed his own signature sneaker, the Nike Air Jordan, and accompanying merchandise.[69]

Another version of this story says Jordan's mom had to persuade him to sign with Nike rather than Adidas.[70] This version is the context for the 2023 film *Air*, starring Academy Award winners Matt Damon as Vaccaro, Ben Affleck as Knight, and Viola Davis as Deloris Jordan. In the film, Vaccaro makes a surprise visit to the Jordans' home and sparks a relationship with Mrs. Jordan. The film ends with Mrs. Jordan persuading Vaccaro to meet Jordan's unique financial demands. Nike signed Jordan to a seven-year, $18 million contract that guaranteed royalties on every pair of sneakers sold. The goal was to sell $3 million worth of merchandise within four years. The company's total annual sales between the late 1970s and 1984 were $150 million. In its first year, the Air Jordan line amassed $126 million of Nike's sales.[71]

The debut pair of Air Jordans were a hit partly because of the myth associated with them. The standard sneakers worn by NBA players in the '80s were white and had little color. Jordan stepped on the court for the first time in a pair of black-and-red high-tops. The dominant myth until the

2010s was that those were the Air Jordan 1 Bred colorway. However, they were the Nike Air Ships, which the first pair of Jordans was modeled after. The NBA informed the Bulls that Jordan would be fined $5,000 for wearing those shoes. Nike made up a story about the NBA banning the Air Jordans and used that to promote the sneakers. In a 1985 commercial, a sweaty Jordan appears standing up, moving a basketball from hand to hand. He is wearing a black T-shirt, a red Nike cut-off T-shirt over it, black-and-red Nike gym shorts, white socks, and *the shoes*. As the camera slowly pans from his face down to his shoes, a voice speaks these famous words:

> On September 15th, Nike created a revolutionary new basketball shoe. On October 18th, the NBA threw them out of the game. Fortunately, the NBA can't stop you from wearing them—Air Jordans from Nike.[72]

When the narrator said sneakers were banned, two large black boxes appeared on the screen covering each shoe. The 35-second ad concluded with the iconic Air Jordan wings logo in a varsity red-and-black background. Nike promoted Jordan's debut sneakers for five months before releasing them to the public. The first time Jordan wore the shoes in public was at an exhibition game in New York. The Jordan 1s were marketed as a fashion must-have for individuals who were rebellious and anti-establishment. "Once anything gets banned, it becomes the coolest thing in the world," says sportswriter Bomani Jones.[73] Rapper LL Cool J (James Todd Smith) wore a pair on the back cover of his debut album, *Radio* (1985). Jordan, three dangling gold chains around his neck, sported the kicks (shoes) in the 1985 NBA All-Star weekend Slam Dunk Contest. The bold red, black, and white colorway that matched the Chicago Bulls' uniform colors became an instant classic after Jordan dropped 63 points on the Celtics at the Boston Garden in the 1986 playoffs.

Jordan almost left Nike to sign with Adidas after Nike's Air Jordan 2 silhouette was released. However, the introduction of Tinker Hatfield, Jr., an architectural designer at Nike, resulted in an uber-successful marriage that still exists today. Hatfield took inspiration from foreign luxury automobiles, World War II fighter planes, West African Kente cloth, tuxedo dress shoes, and other things. Marketing was just as significant as the design. Spike Lee, an emerging Black American film director in his 20s, was hired to direct the Air Jordan 3 commercial. Lee would become a staple in Jordan commercials for the next decade and beyond. "Is it the shoes? Money it's gotta be the shoes," became the famous catchphrase of the fictional character Mars Blackmon portrayed by Lee in the commercials. Lee first introduced this character, a B-boy from Brooklyn, in his debut film *She's Gotta Have It* (1986). Mars loved Jordans so much that he kept them on when he made love to his girlfriend, Nola Darling, in the movie.

B-boy was a nickname given to the Black and Latina kids in the hood who participated in a new subculture called hip-hop. B-boys, along with B-girls, were the kids who breakdanced. Lee and Nike were able to market Jordans to "the hood" and poor kids in urban America. A fresh pair of Js became the Holy Grail for Black and brown youth in the 1980s. Many of the new rappers wore them in pictures. They became socioeconomic status symbols for the local drug dealers and dope boys on the corner. "This particular sneaker brought with it a kind of heroism that made it desirable at an unprecedented level," says Elizabeth Semmelhack, senior curator of the Bata Shoe Museum in Toronto, Canada.[74] "For Black people, we were constantly told we were less than, we didn't matter. And I think there's a direct correlation between that and a little Black boy wanting a coveted pair of sneakers.... When he puts them on, he feels more than. He feels free," says filmmaker Lena Waithe.[75] By 1990, they were so coveted that *Sports Illustrated* published a cover story about the increasing numbers of youth being robbed and killed for their Js.[76]

Historian Walter LaFeber dissects the rise of Nike as a transnational corporation in his 2002 book *Michael Jordan and the New Global Capitalism*. Jordans became the top-selling American-based commodity, along with Coca-Cola, for teenagers in Japan in 1989. Historian Donald Katz says Phil Knight's goal was to make Nike the sports apparel equivalent of John D. Rockefeller's Standard Oil Company. Knight wanted to conquer the market domestically and overseas. Nike launched a $20 million global campaign in 1991 for its new Air Max 180 running shoe designed by Hatfield. The 180s debuted during that same Super Bowl game famous for Houston's renowned national anthem performance. Ads ran in multiple countries except South Africa due to the anti-apartheid movement. Globalization contributed to Jordan's earning $25 million off the court in 1992. A worldwide commercial starring cartoon legend Bugs Bunny introducing the new Air Jordan 7s in the Bordeaux and "Hare" colorways premiered during the 1992 Super Bowl.[77] These Nike ads were perfect bookends to Gatorade's "Be Like Mike" campaign.

Kareem Abdul-Jabbar accused Jordan of choosing "commerce over conscience," meaning that making money for himself and Nike became his primary focus.[78] In 1990, Harvey Gantt, a Black Democrat, challenged Republican incumbent Jesse Helms for his Senate seat. Gantt would have made history as North Carolina's first Black U.S. senator. Helms, a staunch segregationist, staged a filibuster to prevent the extension of the 1965 Voting Rights Act. He voted against establishing the King holiday and creating a national Black history museum. It should have been easy for Jordan to back Gantt's campaign, but he refused, saying in jest, "Republicans buy sneakers, too." For Jordan, it was safer and more lucrative to take Booker T. Washington's accommodationist approach rather than rocking the boat with politically charged agitation that might cost him white consumers. Sportswriters Dave Zirin and William Rhoden, author of *Forty Million Dollar Slaves* (2007), took Jordan to task for his apathy. "Had he said 'jump,' had he said 'protest,' most athletes would have jumped; most would have protested. Instead, Jordan said, 'Be like Mike.'"[79]

The Last Dance sparked a renewed interest in Jordan's refusal to be a leader for the Black community. "America is quick to embrace a Michael Jordan, Oprah Winfrey, or Barack Obama so long as it's understood you don't get too controversial around broader issues of social justice," said former President Obama.[80] Jordan responded to his detractors with the following statement:

> I do commend Muhammad Ali for standing up for what he believed in, but I never thought of myself as an activist.... When I was playing my sport, I was focused on my craft. Was that selfish? Probably, but that's where my energy was.... The way that I go about my life is that I set examples. If it inspires you, great. If it doesn't, then maybe I am not the person you should be following.[81]

This critique finally brings me back to the gold medal ceremony in Barcelona. Reebok was the official sponsor for the American Olympic team. This reality put Jordan in a bind because he was expected to wear the Olympic warm-up jacket with a big Reebok logo on the chest. Footage from *The Last Dance* captures Jordan in a car the night before the gold medal game, sharing his thoughts on the matter with a friend.

> Harvey Schiller. What a dick. The guy who said if we don't wear our uniforms, we can't accept our gold medal and all that stuff.... They said they gonna try to hide the Reebok logo, but they can't hide it like I'm gonna hide it. They in for a big fucking surprise.[82]

Jordan's selfish gesture was a microcosm of the underlying reasons for the NBA's involvement in the summer games. Competition and capitalism meant much more than patriotism and love of sport in the New World Order. "I think we have a great American product, and we'd like to market on a global basis with as much class and success as we possibly can," Commissioner Stern told a reporter.[83] Do not be fooled by the fond reflections of the Dream Team players today. This was about marketing the NBA and brand-building on a global stage. Players like Jordan had the most to gain. Nike placed a large billboard of Jordan in a pair of Jordan 7 Bordeaux in Barcelona. "It was the first time sports were being sold culturally. We were selling Americana, and what was attached to it was this incredibly handsome, successful player. And people wanted to be part of that," said Adam Silver.[84]

The Barcelona games made Michael Jordan the most recognizable and beloved athlete on the planet. Only Muhammad Ali and soccer legend Pelé may have been more popular at the time. This newfound level of celebrity brought intense scrutiny of Jordan as the Bulls strived for a third consecutive championship in the 1992–93 season. The media exposed his potential gambling addiction. Richard Esquinas claimed in his book, Michael & Me: Our Gambling Addiction ... my cry for help, that Jordan owed him over $1.2 million from betting on their golf matches. And then there was Jordan's relationship with James "Slim" Bouler, who was accused of drug and money laundering. Jordan admitted in court to writing Bouler a check for $57,000 to pay off gambling debts on the golf course.[85] Then, on August 3, 1993, Jordan's father's decomposed body was found by a fisherman. Daniel Green and Larry Demery, two minority teenage boys, were charged with stealing James Jordan's red Mercedes-Benz and killing him. Nearly two months later, Jordan stunned the world by retiring. He cited losing his passion for basketball after his father's death. Conspiracy theorists suggested that Stern secretly suspended him for betting on games. Others even dared to connect his father's murder to unpaid gambling debts.[86]

Not long after his retirement, Jordan announced that he would pursue his father's dream of seeing him play Major League Baseball. Baseball was Jordan's favorite pastime before he excelled at basketball. Nike marked his career transition by releasing the Jordan IXs, a high-top basketball sneaker modeled after baseball cleats. The sneakers also highlighted Jordan's role in the globalization of basketball with an image of a small globe on the back and different languages appearing on the sneaker's sole. Jordan played Minor League Baseball with the Birmingham Barons for a $1,200 monthly salary and later the Scottsdale Scorpions for a year and a half. His results on the baseball diamond were mixed. "Bag it, Michael," was one *Sports Illustrated* reporter's advice to the legend. The reporter got his wish. On March 19, 1995, Jordan sent a fax that read, "I'm back." Two nights later, he laced up his Nike Air Jordan X sneakers to play against Reggie Miller's Indiana Pacers. Despite an embarrassing second-round playoff elimination, a motivated Jordan led the Bulls to a second three-peat between 1996 and 1998. He starred in the blockbuster film *Space Jam*, which earned $250.2 million worldwide, making it the 10th-highest-grossing film of 1996.

By Jordan's final season with Chicago in 1997–98, the Bulls had become international rock stars. They opened their preseason at the McDonald's Open in Paris. Bulls games could be seen over communication satellites in 175 countries and 40 languages. When they defeated the Utah Jazz in the 1998 finals, Chinese television aired the final game three times. Jordan finished second in a poll conducted by a Chinese firm of the best-known Americans in the country.[87] Jordan unretired in 2001, a month after the September 11 attacks, to play two seasons with the Washington Wizards. He purchased the Charlotte Bobcats basketball team in 2010. Much of the fortune that allowed him to become the first Black majority owner (governor) of an American professional sports franchise came from the salary he made off the court. According to *Forbes*, Jordan earned $90 million in career salary. However, he received $1.8 billion in endorsements. Nike was his most lucrative endorser. Phil Knight's brand owes its success to Jordan's international appeal. The company earned $5.1 billion off Jordan's sales alone in 2022 (21 years after Jordan's final retirement).[88]

The 1992 Dream Team left an indelible imprint on the world that would extend into the millennium. Michael Jordan created the archetype for the modern athlete to achieve commercial success on and off the court. Many of the NBA's future American stars, including Kobe Bryant and LeBron James, were kids watching the Dream Team play on television during their summer break from school. Overseas, young boys named Tony Parker, Manu Ginobli, Pau Gasol, Marc Gasol, Tim Duncan, Steve Nash, Dirk Nowitzki, and Yao Ming were inspired to learn the game. Both Parker (from France) and Pau Gasol (from Spain) referenced the Dream Team in their 2023 Hall of Fame induction speeches. This new generation of players became the next iterations of Jordan, Johnson, Bird, Barkley, and Robinson, helping to transform the NBA into the most global American professional sports league by the 2020s.

2

Redemption Song

> *"I think winning a gold medal is more important [than an NBA title] because you're playing for your country."*
> —Kobe Bryant[1]

The Dream Team's success in Barcelona was a gift and a curse for the NBA. It introduced the NBA's product and incredible talent pool to the world. Basketball rapidly became the world's second-most-popular sport, behind soccer. Consequently, the world caught up with the U.S. by the mid-2000s. While the Dream Team and its early successors embarrassed all foreign competitors who played in awe of them, this was no longer the case by 2004. A poor bronze-medal-winning performance in the 2004 Olympics led to the creation of a new USA Basketball program and the formation of the "Redeem Team" at the 2008 Summer Olympics in Beijing, China. This chapter explores how this team, led by America's most respected college coach, Mike Krzyzewski (Coach K), succeeded in reestablishing the U.S. as a world leader in basketball and carrying out a larger objective—selling American patriotism in a post-9/11 world. The chapter also focuses on the ascension of the team's two headliners, Kobe Bryant and LeBron James, to global stardom.

Welcome to Atlanta, Where the Players Play

On September 18, 1990, the International Olympic Committee (IOC) selected Atlanta, Georgia, as the site for the 1996 Summer Olympics. The choice of Atlanta surprised many observers who thought Greece, the birthplace of the Olympics, was the ideal location for the centennial games. These were the first games held in the United States since 1984. As a kid in 1996, I fondly remember rushing home from summer track practice to watch the various athletic competitions. Those Olympics had several consequential storylines. American sprinter Michael Johnson shattered world records in the 400-meter and 200-meter races. The U.S. women's gymnastics team, nicknamed the Magnificent Seven, won the country's first gold medal in the women's team competition. Gymnast Kerri Strug provided the most dramatic moment of the summer games by nailing her landing on a vault with a severely sprained ankle.[2] Her teammate Dominique Dawes paved the way for future Black gymnasts Gabby Douglas and Simone Biles 20 years later. The games were nearly overshadowed when a pipe bomb was detonated at Centennial Olympic Park on July 27, killing two people and injuring another 111 individuals. Security guard Richard Jewell was initially blamed for the bombing but was later declared innocent.[3]

The 1996 games introduced the world to two new versions of the Dream Team, one for men and another for women. The women's team was undoubtedly more significant than its male counterpart. Unlike Jordan and his crew, who humiliated their foreign opponents in Barcelona four years earlier, the 1992 women's team struggled to win bronze. This was the first time they did not return home with the gold. The women also lost to Brazil 110–107 in the 1994 World Championships in Australia. At the time, America's female basketball players could play overseas or in the Olympics only once they completed college. NBA commissioner David Stern saw the emergence of the women's collegiate game in the early '90s and the potential for future financial success. NBA deputy commissioner Russ Granik began asking what if they invested in women's USA hoops as they did with the Dream Team. The plan was to put the women's team on a 10-month barnstorming tour to test the waters. If that tour were successful, the NBA would commit to starting a professional women's league.[4]

The women's select team included the country's best players, such as Lisa Leslie, Rebecca Lobo, Ruthie Bolton, Teresa Edwards, Sheryl Swoopes, and current University of South Carolina women's head coach Dawn Staley. Led by Stanford University's head coach, Tara VanDerveer, they embarked upon a 52-game tour spanning four continents and 7,775 miles. NBA Entertainment shot 500 hours of footage that was never publicly released until 2022. The women did everything to connect with the fans. "We were auditioning for the world," said Ruthie Bolton. She and her late teammate Nikki McCray would sing the national anthem before the games. They often dealt with extreme weather conditions and poorly heated gyms abroad. Carla McGhee said they had to practice with gloves on in Siberia. You could see their breath when they spoke. The women always flew coach and shared rooms in dingy, rat-infested hotels. Despite the inhumane conditions, they went undefeated on the tour, leading Stern to announce the establishment of the Women's National Basketball Association (WNBA) on April 26, 1996, 85 days before the start of the Olympics.[5]

The women's team routed Brazil 111–87 in the 1996 Olympic gold medal game. Their closest margin of victory throughout the games was 17 points. As the women reclaimed gold for the U.S. and planted the seeds for the WNBA, the men were looking to repeat the magic of their predecessors from Barcelona. The men were nicknamed Dream Team III. A lesser-known team that won gold at the 1994 FIBA World Championship in Toronto had previously used the Dream Team moniker. The 1996 team's roster had a few familiar faces from 1992: Charles Barkley, Scottie Pippen, David Robinson, John Stockton, and Karl Malone. Newcomers included Gary Payton, Mitch Richmond, Reggie Miller, Grant Hill, Anfernee "Penny" Hardaway, Shaquille "Shaq" O'Neal, and Hakeem Olajuwon. Olajuwon was born in Nigeria and was the league's first MVP from Africa. His dual citizenship allowed him to play for the U.S. Lenny Wilkens, the Atlanta Hawks' head coach and Dream Team assistant coach, replaced Chuck Daly. The team's average margin of victory was nearly 30 points. They defeated FR Yugoslavia 95–69 in the gold medal game.

Dream Team III failed to capture the luster of its predecessors. Barkley revealed his distaste for the experience in the final episode of Jack McCallum's 2020 podcast series, *The Dream Team Tapes*. "'96 was a fucking nightmare," he said.[6] Apparently, the team lacked the camaraderie they had four years earlier. Coach Wilkens was unable to bring the players together as Daly had done before him. The absence of Johnson, Bird, and Jordan was the biggest reason for the lack of enthusiasm surrounding the team. Furthermore, the novelty of seeing the NBA's best players for the first time on a global stage was gone.

The U.S. did not send NBA players to compete in the 1998 FIBA World Championship. Professional players returned in 2000 for the next Olympics in Sydney, Australia. The highlight of the games was Vince Carter, the 6'6" shooting guard from the NBA's first expansion team in Canada, literally jumping over a 7'2" center from France for an explosive slam dunk. The U.S. beat Russia by 15 points in the quarterfinals and squeaked out a two-point victory over Lithuania in the semifinals. They beat France 85–75 in a nail-biting gold medal game. For comparison, the 1992 Dream Team's average margin of victory was 50 points. These close, unimpressive victories were indicative of a few things. First, the U.S. was no longer sending its best players. The 2000 team did not even use the Dream Team moniker. While the roster featured six future Hall-of-Famers, the remaining players were not perennial All-Stars. The names of the players who withdrew from the team were far more impressive: Kobe Bryant, Tim Duncan, Allen Iverson, Shaquille O'Neal, David Robinson, Scottie Pippen, Paul Pierce, Reggie Miller, Chris Webber, John Stockton, and Karl Malone.

The second lesson that should have been learned from the Sydney games was that the world was finally catching up to America in basketball. International players were so in awe of Jordan and his teammates that they could have genuflected after each basket scored. The opposing players sitting on the bench took pictures of the Americans during the games. Brazil's Oscar Schmidt, one of the greatest international basketball players in history, said his goal was to get every Dream Team member's autograph while he was in Barcelona.[7] There were only 23 foreign-born players in the NBA in 1992. In 2000, there were 57. The number jumped to 109 by 2008. Unsurprisingly, the international teams improved with the increasing number of foreigners making NBA rosters. These players no longer feared their American counterparts or placed them on a pedestal. This new attitude was never more evident than in Athens four years later.

When It All Falls Down

On December 12, 2000, the United States Supreme Court voted to end a recount in Florida over disputed ballots in the presidential election. Although the Democratic candidate, former Vice President Al Gore, won the popular vote by nearly 500,000, he did not have enough Electoral College votes to win the election unless he won Florida. The national news media declared his Republican challenger, George W. Bush, son of former President George H.W. Bush, the next president. Before Gore could give his concession speech, his advisers told him to ask for a recount because there were reports of several ballots that were either miscounted or thrown out. After weeks went by, Bush's lawyers asked the Supreme Court to intervene. The majority conservative court voted 7–2 to declare Bush the winner on the grounds that the recount violated the Equal Protection Clause of the U.S. Constitution.[8]

President Bush's first year in office was rather mundane in the beginning. He supported oil drilling in the Arctic National Wildlife Refuge, barred federal funding for stem cell research, attempted education reform with his controversial No Child Left Behind Act, and pushed through the largest tax cut in history to stimulate the economy in the wake of the dot-com bubble burst.[9] Then, on the morning of Tuesday, September 11, 2001, as he was reading a book titled *The Pet Goat* to a group of second graders at Emma E. Booker Elementary School in Sarasota, Florida, his chief of staff, Andrew Card, whispered in his ear that the nation was under attack by foreign invaders.[10] To quote the rapper Drake, from that point forward, "Nothing was the same."[11]

At approximately 8:46 a.m., American Airlines Flight 11 crashed into the North Tower of the World Trade Center Building in New York

City between the 93rd and 99th floors. Ninety-two people died on board that flight. Four minutes later, American Airlines Flight 77 was hijacked. United Airlines Flight 175 crashed into the building's South Tower between the 77th and 85th floors at 9:03 a.m. Fifty-six passengers died on board that plane. Hundreds of people jumped out of the burning building to their deaths. Others died trapped inside or, in the case of the first responders from the police and fire departments, trying to rescue victims. Flight 77 crashed into the Pentagon building in Arlington, Virginia, near Washington, D.C., at 9:37 a.m., killing 64 passengers and 125 people inside the building. Hilda Taylor, a faithful member of my father's church, Ryland Epworth United Methodist, was on board that plane. United Airlines Flight 93, hijacked at 9:28 a.m., was intended to crash into the U.S. Capitol building, but brave passengers overpowered the hijackers, forcing the plane to crash in Somerset County, Pennsylvania. All 44 passengers were killed in the crash. On September 11, 2,996 people died, including the 19 hijackers who committed murder-suicide.[12] Scholar Pu Haozhou believes that globalization helped to spread anti–American sentiment within countries that did not benefit and despised the West.[13]

The attacks were orchestrated by Osama bin Laden, leader of al-Qaeda, a Middle Eastern Islamic extremist organization who believed they were engaging in jihad against their satanic enemies in the West. This conflict had been brewing since the Soviet Union's 1979 invasion of Afghanistan during the Cold War. The Soviets remained in Afghanistan until 1989. The invasion led to the formation of another extremist group called the Taliban. Bin Laden traveled to Afghanistan during the war to help defeat the Soviets. Bin Laden, a Sunni Muslim and the son of a wealthy Saudi Arabian businessman, had his citizenship in Saudi Arabia revoked in 1991 for publicly speaking out against the country's partnership with the U.S. Bin Laden relocated to Sudan, where he helped to form al-Qaeda, meaning "the foundation" or "the base." Bin Laden was one of the few people to recognize the legitimacy of the Taliban regime in Afghanistan. His respect for the Taliban earned him their support.

In his speech to a joint session of Congress on September 20, President Bush stated that America was targeted by these terrorists because "we love freedom. And they hate freedom."[14] Bush announced his new foreign policy titled the Bush Doctrine, which declared that America would go to war with terrorism (making little distinction between the terrorists and the foreign nations that harbored them). "Either you are with us, or you are with the terrorists," he said.[15] The U.S. launched its first airstrikes in Afghanistan on October 7. Some officials believed that the Taliban was harboring bin Laden and may have helped him plan the attacks. Following the airstrikes, American ground troops chased out the Taliban and established a new pro–West government led by American ally Hamid Karzai. Under Karzai, many of the Taliban's repressive policies were prohibited. Women and girls were now free to attend school and serve in parliament. Fewer than 100 American troops died in this initial part of the war in Afghanistan, although it would end up lasting until August 30, 2021, and result in 2,456 American casualties.[16]

By January 2002, President Bush expanded the scope of the war on terror by declaring that Iran, Iraq, and North Korea were an "Axis of Evil" that harbored terrorists out to get us. On March 20, 2003, the U.S. invaded Iraq. What did Iraq have to do with 9/11 and the war in Afghanistan? Well, according to Bush and his vice president, Dick Cheney, Iraqi leader Saddam Hussein was stockpiling chemical weapons of mass destruction to use against the U.S. Some believed that he *could have* been secretly tied to the September 11 attacks. Neither of these claims has been verified after more than 20 years. Some political scholars believe that Bush and Cheney's obsession with Hussein stemmed back to Bush's father's decision not to remove him from power when he had the chance in 1991 during the Persian Gulf War.[17] The U.S., Great Britain, and a coalition of allies much smaller than the one in 1991 went to war with Iraq. Within a month, the capital city of Baghdad was captured, Hussein was dethroned, and a new pro–American government was established. Bush proclaimed "Mission Accomplished" on the aircraft carrier USS *Abraham Lincoln* on May 1, 2003.[18] Unfortunately, Bush gravely underestimated his opposition. Fighting would continue due to an Iraqi insurgency. By 2006, the country had become a haven for Islamic terrorists. The war dragged on until 2011, costing the U.S. $728 billion and the lives of 4,492 servicemembers.[19]

With the backdrop of the war on terror came the 2004 Summer Olympics. Many players and their agents had safety concerns about being overseas due to the growing anti–American sentiment. Like the 2000 Olympics, the names of the nine players who either dropped out or declined the invitation to participate were far more impressive than the final roster. Shaquille O'Neal, Kevin Garnett, Vince Carter, Tracy McGrady, and Jason Kidd were among the most prominent names.[20] Kobe Bryant wanted to play but could not participate for reasons I will discuss later. The squad in Athens consisted of Tim Duncan, Allen Iverson, Stephon Marbury, Carlos Boozer, Shawn Marion, Lamar Odom, Amar'e Stoudemire, Emeka Okafor, and Richard Jefferson. The final three additions to the team were rising sophomores Carmelo Anthony, Dwyane Wade, and LeBron James. While every Dream Team member, minus Christian Laettner, was a future Hall-of-Famer, the 2004 roster had only five future inductees. Larry Brown was named head coach, fresh off leading the Pistons to an upset over the Lakers in June's NBA Finals.

The team held its first practice in Jacksonville, Florida, three weeks before the Olympics began. Carmelo Anthony, then a 20-year-old rising star on the Denver Nuggets, reflected on his first day of practice. "It was like two different teams. You had A.I., Marbury, Tim Duncan, and then you had the younger guys who were just coming into the league," said Anthony. "There was a disconnect between both groups."[21] Before the games started, some media members wondered if the team could win a gold medal. The players and their families did not stay in the Olympic Village with the rest of the Olympic athletes. Instead, they were housed in the *Queen Mary 2*, a luxury cruise ship with five swimming pools, a double-deck sauna and spa, an arcade, 14 decks with sports courts, and plush private staterooms with blond-wood paneling. They had catered meals 24 hours a day. Back in the Village, free Wi-Fi was a luxury.[22] Greek and American police protected them. Despite all these amenities, some players, such as Carlos Boozer, felt detached from everyone else. "We are not even in the Olympic Village. We're not by the Olympians. It did not feel like we were a part of the Olympic experience."[23]

The team's first test came on August 15, 2004, when they faced Puerto Rico in the preliminary round. Most American reporters were off covering other Olympic events because the game was supposed to be an afterthought. Doug Collins, the star of the 1972 team that lost to the Russians, was broadcasting the game for NBC. Early on, he looked at his partner, Mike Breen, and said, "Uh-oh! We're in trouble." Puerto Rico's 21–20 lead quickly ballooned to 49–27 by halftime. Their 6'1" starting point guard, Carlos Arroyo, who was also a member of the Utah Jazz, had the game of his life. He went off for 24 points and seven assists. His teammate Eddie Casiano added another 18 points. José Rafael "Piculín" Ortiz Rijos, a former Oregon State University college player, scored eight points and grabbed six rebounds. The final score was 92–73, making this the first loss for an Olympic team made up of NBA players and the third Olympic loss in the long history of USA Basketball.[24]

Carmelo Anthony summed up Team USA's stunning loss like this: "That first game against Puerto Rico really let us know, we fucking around. We gotta get our shit together."[25] One news anchor for MSNBC joked the following day that they were no longer the Dream Team. They had become the Cream Team. Unfortunately, the bleeding did not cease with Puerto Rico. Team USA suffered another loss in the preliminary round, this time to Lithuania 94–90. They managed to reach the semifinals by defeating Angola, 89–53, and Spain, 102–94. But they were not ready for Argentina in the semifinals. Argentina, led by current and future NBA players Manu Ginobili, Luis Scola, Andres Nocioni, Juan Ignacio Sanchez Brown (Pepe Sanchez), Carlos Delfino, Walter Herrmann, and Ruben Wolkowyski, won

89–81. When interviewed after the game, Argentina's point guard, Pepe Sanchez, told reporters the U.S. had the best individual talent but international basketball is a team sport. Boozer and his American teammates marveled at their opponent's chemistry on the court.

The U.S. clinched a bronze medal by beating Lithuania 104–96. Nevertheless, their third-place finish was embarrassing and a national disgrace. "We were just a bunch of bullshit thrown together and told to go out there and win us a gold medal. There was no culture at all," said Anthony. "It was ugly to watch and terrible to be a part of," said Wade.[26] The players were a perpetual object of ridicule upon their return to America. "Why Team USA keep getting blown out," Jadakiss rapped on his 2004 *Billboard* hit single, "Why."[27] Late-night talk show host David Letterman mocked them on his countdown segment. While the banter from Letterman and Jada was subtle, Jack McCallum and J.A. Adande spotted something more sinister when discussing the team in their 2021 podcast, *The Dream Team Tapes*, season two. McCallum detected a tone of racism in many of the critiques written by white American journalists. According to Adande, this was a microcosm of a growing disconnect between the NBA and white fans and mainstream media at the time.[28] Team USA was all Black, unlike their predecessors in 1992 and 1996. Although the 2000 roster in Sydney was all Black, those players were deemed respectable and nonconfrontational. They were following in the footsteps of Jordan, Johnson, O'Neal, and Hill. However, the 2004 squad was composed of younger players who represented a new rebellious attitude associated with the urban youth culture of the hip-hop generation.[29]

The 2004 team was led by Allen Iverson, Tim Duncan, and Stephon Marbury. The team's rebounding leader, Duncan, was this trio's most accomplished player. He was the MVP of the NBA Finals in 1999 and 2003. By the time his career ended in 2016, he had won five NBA titles. The San Antonio Spurs drafted him with the overall number-one pick in the 1997 draft. Duncan honed his skills during a four-year stint at Wake Forest University in North Carolina. A native of the Virgin Islands, the 6'11" power forward/center was always shy and reserved in public. He displayed little emotion on the court. His calm, nonthreatening, bland demeanor earned him the nickname "The Big Fundamental," a perfect fit for the Spurs dynasty of the 2000s and 2010s.

Iverson and Marbury were much flashier and more popular players than Duncan. Marbury was the team's leader in assists. The Coney Island, Brooklyn, native had been ballyhooed since he was an "NYC point god" at Abraham Lincoln High School. Spike Lee based his fictional character Jesus Shuttlesworth, played by Ray Allen, on Marbury in his 1998 film *He Got Game* starring Denzel Washington. After his first year at Georgia

Tech, the Milwaukee Bucks selected him with the fourth pick in the 1996 draft. The Bucks traded him on draft night to the Minnesota Timberwolves. Between 1996 and 2004, Marbury played on four different teams and was perceived as selfish. He joined the New York Knicks in January 2004, a year before Larry Brown was hired to coach the team. Marbury and Brown had a combustible relationship that began in Athens. At one point, Brown threatened to send him home.[30]

And then there was Iverson. Allen Iverson, affectionately known as AI, was the face of the 2004 Olympic team. He was the opposite of the media darling Jordan. Michael Jordan grew up in a stable, middle-class household with a mother and father. His parents stressed education and the values of middle-class respectability. Iverson grew up in the housing projects of Hampton, Virginia. He was raised by a single mom who had him when she was 15. He was the state's best football and basketball player as a high school junior. In the summer before his senior year, he and a group of friends were arrested for their involvement in a racially motivated bowling alley brawl involving a group of white teenagers. He was charged with maiming by a mob, a state law passed decades earlier to protect Black people from white lynch mobs. Iverson was sentenced to five years in 1993 but served only four months because he was granted clemency by Douglas Wilder, Virginia's first Black governor.[31]

For two years, Iverson played college ball for Coach John Thompson, coach of the 1988 Olympic team, at Georgetown University in Washington, D.C. The Philadelphia 76ers selected him as the number-one pick in the 1996 draft, making him the first point guard to go first overall since Magic Johnson in 1979. Iverson was the most coveted player of a draft class that was arguably the second best in the league's history behind Jordan's 1984 class. Iverson stood 6'0" with shoes on his feet and barely weighed 165 pounds. His small stature among a league of giants made him a fan favorite and youth idol. He led the league in scoring three times, was a three-time All-NBA first-team member, and was league MVP in 2001. Iverson carried an average Sixers team to the NBA Finals in 2001. His cultural impact off the court was even more impactful. He was the first NBA superstar to wear cornrows and have his body covered in tattoos. His gaudy platinum jewelry made him a walking billboard for hip-hop's bling era in the late 1990s and early 2000s. Commissioner Stern instituted a dress code partly because his attire was too "urban" for the league's middle-aged white consumers. He was the quintessential symbol of the hip-hop culture and an anti-establishment ethos.[32] Music personality Sway Calloway described him as 2Pac (Tupac Shakur) in basketball shorts.

Although Iverson was never politically active, his refusal to conform to mainstream standards of respectability earned him the respect of Black youth. Sports journalist Dave Zirin called Iverson the bridge between the earlier generation of Black athletes who were racial accommodationists and today's activist athletes. This posture was not popular in 2004. Iverson's demeanor, attire, and run-ins with the law caused many whites and conservative Blacks to label him a thug. He was a shooting guard in an undersized point guard's body who modeled his game after Jordan's one-on-one style of play from the earlier years of his career. The Sixers surrounded him with less talented players willing to let him carry the scoring load. Barkley described his style as "me, myself, and Iverson." His inability to follow the rules of Larry Brown, an older Jewish white man and his coach in Philadelphia from 1997 to 2003, fueled more criticism. Although Adande says Iverson was a model citizen in Athens and the hardest-working team member, the media scapegoated him as the reason for the Olympic team's misfortune.[33]

Team USA's lackluster performance in Athens put the country and the NBA on alert. One morning in January 2005, the phone rang at Jerry Colangelo's home. When Colangelo picked up the phone, Stern was on the other end, asking him to spearhead a new USA Basketball program. It did not take much convincing for Colangelo to accept, but he made two demands. He had to have complete control of the selection process for players and coaches, and cost could not be a factor.[34] Stern and Russ Granik oversaw USA Basketball; however, Colangelo was the ideal fit for this new position as the director of USA Basketball. He owned the Phoenix Suns and Phoenix Mercury (WNBA), the Arizona Diamondbacks (MLB), the Arizona Sand Sharks of the Continental Indoor Soccer League, and the Arizona Rattlers of the Arena Football League. He helped relocate the Winnipeg Jets to Phoenix to become the Coyotes of the National Hockey League (NHL).

Colangelo was named NBA Executive of the Year four times during his tenure with the Suns. He chaired basketball operations for the Philadelphia 76ers years and the NBA Board of Governors years later. Colangelo has chaired the Naismith Memorial Basketball Hall of Fame since 2009. Grand Canyon University opened the Colangelo School of Sports Business in 2012. His son Bryan followed in his footsteps, serving as the general manager for the 76ers, the Suns, and the Toronto Raptors. Colangelo expressed his feelings for accepting the job:

> I am proud to be an American. I was unhappy about the way people were looking at us as athletes, in particular, our basketball people in Greece. It was a little shameful. The opportunity to represent your country is a lot different from the city, the state, and not just something domestic. This was representing your country on the world stage and having a chance to make a statement.[35]

Colangelo accepted this new role at a tumultuous time in his personal life. He sold the Suns and Diamondbacks in 2004. Months later, he beat off two muggers who assaulted his wife while they were vacationing in Paris. At the end of the year, the 65-year-old mogul was diagnosed with prostate cancer. His first order of business with Team USA was to hire a head coach. Colangelo organized a meeting in Chicago with 35 former Olympic coaches and NBA players, including Jordan, Pippen, John Thompson, Jerry West, and Dean Smith. He asked each attendee to describe their Olympic experience and provide suggestions for team members and a coach.[36] Smith, the Hall-of-Fame coach at the University of North Carolina at Chapel Hill who coached Jordan in college, surprisingly recommended Mike Krzyzewski (Coach K). He and Krzyzewski were bitter rivals in the Atlantic Coast Conference (ACC). By the mid–1990s, Krzyzewski's Duke University teams replaced UNC as the crème de la crème of the ACC. Duke reached the Final Four five consecutive seasons between 1988 and 1992 and again in 1994, 1999, 2001, and 2004. By the time Krzyzewski retired in 2022, he had taken Duke to 13 Final Four appearances and five national championship wins.

The other candidates for the job were Pat Riley and Gregg Popovich. Riley was the architect of the Showtime Lakers dynasty in the 1980s. In the 1990s and early 2000s, he transformed the New York Knicks and Miami Heat into championship contenders. The Knicks advanced to the finals in 1994, and the Heat won their first title in 2006. Popovich had already won championships with the Spurs in 1999, 2003, and 2005. Surprisingly, Phil Jackson was not considered, although he won six championship rings with Jordan's Bulls between 1991 and 1998. After leaving Chicago, Jackson won three consecutive titles with the Lakers between 2000 and 2002. He may not have been considered because he declined an offer to coach the team in the '90s, citing the need to spend time with his five children in the summers.

Colangelo disagreed with the politically outspoken Popovich over the years, about basketball matters, and did not endorse his candidacy. He says Popovich expressed little enthusiasm for the position when they spoke over the phone. Popovich's role on Larry Brown's coaching staff in 2004 did not strengthen his chances; there was an underlying push to disconnect entirely from that Athens experience. Jordan joined Smith in his support for Krzyzewski.[37] Based on Jordan's competitive nature, it would not surprise me if he rejected Riley because he coached the Knicks, one of his hated rivals. The Knicks were the equivalent of the Detroit Pistons from the '80s in terms of their physicality and abuse of Jordan on the court. Ultimately, Krzyzewski was chosen for the task. Although he had never coached an NBA team, he was the most respected college coach in American athletics and was an assistant to Chuck Daly in Barcelona.

Proud to Be an American

The 1992 Dream Team was a star-studded collection of the NBA's premier talent assembled to restore honor to the U.S. after a devastating Olympic loss to the Soviets in 1988. They were basketball's equivalent of Marvel's Avengers and DC Comics' Justice League. These were America's best and brightest superheroes working together to save the world as we knew it. National pride was crucial to the coaches and players associated with the Dream Team, but it would be naive to assume that patriotism was the cornerstone of that Barcelona experience. Commissioner Stern saw the 1992 Olympics as an opportunity to promote his league overseas to new markets. "I think we have a great American product, and we'd like to market on a global basis with as much class and success as we possibly can," he told an NBC reporter.[38] The Dream Team was equally important to emerging transnational companies like Nike and Reebok looking for opportunities to sell sneakers and apparel abroad. Who can forget Jordan draping himself in the American flag when he received his gold medal to hide the Reebok logo on his warm-up jacket? MJ was Nike's top spokesman, and being caught in Reebok was sacrilegious. Capitalism outweighed patriotism in 1992. This attitude was not the case in 2008, mainly due to Coach K.

Mike Krzyzewski was born in Chicago on February 13, 1947, to Polish immigrants William and Emily Krzyzewski. He grew up working-class on the West Side of Chicago in a neighborhood called Ukrainian Village due to its sizable Ukrainian immigrant population. Krzyzewski likes to refer to himself as a guy from the block. "They don't expect me to say, come on motherfuckers, we gotta win this gold," he said.[39] Coach K was quite fond of using the F-bomb around his players. After matriculating through Catholic private schools, he attended the United States Military Academy at West Point, New York. As a cadet, he played basketball for a young Richard "Bobby" Montgomery Knight.[40] After Krzyzewski graduated from West Point, he served as an officer in the U.S. Army from 1969 to 1974, achieving the rank of captain when he was honorably discharged from active duty. In 1974 he joined Bobby Knight's coaching staff at the University of Indiana. Indiana went 31-1 in his only season as an assistant coach. After the season, 28-year-old Krzyzewski left Knight's bench to become the head coach at West Point. He coached his alma mater for five years before accepting a job offer from Duke in 1990.[41]

Krzyzewski stressed patriotism more than any American basketball Olympic coach in recent memory. This belief was the bedrock of his coaching philosophy with Team USA. Their identity would no longer be defined by the individual names on the back of jerseys or the sneaker companies sponsoring the team. Instead, it would be modeled after that tiny American flag and the letters *USA* written on the front of the jersey. The team held its first training camp in Las Vegas, Nevada, in July 2006. Patriotism and respect for the military were quite noticeable during the 35-day camp. The team wore camouflage warm-ups to visit soldiers at a military base. Service members and their families were invited to watch practices. Veterans and high-ranking officers were among the team's guest motivational speakers.

Colonel Bob Brown from the U.S. Army lectured the players on the concept of "selfless service," which means putting the needs of others before your own. On the basketball court, selfless service means diving for a loose ball or sacrificing your body to take a charge.[42] On the battlefield, it means running into a line of bullets to sacrifice yourself to save another's life. Brown gave each player a flag worn on the uniform of a soldier who had fought in Iraq. One of those brave heroes was Captain Scott Smiley, who accompanied him. Smiley lost both eyes when he was hit by shrapnel on the battlefield. Dwyane Wade said meeting Smiley manifested the privilege of wearing that Olympic jersey. He communicated with Smiley, using a lapel microphone, during practice. Chris Bosh reflected on meeting the soldiers: "You saw how important it was to represent the United States of America. Who was watching, and what it meant to those people."[43] "Hearing those stories opened the players' hearts, and consequently, they became the U.S.," said Krzyzewski.[44]

I would never question Krzyzewski's sincerity. We are all products of our environment and upbringing. Clearly, his worldview was shaped by his time at West Point and serving in the army. One of his biggest concerns coming into the Olympics was getting his players to leave their egos at the door. The military analogies were a useful means to drive home this point. Meeting the soldiers and wounded veterans was the inspirational tool to help these "pampered" young millionaires play selflessly for the flag and represent the country with the utmost reverence. But I would be remiss to ignore the historical context of 2006. The U.S. was engaged in two wars—Afghanistan and Iraq—for the previously discussed reasons. Cable news networks dedicated much of their coverage to the war on terror. The Fox News Channel built its empire by emphasizing the war, the military, and the idea of being a true patriot.[45]

The increasing emphasis on patriotism in popular culture impacted professional sports. Howard Bryant, a prominent Black sports journalist, documents this in his 2021 book on sports and race, *Full Dissidence: Notes from an Uneven Playing Field*. Bryant analyzes how the U.S. military partnered with the National Football League (NFL) after 9/11. Sports broadcasters wore American flag pins on their suit jacket lapels. The military aired commercials during the games. Fans rose to their feet to applaud the countless soldiers being honored at the games. Teams sold camouflaged gear in their stores at stadiums and online. Bryant says Sunday afternoons provided the military with the perfect marketing platform.[46] According to a joint oversight report released by the late Arizona senator and 2008 Republican Party presidential nominee John McCain, the Pentagon spent $6.8 million to pay for these patriotic displays at NFL, MLB, NHL, and MLS (Major League Soccer) games. In the words of some U.S. senators, it amounted to "paid patriotism."[47]

Why was the NBA left off the Pentagon's list? The league has never been seen as representing "America's pastime" primarily because it is a predominantly Black workforce. Despite notable exceptions, most players did not transcend race like Michael Jordan and Magic Johnson. While the NFL and MLB are associated with country and rock music, which for some people are as American as apple pie, the NBA has been linked to hip-hop since the mid–1990s. Some might argue the genesis of the league's connection to hip-hop was when the Cold Crush Brothers challenged the Fantastic Five to a basketball game in the 1983 hip-hop classic film *Wild Style*. Rap pioneer Kurtis Blow released his seminal song "Basketball" a year later. Hip-hop is supposed to be ghetto, lower-class, rebellious, thuggish, and unpatriotic. Hip-hop was scapegoated for the shameful 2004 "Malice at the Palace," an incident involving Black players from the Indiana Pacers rushing into the stands in Detroit to fight white fans. Thus, having the overly patriotic Coach K, who represented both the military and elite higher education, as the face of the new Olympic team was an excellent way for the NBA to market its new generation of rising stars as legitimate and beloved pillars of Americana.

All Hail the New King in Town

The U.S. needed to win the gold or silver medal at the FIBA world championships to qualify for the 2008 Olympics in Beijing, China. They traveled to Sapporo, Japan, for the tournament in August 2006, losing to Greece 101–95 in the semifinals. Krzyzewski called it the worst loss in his career. The players were embarrassed to receive their bronze medals. Neither Krzyzewski nor his players were accustomed to the differences in FIBA rules or the variation in the style of play internationally. FIBA games had shorter 10-minute quarters. The size of the court was 91'9" × 49'2". The standard NBA court is 94' × 50'. Players could walk across the court while someone was shooting foul shots. The ball used had 12 panels instead of eight. The Americans had to learn a different game. The U.S. needed more than their talent to overcome this learning curve that summer. They regrouped the following summer in Vegas to prepare for another qualifying FIBA tournament. The version of the team that lost to Greece was not the one that eventually traveled to Beijing, but many of the core players were already in place. The team's headliner was the player many basketball aficionados and fanboys were eager to crown as the NBA's new king.

LeBron James was destined to become Michael Jordan's heir apparent and a global icon when *Sports Illustrated* dubbed him "The Chosen One" in 2002 when he was a 17-year-old high school phenom at Saint Vincent-Saint Mary in Akron, Ohio. Several biographies about the NBA's millennium messiah are available, including Jeff Benedict's *New York Times* bestseller *LeBron* (2023) and Brian Windhorst's *LeBron, Inc.: The Making of a Billion-Dollar Athlete*. Windhorst has written four books about him. Two films, *More Than a Game* (2009) and *Shooting Stars* (2023), are dedicated to his high school team. LeBron Raymone James, Sr., or simply LeBron, was born on December 30, 1984, in Akron. His childhood was far from ideal. His mother, Gloria James, gave birth to him when she was only 16. LeBron had little contact with his father, Anthony McClelland, who was incarcerated. They lived with his maternal grandmother, Freda James, until she suffered a fatal heart attack on Christmas Day, a week before LeBron's third birthday. He and his mom struggled to make ends meet, moving from one apartment or friend's home to the next following his grandmother's death. LeBron missed nearly 100 school days as a fourth grader due to the lack of stability and permanent residence.[48]

LeBron and Gloria moved 10 times between his third and eighth birthdays. Their saving grace came in the form of Frank and Pam Walker. Mr. Walker worked for the Akron Housing Authority and Akron Urban League. His wife was a congressional aide to state politician Tom Sawyer. LeBron lived with the Walkers for a year and a half until Gloria secured a stable home. As a child, LeBron watched television shows like *The Cosby Show*, *Family Matters*, and *The Fresh Prince of Bel-Air* about fictional elite and upper-middle-class Black families with happy two-parent households. The Walkers provided the closest thing to that fantasy. Organized basketball and football also opened a new world for him. When LeBron was in the fifth grade, the Walkers introduced him to Dru Joyce II. Eventually, LeBron began spending considerable time at Joyce's home, hanging out with his son Dru III. Joyce ended up coaching LeBron and Dru III on the varsity basketball team at Saint Vincent-Saint Mary. More importantly, Joyce became a surrogate father figure to LeBron. Since he was an only child, LeBron's teammates became his siblings and extended family.[49]

Saint Vincent-Saint Mary, a predominantly white Catholic school, was a culture shock for a young LeBron. "I'm not fucking with White people," he told his guests on his former HBO television series *The Shop*, describing his earliest encounters at the school. Many Akron residents wondered why he went there instead of John R. Buchtel, the Black public high school.[50] As a 6'2" freshman, LeBron averaged 21 points and six rebounds. He led the varsity team to a 27–0 record and a Division III state championship. LeBron was equally outstanding in football, being named to the All-State team in his sophomore and junior years. He received scholarship offers to play wide receiver for college blue bloods—Ohio State and Notre Dame.[51] An epic matchup with Lenny Cooke, the top-rated high school basketball player in the country, at the Adidas ABCD camp in the summer of 2001 introduced him to the rest of the country. At the camp, he met future Olympic teammate Carmelo Anthony, a rising senior at Oak Hill Academy in Virginia.[52]

Slam magazine, a national basketball publication aimed at hip-hop fans, devoted a cover-story article to LeBron that same summer as the camp. LeBron then appeared on the cover of *Sports Illustrated* during his junior year of high school. The magazine's front page read "The Chosen One." The article opened with a story detailing LeBron's first meeting with his idol, Michael Jordan, at a Washington Wizards game. "Remember that photograph of a teenage Bill Clinton meeting JFK? Same vibe. Here, together, are His Airness and King James, the 38-year-old master and the 17-year-old prodigy," wrote Grant Wahl.[53] William "Worldwide Wes" Wesley, a mysterious basketball powerbroker, arranged this historic meeting of basketball GOATs.[54] During his senior season, Time Warner Cable offered his games on pay-per-view. ESPN2 aired LeBron's game against the nation's number-one team, Oak Hill. Saint Vincent-Saint Mary eventually had to move their home games to the University of Akron's 5,100-seat James A. Rhodes Arena. The Fighting Irish games doubled the attendance of the university's men's team. Tickets were going for $120 on the aftermarket. On a lucky night, you could find Jay-Z sitting in the stands.[55]

LeBron opted to skip college and declare for the NBA draft. Sonny Vaccaro offered him a lucrative sneaker deal with Adidas. However, LeBron signed a $90 million contract with Nike before he graduated from high school. On June 26, 2003, the Cleveland Cavaliers drafted the 6'8", 240-pound recent high school graduate. LeBron took the league by storm, winning the Rookie of the Year award. He had Magic's passing ability and Jordan's scoring and athleticism. His charisma on and off the court was equal to Johnson's and Jordan's. He was selected as a reserve for the 2004 Olympic team but received little playing time. He guided the Cavaliers to the Eastern Conference finals in his fourth season. In the fifth game against the Detroit Pistons, LeBron scored 29 of the Cavalier's final 30 points. He finished the game with 48 points. The Cavaliers were swept by the Spurs in the NBA Finals that season. Tim Duncan was overheard on camera at the series' conclusion telling LeBron the league would soon belong to him. A month later, LeBron was in Vegas training for FIBA. Despite Duncan's proclamation, King James's ascendance to the throne had to wait a few more years. There was another alpha dog who was the world's reigning best player, and he had finally arrived in Vegas with something to prove.

The Black Mamba

Before LeBron, there was Kobe! Arguably, no player since Jordan propelled the NBA's popularity overseas more in the early 21st century. Kobe Bean Bryant's origin story began in Rieti, Italy, 50 miles from Rome, where he resided with his parents and older sisters, Sharia and Shaya, for seven years. He was six when his father uprooted the family to play for Sebastiani Rieti, an Italian professional basketball club. Kobe's dad, Joe "Jellybean" Bryant, was a star in his own right for a period. Joe was one of Philadelphia's top high school players during the early 1970s. Local reporters covered him as if he were already in the NBA. Joe met his wife and Kobe's mom, Pamela Cox, when he was a star player at La Salle University in Pennsylvania. After his junior year, Joe turned professional to support his family because an injury prevented his father from working. He signed with the 76ers expecting immediate stardom; however, he sat on the bench once the team signed ABA star Julius "Dr. J" Erving.

Joe's NBA career quickly dissipated after his parked white Datsun 280Z was spotted shortly after midnight on May 5, 1976, with a blown taillight. Two white police officers found him in the car with a woman who was not his wife. When they asked him to show his license and registration, he drove off, leading the officers on a three-mile chase. Joe lost control of the car and crashed into a sign and a wall. He jumped out of the vehicle and fled on foot. When the police caught him, a search of his car uncovered two vials of cocaine. He was charged with possession of illegal narcotics, reckless driving, and resisting arrest. Luckily, a judge ruled that the illegal search of his car was racially biased, and most charges were dismissed. Kobe was born two years later. His name was derived from the Kobe Japanese Steakhouse, where his mother loved to eat. The Sixers traded Joe to the San Diego Clippers, which sent him to Houston. His first year with the Houston Rockets was so dismal that the team's governor offered him an alternative job at a car dealership he owned. Rather than remain in Houston, Joe opted to repair his career in Europe.[56]

The Bryants initially felt isolated when they arrived in Italy due to the language barrier and the lack of other Black people. The kids learned Italian in school and quickly became fluent speakers. At times the family was treated as if they were famous because they were American and Black. Kobe could always find solace in basketball. His maternal grandfather sent him VHS tapes of NBA highlights to study. He attended Joe's practices on Sundays and mopped sweat off the floor. As his game matured, the Italian junior teams recruited him to play. Many of the boys he competed against were three years his elder. Kobe's mythic work ethic was forged as a youth in Italy. He arrived for his 9:00 a.m. practices three hours early to put in extra work. When he broke his right hand, he learned to dribble and shoot with his left.[57]

Joe retired in 1992 and relocated the family to Lower Merion, a majority-white suburb in Montgomery County, Philadelphia. Kobe was 13 then and struggled to fit in with his new American peers. "He didn't know any of the new slang kids were using, and he didn't have the shared cultural references in TV or music.... Even the clothes he brought back from Italy made him the subject of ridicule," says Mike Sielski, author of *The Rise: Kobe Bryant and the Pursuit of Immortality* (2022) and host of the *I Am Kobe* podcast.[58] Kobe and his sister dressed like they still lived in Europe. One of Kobe's teachers told his mother he had dyslexia because he could no longer spell in English.[59]

After Kobe completed a year at Bala Cynwyd Middle School, he enrolled in Lower Merion High School, where he became one of the top prep players in the nation. He won the MVP award at the Adidas ABCD camp the summer before his senior year. During the school year, he was named to the McDonald's All-American team, was the Gatorade National Player of the Year, and led his school to its first state championship in 53 years. Although he received scholarship offers from UNC and Duke, he announced to his school's packed auditorium that he had decided to skip college and take his talents to the NBA. Ironically, LeBron borrowed Kobe's phrasing when he announced his decision to leave Cleveland and take his talents to South Beach (Miami) in 2010.[60]

Kobe was already a star before he was drafted. Sonny Vaccaro moved to Philadelphia to befriend and woo Kobe. Vaccaro eventually signed him to a $48 million sneaker deal with Adidas. He believed Kobe could be for Adidas what Jordan was for Nike. Brandy, a chart-topping R&B singer and actress, escorted him to the prom. He appeared on Brandy's television series *Moesha* (1996–2001) four months later. Typically, most NBA general managers and coaches were skeptical of drafting a high school player; however, that was not the case with Lakers general manager Jerry West. The Minnesota Timberwolves selected Chicago prep star Kevin Garnett with the fifth overall pick a year earlier. Garnett's success proved that picking Kobe was not such a gamble. On June 23, 1996, West arranged a secret workout between Kobe and retired Lakers legend Michael Cooper. It only took a few minutes of the teenage phenom dominating the retired five-time champion for West to make his mind up. After the Charlotte Hornets selected Kobe as the 13th pick, West traded Vlade Divac, the Lakers' starting center from Serbia, to Charlotte for him.[61]

The Lakers signed Orlando Magic free agent Shaquille O'Neal in the summer of 1996. The new dynamic duo of Kobe and Shaq struggled initially when the Lakers replaced head coach Dell Harris with Phil Jackson. Under Jackson's mentorship, the Lakers won three consecutive championships between 2000 and 2002. They lost to the Detroit Pistons in the 2004 NBA Finals. Although O'Neal was the team's marquee attraction, Kobe rapidly emerged as one of the league's top five players. He mimicked Jordan both on and off the court. Kobe demanded the ball late in games like Jordan, even if it resulted in three consecutive air balls, as was the case against Utah in the 1997 playoffs. He copied his moves, won the Slam Dunk Contest like Jordan, wore an armband like Jordan, shaved his head bald like Jordan as a rookie, and spoke like Jordan in interviews.

Kobe's youth and obsessive determination to be great did not earn him many friends in the Lakers' locker room or around the league. Many of his teammates thought he was selfish on the court and too serious off it. Teammates say he would put headphones on and pretend to be listening to music so that he could hear if they were secretly insulting him. His growing feud with O'Neal, whom he viewed as lazy and immature because of how he handled a toe injury that cost the Lakers a fourth championship, became tabloid fodder.[62] Peers may have disliked him at the start of his career, but the mainstream media adored him. His pristine image, charisma, good looks, and amazing athleticism made him a spokesman for multiple corporations and the undeniable heir apparent to Jordan to lead the NBA into the millennium. On April 18, 2001, he married Vanessa Laine, a younger Latina model he met on the set for a music video for a rap album he planned to release. In January 2003, they welcomed Natalia, their eldest of three daughters. Kobe's life was on a steady upward trajectory until that summer. After receiving offseason surgery on his right shoulder, Kobe went to Eagle, Colorado, for physical therapy.

On the night of June 30, Katelyn Faber, a 19-year-old White employee at the Lodge & Spa at Cordillera in Edwards, Colorado, accused Kobe of rape and false imprisonment. According to Faber, she was asked to give him a tour of his hotel room around 10:00 p.m. When she proceeded to leave, he began kissing her. Faber says she consented until he removed his pants. As she tried to leave the room, he choked her and anally penetrated her. Kobe was arrested and released on bail. He publicly apologized to his wife for committing adultery but denied all criminal charges. He was facing life imprisonment if found guilty.[63] During the 2003-2004 season, Kobe would fly back and forth between meetings with his lawyers and games. A week before the start of his criminal case in September 2004, the case was dismissed after Faber declined to testify. She filed a civil lawsuit and agreed to drop the charges if he apologized to her in the courtroom. Kobe's lawyer read an apology on his behalf.[64]

The accusations sullied Kobe's pristine reputation and cost him endorsement deals with McDonald's and Nutella. Yet he maintained sponsorships with Nike, Sprite, and other brands.[65] His wife experienced a miscarriage amid the pressure of the trial. Dealing with the negative media scrutiny and growing disdain from the public outside of Los Angeles led Kobe to create his Black Mamba alter ego. The Black Mamba, a name taken from a villain in Quentin Tarantino's 2004 action film *Kill Bill: Volume 2*, was a scowling figure on the court and in press conferences who destroyed anything in his path. Over the next four seasons, Kobe became the world's most outstanding player, scoring 81 points in a game and winning league MVP in 2008.[66]

The ensuing trial prevented Kobe from joining the 2004 Olympic team in Athens. There was much to prove when he joined the pending Olympic squad in June 2007 for the World Championships. He was unpopular with his peers and had few friends. Many sports reporters blamed him for Shaquille O'Neal's departure to the Miami Heat. Phil Jackson, who retire after the Lakers lost in the 2004 NBA Finals, called him "uncoachable" in his 2005 book *The Last Season: A Team in Search of Its Soul*.[67] Kobe expressed his desire to be traded from the Lakers while he was in a Ralph's grocery store parking lot and then restated his wish during interviews with Stephen A. Smith and Jim Gray. When Kobe arrived in Vegas, he sat alone during his first Team USA meeting. Would he put his enormous ego aside, commit to Coach Krzyzewski's selfless philosophy, and get along with his teammates? Could he and LeBron work together to win gold? "I don't want to force a relationship. You sensed Kobe as someone who doesn't really want to be fucked with," said LeBron.[68]

The Redeem Team

Los Angeles journalist Bill Paschke describes the Olympic experience as the genesis of the second chapter in the Kobe Bryant narrative. Players immediately felt his presence during the Olympic training camp. One night, all the players, except Kobe, went to Tryst, a famous nightclub in Vegas, to party. It was nearly 5:30 a.m. when they returned to their hotel,

The Wynn, for bed. As they were heading to the elevators, who did they see sweat-drenched on his way to the gym for a workout? Kobe. From that morning forward, almost every player on the team joined him for predawn workouts and breakfast afterward. This new "Breakfast Club" ritual united the players and thawed the ice between Kobe and his teammates, especially LeBron.

Rather than bringing in more military veterans for training camp, Coach Krzyzewski invited Doug Collins to speak to the team. Collins was scheduled to announce the games in Beijing for NBC, and his son, Chris, was one of Coach K's assistant coaches. Collins was also the star of the 1972 Olympic team that the USSR robbed of its gold in Munich. He shared that horrific story with the players. Many of them did not know this story. Collins told them that he wanted the national anthem to be the last song they heard playing while standing on the medal stand. He wanted their team to bond in joy, not the pain his teammates experienced almost 40 years earlier. Collins felt a special connection to this team; he broadcast LeBron's first NBA game and played with Kobe's dad in Philadelphia. Consequently, his message to the team was very personal. The final thing Krzyzewski did to motivate his players was to have them watch Marvin Gaye's soulful performance of the national anthem at the 1983 NBA All-Star Game.[69] Chris Paul says hearing that song made them remember the countless Black Americans who sacrificed their lives for their country's freedom.

Team USA went undefeated in the FIBA tournament and defeated Argentina 118–81 to qualify for Beijing. The final Olympic roster consisted of Kobe Bryant, LeBron James, Dwyane Wade, Carmelo Anthony, Jason Kidd, Carlos Boozer, Chris Bosh, Dwight Howard, Chris Paul, Deron Williams, Michael Redd, and Tayshaun Prince. Eight future Hall-of-Famers were in this Olympic squad, nicknamed the Redeem Team. When they arrived in Beijing, they quickly learned that the three most prominent attractions in town were American swimmer Michael Phelps, Jamaican sprinter Usain Bolt, and Kobe. "I thought I was famous until I got to China," said LeBron. Kobe was arguably more popular in China than he was stateside. Wade recalled the love he received in Beijing being like nothing he had ever witnessed. "Kobe's celebrity in China was like Michael Jackson about to go on tour. A girl fainted right in front of us trying to get to him," said Boozer.[70] "It was thousands of fans waiting at the hotel to take pictures of our bus because they knew Kobe was on the bus," said Howard.[71]

The Redeem Team blew out China and Angola in the preliminary round. Their third opponent was the Greek team that beat them in 2006. The U.S. overcame a slow start to win 92–69. Next, they routed Spain and Germany. They defeated Australia by 31 points in the quarterfinals.

Krzyzewski demanded that his players display class in victory. There would be no repeats of Charles Barkley elbowing an Angolan competitor. Krzyzewski's goal was to respect all opponents and gain the world's respect for America. Unlike their predecessors in 2004, the Redeem Team lived in the Olympic Village and interacted with the other domestic and international athletes whenever possible. They cheered on Phelps as he swam for one of his eight gold medals. Kidd was present for the U.S. women's beach volleyball gold medal game.

The Redeem Team's opponent for the quarterfinals was Argentina, which had danced on the court as they beat the U.S. in Athens four years earlier. In this game, Argentinian star Manu Ginobili, the sixth man for the San Antonio Spurs, was hailed in the media as the best shooting guard in the world. Krzyzewski played mind games to motivate his players for that matchup. He played a highlight tape of Ginobili in practice. On game day, he placed news clippings in everyone's seat praising the Great Manu. Kobe and Wade were infuriated by the disrespect. "You saw him go from Kobe Bryant to the Black Mamba," said Anthony.[72] The entire game, Kobe focused on Ginobili as aggressively as Jordan and Pippen on Toni Kukoč in Barcelona. After Ginobili was forced to exit the game early with an injury, the team lost its intensity. Suddenly, a 21-point lead dwindled down to four. The team regrouped and cruised to a 101–81 victory.

The players celebrated Kobe's birthday the night before the gold medal game. LeBron serenaded him as he brought out a birthday cake. This moment was symbolic of how far they had come since Vegas. They were brothers in arms, a family, not just a bunch of parts thrown together as in Athens. They would need each other more than ever to defeat Spain in their grand finale. Team USA and Spain met on August 24 for one of Olympic history's most competitive gold medal games. Spain was led by Kobe's Laker teammate Pau Gasol and his younger brother Marc, who played for the Memphis Grizzlies. Future NBA guard Ricky Rubio was Spain's starting point guard. Early foul trouble for Kobe and LeBron caused Team USA to struggle in the first half. Wade carried the scoring load with 18 points off the bench. They led 69–61 at halftime. Spain's Rudy Fernandez hit a three-pointer to make the score 91–89 with 8:14 minutes left to play. Krzyzewski called a time-out. Before he could open his mouth, Kobe told everyone not to worry. Coming out of the time-out, Kobe scored or assisted on almost every play for the U.S. At one point, he knocked down a three-pointer, turned toward the pro-Spanish crowd, and placed his finger over his lips to "shush" them. Spain would not back down no matter how many clutch shots Kobe hit. Finally, another Kobe basket put the U.S. up by eight with under a minute left. The game's final score was 118–107.

As the game ended, all the players approached Doug Collins, sitting at the scorer's table, calling the game, to hug him. They ran into the locker room, joyously celebrating and hugging each other. Afterward, the players returned to the court to receive their medals. Each of them smiled like little kids receiving presents from Santa on Christmas. In the final episode of *The Dream Team Tapes* podcast, J.A. Adande astutely reminded listeners that this moment reflected how much simpler these times were for Black NBA players in America. Barack Obama would become the first Black nominee for a presidential campaign three days later. Obama's campaign and presidency sparked a feeling of change and hope for young Black men like the guys on this team. The year 2008 was five years before Trayvon Martin's death ignited the birth of the Black Lives Matter movement. This triumph was eight years before the rise of Donald Trump's MAGA movement and increased White nationalism.[73] San Francisco 49ers quarterback Colin Kaepernick had yet to take a knee, and the NBA had yet to become America's "wokest" professional sports league.[74] LeBron, Wade, Paul, and Anthony had yet to address racial issues and police brutality against unarmed Black people at the ESPY Awards show. There was a beautiful naivete that allowed these players to clutch their medals and display unbridled exuberance and patriotism as the national anthem blasted from the loudspeakers.[75]

Legacy

The Redeem Team is the most outstanding American Olympic basketball team after the Dream Team. Nearly everyone associated with that team would go on to achieve greatness. Coach Krzyzewski won three more Olympic gold medals and two more NCAA titles. LeBron left Cleveland as a free agent in June 2010, joining forces with Olympic teammates Wade and Bosh on the Miami Heat. The Heat made four consecutive appearances in the NBA Finals, winning titles in 2012 and 2013.[76] LeBron clinched two more championships with the Cavaliers and Lakers, respectively, in 2016 and 2020. Off the court, he became an outspoken social activist in the fight against racial profiling and voter suppression, opened a charter school, became a mogul in television and film, and was named a billionaire in 2022.[77] He broke the NBA's all-time scoring record. The Lakers drafted his eldest son, Bronny. LeBron's former running mate, Dwyane Wade, became the face of Jordan Brand from 2009 to 2012. He left Jordan in September 2012 to sign a lifetime contract as the chief spokesman for Li-Ning, a Chinese athletic apparel and sneaker company.[78] Wade, currently a minority owner of the Utah Jazz and WNBA's Chicago Sky franchise, was enshrined in the 2023 Hall of Fame class.

As for Kobe, his post–Beijing narrative exceeded the first chapter of his life. He won consecutive NBA championships in 2009 and 2010, giving him a total of five rings, one behind his muse, Michael Jordan. His new number 24 jersey was the league's top-selling jersey in the U.S., China, Latin America, and Europe. Debilitating injuries stole much of his athleticism and ended his career early. He was honored in every city the Lakers visited during his farewell season before scoring an awe-inspiring 60 points in his final game on April 13, 2016. The Lakers retired both of his jersey numbers, 24 and previously 8, a year later.

Kobe showed the world a completely different image in retirement. He was loved by all the younger players in the NBA. Many of them called him their generation's Jordan. He delighted in mentoring upcoming superstars Kyrie Irving, Devin Booker, and Jayson Tatum. The hip-hop community embraced him as they had once done Iverson. Kobe was portrayed as the perfect "girl dad" to his two daughters and a devoted husband. He became a staunch advocate for women's and girls' athletics. He made history as the first retired athlete to win an Academy Award and a Sports Emmy Award for his 2017 animated short film *Dear Basketball*. After all those achievements, he was nominated to headline an exemplary Hall of Fame class in 2020.

On Saturday, January 25, 2020, LeBron surpassed Kobe for third place on the NBA's all-time scoring list. By this point, LeBron was in his second season playing for the Lakers. He spent his postgame interview praising Kobe for the inspiration he had been in his career. Kobe sent him a congratulatory tweet and a special bottle of wine after the game. The next morning, the Lakers were on the plane flying from Philadelphia to Los Angeles when Anthony Davis abruptly woke LeBron to show him some devastating news on his cell phone. Kobe and his 13-year-old daughter, Gianna (Gigi), were killed in a helicopter crash in Calabasas, California. They were on board the flight with seven other individuals killed on their way to Gianna's basketball game at Kobe's Mamba Sports Academy. A memorial service was held at the Staples Center on February 24. Pop stars Beyoncé, Alicia Keys, and Christina Aguilera performed at the ceremony. Michael Jordan, Shaquille O'Neal, and Pau Gasol delivered tearful reflections. His wife, Vanessa, gave the eulogy. Kobe was only 41 years old.

The outpouring of love for Kobe and Gianna worldwide was momentous. Catholic priests in African nations, such as Bishop Eduardo Hiiboro Kussala of Sudan, paid homage and mentioned that Kobe, who was Catholic, attended Mass the morning he died.[79] A mural honoring Kobe, standing 39 feet wide and 19 feet tall, was erected in the European nation of Bosnia and Herzegovina.[80] Fans made their own memorial for Kobe in Toronto, Canada. A basketball court in Manila, the capital city of the

Philippines, was painted over with an image of Kobe and Gianna. He had visited that country multiple times during his lifetime. Luca Vecchi, the mayor of the northern Italian city of Reggio Emilia, posted a moving salutation on his Facebook page. Kobe received the most love in China.

NBA commissioner Adam Silver tried to explain why Kobe was so beloved around the world.

> Kobe came of age almost at the exact moment that we became a digital league. I believe we launched NBA.com the year before Kobe came into the league. And Kobe embraced all things digital. In China, he realized he could be virtually present around the world by providing content to websites. He saw an opportunity to make himself universal.... Kobe showed how big the NBA was becoming in China. I think Kobe recognized that he was a product of his time.[81]

Kobe Bryant was truly a cosmopolitan. He spoke English, Spanish, and Italian fluently and once trash-talked current Dallas Mavericks star Luka Dončić in his native Slovenian language. He owned a 50 percent stake in Olimpia Basket Pistoia, an Italian basketball club his father played for between 1987 and 1989. In 2018, he and Chinese American basketball player Yao Ming were appointed global ambassadors for FIBA's Basketball World Cup.[82] Kobe will always be linked to the league's ascendance as a global empire.

The Redeem Team Part Two

The Redeem Team's relevance cannot be overstated. They restored American dominance worldwide. The U.S. won gold in the next three Olympic games under the leadership of Coach K and then Coach Gregg Popovich. They proved that the NBA was just as patriotic as the NFL and MLB. The Redeem Team, like the 1992 Dream Team, sold the NBA to a global audience and inspired the current generation of foreign-born players. Giannis Antetokounmpo, the 2021 NBA Finals MVP, was one of those kids watching his favorite NBA players in 2008. He, along with Serbia's Nikola Jokić and France's Victor Wembanyama, now carry that torch passed on by Kobe, LeBron, and the Redeem Team to grow the NBA and the game of basketball internationally.

Globalization has a downside for individuals who bleed red, white, and blue and profess that it is America's birthright to reign supreme in basketball. Five regular season MVP awards went to foreign-born NBA players between 2019 and 2023. The 2023 FIBA World Cup proved that the U.S. can no longer roll out 12 NBA players and expect to dominate the competition. Grant Hill replaced Jerry Colangelo, after his retirement in

2021, as the head of USA Basketball. Hill failed to adopt Colangelo's model of getting the league's top stars to commit their summers leading up to the Olympics. The 2023 World Cup roster had only two All-Stars from the previous season. The team lost to Germany 113–111 in the semifinals and followed up that sobering defeat with a 127–118 loss to Canada in the bronze medal game.[83] The U.S. has not won gold at the World Cup since 2014, mainly because a different roster has represented the country each time, with the premier players sitting out until the Olympics.

The World Cup ignited a call to arms for a new Redeem Team of sorts to restore order. The result was a historic collection of talent led by LeBron, Stephen Curry, and Kevin Durant to represent Team USA at the 2024 Olympics in Paris. The media proclaimed this roster superior to the 1992 and 2008 teams. Nevertheless, this "Supreme team" struggled to beat South Sudan, a team from an African country so poor it could not afford indoor basketball courts, 101–100, in a pre–Olympic exhibition. The U.S. was favored to win the game by 41 points. Despite defeating France to win gold, it took an epic 13-point fourth-quarter comeback, fueled by LeBron and Curry, to survive Nikola Jokić's Serbian squad in the semifinals. The day is nearing when America's best is no longer a match for the world's best.[84]

3

Views from the 6ix

"Been flowin' stupid since Vince Carter was on some through the legs, arm in the hoop shit."

—Drake[1]

December 20, 2005, is not a date that most basketball fans remember, but something special happened that Tuesday evening in Los Angeles. The Lakers were hosting the Dallas Mavericks, and Kobe was having one of those nights. He shot 18-of-31 from the field and 22-of-25 from the foul line. Kobe outscored the eventual runner-up in that season's NBA Finals 62–61 through three quarters. With the Lakers leading 95–61 at the start of the fourth quarter, their coach, Phil Jackson, chose to sit his star for the rest of the night. Before Jackson made the call, he had Lakers point guard Brian Shaw ask Kobe if he wanted to remain on the floor. "Hey, coach wants to know if you want to stay in for the first few minutes of the fourth quarter, get 70, and then come out," asked Shaw. Kobe responded, "Nah, I'll get it another time."[2]

For most people, the Lakers' game against the Toronto Raptors weeks later, on Sunday night, January 22, 2006, was an afterthought. The NFL's conference championships were that day and dominated all sports media coverage. Joel Meyers, the Lakers' television play-by-play announcer, was in Seattle covering one of the football games. Andrew Bernstein, the team's photographer, was at home with his children. Even die-hard celebrity fan Jack Nicholson was absent. Kobe, who celebrated his eldest daughter Natalia's third birthday the previous day, was dealing with a sore knee. Ironically, his grandmother chose this night to attend her first and only of his professional games. The Lakers' record entering that night was a mediocre 21-19. The 14-26 Raptors were far less impressive. Nevertheless, the Raptors led 63-49 at halftime. As the Laker players walked off the court into the locker room for halftime, a chorus of boos came down from the fans in the stands.

When the game resumed, Kobe Bryant transformed into the Black Mamba. "We made him pick his dribble up; he pump-faked and then [did] a 360-fade-away-jump-shot. All net. And I'm sitting here with my hands on top of my head like what else can a defender do?" said former Raptors head coach Sam Mitchell.³ Mitchell threw his best defenders, Morris Peterson and Jalen Rose, at Kobe, but they could not stop him. Raptors forward Chris Bosh, reflecting on that night, added, "It just seemed like they were multiplying his points. They added up so fast. I'm sitting there thinking: 'I just ran up and back twice, and he went from 50 to 60. What the hell?'"⁴ I was at home that evening when I came across this game on television. I nearly fell out of my seat with every jaw-dropping shot he hit. The Lakers rebounded to win 122–104. Kobe finished with a record-setting 81 points, the second highest in NBA history, behind Wilt Chamberlain's 100-point night in 1962. If social media had existed in 2006, this certainly would have been a viral moment that broke the internet. Kobe blamed his teammate Lamar Odom for his historic scoring outburst. When he would return to the bench, Odom would say, "You can't score 50." Later, Odom would tell him, "You can't score 60." By the time Kobe reached 70, Odom said, "Go on and score 80."

Kobe's 81 made him the toast of the town and further cemented his acclaim as the best player on the planet. The Phoenix Suns would eliminate the Lakers in the playoffs' first round later that season. As for the Raptors, they became a proverbial punch line. They finished the season with a dismal 27–55 record. But better days were ahead for this expansion team from north of the border. They won 47 games the following season, and Mitchell was named NBA Coach of the Year. Despite this success, Raptors general manager Bryan Colangelo fired Mitchell after three games the following season. At the time, few people would have predicted a championship parade celebration in Toronto a decade later.

In 1995, the NBA created two new teams in Canada, the first since the inaugural 1946–47 season: the Toronto Raptors and the Vancouver Grizzlies. The Grizzlies eventually relocated to Memphis after six losing seasons. The Raptors became Canada's team and one of the world's most popular sports franchises thanks to American-born players like Vince Carter; their crafty Nigerian general manager, Masai Ujiri; a devoted native and immigrant fanbase; and their connection to Canada's homegrown global hip-hop sensation Drake. The Raptors' success culminated with a stunning defeat of the league's reigning dynasty, the Golden State Warriors, in the 2019 NBA Finals to capture their first world championship. This chapter assesses the NBA's expansion into the northern border by analyzing the following questions: Why did basketball fail in Vancouver? How did the Raptors teams of the 1990s inspire an entire generation of Canadian-born players who eventually made their mark in the NBA by the 2010s? How did immigration and hip-hop help the NBA eventually succeed in Canada? What do the NBA's mixed results in Canada mean for future international expansion in other parts of the world?

Canada and the Birth of the NBA

Basketball began in Canada! While this statement is not entirely accurate, the game as we know it owes a lot to Canadians. Basketball's founder, Dr. James Naismith, was born and raised in Ontario, Canada. Naismith was an accomplished athlete who participated in football, lacrosse, rugby, soccer, and gymnastics at the collegiate level. He taught physical education at his alma mater, McGill University in Montreal, before relocating to the United States in 1890. He found work at the Young Men's Christian Association (YMCA) International Training School in Springfield, Massachusetts. The lack of organized recreational activities between football and baseball seasons left the boys at the school with too much idle time. The school's instructors began complaining about their students' rebellious behavior and constant fighting. Dr. Luther Gulick, the head of the physical education department, looked to Naismith to find a solution to this festering problem. Gulick ordered him to find an "athletic distraction" to keep the boys busy.[5] The activity needed to embody the YMCA's mission of Muscular Christianity, which utilized sports to shape a young man's mind, body, and soul.[6]

Since it was winter in Springfield, Naismith had to find something for the boys to do indoors. After unsuccessful attempts to develop variations of lacrosse and football, he opted to come up with something from scratch. Naismith began writing the 13 rules for this new form of athletic competition.[7] He divided his 18 students into two teams of nine players. A team scored points by shooting a soccer ball into a peach basket he found in a nearby orchard. The basket was attached to the gymnasium's balcony, which was 10 feet high. Before a basket was scored, players had to pass the ball to each other by throwing it over their heads. They could not pick up the ball, run, or kick it.[8] Naismith did not include dribbling the ball in his rules. After each score, a jump ball was taken in the middle of the gymnasium court. One of his students called this new game basketball. The students played the first game on December 21, 1891. "I showed them two peach baskets I'd nailed up at each end of the gym, and I told them the idea was to throw the ball into the opposing team's peach basket. I blew the whistle, and the first game of basketball began," said Naismith in a 1939 radio interview with WOR-AM in New York.[9]

Naismith left Springfield to complete a medical degree at the University of Colorado. In 1898, he was hired to be the chapel director and teach physical education at the University of Kansas. The university eventually hired him as the school's first basketball coach. One of his players, Forrest "Phog" Allen, succeeded him as the head coach and turned Lawrence, Kansas, into a mecca for college basketball. Future Hall of Fame coaches Adolph Rupp and Dean Smith grew from Allen's coaching tree. As for basketball, it continued to evolve at the men's and eventually women's collegiate levels between the late 19th and early 20th centuries. The number of players on opposing teams was reduced to five. Teams no longer lined up for a jump ball after every basket. Dribbling was introduced to the game. The Naismith Memorial Basketball Hall of Fame was established in 1959 to honor the most exceptional players, coaches, and contributors to the game at all levels.

Naismith's game did not take long to spread globally, thanks to YMCA affiliates in Australia, Brazil, China, and France. After the game was introduced in those destinations, it spread throughout Europe, Latin America, and the Caribbean. World War I further contributed to the game's growing popularity. The YMCA used basketball to promote the health and wellness of American and Allied soldiers stationed in Europe. An international basketball organization consisting of nine European nations was established in 1932. It served as the predecessor to FIBA.[10]

The National Basketball League (NBL), founded in 1898, was the first professional basketball association. The NBL consisted of six teams from Philadelphia and central New Jersey until it dissolved in 1904.[11] General Electric, Firestone, and Goodyear formed the Midwest Basketball Conference (MBC) in 1935. They renamed their association the new National Basketball League (NBL) two years later. On June 6, 1946, the Basketball Association of America (BAA) was formed. The BAA quickly became the NBL's chief competitor and had 16 teams, including inaugural champions the Philadelphia Warriors, the Baltimore Bullets, and the Minneapolis Lakers. On August 3, 1949, the BAA merged with the NBL to form the National Basketball Association (NBA).[12]

Although the NBA's inaugural season was in 1949, it included the BAA's previous three seasons as part of its history. Consequently, the NBA counts the BAA's inaugural game played in Canada on November 1, 1946, as its first competition. The New York Knickerbockers traveled by train to Toronto to face the Toronto Huskies. When the train stopped in Niagara Falls for Customs and Immigration inspection, the uniformed officer was startled when he saw so many tall guys. He asked the Knickerbockers' coach who they were supposed to be. The officer was familiar with the New York Rangers professional hockey team but had never heard of them. He told the coach that he should not expect to find too many basketball fans in Canada. Unfortunately, for the Knickerbockers and the Huskies, he was right.[13]

The Knickerbockers defeated the Huskies 68–66 in front of 7,090 attendees at the Maple Leaf Gardens arena. Anyone taller than the Huskies' tallest player, George Nostrand, who stood 6'8", received free admission. The Huskies, valued at $150,000, were owned by Eric Craddock, co-owner of the Montreal Alouettes, a Canadian professional football franchise, and his business partners Harold Shannon and Ben Newman oversaw the team's operations. The team was initially coached by their best player, Ed Sadowski, until he resigned a month into the season. Red Rolfe, an American Major League Baseball player who had played third base for the New York Yankees, replaced Sadowski.

According to the *Toronto Star*, the Huskies lost $100,000 in their first season due to poor ticket sales. The team folded after one year of operation. Although ice hockey did not originate in Canada, it has been the country's national pastime since the late 19th century when organized leagues were formed. Montreal hosted the first organized hockey game on March 3, 1875.[14] Basketball finally succeeded in Canada in the late 20th century due to NBA expansion and the arrival of an immigrant population not raised on hockey.

Grizzlies Rising

In 1988, the NBA expanded by establishing teams in Florida, North Carolina, and Minnesota. The success of these markets opened the doors for further expansion north of the border by the mid–1990s. Why did the NBA choose Canada? As stated in Chapter 1, David Stern was the ultimate capitalist who realized the league's potential for growth by selling its product internationally. His goal with Canadian expansion was to see the children of hockey fanatics grow up wearing basketball jerseys instead of hockey sweaters. Sending the Dream Teams to play in FIBA and the Olympics did not have the same impact as having a permanent team outside the United States. A flight from New York to Canada was only 90 minutes; therefore, American fans could easily attend games if they chose to travel. Despite Mexico's proximity to the U.S., that country did not have historical ties to basketball.[15] The U.S. and Canada have also had strong foreign policy ties since the Cold War.

The NBA's Expansion Committee and the Board of Governors approved the creation of the Toronto Raptors on September 30, 1993. Vancouver was awarded a team on April 27, 1994. Toronto and Vancouver each paid $125 million to join the league, a steep price hike from the $32.5 million the new expansion teams paid a few years earlier.[16] Many American basketball fans may have forgotten the story of the Vancouver Grizzlies because of their abbreviated existence and the Raptors' success. Vancouver is the third-largest city in British Columbia, the westernmost province of Canada. The grizzly bears that roamed British Columbia inspired the team's nickname.[17]

Nelson Skalbania, a local businessman, unsuccessfully tried to bring the NBA to Vancouver in the 1980s. In 1993, Arthur Griffiths, owner of the Vancouver Canucks NHL team, began building a 20,000-seat arena to be home to a potential new basketball team. On October 28, 1995, Stu Jackson was hired as the team's first general manager. Jackson, the head basketball coach at the University of Wisconsin, had previous NBA experience coaching the New York Knicks from 1989 to 1991. He was the second-youngest (33) coach in league history at the time. In his new role with Vancouver, Jackson had the arduous task of reintroducing basketball to Canada and developing a winning culture. Brian Winters, a retired NBA player and former assistant coach at the NBA and collegiate level, was the first of five head coaches in Vancouver between 1995 and 2000.

The NBA held its 10th expansion draft on June 24, 1995, in Toronto. The Grizzlies and the Raptors were allowed to fill their rosters by selecting players from the league's 27 teams. Each existing team was allowed to prohibit eight players from their rosters from being taken, and only one of their unprotected players could be drafted. The Grizzlies won a coin flip but allowed the Raptors to pick first. They used their first draft pick on New York Knicks point guard Greg Anthony.[18] Other notable draftees included Byron Scott, Gerald Wilkins, Theodore "Blue" Edwards, and Benoit Benjamin. The NBA held its traditional draft four days later in Toronto. Neither the Grizzlies nor the Raptors could receive the top pick due to their expansion status. The Grizzlies drafted Bryant "Big Country" Reeves and Lawrence Moten with the sixth and 36th picks, respectively. Reeves, a 7'0" 250-pound center from Oklahoma State University, led his college squad to the NCAA Final Four in his senior year.[19]

The Grizzlies played their first game against the Raptors in a preseason exhibition called the Naismith Cup.[20] More than 11,000 attendees watched the Grizzlies lose 98–77. They defeated the Portland Trailblazers 92–80 in their regular-season debut. The Grizzlies beat the Minnesota Timberwolves, 100–98 in overtime, two nights later in the home game opener. The initial excitement and euphoria of this impressive start quickly faded with 19 straight losses. The Spurs beat them 111–62 in November. The Grizzlies set a league record by losing 23 consecutive games from February to April. Their inaugural season concluded with a bleak 15–67 record and the league's lowest winning percentage. They averaged just slightly over 17,000 fans per game. Meanwhile, the city's hockey team advanced to the Western Conference semifinals of the NHL playoffs.

Big Country Reeves averaged 13 points and seven rebounds in his rookie season. The next season opened with promise after the Grizzlies obtained University of California star Shareef Abdur-Rahim with the third overall pick in a historic draft. Abdur-Rahim was taken ahead of future first-ballot Hall-of-Famers Ray Allen, Steve Nash, and Kobe Bryant. Abdur-Rahim had only one All-Star appearance during his eight seasons in the NBA. The Grizzlies won 14 games in their second season. Coach Winters was fired in the middle of the season and replaced by Stu Jackson, who did not fare any better in an interim role. Brian Hill was named head coach in season three. Hill had taken an upstart Orlando Magic team led by Shaquille O'Neal and Penny Hardaway to the 1995 NBA Finals. Hill's Magic was the only team to eliminate Jordan's Bulls in the playoffs during their dynastic run. The Magic joined the NBA as a part of the 1989 expansion. Vancouver ownership hoped Hill could repeat his success with the proper draft picks and free-agent signings.

A collective bargaining dispute over changes to the league's salary cap caused the NBA to be locked out from July 1, 1998, to January 20, 1999. The regular season was reduced to 50 games that year.[21] The Grizzlies could muster only eight wins in the abbreviated season and set a record for the lowest winning percentage (.160) in NBA history. The consolation prize for their dismal record was the second overall pick in that summer's draft. The Grizzlies selected Steve Francis, an athletic point guard from the University of Maryland. Francis had one of the most unlikely paths to the NBA. He sold crack cocaine as a teenager and attended six high schools before dropping out and completing a General Educational Development (GED) exam. Francis received an offer to play at San Jacinto College, a two-year community college in Texas, despite playing only two high school varsity games. He spent a year at San Jacinto College and another year at Allegheny College of Maryland before transferring to the University of Maryland in College Park. He helped the Terps earn a top-five national ranking and a trip to the Sweet Sixteen in the NCAA Tournament.[22]

Francis appeared destined for superstardom coming out of college. He was a flashy little guard who could jump out of the gym and play with the swagger of Allen Iverson. Francis and his agent had no desire to have his career *wasted* in Canada. In interviews, he fed the press a bevy of excuses for wanting to be traded: the distance from his family, lack of sponsorship opportunities outside the U.S., and high taxes. He even told one reporter that it was "God's will" for him to play in America. The Grizzlies traded him to the Houston Rockets in a historic three-team deal involving 11 players and future draft picks. At the time, this was the most extensive trade in NBA history.[23]

While Francis became a three-time All-Star in Houston, playing alongside Chinese center Yao Ming, the Grizzlies' fortune worsened. The team was unable to recover financially from the lockout. Vancouver had the league's third-lowest attendance and dwindling fan support. The team was sold to John McCaw, Jr., an American entrepreneur, in 1995. McCaw then sold the team in September 2000 for $160 million. The Grizzlies' new owner, Chicago industrialist Michael Heisley, relocated the team to Memphis, Tennessee, in 2001. Heisley lost $87 million in his first year of ownership, including the league's $30 million relocation fee.[24] The Memphis Grizzlies are currently one of the NBA's premier young teams. They have a rabid fanbase and an imposing home-court advantage. Rappers and other celebrities like Usher frequently sit courtside at games to watch the team's All-NBA point guard, Temetrius Jamel "Ja" Morant. In the past two decades, Canadian basketball enthusiasts have suggested Montreal, Ottawa, Winnipeg, Edmonton, and Calgary as potential homes for a new NBA franchise.[25] The Vancouver Grizzlies had an overall record of 101–359 during their existence.[26]

Welcome to Jurassic Park

In the summer of 1993, the most spectacular film on the planet was Steven Spielberg's adaptation of Michael Crichton's 1990 novel *Jurassic Park*. The film told the fictional story of a Central American island near Costa Rica where de-extinct dinosaurs roamed.[27] Exceptional storytelling, great marketing, and computer-generated dinosaurs propelled *Jurassic Park* to earn over $914 million worldwide, making it the highest-grossing film in history as of 1993.[28] Raptor mania was contagious and infected the young basketball fans in Toronto. The Toronto Raptors were born on November 4, 1993, when the NBA Board of Governors voted to make them the league's 28th franchise. Canadian entrepreneurs John Bitove and Allan Slaight, a former magician and radio personality, were the team's majority owners.

Fans could choose the team's name from a list of 10 options: Beavers, Bobcats, Dragons, Grizzlies, Hogs, Scorpions, T-Rex, Tarantulas, Terriers, and Raptors. The Raptors nickname was announced on May 15, 1994. A logo featuring a dinosaur dribbling a basketball surfaced days later. The team's official colors were purple, red, black, and "Naismith" silver in recognition of Dr. Naismith.[29] The team had a dinosaur on the front of their jerseys. Their mascot was the Raptor, a large red dinosaur that resembled a more athletic version of the beloved children's television character Barney. Raptor was born by hatching from a gigantic egg on the basketball court. Two decades later, the team renamed the street area outside its arena Jurassic Park. Fans unable to purchase tickets could watch games on a jumbotron and enjoy an unforgettable block party experience.

The Raptors played their home games at the SkyDome until 1999, when they moved to the Air Canada Centre. The SkyDome hosted the 1995 expansion and traditional drafts. NBA legend Isiah Thomas was the team's first general manager and vice president. Thomas, who owned a minority stake in the team, had recently retired from the Pistons and possessed no managerial experience. The Raptors' early struggles and coaching carousel were partly attributable to Thomas's inexperience.[30] Thomas selected Damon Stoudamire with the seventh overall pick in the 1995 draft. Stoudamire, a 5'10" All-American point guard, took the University of Arizona to the 1994 Final Four. His diminutive stature and speed earned him the nickname "Mighty Mouse." He even tattooed the pint-sized animated hero on his right arm. While other teams passed on Stoudamire because of his size and age, he was a 21-year-old senior; Thomas recognized a bit of himself in the young man.

Toronto fans booed when David Stern read his name on draft night. They expected the team to pick Ed O'Bannon, a 6'8" power forward and the national College Player of the Year. Thomas's gamble on Stoudamire paid off in the beginning. He posted 20 points, 11 assists, and 12 rebounds in the team's first and only nationally televised game that inaugural season. He set a rookie record for three-pointers in a season with 133. He hit six three-pointers in the Raptors' shocking upset of the Bulls' team that won an NBA record 72 regular-season games. Stoudamire averaged 19 points and nine assists, won the MVP award at the Rookie All-Star Game, and was named NBA Rookie of the Year.

Damon Stoudamire's surprising exploits on the court were not enough to make the Raptors competitive. They won 21 games and suffered 61 losses. Thomas fired the team's first head coach, Brendan Malone. Heading into the 1996 draft, the Raptors won the second overall pick in the draft lottery. Philadelphia was expected to use the first overall pick on Georgetown's Allen Iverson. The Raptors had a pool of riches from which to choose, including Kobe Bryant and Canadian point guard Steve Nash. However, they went with Marcus Camby, a skinny 6'10" sophomore center from the University of Massachusetts (UMass). Camby set an NCAA tournament record of 43 blocked shots between his freshman and sophomore seasons. He won the Naismith College Player of the Year Award and helped UMass reach its first Final Four in his final season. Most NBA scouts thought he was the obvious choice for the second pick.[31] Toronto finished Camby's rookie season with a 30–52 record. The Camby-Stoudamire tandem was short-lived. After Thomas departed Toronto on bad terms, an increasingly disgruntled Stoudamire was traded to Portland in 1998. Camby was traded to New York that same year.

Basketball was still new to Toronto fans in the beginning. Leo Rautins, a commentator for Raptors' games since 1995, remembers how fans made noise and waved signs when their players were shooting free throws instead of when the opposing players were at the foul line. Game tickets sold for $5 at Pizza Pizza, a local food chain, and the Shoppers Drug Mart. Cross-promotional efforts like "buy a ticket to a Raptors game and get a ticket to Toronto Maple Leafs' hockey game" were used to increase attendance. Doug Smith, author of *We the North: 25 Years of the Toronto Raptors*, documents many early challenges to basketball succeeding north of the border. Visiting NBA teams had to fill out customs forms whenever they arrived. According to Smith, most American-born players viewed playing in Toronto as if they were going to a third-world country. "It's bias born out of ignorance. I sometimes think about how these players who come to Toronto don't appreciate all the good that comes from getting out of the United States. Back then, your contract was paid in American dollars, but you spent everything here in Canadian dollars. It was like getting a 33 percent raise," says Smith.[32]

Tha Carter Effect

Before Victor Wembanyama, there was Frederic Weis. The New York Knicks selected the 7'2" French center with the 15th pick in the 1999 draft. His American arrival was far different from today's young French phenom. When Weis came to the Big Apple for training camp, he quickly realized that neither Knicks' fans nor coaches were ecstatic to have him. He was virtually unknown outside of Europe. Weis never played a game in the NBA and his story nearly ended tragically with a failed suicide attempt.[33] When the *New York Times* profiled him for a 2015 story, I doubt that most readers would have remembered Weis had it not been for the 2000 Summer Olympics.

On September 25, 2000, Team USA played France at the Olympic games in Sydney, Australia. Team USA led 69–54 in the fourth quarter when Vince Carter, a 6'6" shooting guard from the Raptors, intercepted a behind-the-back pass, disrupting a French fast break, and then preceded to dunk on the much taller Weis. However, Carter did not simply dunk on Weis. He literally jumped over him, as if he were shot from a cannon, and threw down a rim-rattling, one-handed dunk. The French press dubbed this dunk "La Dunk De La Mort," translated as "The Dunk of Death." Carter feared not scoring the basketball if he did not attack the rim with such ferocious fervor. As his feet landed on the floor, he threw his head back, let out an enthusiastic scream, and emphatically pumped his fist in the air. His Olympic teammate Kevin Garnett shoved him in the chest to further punctuate the moment. Carter says he was unaware of what had happened until someone showed him a video of the dunk after the game.

During a 2022 interview with the *I Am Athlete Tonight* podcast, Carter told the hosts his embarrassing dunk was responsible for Weis's failed NBA career and suicide attempt. This hyperbolic statement was far from the truth. Weis struggled with depression and drug abuse after his son was born with autism.[34] His personal problems were the impetus for his troubles. But what cannot be understated is Carter's role in the evolution of Canadian basketball and the rise of Toronto in global popular culture. For a generation of basketball fans and current NBA players under 30, Carter was their version of MJ and Kobe.

Vincent Lamar Carter, Jr., was born in Daytona Beach, Florida, on January 26, 1977. His uncle Oliver Lee introduced him to basketball when he was two years old. Uncle Oliver played college ball at Marquette University in the 1970s. He was drafted by the Milwaukee Bucks and played for the Bulls and Spurs. Uncle Oliver taught Carter to make his first basket on a 10-foot hoop. He did not lower the rim or pick up his nephew to help him shoot into the basket. Carter dunked a basketball with one hand for the first time on an outdoor court at Ormond Beach Middle School when he was only in the sixth grade. He taught himself to dunk by performing various drills such as touching the rim, dunking a golf ball, dunking a tennis ball, dunking a volleyball, dunking a girls' basketball, and finally, a men's regulation-size basketball.

Vince Carter's parents, Vince, Sr., and Michelle, divorced when he was seven. His mother remarried, but she was his primary guardian. She stressed academics over athletics. On game days in high school, most of the guys on the varsity basketball team would stay after school to watch the junior varsity or the girls play before their contest. Carter's mom required him to come home to finish his homework before playing that evening. She also encouraged him to nurture other interests beyond basketball. Carter excelled in music, joining the marching band at Mainland High School, where he amazed audiences with skills on the saxophone, trumpet, tuba, and drums. He wrote music and choreographed the band's dance routines. His musical repertoire can be partially credited to his stepfather, Harry Robinson, a retired band director. Carter became drum major his senior year. "He's tall and thin, so anything he put on looked good. He had one of those tall white hats that made him look even taller and a white uniform with gold buttons. He just looked terrific," said his mom.[35] Florida A&M University and Bethune-Cookman College, two prominent HBCUs in Florida, offered him band scholarships.

Vince Carter's musical exploits took a back seat to what he was doing on the basketball court. Before NBA fans knew him as "Vinsanity" and "Half man, half amazing," he earned the nickname "UFO" at Mainland.

Carter says he was jumping higher in high school than in the pros. His head even touched the top of the basket on a few dunks, causing kids and local sportswriters to say he was levitating like a UFO. Some of his dunks in the McDonald's All-American high school dunk contest were better than those in the NBA contest. All the major collegiate basketball programs across the nation recruited him. His mother set strict guidelines for the 80 schools pursuing him. No coach could call their home after 10:00 p.m. He had to finish his homework or get ready for bed because he had school the next morning. Coaches who failed to abide by her rules were immediately removed from consideration. The University of North Carolina at Chapel Hill was among the last schools to recruit him. When UNC coach Dean Smith came to Florida on a recruiting visit, he had to wait on a field two miles from the International Speedway before they met. Carter was busy leading the band in a practice performance of Survivor's memorable anthem "Eye of the Tiger" from *Rocky III*. Smith's patience and persistence paid off in getting Carter to accept his scholarship offer.[36]

From the first day Carter arrived at Chapel Hill in 1995 for his freshman year, ESPN college basketball analyst Dick Vitale hyped him up as a "Diaper Dandy." Carter joined Antawn Jamison, another freshman and McDonald's All-American, on the varsity squad. Carter and Jamison became the foundation for UNC Tarheel basketball for the next three seasons. Coach Smith was famous for being the only coach who could hold Michael Jordan's scoring average below 20 points. Jordan starred at UNC from 1981 to 1984. Carter was often compared to him because of his tremendous athleticism, dynamic dunks, slender 6'6" frame, and bald head. Smith stressed that all his student-athletes learned to play the "Carolina way," which meant team-first basketball. Carter, like Jordan, was not allowed to be the scintillating scorer and highlight-reel dunker he would become in the NBA while he played under Smith's system.

Carter averaged 12.3 points per game while he was at UNC. During his junior year, the Tarheels advanced to play the University of Utah in the Final Four. He declared for the NBA draft a week after Carolina's loss to Utah. That year's draft was held on June 24, 1998, at General Motors Place in Vancouver. Michael Olowokandi, a Nigerian-born center who played for the University of the Pacific, was selected by the Los Angeles Clippers as the first overall pick. Carter was taken fifth by the Golden State Warriors, but he changed team hats before the night ended. The Warriors traded Carter to the Raptors for Antawn Jamison. On draft night, there was a rumor that Golden State desired Jamison; however, they feared Toronto would draft him with the fourth overall pick and trade him to Milwaukee, drafting ninth. To protect themselves, Golden State asked Toronto to take Jamison and trade him for Carter.

Vince Carter's rookie season coincided with the NBA lockout that shortened the regular season and canceled the annual All-Star weekend. Carter loved his new surroundings, unlike most American-born players who hated moving to Canada. I attribute this to his upbringing. His mother raised him to think outside the box and have a larger worldview. While his peers saw desolation north of the border, he saw an opportunity on and off the court. His transition on the court was smoother, thanks to the presence of an unlikely teammate. Tracy McGrady (T-Mac), a 6'8" small forward, was discovered by Sonny Vaccaro at the Adidas ABCD camp the summer before his senior year of high school. He jumped from being ranked 150th to first in the nation. McGrady left his home in Florida and transferred to Mount Zion Christian Academy in Durham, North Carolina. It was a widely known secret that he planned on following Kobe's footsteps to skip college for the NBA. The Raptors drafted him with the ninth pick in that summer's draft.[37]

McGrady and Carter were predestined to be the duo that would make the Raptors one of the league's marquee franchises. The two already knew each other from playing on AAU teams in Florida as kids. McGrady played on the junior Florida team, while Carter played for the senior Florida team. McGrady also played at Auburndale High School, two hours away from Mainland, before transferring to Mount Zion. A week before his draft, McGrady went to UNC to work out. Carter let him borrow his locker while he was on campus. On Thursday, McGrady informed Carter that he would head home to Florida that weekend for a family reunion. While McGrady was at the reunion, his grandmother Roberta introduced him to an older cousin who said she had a grandson named Vincent enrolled at UNC. It turned out that he and Carter were third cousins. Carter's grandmother immediately called him and put McGrady on the phone. "What up, cuz!" McGrady said happily. "Who the hell is this?" Carter replied. "Boy, this T-Mac! Bro, you ain't gonna believe this. We're family, bro!"[38]

By the culmination of his rookie season, Carter had exceeded the pre-draft predictions of the NBA scouts. No longer constrained by Dean Smith's rules, he was finally free to exhibit an athleticism and style of play tailor-made perfectly for the NBA. Even though the Raptors still were not a draw on American television, Carter's highlights were featured prominently on ESPN's *SportsCenter* almost nightly. Puma named his debut sneaker Vinsanity, a catchphrase used by a sportscaster to describe one of his dunks.[39] Carter, who played 22 years in the NBA, is destined to be inducted into the Naismith Memorial Hall of Fame. He was the oldest player in the league, 43, when he retired in 2020. All his accomplishments on the court pale compared with the night the world discovered him. On Saturday, February 11, 2000, the NBA hosted its All-Star weekend Slam

Dunk Contest at The Arena in Oakland, California, the then home of the Golden State Warriors. Carter made his first and only appearance in the contest.

In 1976, the NBA merged with its rival, the American Basketball Association (ABA). The ABA played a much more upbeat, "urban" or "Blacker" style of basketball. The slam dunk was a prominent feature in the ABA. Historically, the dunk has been a racialized aspect of the game because it was associated with Black athletes believed to be naturally more athletic than their white competitors. Players like Philadelphia's Darryl Dawkins, who nicknamed his dunks and shattered two backboards, made dunking an essential part of their game. Critics associated the dunk with showboating and "streetball." The NCAA banned dunking from 1967 to 1976. "I don't think there's any question that some of those rules were racially motivated," said sports historian Randy Roberts.[40] On January 27, 1976, the ABA staged the first slam dunk contest, at McNichols Sports Arena in Denver, Colorado. The contest featured a who's who of ABA talent and prolific nicknames: Artis "A-Train" Gilmore, George "Iceman" Gervin, Larry "Special K" Kenon, David "Skywalker" Thompson, and Julius "Dr. J" Erving. Dr. J, who was arguably more prominent than any NBA player at the time, won the contest by jumping from the free-throw line and dunking the ball. His prize for winning was $1,000 and a brand-new stereo.

The NBA held its first dunk contest in 1984. Over the next decade, the competition became the premier event of All-Star weekend and one of the most anticipated nights on the professional sports calendar in America. In 1986, 5'7" guard Anthony Jerome "Spud" Webb shocked the world by winning the contest. He beat 6'8" forward Dominique "The Human Highlight Film" Wilkins, the 1985 contest winner and his teammate in Atlanta. Two years later, Michael Jordan dueled in Chicago with Wilkins in the greatest dunk contest. Millennials and Generation Zers probably would choose Zach LaVine's iconic match with Aaron Gordon in 2016 over Jordan v. Wilkins. Jordan won the 1988 contest by copying Dr. J's free-throw-line jam. The image of Jordan *flying* from the free-throw line with his legs spread birthed Nike's famous Jordan brand logo. During the '90s, there were many memorable contest winners, such as Dee Brown, who pumped up his Reebok sneakers before every dunk, and Cedric Ceballos, who dunked the ball blindfolded. Kobe won as a rookie in 1997. His victory marked the final time the event was held until 2000.

By 1998 fans were growing tired of the Slam Dunk Contest. A major complaint was its lack of star power. Most contestants were rookies and lesser-known role players who had been in the league for a few years. No one expected Kobe to become a world-famous legend in 1996. It had been a decade since there was anything close to Jordan v. Wilkins. A *New York*

Times columnist, Mike Wise, said the contest was done. According to Rod Thorn, the contest had grown stale because we had already seen all the creative dunks. "Let's give it a rest," said Commissioner Stern in 1998.[41] The contest was canceled again in 1999 due to the lockout. When it returned in 2000, no one knew what to expect except for the man from Toronto.

The 2000 Slam Dunk Contest participants were Vince Carter, Tracy McGrady, Ricky Davis, Jerry Stackhouse, Larry Hughes, and Steve Francis. There was a buzz in The Arena that night as the NBA's brightest stars rubbed shoulders with Denzel Washington and Halle Berry courtside. Shaquille O'Neal held a huge camcorder, which looked miniature in his colossal hands, to film the night's festivities. Basketball legends Isiah Thomas, Cynthia Cooper, and Kenny Smith were among the event's judges. "We knew he [Carter] was athletic. We just didn't know what to expect from him," said four-time WNBA champion Cooper.[42] TNT broadcast the contest. Cheryl Miller, the older sister of Reggie Miller and arguably the most outstanding women's college basketball player in history, was the network's sideline reporter. Carter says winning this contest was his second-most-important achievement after being drafted. He accepted the invitation to participate without any hesitation. McGrady was less eager to join his cousin in Oakland because he did not see himself as an elite dunker. There was little time to practice for the event. Butch Carter, the Raptors' head coach, fined players $500 for dunking in practice. Carter knew he was the best dunker in the contest, but he would only be satisfied with a performance on par with that of Jordan, Wilkins, and Dr. J.

It was raining heavily on the day of the contest. Carter had stitches in his middle finger from an injury. Although the event was in Oakland, Carter and McGrady stayed at a San Francisco hotel. The car scheduled to pick them up for The Arena did not arrive on time. Instead, they rode in a sedan with two other guys weighing at least 275 pounds. They rode across the Bay Bridge in the tiny car packed in like sardines. McGrady, still anxious about participating, sarcastically told his cousin God was sending them a sign to turn around and go home. They did not arrive until 30 minutes before the contest began. The sight of the crowd raised Carter's adrenaline level to an all-time high. His first dunk was a 360-degree windmill. In layperson's terms, this type of dunk requires a player to leap and complete a full midair spin before dunking. The 360 is difficult enough, but he added a windmill, which means he brought the ball up to his waist before moving his arm straight back and up in a circular motion until he dunked the ball over his head. Carter did all these moves rapidly in one seamless motion. He bounced off the floor so high after the dunk that he believed he could have completed another windmill. "The crowd was going nuts. I think I punched somebody in the ribs," said Dallas Mavericks German forward

Dirk Nowitzki.[43] Judging the contest and reporting for TNT, Kenny Smith screamed, "Let's go home!!! Let's go home, ladies and gentlemen."

Carter changed his routine for his first dunk while warming up on the layup line. He saved his original dunk for his second routine. It was a windmill off one step toward the basket. Carter described his thought process behind that move to Steve Smith during a 2016 interview for NBA TV. "What I was trying to accomplish was the windmill doing the one step while turning my body, still trying to find the rim while getting the height and the proper distance with the dunk."[44] He received all 10s from the judges except for a nine from Kenny Smith, who said afterward that the bar was set too high with the first dunk. Carter was upset with his fellow UNC alum who blocked him from earning a perfect score for every round. "We're like, 'Are you kidding me?' [Smith] almost got banned from future judging for that," said Cheryl Miller.[45]

The third dunk was something that Carter had never done before in a game or practice. The contest's new format required each participant to perform a dunk with a teammate's assistance. Carter, who had his cousin assist him, was unaware of this rule change until he arrived that night. The first time McGrady bounced the ball, it was too high. Carter jumped halfway in the air and landed without completing an attempt to avoid penalization. He walked off the steps again and told his cousin to bounce the ball waist-high and move. The second bounce was perfect. He caught the ball in midair, moved it from his left to right hand between his legs, and slammed it with his right hand. As Carter landed, he pointed to the sky like Jamaican sprinter Usain Bolt's victorious lightning bolt pose after he crossed the finish line. Carter walked off the court, motioning to the crowd with his hands that the contest was done. "It's over! It's over, ladies and gentlemen!" declared Kenny Smith.

For his fourth dunk, Carter pulled from something he had done the previous year at Gary Payton's annual celebrity game in Seattle, Washington. Carter had been playing around in the layup line at Payton's event, jumping up and placing his hand through the net. Fast-forward to round four in Oakland. Carter dunked the ball, placed his entire elbow inside the net, and hung there on the rim for a few seconds. The room was dead silent, unlike the previous dunks that garnered a raucous reaction. Carter slowly walked away hoping that the crowd was so in awe of what he did that their silence would speak volumes. He faced former Vancouver malcontent Steve Francis in the finals. At this point, it was a foregone conclusion about who the winner would be. Carter played it safe for his fifth and final dunk with a less spectacular two-handed dunk from the free throw line. This move was his rendition of the dunk Dr. J and Jordan made iconic.

The next generation of Canadian basketball was born that night. Cory

Joseph, Tristan Thompson, and Nik Stauskas were among the little kids back home in Canada, marveling at Carter's feats. All would play in the NBA between the 2010s and 2020s. Carter's performance placed the Raptors on the map globally and inspired several future NBA players raised in Canada. The Cleveland Cavaliers selected Anthony Bennett as the number-one pick in the 2013 draft. Fellow Canadian Andrew Wiggins went number one in the next year's draft. Wiggins was the unsung hero of the Golden State Warriors in the 2022 NBA Finals. There were 22 Canadians on NBA rosters at the beginning of the 2022–23 season, including Shai Gilgeous-Alexander and Jamal Murray. SGA was first-team All-NBA in 2023 and 2024 and a finalist for the MVP award the latter year. Murray was the second-best player on the Denver Nuggets when they won the 2023 NBA championship. He recorded a 34-point triple-double in game three of the finals. He and teammate Nikola Jokić became the first duo to post a triple duo in the same finals game.

Carter's life changed forever after All-Star weekend. Nike signed him to a signature sneaker deal. His jersey sales rivaled the game's elite players, including Jordan, who unretired in 2001 to play two seasons with the Washington Wizards. [Fans voted Carter to start over Jordan in the 2003 All-Star Game. Carter declined the offer because it was Jordan's final All-Star appearance.] Raptors' games began airing on American television. Carter scored 51 points against the Suns in his American television debut. He never competed in another Slam Dunk Contest after that magic night in Oakland because he wanted to be viewed as an all-around player capable of leading a team to a championship.

The Raptors reached the playoffs for the first time that same season. Ironically, their opponent was the New York Knicks, the same team that faced the Toronto Huskies. The Knicks swept them in three games in the first round. Coach Butch Carter was fired at the end of their playoff run. Tired of playing in his cousin's enormous shadow, McGrady signed with the Magic that summer. He eventually became a better player than his cousin, one of the best scorers in league history, and a Hall-of-Famer. The Raptors continued to improve despite McGrady's absence. They reached the Eastern Conference semifinals in May 2001, where they faced the Philadelphia 76ers. The highly competitive series went a full seven games but was overshadowed by an event that had nothing to do with basketball.

Education had always been more important than athletics to Vince Carter's mother. Despite leaving college early, he continued his education at UNC during the offseasons. Carter was due to graduate with a bachelor's degree in African American studies in May 2001. His commencement ceremony was the same day as the final game of the Philadelphia series. Rather than skip graduation, he flew to Chapel Hill in a private jet provided by the Raptors' governor to reach campus at 9:00 a.m. After signing a few autographs and posing for pictures, he walked across the stage with his classmates. When asked why he returned, Carter referenced the importance of fulfilling that dream for himself and his mother.

The ceremony concluded at 11:00 a.m. Carter flew to Philadelphia, arriving about five hours before game time. He and Philadelphia guard Allen Iverson staged one the best duels in playoff history. In the end, Iverson walked away victorious. The Sixers eventually lost to the Lakers in the NBA Finals. Carter shot 6-of-18 from the floor that night. In the game's final seconds, he received a pass from teammate Dell Curry, father of future four-time NBA champion Stephen Curry, and took the game-winning shot. He missed a three-pointer from the corner as the buzzer sounded. Critics blamed his extra travel time that day for his play. Carter scored 50 and 39 points in previous games.[46]

Over time, the responsibility of being the face of the Raptors and winning a championship began weighing on Carter like a ton of bricks. Significant changes in management and the coaching staff did not improve his relationship within the franchise. Making matters worse, a slew of injuries grounded "Air Canada." Jalen Rose, Carter's teammate from 2003 to 2004, says rumors began leaking that he no longer wanted to play in Toronto, soiling his relationship with the local fanbase. After he stopped dunking in games, he told reporters dunks were overrated. Years later he admitted to not playing hard during his final season with the Raptors.

The Raptors traded Carter to the New Jersey Nets for center Alonzo Mourning on December 17, 2004. The fans booed him unceasingly each time he returned to Toronto to play for the next four years. He played for New Jersey, Orlando, Phoenix, Dallas, Memphis, Sacramento, and Atlanta after departing Toronto. Injuries and old age eventually transformed him into a reliable role player and respected mentor to his younger teammates. Carter, who retired at 43, is the only NBA player with a career spanning four decades. He currently works as a basketball analyst and broadcaster for ESPN. Ironically, when Carter returned to Canada in 2014 as a Memphis Grizzlies member, Toronto fans finally forgave him. He was unable to control the tears running down his face while receiving a lengthy standing ovation and a heartfelt appreciation video.[47]

Vince Carter's impact on Toronto extended beyond the basketball court. When he arrived in the city, there were only three nightclubs. He partnered with a young White entrepreneur, Travis Agresti, to open a new club called Inside. Carter saw the club as an outlet for other NBA players when they were in town for road games or during the offseason. "Whether you were at Vince's club or Vince was somewhere else. Whether you were just out, and Vince wasn't there, his presence was felt because the city was just on," says Toronto rapper Drake.[48] "This was the first time that you're seeing these superstars party with everybody. At that time, the vibes that were in this city were out of control," says Kardinal Offishall, the first mainstream Canadian rapper famous for blending Jamaican reggae and dancehall with rap.[49]

Carter befriended many upcoming hip-hop stars growing up in Toronto in the early 2000s. One of those newfound friends was Julien Christian Lutz, better known by various monikers: Little X, Director X, or X. Lutz replaced Harold "Hype" Williams as the leading director for hip-hop music videos since the 2000s, working with Jay-Z, Usher, Rihanna, Drake, Future, and Kendrick Lamar. Carter's reputation around the city benefited immensely from befriending Mona Halem, a beautiful young Egyptian American woman and the founder of Lady Luck Entertainment. At the time, Halem was Toronto's premier party promoter. Whenever famous NBA players came to town, they knew to call her or Carter if they wanted to have a good time.

The growing presence of NBA celebrities in the city resulted in another significant development. Carter and Agresti challenged local liquor licenses to allow them to provide bottle service in their club. Anyone who has ever gone to a plush nightclub or lounge is familiar with the practice of bottle service. Patrons with money have large bottles of expensive alcohol brought to their private tables or sections in the VIP (very important person) area. NBA players were accustomed to this service in the U.S., but Canadian clubs had it only after being introduced at Carter's Inside. Carter also held a celebrity basketball game during Caribana, Toronto's annual Carnival, to celebrate the city's Caribbean culture. According to Halem, NBA players and other young celebrities who began visiting Toronto quickly fell in love with the city because of its diversity in people, music, and culture. "When you grow up in certain American cities, and you're only surrounded by one type of culture or one type of language, and then you come to Toronto, you going to come here and think 'oh my God, this is so exotic.'"[50]

Toronto was a mixing bowl for basketball, hip-hop, and multiculturalism at the dawn of the millennium. This level of diversity was not caused by happenstance or due to the celebrity of Vince Carter. Enslaved Africans arrived in Canada between the 17th and 18th centuries. Over 3,000 enslaved Black people and free Blacks of African descent in the U.S. who remained loyal to the British crown migrated to Canada after the Revolutionary War. At least 30,000 enslaved Black people migrated to Canada after 1793 following the passage of the Fugitive Slave Law. They arrived by way of the Underground Railroad, a series of escape routes to freedom from slavery in the American South, and with the help of "conductors" like Harriet Tubman and William Still. Canada's Immigration Act of 1910 prohibited the immigration of "undesirable" persons until 1967, curtailing the number of Black migrants.[51]

Toronto's Black population was 40,000 in the 1960s. Many residents were immigrants from Barbados, Jamaica, and Trinidad and Tobago. Ontario-born Black Canadians established Caribana in 1967 by merging their Emancipation Day celebration with the Trinidad and Tobago celebration of Carnival. During the 1980s and 1990s, Toronto received an influx of arrivals from Eritrea, Ethiopia, and Somalia. Nigeria has become a primary source of immigration to Toronto in recent years. Surprisingly, Blacks make up only a small percentage of the city's population. Since 2016, the city's largest ethnic groups have been South Asian (12.6 percent), East Asian (12.5 percent), and Black (8.9 percent). Most of the East Asian population is Chinese. Many South Asian immigrants are from India, Pakistan, and Sri Lanka.[52] This diverse population made Toronto the most likely place for basketball to succeed in Canada. This new generation of Black, brown, and yellow children did not grow up playing the majority-White sport of hockey. The NBA players were more relatable for many of them. It was also easier and cheaper to hang up a hoop to shoot baskets than to learn to ice-skate.

We the North

Vince Carter's departure left the franchise with a void of star power. Chris Bosh, the team's fourth overall draft pick in 2003, was expected to take the baton. Bosh was different from your typical professional athlete. The Dallas, Texas, native grew up fascinated by science and computers. He majored in graphic design and computer engineering during his one year at Georgia Institute of Technology (Georgia Tech). In 2020, he was named the dean of the Drone Racing League (DLR) Academy, the league's digital youth science, technology, engineering, and mathematics (STEM) system. While a student at Lincoln High School, he joined the National Honor Society and student engineering organizations. His love for STEM came from his mother, Freida, who worked at Texas Instruments, and his father, Noel, an engineer.[53] While basketball was his best sport, he also participated in baseball, gymnastics, and karate.

Bosh averaged 16 points and nine rebounds in his first season playing without Carter. He scored 18 points and grabbed eight rebounds in Kobe's historic 81-point game. The Raptors received less television coverage outside Canada once Carter departed. Consequently, Bosh had to take unconventional measures to get noticed by non–Raptors' fans and the American press. In 2008, he posted a quirky, one-minute promotional video on YouTube to get voted onto his first All-Star Game team. Bosh dressed up like a cowboy and spoke with an exaggerated Western accent. He and his chipped-tooth, cow-tipping friend, Bubba, informed viewers that the cost to vote for him was not "$20, $10, or even $5 ... it's free." At the ad's conclusion, viewers were given the option to vote at www.nba.com or www.chrisbosh.com. His goofy antics paid off as he was selected to be a reserve for the Eastern Conference.

Bosh averaged a career-high 24 points in the 2007–08 season. That summer he helped the Redeem Team win gold at the Olympics. His summer in Beijing allowed him to bond with Olympic teammates LeBron James and Dwayne Wade. He signed with the Miami Heat as a free agent two summers later. He was the third member of the "Heatles" super team headlined by LeBron and Wade. Miami made four straight appearances in the NBA Finals between 2011 and 2014, winning championships in 2012 and 2013. Bosh, forced to retire in 2019 because of a blood clot in his calf, was inducted into the 2021 Hall of Fame class. He was the first Raptor to receive such an honor. During a town hall with Sirius XM before his induction, he admitted that he thought he needed a championship on his résumé to be considered one of the greats. He knew his chances of winning a ring were greater in Miami than in Toronto.[54] Vince Carter was enshrined in the Hall of Fame on August 17, 2024.

Bosh's departure left the team's future in the hands of three newcomers: DeMar DeRozan, Kyle Lowry, and Masai Ujiri. The Raptors drafted DeRozan with the ninth pick in 2009. DeRozan, an athletic scoring guard from Los Angeles, was joined in the backcourt by Lowry in 2012. Lowry, a stocky point guard from Philadelphia, began his career with the Memphis Grizzlies and Houston Rockets before coming to Toronto. The pair spearheaded a rejuvenated squad that was making incremental improvements each year. Their version of the Raptors had the misfortune of playing during LeBron's reign over the Eastern Conference as a member of the Cleveland Cavaliers. The Raptors lost to the Cavaliers in the 2016 conference finals and again in the 2017 and 2018 conference semifinals. When LeBron left Cleveland to play for the Lakers in the summer of 2018, it opened the door for Toronto to advance to the NBA Finals. But for that to happen, drastic changes had to be made.

Bryan Colangelo, son of Jerry Colangelo and the team's general manager, hired 36-year-old Masai Ujiri in 2007 to be the Raptors' director of global scouting. Ujiri is one of the most successful and intriguing people in today's NBA. He was born in Bournemouth, England, in 1970. His parents moved the family to their native country, Nigeria, when he was two. His mother, Paula, worked as a doctor, and his father, Michael, was a nursing educator and administrator at a local hospital. As a boy, Ujiri developed a love for basketball by watching NBA games on VHS tapes. His earliest memories are of watching the Celtics-Lakers rivalry during the 1980s. He especially admired Hakeem Olajuwon, the Nigerian-born center who won league MVP and championship rings with the Rockets in 1994 and 1995.[55]

Ujiri says that as a child, he knew that basketball would be his future, but few—even his parents—could envision this coming to fruition. He migrated to America to pursue his dreams, playing basketball for two years at Bismarck State College in North Dakota. His goal was to make the NBA, but he bounced around to various lower-level professional leagues in Belgium, England, Finland, Germany, and Greece. Ujiri found himself jobless and penniless at 31 years old, 5,000 miles away from home. Unwilling to give up on his dream, he started hustling around the globe to earn a spot in the NBA, not as a player but as a talent scout. While living in Nigeria, he encountered countless kids with the potential to play in the pros. He sought to find the NBA's next African sensation. In 2003, he launched Giants of Africa, a summer basketball camp in Nigeria for the country's best and brightest youth.[56]

Ujiri's NBA career began a year before he founded his first camp. While accompanying a professional prospect from Nigeria at tryouts for the Orlando Magic, he met Magic scouting director Gary Brokaw, head coach Glenn "Doc" Rivers, and general manager John Gabriel. He impressed the group enough to earn an unpaid scouting job with the team. Ujiri did not mind paying for his own accommodation or sharing rooms with other scouts and players on trips. These sacrifices resulted in a salaried position with the Denver Nuggets as an international scout in 2003. Ujiri joined the Raptors four years later. In 2008, he was promoted to the position of assistant general manager. After only two years in this post, Denver hired him as their general manager and executive vice president. Ujiri is the first general manager of African descent in any American sports league. Under his leadership, the Nuggets amassed a franchise record of 57 regular-season wins. He became the first non–American to be named NBA Executive of the Year.

Ujiri replaced Colangelo as Toronto's general manager and executive vice president in May 2013. He signed a five-year contract worth $15 million, quite a leap from his early days with the Magic. From his first day on the job, he galvanized the fanbase with an attitude and swagger missing in the past. When he addressed thousands of eager fans standing outside the arena in Jurassic Park before a playoff game with the Brooklyn Nets, he shouted, "Fuck Brooklyn!" Two years later, he was fined $35,000 for shouting out to fans, "We don't give a shit about it," before a playoff game with the Washington Wizards. His profanity was a response to a comment made by Wizards star Paul Pierce. Ujiri may have been profane, but he was an exceptionally hard worker who produced results. He was a ruthless executive who placed winning above all things, even loyalty.

Dwane Casey was the first Raptors head coach to provide stability to the team. Before his hiring in 2011, there was a revolving door of coaches. Under his direction, the Raptors reached the Eastern Conference finals in 2016. He won the NBA Coach of the Year award in 2018. The Raptors were eliminated by the Cavaliers in the semifinals later that season. Despite the team's success, Ujiri fired Casey after the playoff loss and replaced him with assistant coach Nick Nurse. While some people might see this hiring as another example of a Black coach being fired and his White successor reaping the benefits of an eventual championship (see the 2002–03 Tampa Bay Buccaneers and the 2014–15 Golden State Warriors), Ujiri was not concerned with the optics. Ujiri demonstrated the same callous behavior two months later when he traded fan favorite DeRozan to the Spurs for their mercurial, young all-star Kawhi Leonard, who had only a year remaining on his contract.[57]

The 2018–19 Raptors' roster had a heavy dose of international flavor, starting with coach Nick Nurse. Before the Raptors hired him in 2013 to be Casey's assistant, he coached 11 years in Europe's British Basketball League (BBL), where he was a two-time Coach of the Year. Nurse coached the Birmingham Bullets and the Manchester Giants to championships in 1996 and 2000, respectively. He was an assistant coach for the Great Britain national team at the 2012 Summer Olympics. These experiences prepared him to coach a diverse roster with four key players of international descent. The Raptors acquired Marc Gasol from Memphis in 2019. The 6'11" center from Barcelona, Spain, was the younger brother of Lakers champion center Pau Gasol. Besides his time in the NBA, Gasol was a member of Spain's national team. He won a FIBA EuroCup in 2007 and was the Most Valuable Player of his Spanish league in 2008.

Other international players on the Raptors' 2019 roster were Serge Ibaka, Pascal Siakam, and Jeremy Lin. Ibaka was a 6'11" power forward from the Democratic Republic of Congo. The third youngest of 18 children, he was drafted by the Oklahoma City Thunder in 2009 after playing overseas. He joined the Raptors in 2017. Siakam, a 6'8" power forward from Douala, Cameroon, migrated to the U.S. for high school and college. The Raptors drafted him out of New Mexico State University in 2016. He was a vital contributor to the team's 2019 playoff run. Lin was born in California and attended Harvard University. But his parents migrated to the U.S. from Taiwan in the 1970s. Lin became a symbol for the Asian-American community and a popular culture icon when he led the New York Knicks in scoring for a brief period in 2011–12. "Linsanity" became a catchphrase to describe the world's fascination with him during that magical run. Lin's games were watched in the U.S. and China. He and Ibaka played minor roles for the Raptors in the playoffs.

We Need Some Really Big Rings

The Raptors achieved a 58–24 record in the 2018–19 regular season, finishing second in the Eastern Conference. It took them only five games to eliminate Orlando in the first round of the playoffs. Their second-round series with Philadelphia came down to a decisive game seven. With the score tied at 90, Marc Gasol inbounded the ball to Kawhi Leonard with 4.2 seconds left to play. Leonard dribbled the basketball to the far-right corner of the court and pulled up for a game-winning shot over 7'0" Philadelphia center Joel Embiid. The ball bounced slowly off the rim four times before miraculously going in. Leonard, who always appears emotionless, let out a victorious roar as his teammates rushed over to celebrate as he fell to the floor. Leonard, who scored 15 of his 41 points in the final quarter, reflected on the moment in an oral history about "the shot" conducted by *The Ringer*.

> I'm a guy that acts like I've been there before. So, probably the last time you probably seen me screaming was like when [the Spurs] won [the 2013–14 NBA championship]. So whenever there's a moment where I haven't really experienced [something], I try to give some emotion, show some emotion, and let it just come out. [Game 7] was one of those nights. I'd never been in that situation before ... it's the first shot somebody hit a game-winner in Game 7. So, I just showed emotion. And it was great. It's a great feeling.[58]

The Raptors defeated the Milwaukee Bucks in the next round to advance to the NBA Finals, where the back-to-back defending champion Golden State Warriors, starring Steph Curry and Kevin Durant, were waiting. Throughout Toronto's playoff run, two "superfans" were noticeable at most games, garnering the media's attention. Nav Bhatia is an immigrant from India who migrated to Canada in the 1980s due to anti–Sikh riots in his native land. Bhatia was a mechanical engineer in India but had to work as a car salesman in Toronto because employers were uncomfortable hiring someone with a long beard and turban. After selling a record 127 cars in his first 90 days, he became a general manager at one of the city's largest dealerships. His earnings allowed him to purchase season tickets to the Raptors' games during their inaugural season. Soon Bhatia was a fixture at Raptors games. Isiah Thomas nicknamed him "superfan" because of his exuberant support for the team. It took a historic pandemic to keep him from cheering on his beloved Raptors. Bhatia never missed a home game until he contracted Covid-19 attending a game against the Wizards in December 2021.

Bhatia is on a short list of NBA fans, such as Spike Lee, Jack Nicholson, Clipper Darrell (Darrell Bailey), Jimmy Goldstein, and rapper E-40, who are more famous than some players. On May 15, 2021, he became the first superfan inducted into the Naismith Memorial Hall of Fame. Actor Kal Penn is producing and starring in a forthcoming biopic about him.[59] The Raptors' other famous superfan is *Billboard* chart-topping rapper Drake. Aubrey Drake Graham was born in Toronto in 1986 to a white Jewish mother and a Black American father from Memphis. A year after his Bar Mitzvah, Drake joined the cast of the Canadian teen drama *Degrassi: The Next Generation*. From his role on *Degrassi* as Jimmy Brooks, who uses a wheelchair, he went on to record successful rap mixtapes *Room for Improvement* (2006), *Comeback Season* (2007), and *So Far Gone* (2009) before signing with Lil Wayne's Young Money Entertainment. Wayne was arguably the hottest emcee in the world when he gave Drake his stamp of approval. Drake joined Wayne's label alongside emerging hip-hop stars Nicki Minaj and Tyga. Between 2010 and 2020, Drake was Spotify's most-streamed artist, with over 28 billion streams. All his albums topped the *Billboard* 200 charts.[60] His hybrid style of rapping and singing crosses genres of hip-hop, R&B, pop, Afropop, dancehall, and Latin Trap, reflecting Toronto's musical diversity. His everyman persona brought international acclaim and ridicule from rival emcee Kendrick Lamar who accused him of cultural appropriation.

Drake credits Vince Carter with his success in music. When he was a kid, Carter gave him the VC15 armband he wore after a home game. "Without Vince, I don't know if any of us would have had that feeling that this city was a place people would pay attention to," says Drake.[61] The Raptors named Drake their global ambassador in 2016. He served as the city's official host when the NBA held its first All-Star weekend in Canada. Drake became the quintessential promotor for the team and his city. In songs, it was common to find him name-dropping Raptors players or the 6ix, the city's nickname.[62] He sat atop the CN Tower, a local landmark, for the cover art of his fourth studio album, *Views*, initially titled *Views from the 6*. The self-proclaimed "6ix god" appeared on the March 2016 cover of *Slam* magazine alongside Lowry and DeRozan. He and LeBron produced the 2017 documentary *The Carter Effect*, about Vince Carter's effect on Toronto. His 2019 signature Nike Air Jordan 4 sneaker came in a black, purple, and red colorway inspired by the Raptors' original uniform.

Drake never shied away from making himself a part of the games as he sat courtside. During the 2019 Eastern Conference finals, he was caught on camera massaging Coach Nurse's shoulders to relax him.[63] He called Warriors forward Draymond Green "trash" as he walked off the court at the end of game one in the NBA Finals. He taunted Green in game five for receiving a technical foul. Toronto won a tightly contested game six 114–110 to clinch their first championship.[64] Drake delivered a passionate, drunken victory speech after the game. "This is poetic.... The 6ix in six.... I want my chips with dip," he told reporters.[65] Drake and Bhatia both attended the championship parade on June 17, 2019.

An estimated crowd of nearly two million people clogged the streets of Toronto to celebrate the championship victory. Ujiri, who was wrongfully charged with assaulting an Oakland police officer who did not realize he was the team's vice president trying to join his players on the court at the end of game six, was embraced by Canadian Prime Minister Justin Trudeau at the parade. That glorious day in June was a testament to the success of NBA expansion in Canada. The Raptors clinched their first title on the same court in Oakland where Vince Carter captivated the world at the dunk contest 19 years earlier. Despite the Grizzlies' departure to Memphis and the Raptors' initial struggles, David Stern's dream was finally a reality.

What does the Raptors' success mean for NBA expansion moving forward? In 2023, Commissioner Adam Silver teased potential expansion in Las Vegas and Seattle. The Supersonics franchise existed in Seattle from 1967 to 2008 and were the 1979 champions. Jordan's Bulls defeated the Supersonics in the 1996 NBA Finals. The Supersonics are now the Oklahoma City Thunder. Las Vegas has become a likely destination for expansion in recent years due to the legalization of sports betting, the growing popularity of the NBA's annual Las Vegas Summer League tournament every July, and the success of the WNBA's Las Vegas Aces.[66] Will the league ever attempt to expand internationally again? Can it repeat Toronto's accomplishments in Montreal, Quebec, or another part of the globe? International expansion comes with many challenges. Players do not always want to play and live overseas. Most free agents are not clamoring to play in Toronto. Travel time could be an issue for destinations outside North America. The Grizzlies failed partly because they were introduced to a fanbase that was new to the sport. The game is much more global today, so this is not a significant issue. Nevertheless, the league would be wise to avoid establishing a franchise in an area likely to have a constant uphill climb to attract a fanbase.

The Raptors created the blueprint for successful international expansion, but their success was unique. No one could have predicted that Vince Carter would become a cultural icon. They were lucky to draft Tracy McGrady and Chris Bosh, although neither player re-signed with the team when they entered their prime. If the Raptors had not hired Masai Ujiri, who traded their best player, DeRozan, for Leonard, they would still be searching for their first title. Leonard signed with the Los Angeles Clippers less than a month after the parade. On May 23, 2024, WNBA commissioner Cathy Engelbert announced "the W's" first international expansion team would reside in Toronto beginning in 2026. Canadians may have another basketball championship to celebrate soon.[67] The NBA's success in Toronto, not just with the Raptors but also in developing notable current and future players, manifests how the league benefits from globalization.

4

The Joker

> "*Europe's best young players are now the world's best young players. Their guys will have titles. [American] guys will have clout.*"
>
> —Colin Cowherd[1]

Back in the day when Magic and Bird were the NBA's main weekend attraction, short basketball shorts were still in vogue, and Michael Jordan had hair and two (gold) chains dangling from his neck in the dunk contest, the sports media landscape was quite different. Fans relied on local sports beat writers to follow their favorite teams and athletes. *Sports Illustrated* was the quintessential source of national sports news. By the 1990s and 2000s, ESPN and sports talk radio dominated media coverage and shaped sports discussions at the barbershop, office water cooler, and anywhere else folks gathered. When ESPN launched a new television series called *Pardon the Interruption* on October 22, 2001, starring former *Washington Post* sports columnists Tony Kornheiser and Michael Wilbon, they probably had no idea they were creating the paradigm for sports programming today. Kornheiser and Wilbon debate popular sports topics of the day. While the debates on *PTI* are relatively tame, that is not true of the sports debate shows that have followed it.

PTI is the standard bearer for all sports debate shows, but it is not the most popular with television viewers and social media followers. That title belongs to another ESPN series, *First Take*. The two-hour morning debate show originally aired on ESPN2 from 2007 to 2016 before moving to ESPN in 2017. After the first five years of modest success, Queens, New York's loquacious sports journalist Stephen A. Smith joined the show alongside Skip Bayless, arguably the chief provocateur of the sports media landscape. Smith and Bayless built an empire that lasted into the 2020s and spawned multiple imitations, such as FS1's *Undisputed* (2016–2024), initially hosted by Bayless and NFL Hall-of-Famer/*Club Shay Shay* podcaster Shannon Sharpe.

First Take's more contentious debates make the most noise on Twitter (now X) and other social media platforms, which helps to boost television ratings. One such debate occurred on March 7, 2023, between retired NBA players turned media darlings Kendrick Perkins and JJ Redick. Perkins was a member of Boston's 2008 championship team. Reddick, a 15-year NBA veteran, was hired to coach the Los Angeles Lakers in 2024. Before leaving the media to coach, he had burned bridges with numerous NBA legends from Bob Cousy to Dominique Wilkins for downplaying the skill level of the men who played in the NBA before the year 2000 and calling "old school" basketball overrated based upon the hours of past games he watched on YouTube.

The Perkins-Redick debate had nothing to do with generational differences about what constitutes great basketball. Their discussion opened a wound surrounding an uncomfortable subject that cannot be adequately dissected in 10-minute segments aimed at defeating one's opponent with the cleverest hot take. Redick began the segment by apologizing to Stephen A. Smith for anything he was about to say that might be offensive. Redick was irate and wanted to set the record straight with Perkins, who insinuated on a previous episode that racial bias was why Nikola Jokić was on the verge of winning a third consecutive league MVP award. Jokić is a 6'11" 245-pound Serbian center for the Denver Nuggets. His former Denver teammate Mike Miller began calling him Joker because he had trouble pronouncing his last name. Jokić is the most improbable MVP winner in league history. He was the 41st overall pick in the 2014 draft. He is often body-shamed for having the stereotypical physique of a 40-year-old dad who shoots hoops at the YMCA on the weekends for exercise.[2]

Jokić, a reserved guy, does not dance like Steph (Curry) after he hits three-point daggers. He lacks the "handles" of Kyrie (Irving) and cannot leap out the gym like Ant (Anthony Edwards) or Ja (Morant).[3] Vince Carter's vertical jump was 43 inches during his peak years. Jokić has a five-inch vertical. If you enjoy watching a fundamentally sound play, the Joker is your guy! Otherwise, you may find his two rowdy older brothers, Strahinja and Nemanja, more fascinating. Jokić may not win a popularity contest among the cool kids on social media, but there is no denying his ability. He has led the Nuggets in scoring, rebounding, and assists the past three years. He is the first center with the passing and scoring ability of a point guard. In a frustrating "load management" era where players frequently sit out for "rest," he seldom misses games. Many sports media members believe Jokić is the best basketball player in the world. Perkins was not one of those people. He accused Jokić of "stat padding," which means piling up statistics in different areas of the game, like points, assists, and rebounds, for personal prestige. Point guard Russell Westbrook, the league's all-time leader in triple-doubles, has been accused of this for years. Yet Jokić is praised for his triple-doubles. Reddick reminded Jokić's "haters" that the Nuggets were 23–0 in the 2022–23 season when the Joker recorded a triple-double.

The first minute of Redick and Perkins' debate went as follows:

> **REDICK:** What you are implying is that the white voters are racist, that they favor White people.
> **PERKINS:** I did not. I did not.
> **REDICK:** Yes, you did! Yes, you did! That is exactly what you implied, Kendrick Perkins.
> **PERKINS:** I did not. I STATED THE FACTS! I STATED THE FACTS! And you are not about to sit up here (inaudible sound) ... IT'S THE FACTS! IT'S THE FACTS!!!!⁴

In a previous episode, Perkins mentioned that Jokić, Steve Nash, and Dirk Nowitzki were the only players in the NBA to win the MVP award without being among the top 10 scorers in those seasons. Nash and Nowitzki were White international players from Canada and Germany, respectively.⁵ In the season in which Kobe Bryant scored 81 points against Toronto and led a depleted Lakers roster to the playoffs, Nash repeated as league MVP. Some basketball analysts believe Nash *stole* one of Shaquille O'Neal's MVPs. Redick pointed out Black players like Magic Johnson, who also won the award despite having low scoring averages. Perkins, rolling his eyes as Redick referenced analytical data to justify his argument, began yelling to get his point across as Redick tried to talk over him.

Bomani Jones, a former ESPN personality and host of HBO's *Game Theory with Bomani Jones* (2022–23), weighed in on the matter during a taping of *Game Theory* before a live audience: "If you're trying to make the argument that something doesn't involve race, might not be the best look to talk over a Black man on live television, tell him his argument was flat out wrong, and cut him off over and over again."⁶ Jones further reiterated his feelings on Twitter (X):

> Nobody patronizes White hoopers more than White dudes. But when they're excellent? Well, that's a little different. It can sometimes go too far. That causes an obvious dissonance, and when things get dissonant, and it sounds like White people are going a little far to hype up a White dude.... You're acting like Perk's crazy for bringing it up.... But chastising us for saying something might be racist in the land where racism was perfected, that's how you get pats on the back from folks I know JJ Redick does not want on his side.⁷

In the early 1980s, with the NBA on the verge of collapse, globalization was an unlikely pipe dream. Critics lambasted the league for being "too Black" and full of entitled, thuggish cocaine abusers who scared off a white fanbase. The league's lifeline came with the introduction of "safe" and "nonthreatening" Black stars Earvin "Magic" Johnson and Michael Jordan and the Boston Celtics' newest leading man, Larry Bird. Bird, unwillingly, became the NBA's version of the Great White Hope. His retirement in 1992, shortly after his Dream Team appearance, marked the beginning of the end for the American-born White superstar in the NBA. Over the next three decades, fewer American White players were drafted. Globalization *unintentionally* became the cause and solution to the growing absence of White American players. Europe has produced the league's highest number of foreign-born players since the 1990s. By the start of the 2021–22 season, 321 Europeans played in the league. Despite the success of these Europeans, the most popular players are still Black, and none of them has achieved the American mainstream status of Bird. In recent years, some current and retired Black players and Black media members have called out racial bias in the coverage and praise of certain White European players. This chapter analyzes the evolution of the NBA's White European talent pool and this polarizing debate over racial bias.

Make the NBA Great Again

In January 2019, I interviewed Kevin Lloyd for the Virginia Interscholastic Association (VIA)'s oral history project and digital archive. Kevin's late father, Earl Lloyd, was a VIA legend and, as Kevin told me, "the NBA's Jackie Robinson."[8] Mr. Lloyd was drafted by the Washington Capitals in 1950. The Alexandria, Virginia, native was the first Black American to play in an NBA game and the league's first Black bench coach. Lloyd was among the trinity of the NBA's first Black players, which included Chuck Cooper and Nat "Sweetwater" Clifton. The Celtics drafted Cooper on April 25, 1950. The Knickerbockers signed Clifton on April 25, 1950, making him the first Black player under contract.[9]

"People don't realize it now, man, but the NBA was virtually lily-White. If you look at all those early pictures, it was a predominantly White league," noted sports journalist and writer William C. Rhoden.[10] Throughout the first 50 years of the 20th century, nearly all professional sports in America were segregated by a strict color line. Call it the "Jockey Syndrome," a term coined by Rhoden in his book *Forty Million Dollar Slaves* (2006) to describe efforts by Whites in thoroughbred horse racing to ban the triumphant Black jockey Isaac Murphy from their sport because, as the kids say, "he was him." Murphy's three Kentucky Derby victories were an affront to white supremacy.[11] Horse racing's color line spread to boxing, baseball, football, golf, hockey, tennis, and basketball. The Black Fives Era from 1904 until 1950 refers to the period in which all-Black basketball teams existed before integration. These Black teams emerged throughout Northeastern and Midwestern cities. Edwin Henderson, nicknamed "the grandfather of Black basketball," is credited with introducing the game to the Black community in 1904 while teaching physical education in Washington, D.C.[12] The best Black players not involved with the Black Fives played for the Harlem Globetrotters.

The NBA's unwritten quota system after integration was that teams could keep one Black player on their roster. Eventually, teams allowed two Blacks to avoid having integrated rooms on road trips. Boston's decision to draft Cooper came from their head coach, Arnold Jacob "Red" Auerbach, who did not care if a player was green if he contributed to winning.[13] The Celtics, the NBA's first great dynasty, were led by their 6'1" White point guard Bob Cousy. The son of French immigrants who migrated to Manhattan, Cousy was the NBA's first superstar at the guard position. Fans called him "the Houdini of the Hardwood." "If you stopped the average man on the street in America in the fifties and said, okay, name a basketball player, more people would say Bob Cousy," says *Boston Globe* columnist Bob Ryan.[14] SiriusXM NBA Radio host Justin Termine credits Cousy with originating behind-the-back, no-look passes and fancy dribbling. This attribution sounds overly hyperbolic, considering the moves the Globetrotters were already doing in the 1940s and the moves amateur Black players were exhibiting on playgrounds across the country. Cousy's ball-handling wizardry paled compared with that of Globetrotters Marques Haynes and Frederick "Curly" Neal.

Bob Cousy's Celtics were stellar offensively; however, they lacked defense and never won a championship until they drafted Bill Russell, a 6'10" Black center, in 1956. Auerbach convinced Celtics owner Walter Brown, who owned stock in the Ice Capades, to promise the owner of the Rochester Royals free Ice Capades shows in his arena if he did not take Russell with the first pick in the draft. Russell, the only Black player on the Celtics when he was drafted, was the target of rampant racism in opposing cities. Conditions were not much better for him in Boston. When he and his first wife, Rose, purchased a home in the all-White town of Reading, the "raccoons" routinely tipped over their trash cans on their lawn. Vandals broke into Russell's house, wrote *nigger* on the wall, and defecated in their bed. "Boston was the least liberal city in the NBA when I got there," said Russell, who called the city a "flea market of racism."[15] He became an active member of the Civil Rights Movement to help change society.[16] Cousy remained the fan favorite, but the defensive-minded Russell was the Celtics' cornerstone to 11 NBA championships between 1957 and 1969.[17] Boston drafted more Black players during their dynastic run and named Russell the NBA's first Black player-coach in 1967.

4. The Joker

The Celtics defeated the Los Angeles Lakers seven consecutive times in the NBA Finals between 1959 and 1969. The Lakers, starring Wilt Chamberlain and Jerry West, lost the 1969 championship series in seven grueling games. West became the first and only finals MVP on the losing team. His performance in that series was the stuff of legend. To quote OutKast's Andre 3000, West was "Ice Cold!" He scored 51 points and dished 10 assists in game one. A hamstring injury in game six *limited* him to 42 points, 12 assists, and 13 rebounds in the series finale. A silhouette of West dribbling a basketball became the league's official logo that season.[18]

NBA history cannot be told without Jerome Alan West. He is responsible for the Lakers' success in the 1970s. It was his idea to trade Vlade Divac for a high school kid named Kobe in 1996. He brought Kevin Durant to the Golden State Warriors in 2016, resulting in back-to-back championships. West never basked in his stardom. The painfully shy and introverted shooting guard was plagued by depression since the age of 12 when his older brother Davis was killed in the Korean War. An abusive childhood contributed to his mental health problems. He kept a shotgun under his bed as protection from his father's belt and beatings. The basketball court was one of the few places West could find solace.[19] As a junior at West Virginia University, he scored 116 points in five games during the NCAA tournament. He was named the co-captain of the 1960 U.S. Olympic basketball team in Rome. The Lakers drafted him that same year. In his sophomore season, the Lakers had a 33-game winning streak and won 69 regular-season games and the NBA Finals. The 69-game record stood for 24 seasons until Jordan's Bulls went 72–10 in the 1995–96 season.

The Lakers beat the Knicks in the 1972 finals, setting up a rematch the following year. The Knicks avenged the loss, winning the championship series in five games. This was New York's second championship in three seasons and the last one in franchise history. Those championship teams had a who's who list of Black players, including Walt "Clyde" Frazier, Earl "The Pearl" Monroe, Cazzie Russell, and Willis Reed. However, a moderately athletic White player from Princeton University received the most attention and transformed their home arena, Madison Square Garden, into the "hot spot" to attend a professional sporting event in the '70s.

The Knicks drafted Bill Bradley, the Ivy League All-American small forward, with the first overall pick in 1965. Rather than turn professional, Bradley took a two-year hiatus to pursue a Rhodes scholarship at Oxford University in England. When Bradley joined the team, he signed a four-year $500,000 rookie contract, comparable to the contracts of Wilt Chamberlain and Bill Russell, arguably the league's most dominant players. Teammates sarcastically nicknamed him "Dollar Bill."[20] Magazines that did not cover sports began sending reporters to the Garden to write stories about him. One journalist predicted he would run for U.S. president (which he did in 2000 after serving 18 years in the U.S. Senate representing New Jersey). Bradley's home game debut against the Pistons drew a sellout crowd of 19,500, at the time the largest crowd in NBA history. Walt Frazier reflected on Bradley's Garden debut: "If he made a layup, the crowd would cheer. If he tied his shoe, they cheered."

Bill Bradley, who admitted to disliking the undeserved attention, was the NBA's first example of "a Great White Hope." Adam J. Criblez discusses this phenomenon in his 2015 article "White Men Playing a Black Man's Game: Basketball's Great White Hopes" of the 1970s.[21] Bradley represented a savior figure for countless White sports fans and media members uncomfortable with the changing demographics of the league. The Great White Hope mythology dates to Jack Johnson, the first Black heavyweight champion in professional boxing.[22] At a time when Whites ran everything, Jack Johnson took orders from no one. While the Black masses struggled to make ends meet, Jack Johnson was wealthier than most Whites. When Black men were expected to kowtow to White men, Jack Johnson reveled in beating them to a bloody pulp inside the boxing ring. And at a time when Black men could be lynched for merely flirting with a woman, Jack Johnson slept with whomever he pleased.[23] Historian Theresa Runstedtler describes Johnson in her book *Jack Johnson, Rebel Sojourner* (2013) as a Black man who challenged the color line in America and abroad in Africa, Australia, Europe, and Latin America.[24]

At the turn of the 20th century, boxing was one of the three dominant American sports, next to baseball and horse racing. Since people viewed the heavyweight champion as the "Emperor of Masculinity," Black men were barred from title fights. Johnson's first significant bout against a White fighter came on May 16, 1902, against Jack Jeffries, the younger brother of reigning heavyweight champion Jim Jeffries. Johnson knocked him out and helped carry him back to his corner as Jim sat ringside. "You are next," Johnson warned him. But the champ drew the color line, pledging to retire once there were no more worthy White opponents. In the meantime, Johnson continued to knock out all the top Black competition and lesser white opponents. He typically took it easier on Black fighters. But he showed no mercy to the White ones, knocking out one man 20 times in the same fight. Johnson struck one White opponent so hard that an imprint of the man's teeth appeared on his boxing gloves.[25]

After Jim Jefferies retired in 1905, Noah Brusso, a Canadian fighter who later changed his name to Tommy Burns, became the new heavyweight champ two years later. Burns agreed to fight Johnson in Sydney, Australia, on December 26, 1908. The smug Johnson blew kisses to the predominantly White crowd as they hurled racist remarks at him. Burns taunted Johnson in the fight's early rounds. "Fight like a White man," he yelled out. Burns was no match for his indomitable Black challenger. Whenever Burns appeared to be falling to his knees, Johnson held him up to prolong the beating. "Stop the fight, stop the fight," the audience cried out. Before Johnson knocked him out, police officers rushed into the ring and told camera crews to stop recording. A series of "Great White Hope" fighters unsuccessfully tried to dethrone Johnson and restore the white race to its pinnacle of racial hegemony. After two years, Jefferies decided to end his retirement for a bout with the champ. The fight, billed as "the battle of the century," was held on July 4, 1910, in Reno, Nevada, and it would be a celebration of somebody's independence.[26]

Johnson dropped Jefferies to the mat repeatedly in the 15th round. Some Whites, among the 20,000 in attendance, could be heard saying, "Don't let the nigger knock him out! Don't let the nigger knock him out!" Riots broke out across the nation between whites feeling sore about the loss and Blacks jubilant about the win. On a Houston streetcar, an enraged white person slit a Black man's throat because he had cheered for Jack Johnson. In Manhattan, a White crowd set a Black tenement on fire, then tried to block the doors and windows so that no one could get out. Not until the 1968 assassination of the Rev. Martin Luther King, Jr., would there be this level of nationwide racial violence.[27] Johnson was eventually defeated, first in the ring in 1915 and next by the U.S. government, which charged him with taking White women across state lines for sexual activity.[28]

In his journal article "Basketball's Great White Hope and Ronald Reagan's America: Hoosiers," Ron Briley explains how America's beloved sports film *Hoosiers* (1986) was a classic example of Great White Hope mythology and how the film's popularity manifests the blind acceptance of this myth.

> Based upon a screenplay by Angelo Pizzo, who met Anspaugh at the basketball-infatuated Indiana University, *Hoosiers* attempts to reconstruct the so-called "Milan Miracle" of 1954 in which the Milan Indians, a school of only 161 students, defeated Muncie Central, with an enrollment of over 2,000 students, for the one-class Indiana boys' state basketball championship. Milan's victory was a classic David and Goliath story in which the underdog, through hard work, virtue, and cunning, defeats the seemingly invincible adversary.... This storyline resonated well with audiences during the 1980s as President Ronald Reagan attempted to return America to a mythical patriarchal 1950s in which divisions of race, gender, and class did not exist for a homogeneous middle-class nation.[29]

Bill Bradley was not the only White player in New York to capture the media's fascination. The Knicks signed Jerry Lucas in 1971. Lucas, who was as famous for his IQ as for his playing, graduated Phi Beta Kappa from Ohio State University. The press wrote stories about his ability to memorize the entire New York City phone book. When he and Bradley frequently communicated with each other in pig Latin, it was depicted as a sign of their remarkable intelligence. Phil Jackson, the future Hall of Fame coach for the Bulls and Lakers, was a reserve on those Knicks teams. Jackson has long been praised for his impressive IQ. Other White stars dominating the NBA in the 1970ss included Bill Walton, Rick Barry, and "Pistol" Pete Maravich.[30] Walton was aware of and uncomfortable with the media's adoration. "Since his college days, he [Walton] refused to accept the role as the 'great white hope' in a Black-dominated sport.... He regularly highlighted the workings of White male privilege in press interviews," wrote Dave Zirin in *The Nation*.[31]

Soul on Ice

What if I told you the person responsible for the NBA's current image as America's *Blackest* professional sports league was George Mikan? Yes, that George Mikan! Whoever thought a white 6'10" center of Croatian and Lithuanian descent would be associated with crossover dribbles and hip-hop? On the court, Mikan was famous for wearing thick round glasses that made him resemble an extremely tall version of Harry Potter.[32] His tight short shorts did little to compliment his long, 245-pound frame. Mikan was the league's first great big man, paving the way for Russell, Chamberlain, Jabbar, and even Shaq. He won seven NBL, BAA, and NBA championships in nine seasons. His dominance forced the NBA to widen the free throw line and invent the shot clock and goaltending rule.[33] Mikan's professional career began with the Chicago American Gears of the National Basketball League (NBL) in 1946.[34] The NBL was the predecessor to the NBA. A year later, Mikan joined the Minneapolis Lakers, which started in the NBL but left for a rival league called the Basketball Association of America (BAA). The NBL and the BAA merged in 1949, forming the NBA.

Mikan hung up his short shorts in 1956. But retirement did not signify that he was permanently leaving the basketball game. Quite the contrary, in 1967 he became a founder and the inaugural commissioner of the American Basketball Association (ABA), the first rival to the NBA. The ABA marketed itself as a rowdy counter to the mainstream, more conservative NBA. Professor Todd Boyd, the author of *Young, Black, Rich, and Famous* (2008), says the ABA was comfortable embracing urban Black America and street culture. The ABA's Black players were free to play a less structured game more akin to the improvisational style of play popular on the playground. Unlike the NBA, which was based on dumping the ball inside the post to a center like Mikan, their style of play emphasized athletic fast breaks, which required players to sprint up and down the court. The ABA promoted individual stars over teams. Their players had catchy nicknames like The Iceman and The Doctor. In the 2000s, the AND1 Mixtape Tour brought "street ball" from New York City, Atlanta, Chicago, and Washington, D.C., playgrounds to the mainstream. Forty years before anyone heard of an AND1 mixtape, there was the ABA.

The upstart league was fearless in trying new things to distinguish itself from the NBA. It replaced the standard orange basketball with a red, white, and blue ball. ABA innovations were three-point shots, the 30-second shot clock, and the slam dunk contest. Fans wrestled bears at halftime. Yes, full-grown bears. There were halter-top-themed nights and bikini-clad cheerleaders. ABA games were not as ridiculous as depicted in Will Farrell's 2008 comedy *Semi-Pro*, but they were close enough. In 1969, Lew Alcindor (Kareem Abdul-Jabbar) was the most hyped collegiate player preparing to turn professional. Mikan offered to pay him $1 million, more than the Milwaukee Bucks, the team with the number-one pick in the NBA draft. But Mikan forgot to bring the check with him when he met Alcindor. The UCLA All-American signed with the Bucks, becoming the NBA's second-all-time-leading scorer and a five-time champion with the Bucks and Lakers.[35]

The ABA shut down after only nine years. Due to chronic financial woes and administrative mismanagement, the league needed all the gimmicks to maintain attendance. It had seven different commissioners. On the league's opening night, no red, white, or blue balls were available for a game in Pittsburgh. Someone had the brilliant idea to paint a ball. Unfortunately, there was not enough time for the paint to dry before play began, making for a messy night. In 1976, the NBA absorbed six ABA teams: the Denver Nuggets, Indiana Pacers, New York Nets, Kentucky Colonels, Spirits of Saint Louis, and the San Antonio Spurs. The Colonels and Spirits dissolved soon after the NBA-ABA merger. The merger had a significant impact on the NBA. The league adopted the dunk contest, three-point shot, and the Spencer Haywood Hardship Rule, which said players from families facing financial hardship could declare for the draft a year after their high school graduation. ABA players brought a swag(ger) and refreshing performance of Blackness that had been muted to appease White fans in earlier years. Julius "Dr. J" Erving, who had starred on the Virginia Squires and New York Nets between 1971 and 1976, made his long-awaited NBA introduction thanks to the merger. He became the league's ambassador until the mid–1980s. Before the merger, players were paid so little that they needed second jobs in the offseason. Cousy worked as a driving instructor. His teammate Tom Heinsohn waited tables.[36] Salaries increased drastically. But not all the changes were so good.

Four years after the merger, the country entered a new decade. The 1980s were characterized by a conservative revolution, increased emphasis on individualism, a growing wealth gap, backlash to the liberal politics and civil rights gains of the previous two decades, and a "Greed is good" mentality. Powder cocaine became the party drug of choice for the wealthy and upper-class whites in the '70s. New York's Studio 54 disco was infamous for its quaalude and coke-inspired parties filled with dancing, high fashion, casual sex, and celebrities. According to Todd Boyd, by the early 1980s, cocaine was something people aspired to use because it was a status symbol for those who had money.

Professional athletes were receiving the highest salaries in history at that point. The surplus money allowed athletes access to a luxurious lifestyle and forbidden pleasures they could only dream of before. Several NBA players, such as the Atlanta Hawks' Terry Furlow, were becoming cocaine casualties. On May 23, 1980, the night of the NBA Finals, Furlow was driving his blue Mercedes high on coke and weed when he veered off to the right of a tractor-trailer and crashed into a utility pole. The grille of his Benz flew 500 feet down the highway. It took multiple police officers to pry his body out of the car. The autopsy showed that he had never hit the brakes before the crash. Magic Johnson was a pallbearer at his funeral. One of Johnson's teammates, Spencer Haywood, also struggled with cocaine addiction. After Haywood fell asleep during a team workout in the middle of the 1980 finals, he was suspended for the remainder of the series.[37] Richard Dumas, Roy Tarpley, and "Fast" Eddie Johnson received lifetime bans due to drug abuse.

Charles Barkley says the public thought the NBA was nothing but arrogant, rich Black guys getting high all the time when he entered the league in 1984. In the debut episode of *The Last Dance*, Jordan laughed as he described an experience in his rookie season when he walked into a hotel room to find nearly all his teammates snorting cocaine and smoking marijuana with random female companions. On June 19, 1986, Len Bias began having a seizure in his University of Maryland dormitory room. The Celtics had selected Bias with the second overall pick in the draft two days earlier. He died at the hospital from a cardiac arrhythmia caused by a cocaine overdose.[38]

The timing of Bias's death could not have been worse. President Reagan's War on Drugs made young Black men the face of a growing crack cocaine epidemic in urban cities that was contributing to illegal gun violence, death, and the need for mass incarceration. Think FX's 1980s drug-fueled drama *Snowfall*. Bias's death was a severe black eye for the NBA. After the merger, the league's increasingly Black workforce did not sit well with white fans who grew up idolizing Bradley, Cousy, Walton, and West. Fighting was becoming more commonplace in games. While this was a staple of the majority-white NHL, it caused NBA players to be labeled thugs. "I don't enjoy going to the game and seeing all Black guys," one spectator told a reporter during a game.[39]

Professor Theresa Runstedtler, author of *Black Ball: Kareem Abdul-Jabbar, Spencer Haywood and the Generation that Saved the Soul of the NBA* (2023), says mainstream media damaged the reputation of the league by exaggerating the amount of drug use among the players and creating a false narrative that they were all anti-establishment hoodlums. Between 1979 and 1981, seven NBA Finals games were tape-delayed and broadcast at 11:30 p.m. Sixteen of 23 teams were losing money in the early '80s. Rather than fully embracing this new brand of basketball, Runstedler says the NBA was concerned with losing its White fanbase.[40] The league needed a savior; it would come as another Great White Hope.

"Who's Coming in Second?"

On March 26, 1979, Michigan State University squared off against Indiana State University in Salt Lake City for the NCAA national championship. Michigan State won 75–64. Twenty-five years later, this still stands as the most-watched college basketball championship game in history, with an estimated 40 million viewers, a 20 percent increase from the previous year. For a point of comparison, the 2022 national championship game between the University of Kansas and the University of North Carolina at Chapel Hill attracted 10.7 million viewers. The 1979 championship was no better than the countless title games that preceded or followed it. Quite simply, this game was *Rocky* on the basketball court. In the 1976 sports film *Rocky*, Sylvester Stallone played an unheralded Italian American fighter named Rocky Balboa from a working-class white neighborhood in Philadelphia. Rocky received the shot of a lifetime when he earned a fight against the heavyweight champion of the world, Apollo Creed, on Independence Day. Creed was a loudmouth, cocky Black fighter. After months of training and personal growth, the humble Rocky went the distance but lost the fight. However, he won an exhilarating rematch in *Rocky II* (1979). Rocky was slow and unathletic, but his grit, tireless work ethic, and dogged determination propelled him to defeat the naturally athletic Apollo. Rocky was the people's true champ!

Rocky received an Academy Award nomination for Best Picture. Its success spawned five sequels between 1979 and 2006, a musical, and the current spin-off film series, *Creed*, starring Michael B. Jordan as Rocky's mentee and Apollo's son, Adonis Creed. Although *Rocky* is one of my favorite film series, I feel a tingling in my stomach each time I watch Rocky knock out Apollo. Although Apollo becomes a "good guy" in the third film, the depiction of Rocky's new Black antagonist, Clubber Lang (Laurence "Mr. T" Tureaud), is despicable. Stallone's character is Hollywood's Great White Hope.[41] This was no secret. The shady Black promoter, George Washington Duke, refers to Rocky as "the white hope" in *Rocky V* (1990). A similar storyline played out at the 1979 NCAA championship. Michigan State was led by its 6'9" sophomore point guard Earvin "Magic" Johnson, a flashy, charismatic Black player from Lansing, Michigan. Indiana State was led by their sullen, not-so-athletic white star Larry Bird. While much of Black America rooted for Michigan State that night, the rest of the nation supposedly backed Indiana State. The national championship was a prelude to what would come as these two young leading men resurrected the NBA and dominated headlines throughout the '80s. Without Johnson and Bird, there would not have been a Dream Team or globalization in the NBA.

The NBA's White savior did not grow up with a silver spoon. His upbringing mirrored that of many of the Black players he competed against. Larry Bird was raised in a three-room house near a railroad track. His family lived on $50 a week in French Lick, one of the poorest places in Indiana. He was the fourth of Joe and Georgia Bird's six children. The family was so poor that Bird did not realize that other families owned a car. He accepted a scholarship to play basketball for coach Bobby Knight at Indiana University in Bloomington. The 30,000-student population at IU may have been too overwhelming for the bashful and insecure freshman who saw himself as "poor white trash." Bird dropped out of school after 24 days on campus and returned home to take a job hauling trash for the city. Bird claims he dropped out due to financial hardship, not because he was homesick. On February 3, 1975, his father, who struggled with alcoholism and depression, committed suicide.

Bill Hodges, a young coach at Indiana State, convinced Bird to give college one more shot.[42] Bird found a home at his new school, averaging 30 points and 13 rebounds for his collegiate career. Although the Celtics drafted him with the sixth overall pick in the 1978 draft, Bird decided to return to school for his senior year. Bird unanimously won the Rookie of the Year award for his first year in the NBA. When the league signed a new television deal with CBS before the 1982–83 season, the executives decided the best way to boost ratings and move the finals out of tape delay was to sell the public large doses of Bird and Magic. CBS would air regular weekend double headers with the Celtics game preceded by a Lakers game.

The Celtics and Lakers met for the first of three finals series in 1984. The Celtics won in seven games, and the Lakers clinched the next two championships in the trilogy. The Celtics-Lakers rivalry, which has inspired multiple documentaries and the HBO series *Winning Time*, highlighted old racial tropes. The media labeled the Lakers "Showtime" due to their athleticism and flamboyant style of play, which was tailor-made for Hollywood and Gucci Row.[43] The Celtics played a fundamental style of basketball that represented the working-class man. Many Blacks, even working-class Black Bostonians, cheered for the Lakers when the teams played. Several White fans across the country worshipped Bird and the Celtics. These preferences did not mean that Blacks did not like Bird and whites did not like Johnson, but the racial bias was evident. Bird emerged as an increasingly polarizing figure during the conservative Reagan era, symbolizing the rolling back of the civil rights gains of the past two decades. Some Black teenagers did not wear black gym shoes because they did not want to be associated with the sneakers worn by Bird. There was the famous scene in Spike Lee's 1989 film *Do the Right Thing* when a White bicyclist wearing a Bird jersey accidentally scuffs the brand-new "$108 bucks with tax" white cement 4 Air Jordan sneakers worn by Buggin Out, a young Black man in Brooklyn. "GO BACK TO BOSTON!" Buggin Out yells.

"Not to be a racist, but we got a White guy who's the best in the world. It's a predominantly Black sport now, and we got a guy like Larry Bird who can't run, can't jump, but can do everything out there," a young White Celtics fan told a reporter.[44] According to Arsenio Hall, the host of a popular late-night talk show in the 1990s and Magic Johnson's close friend, the media exaggerated Bird's exploits and went out of their way to make him a hero. Hall joked that Bird could be injured, sitting on the bench in a suit with a cast on his arm, and the announcers calling the game would say the following when one of his Black teammates scored. "Larry Bird made that possible. He told him a few weeks ago he could do it, and he did." Hall's response, "They gonna give this muthafucka the assist, and he's not even in the game!"[45]

Larry Bird won three championships and three league MVPs, was a 12-time All-Star and nine-time All-NBA First Team. The more he won, the harder it was for him to escape the Great White Hope hype. In 1987, after the Celtics beat the Detroit Pistons to advance to the finals for the fourth straight year, Detroit forward Dennis Rodman referred to Bird as overrated because he was White. Pistons captain Isiah Thomas added, "I think Larry is a very good basketball player. He's an exceptional talent.

But I have to agree with Rodman. If he was Black, he'd be just another good guy [laughter]."[46] Thomas's comments created a media firestorm. A press conference was held with Bird and Thomas sitting front and center. Despite Thomas's efforts to explain himself, the media villainized him and depicted this as a case of reverse racism. To Bird's credit, he never bought into the hype and did not deny his White privilege. He always credited the older Black guys he played with as a boy with teaching him the game. He even defended Thomas and still does now.

In many ways, Bird was the NBA's version of B-Rabbit (Jimmy), the fictional character played by hip-hop icon Eminem in his 2002 semi-autobiographical film *8 Mile*. Rabbit was trying to earn respect in Detroit's underground battle rap scene, which Black men dominated. Even though Rabbit was better than the Black lyricists, he was often underestimated because of his lack of melanin. Competitors nicknamed him Elvis.[47] Bird's teammate Cedric "Cornbread" Maxwell tells a story about his first practice against Bird. Cornbread assumed that Bird was a "scrub" because he was white. After Bird continued to knock down shot after shot, Cornbread quickly changed his opinion. Bird never backed down from any of his Black opponents. There was the famous fight between him and Dr. J during the Celtics-76ers game on November 9, 1984. Bird was quiet, but he could talk trash with anyone. Before winning the three-point contest at the 1988 All-Star weekend, Bird walked into the locker room and asked his competitors, "Which of you motherfuckers is coming in second?"[48]

The bitter rivalry between Bird and Magic Johnson eventually grew into a beautiful lifelong friendship. They were the co-captains of the Dream Team. As discussed in Chapter 1, the 1992 U.S. men's Olympic basketball team ushered in the era of NBA globalization. A nagging back injury reduced Bird to a ceremonial role in the Olympics. He had to retire nine days after the summer games concluded. He was only 36 years old. Larry Bird was the NBA's last exceptional American-born white superstar. White collegiate players, most notably Duke University's Christian Laettner, the youngest Dream Team member, failed to carry the torch when it was passed on to them.[49]

As the NBA entered the millennium, it was Blacker than ever. The NBA's image of Blackness in the 2000s was reminiscent of the late 1970s–early 1980s. But it differed because the players were much younger, and many were products of a hip-hop culture glorifying hypermasculinity, "the hood," smoking marijuana, misogyny, and extravagant spending. The infamous 2004 brawl between the players of the Detroit Pistons and Indiana Pacers and the fans in the stands at The Palace of Auburn Hills, dubbed "The Malice at the Palace," precipitated historic punishments and a mandatory dress code to counter accusations that the NBA was a professional league for hip-hop wannabe thugs and some actual felons. "There are too many players in this league whose actions speak of a thug-like mentality," said the esteemed sportscaster Bob Costas.[50]

In a 2004 interview, Jim Gray asked Larry Bird if the NBA needed more White superstars to be successful.

> Well, I think so. You know, when I played, you had me and Kevin (McHale) and some others (white standouts) throughout the league. I think it's good for a fan base because, as we all know, the majority of the fans are white Americans. And if you just had a couple of white guys in there, you might get them a little excited.[51]

Bird's interview with Gray came at a transformative time in NBA history. Two years later, the Miami Heat beat the Dallas Mavericks in the finals. The Mavericks' star player was Dirk Nowitzki, a white 7'0" power forward from Germany who eventually became the greatest European-born player to grace the NBA until Denver's Joker. Nowitzki's presence in the 2006 finals was a microcosm of the European revolution underway in the NBA. This revolution was birthed in the early 1990s, nurtured in the 2000s, and fully matured in the 2010s and 2020s.

The Mozart of Basketball

The 2022 film *Hustle* tells the fictional story of Stanley Sugerman, an international scout for the 76ers, played by comedian Adam Sandler. Sugerman has grown tired of being away from his wife and daughter as he travels from country to country in search of the team's next diamond in the rough. During one of his trips to Spain, Sugerman accidentally stumbles upon a 22-year-old kid dressed in construction boots named Bo Cruz, hustling the best players for their money on an outdoor court. Enamored by Cruz's play, Sugerman, like Captain Ahab, believes he has finally found the mythical whale he has been searching for.[52] He brings him back to America, but the Sixers' new owner is unimpressed. With Sugerman's mentorship, familial support, and social media marketing, Cruz proves the Sixers wrong and becomes the most intriguing lottery pick in that summer's draft.

Hustle, produced by LeBron James, stars Juancho Hernangómez as Bo Cruz. Hernangómez is an NBA player from Spain who was drafted by the Nuggets in 2016. He has played for multiple teams, including the Celtics, Spurs, Jazz, and Raptors. Sandler's character represents the countless international scouts who receive little fanfare for their work. Without these scouts, media personalities like ESPN's Fraschilla, who cover foreign prospects for the NBA draft, would be at a loss for words. One such scout is Clarence Gaines, Jr., a talent evaluator for the Knicks and son of the late Hall of Fame coach Clarence "Big House" Gaines. In 2015, the Knicks sent Gaines to Madrid to scout Kristaps Porziņģis, a 19-year-old Latvian basketball player. The long and lean 7'1" Porziņģis could shoot and handle the ball like a guard. Kevin Durant nicknamed him "the unicorn" because his skills were so rare for a man his size. Porziņģis moved to Spain when he was 14 to play professionally and attend school. Gaines expressed the same enthusiasm Sugerman displayed for Cruz when he told the Knicks front office about Porziņģis. The Knicks' new team president, Phil Jackson, worried about Porziņģis' ability to withstand the rigors of the NBA due to his slim build. Nevertheless, the Knicks drafted him with the fourth overall pick.

On draft night, Knicks fans at Brooklyn's Barclays Center booed Porziņģis ferociously when David Stern called his name. They assumed he would be another Frederic Weis, the team's 1999 draft pick who never played a game and is only famous for being dunked over by Vince Carter in the Olympics. Stephen A. Smith, a longtime Knicks fan, shared his feelings about the draft pick on *SportsCenter*: "As a native New Yorker, I'm completely disgusted. We have been hoodwinked, bamboozled, led astray, run amok, and flat-out deceived by Phil Jackson and the New York Knicks."[53] All Smith's soliloquy needed was "We didn't land on Plymouth Rock, Plymouth Rock landed on us," as he blatantly borrowed from Denzel Washington's famous *Malcolm X* film speech to explain his displeasure. Porziņģis proved his haters wrong by becoming one of the top rookies that season. He grew to 7'3" and averaged 17.8 points with the Knicks before he was traded to Dallas in 2019. He joined the Celtics in 2023–24 after one year in Washington.

At the start of the 2022–23 NBA season, there were 58 European players on opening-night rosters. While some players, like Rudy Gobert and Nicolas Batum, were Black, most would be considered White according to American racial standards today. It is important to qualify this because some people might classify these men as French, not White. In the 19th and early 20th centuries, many European immigrants were not considered white when they arrived in America. Historian Noel Ignatiev explored this phenomenon in his 1995 book *How the Irish Became White*.[54]

Hank Biasatti, an Italian native raised in Canada, was the league's first White European player. He played for the Toronto Huskies in the league's inaugural season. Oscar Schmidt should have been the first White European superstar in the modern NBA. There's footage from a 2008 Olympic practice in which Kobe informs his teammates of the legendary Oscar. "Oscar was like my Larry Bird, but I actually like him," he joked. Kobe grew up in Italy admiring Schmidt, who competed against his dad, Joe "Jellybean" Bryant. Schmidt, born in Brazil 12 years after Biasatti played his first game with the Huskies, holds the world record for the longest professional basketball career. He played professionally in Brazil, Italy, and Spain between 1974 and 2003. Most Americans discovered him watching the Summer Olympics and the FIBA World Cup. His 29-points-per-game average in five Olympic appearances helped him score a record 1,093 points. He also holds the scoring record, 843 points, in the World Cup.[55]

Despite being the best non–American player in the world, Schmidt was the 144th pick in the famous 1984 NBA draft, which included Michael Jordan, Charles Barkley, Hakeem Olajuwon, and John Stockton. The New Jersey Nets selected him in the sixth round (the NBA draft lasted seven rounds until 1988). He endured so many rounds due to prevailing stereotypes about Europeans being "too soft" to survive the physicality of NBA games.[56] When Schmidt declined the Nets' contractual offer, it was not because he was soft or doubted his skills. At the time, international players had to sacrifice their amateur status to play in America, and they could no longer play for their national teams in FIBA and Olympic competitions. National pride was more important than an NBA career to Schmidt. Three years later, he led Brazil to the gold medal game of the 1987 Pan American Games. With Brazil trailing the U.S. by 14 at halftime, he scored 35 of his 46 points in the second half to give Brazil a 120–115 victory. Schmidt handed the U.S. their first loss in the Pan American Games since 1971 and their second loss in the event's history.[57] He retired from basketball at the age of 45 with 49,000 points.[58] Schmidt was inducted into the Naismith Memorial Basketball Hall of Fame in 2013.

I wonder how good Schmidt would have been if he played in the NBA during his prime. Would his name come up in debates over everyone's all-time top 10 list? The same can be said of Arvydas Sabonis, the next great European player to attract NBA scouts in the 1980s. The 7'3" Lithuanian center began playing basketball in 1977 when he was 13. Lithuania was still a part of the Soviet Union (USSR) at the time. Consequently, Sabonis's playing career began with the Soviet national junior team. When he was 19, he played for Zalgiris, a professional club in Kaunas, Lithuania, and led the Soviet national team to a bronze medal at the 1983 FIBA Eurobasket.[59] Sabonis contributed to the USSR's silver medal at the 1986 FIBA World Cup.

Cold War geopolitics prohibited Sabonis from leaving Europe; nevertheless, the Atlanta Hawks drafted him with the 77th pick in 1985. Even if the Cold War had ended, Sabonis could not play for Atlanta because he failed to meet the league's 21-year-old age limit. When Portland drafted him the following year, he opted to play for Real Madrid in Spain. By the time he joined Portland in 1995, he was a 30-year-old man with hobbled knees.[60] I still remember hearing NBA analysts say, "You should have seen him in his prime back in Europe." Sabonis was Portland's starting center when they faced Kobe and Shaq's Lakers in the 2000 Western Conference finals. Sabonis was no match for the younger, more athletic, and overpowering Shaquille O'Neal. The Lakers eliminated Portland in seven games, on their way to winning the first of three consecutive NBA championships.

Sabonis retired in 2005 after seven seasons in Portland and two more with Zalgiris. His legacy continues to shape today's NBA. The Orlando Magic drafted his youngest son, Domantas, with the 11th pick in 2016. Domantas was born while his dad was playing in Portland. Although he played for two European professional teams between the ages of 16 and 18, he never signed a professional contract, allowing him to maintain NCAA eligibility. He attended Gonzaga University in Spokane, Washington, for two years before turning professional. The Magic traded him to the Oklahoma City Thunder on draft night. He was on the move again after the Thunder traded him to Indiana in his sophomore season. Domantas made a name for himself in Indiana, being selected to two All-Star teams. He made his third All-Star appearance and was placed on the All-NBA Third Team as a new member of the Sacramento Kings in 2022–23. His impact in Sacramento was felt immediately. The Kings finished that season in third place in the Western Conference, reaching the playoffs for the first time in 16 years.

When the elder Sabonis played for Portland in the '90s, he was among a small group of prominent European players, including Vlade Divac, Toni Kukoč, and Dino Radja. Each player was inducted into the Naismith Hall of Fame because of his exploits in the NBA and overseas. Radja spent four years with the Celtics. The Lakers famously traded Divac to the Hornets in 1996 to draft Kobe. Kukoč was a significant contributor to the Bulls' second three-peat between 1996 and 1998. He will always be remembered for hitting the game winning shot against the Knicks in the 1994 Eastern Conference semifinals after his teammate Scottie Pippen refused to come off the bench in protest. Dražen Petrović, the best European player of the decade, had the shortest career. Petrović, born in Sibenik, Yugoslavia (now Croatia), in 1964, was a basketball prodigy from a young age. His parents envisioned a musical career for him. He was supposed to be the (Wolfgang Amadeus) Mozart of music, not basketball. His parents, Jole and Biserka, placed him and his brother, Aleksander, in music lessons when they were children. He played guitar while Aleksander was on the clarinet. Aleksander routinely skipped his lessons to shoot hoops at a nearby playground. The younger Dražen went to practice but began loosening the strings on his guitar as a diversion. The 30 minutes his teacher wasted restringing his instrument gave him enough time to sneak off to join Aleksander on the playground.[61]

Basketball's hold on the brothers was too strong for their music teacher to compete with. Aleksander played on an under-17 Yugoslavian cadet national team that participated in the 1975 European championships in Greece. Dražen Petrović eventually surpassed his big brother on the court. He began playing for Sibenka, the local professional club, when he was 15, averaging 13.2 points per game. In 1984, the 19-year-old basketball phenom took a break to fulfill a mandatory year of service in the Yugoslav army. Upon returning to the court, he became one of Europe's top scorers as a member of the Cibona club. Petrović's stats sound like something out of an EA Sports video game. He averaged 48 points over four games in the 1986 European Cup. But that paled compared with the 67 points he scored in the first half against Smelt Olimpija from Slovenia. He finished that game with a modest 112 points.[62]

The Yugoslavian national team toured the U.S. in the fall of 1986, playing eight games against American colleges. Petrović scored 35 points against the University of North Carolina, the top-ranked team in the national preseason polls. He exceeded 30 points in another four games. Nevertheless, American scouts were skeptical of his ability to score that much against NBA defenses. When 5'3" Wake Forest University point guard Tyrone "Mugsy" Bogues held him to 12 points in the 1986 World Championships, their doubts appeared justified. Petrović would get another shot at NBA competition in 1988 as a member of Real Madrid. When the Celtics visited Spain for the second annual McDonald's Open, they played Real Madrid in the championship game. Bird posted 29 points and 12 assists. Petrović scored 22 points but took 28 shots to achieve that much. He also struggled against the defensive pressure that Boston rookie point guard Brian Shaw applied.[63]

Two years before he faced the Celtics, Portland selected Petrović with the 60th overall pick in the 1986 draft, but he was legally prohibited from joining the Trailblazers for three years. David Stern and Eduardo Portela, the CEO of the ACB Spanish League, had signed an agreement that prevented either league from negotiating with a player already under contract. Petrović was still signed to Real Madrid when the Trailblazers drafted him. Portland's team governor, Paul Allen, and his lawyer, Allen Israel, engaged in attempts to overturn this ruling. Petrović filed a lawsuit against Real Madrid, the ACB, and the NBA in July 1989. One month later, the three parties renegotiated a deal to buy out his contract with Real Madrid, allowing him finally to join the Trailblazers.[64] Portland reached the NBA Finals, losing to the Pistons in five games, his first season with the team. Petrović did not play much in the finals and had difficulty earning minutes on the court the next season after the team acquired the feisty shooting guard Danny Ainge. He was traded to the New Jersey Nets halfway through the season.[65]

Petrović entered his prime in New Jersey, becoming one of the league's best shooting guards. He played alongside big man Derrick Coleman and point guard Kenny Anderson, who said jokingly that opposing guards struggled to defend his European teammate because he never wore deodorant. The Nets achieved their first playoff berth in six years during the 1991–1992 season. At the end of the season, Petrović flew to Barcelona for the 1992 Summer Olympics. While the NBA Dream Team stole the show at the Olympics, Adam McKay, host of the *Death at the Wing* (2021) podcast, says there was another dream team featuring Petrović that the world never saw play. The collapse of the Soviet Union left Petrović's homeland, Yugoslavia, in a state of flux. Slovenia and Croatia declared their independence from Yugoslavia on June 25, 1991. This action was declared unconstitutional by the Constitutional Court of Yugoslavia. That same year a civil war erupted between Croatia and Serbia.[66] Nearly four million people were displaced and became refugees in a country of 20–22 million. Before the war, the Yugoslavian national team consisted of players from the various republics that made up Yugoslavia. Petrović played alongside fellow countrymen and NBA stars Divac, Radja, and Kukoč. The war broke the team up and shattered longtime friendships. Petrović and Divac stopped speaking to one another. Divac was Serbian, and Petrovic was Croatian. Petrović, Radja, and Kukoč led the Croatian team to the 1992 Olympic gold medal game, losing to the Dream Team 117–85.[67]

Petrović averaged an NBA career-high 22.3 points per game during the 1992–93 season. Despite his impressive play, he failed to receive a roster spot on the Eastern Conference All-Star team. Neither the fans nor NBA coaches thought he was good enough to be on the team. Harvey Araton, a journalist for the *New York Times*, wrote in 1993 that his omission resulted from prejudice.

> Is there an us-versus-them mentality that borders on xenophobia in the NBA? When he was omitted by Eastern conference coaches, Petrovic dismissed the notion of a bias against his European heritage. He pointed out that Indiana's Detlef Schrempf, a German, had made the team for the first time.... Perhaps Petrovic, in time, came to reason Schrempf's acceptance as a result of him being a product of the American collegiate system.[68]

At the season's conclusion, Petrović was poised to negotiate a new contract with the Nets to make him the NBA's second-highest-paid shooting guard behind Jordan. He returned to Europe for his summer vacation.

With his girlfriend, Klara Szalantzy, behind the wheel and a friend, Hilal Haene, in the back seat, they set off on the Autobahn, Germany's federal highway, on their way to Croatia. The road was slick from rain. At 5:20 p.m. on June 7, Szalantzy lost control of the car when a semiautomatic truck cut her off. She and Haene were hospitalized with injuries. Petrović, 28, died in the crash.

The Great Nowitzki

"Drazen was an extraordinary young man, and a true pioneer in the global sport of basketball," said David Stern.[69] In the immediate years after Petrović's tragic death, countless Europeans joined NBA rosters. Perhaps there was none more special than a kid from Germany with long, floppy blond hair. When the Dallas Mavericks drafted a 7'0" power forward from Germany named Dirk Nowitzki in 1998, some may have wondered if he was a tall backup dancer for a boy band due to his *cool* haircut and gold hoop earring. Years later, on the day that it was announced he would be a part of the 2023 Hall of Fame class alongside fellow foreigners Pau Gasol (from Spain) and Tony Parker (from France), he blamed that hairstyle on the popularity of the Backstreet Boys in the late 1990s.[70] Billionaire entrepreneur Mark Cuban is best known to the masses for his role on the popular television *Shark Tank*. NBA fans and Dallas residents know him as the former governor of the Mavericks. In the 1990s, Cuban was a brash, young team governor looking to transform the Mavericks into a perennial title contender. He saw Nowitzki as the missing piece to his puzzle. By pairing him with Steve Nash, his Canadian point guard newly acquired from the Phoenix Suns, the Mavericks were expected to have a generational one-two punch for the next decade.[71]

Dirk Nowitzki was born to a middle-class family in Wurzburg, Germany, on June 19, 1978. His parents, Jorg-Werner and Helga, ran a painting business passed down from his paternal grandfather. Nowitzki was genetically predisposed to succeed in athletics. Jorg-Werner formerly played handball, and Helga formerly played basketball. Both were also decent tennis players. When Nowitzki was a young boy, Germany dominated professional tennis. Little German boys and girls grew up desiring to be the next Boris Becker and Steffi Graf, the country's premier tennis players. Tennis was a social status symbol for German families. Consequently, he grew up playing the sport along with handball.

Basketball did not become an integral part of Nowitzki's life until he was 13. In 1993, he met the man who would alter the trajectory of his life. Holger Geschwindner ran a pecan farm and played basketball professionally in Australia, Bamberg, Gottingen, and Cologne. Geschwindner learned the game when he was 17 from an unlikely source, a Black man from Indiana. Ernie Butler moved to Germany in the 1960s to teach physical education, art, and history at a junior high school on an army base. Butler, the first Black player on Germany's MTV Giessen basketball club, imparted his love for basketball and music to his new mentee. "Basketball is free—like jazz. You can't plan a solo; you have to play it," he often said. Butler took Geschwindner to jazz bars to absorb the music. At the time, Geschwindner, much too young to hang out at these bars, did not know he would one day pass down similar lessons to Germany's first NBA Hall-of-Famer.[72]

Geschwindner wanted Nowitzki to think of basketball as a dance. He imparted Butler's wisdom to him, teaching him to play basketball freely as if he were playing jazz.[73] Butler would sometimes play his saxophone during their workouts. Nowitzki learned to dribble the ball to the rhythm of Butler's melody. Geschwindner gifted Nowitzki a saxophone for Christmas in 2001. Music became such an important part of Nowitzki's game that he would sing David Hasselhoff's "Looking for Freedom" under his breath when he took foul shots during the 2006 NBA Finals. Hasselhoff, best known in America for his television roles in *Knight Rider* and *Baywatch*, was a chart-topping singer in Germany. "He just real goofy. Singing songs. Trying to sing the rap songs. I used to call him the Black German," said Nowitzki's former teammate Nick Van Exel in an oral history for *CBS Sports*.[74] Ironically, House of Pain's "Jump Around" was blaring from the speakers in a local basketball gym when Geschwindner met Nowitzki. Once he proved to the scrawny 6'8", 16-year-old teenager that he was more than just some "old dude," he met his parents. Geschwindner offered to train their son twice a week for as long as they wanted the partnership to continue.

According to Thomas Pletzinger, author of *The Great Nowitzki: Basketball and the Meaning of Life*, their training sessions became a master class on life and the genesis of a lifelong friendship. Besides talking music, the pair read and discussed novels. Pletzinger used mathematics and physics to help Nowitzki develop that one-legged fadeaway jump shot that would make him an NBA champion and league MVP. Their biweekly workouts became daily meetings during the summer of 1994. Pletzinger accompanied Nowitzki when he made his first trip to America in March of 1998 to play against a select team of American collegiate stars.[75]

The Mavericks had the sixth pick in the 1998 NBA draft; however, they traded it to Milwaukee, drafting ninth. The Bucks picked Robert "Tractor" Traylor from the University of Michigan. Traylor had a short stint in the NBA and passed away when he was 34. The Mavericks drafted

Nowitzki, who became the most adored player in franchise history. After Dallas traded Steve Nash to Phoenix in 2004, Nowitzki was left to anchor the load on his own. He proved more than capable of accepting this new challenge, carrying the Mavericks to the 2006 NBA Finals, where they lost to the Miami Heat in six games. Nowitzki, who was labeled "soft" for his play in the finals, received the league MVP award the next season. Besides winning the MVP, he helped the Mavericks earn the top seed in the Western Conference playoffs with a 67–15 regular season record. However, a first-round loss to the eighth-seeded Golden State Warriors intensified the doubts about a European star ever carrying a team to a championship.

In 2011, Dallas faced the Heat for a second time in the NBA Finals. The Heatles, as they were nicknamed, could be described as a traveling All-Star team consisting of future Hall-of-Famers LeBron James, Dwyane Wade, and Chris Bosh. "Not one, not two, not three [championships]," James arrogantly promised Miami fans at a "pre-championship" celebration when the team was formed the previous summer. The Mavericks were supposed to be the sacrificial lambs standing in the way of the Heat's predestined coronation. Unfortunately for "Heat culture" fans, someone forgot to relay that message to Dallas.[76] The Mavericks stunned the immature Heat, winning the series in six games. Nowitzki outplayed Miami's Big Three, leaving no doubt about who was the best player on the court. He averaged 26 points and nine rebounds on his way to being named finals MVP. Nowitzki and his teammates celebrated their championship with rapper Lil Wayne at a $200,000 party held at Miami's famed LIV nightclub.

Nowitzki played his 21st and final season in 2018–19. The Mavericks played two preseason games in China. The country's 300 million NBA fans rolled out the red carpet for the Great Nowitzki. Chants of "MVP" and "China Loves You" welcomed him as he stepped on the court. When Nowitzki was not playing, he led workshops with children in Shanghai and spoke with the local media affiliates. The adoration he received in China was phenomenal, but it did not match his celebrity back home in Germany. German historian Wolf Lepenies said Nowitzki, like other athletes Max Schmeling, Steffi Graf, and Fritz Walter, shaped how the world viewed the country.[77]

Nowitzki shifted the paradigm for perceptions of European players. "It wasn't so much that Nowitzki changed when he got to the league. He remained himself and forced the league to adapt to him," wrote Luke O'Neil in *Deadspin*.[78] Was he the NBA's latest version of a Great White Hope? No. Perhaps his Black Kenyan girlfriend and future wife, Jessica Olson, made him an unlikely candidate. They have three biracial children. Hans Ulrich Gumbrecht, a German American literary scholar at Stanford University, argued that Nowitzki was less popular in America than globally because he was White. According to Gumbrecht, films like *White Men Can't Jump* (1992 and 2023), about athletic stereotypes of white and Black players, caused individuals who resembled Nowitzki to be perceived as less talented and not as cool as their Black rivals.[79] I disagree with that assessment because those stereotypes existed decades before *White Man Can't Jump* was released and did not prevent Bill Bradley or Larry Bird from being adored. Nowitzki's biggest impediment was being born and raised in Germany. He also had to compete for likability with transcendent American stars like Kobe Bryant, Vince Carter, Allen Iverson, LeBron James, and Shaquille O'Neal.

Dallas traded their 2018 draft pick, Trae Young, for a 19-year-old point guard from Slovenia named Luka Dončić in the summer before Nowitzki's final season. In the years since Nowitzki's retirement, Dončić, or simply Luka, has become the heir apparent in Dallas and the NBA's most marketable White player. Luka's game is reminiscent of Larry Bird and LeBron James. He is not exceptionally quick or athletic, but he has an uncanny ability to score and pass the basketball. A great example would be his performance against the New York Knicks on December 27, 2022. Luka's historic 60 points, 21 rebounds, and 10 assists carried the Mavericks to a 126–121 overtime victory.[80] "The way he plays reminds me of the way I play the game. We're triple threats. We rebound, we pass, which is the number one thing on our mind … and we'll put 40 on you too if you disrespect us," said LeBron.[81] Luka made history on the fourth anniversary of Kobe's death by scoring 73 points (41 points in the first half) against the Hawks in Atlanta. Luka's 73-point spectacular was the most points in a game since Kobe's 81 in 2006, tied for the fourth most points in the NBA's history.[82]

Luka was already a five-time All-Star and four-time All-NBA first-team selection by age 25. His Mavericks lost to Boston in the 2024 NBA finals. Thus far, he has had only a few publicized controversies involving race. Montrezl Harrell, a Black player on the Los Angeles Clippers, called him a "bitch ass White boy" during a game in 2020. Unlike the infamous Larry Bird-Isiah Thomas incident in the '80s, this story made headlines for a few days but quickly faded after Luka accepted Harrell's apology.[83] Jamal Crawford, a retired Black player who now works for TNT and NBA TV, questioned why Luka has been praised for the same things for which mercurial guard James Harden is often denounced. Crawford did not bring up race, but Harden is a Black American.[84]

You Are the Real MVP!

By the final weekend of the 2022–23 regular season, the MVP race had come down to three players: Joel Embiid, Giannis Antetokounmpo, and Nikola Jokić. The race had grown quite contentious over the last two months. Antetokounmpo was having his best season since winning back-to-back MVPs in 2019 and 2020. His team, the Bucks, had the league's best record heading into the playoffs. Embiid, leading the NBA in scoring with 33.1 points per game, outplayed Jokić when they squared off on January 28. In a nationally televised game, Embiid impressed with 38 points, 18 rebounds, and five assists. Jokić posted an impressive 24 points, eight rebounds, and nine assists in a losing effort. By mid–February's All-Star break, multiple media members and outlets were ready to hand the award to Jokić for a third straight year. Only Bill Russell, Wilt Chamberlain, and Larry Bird have won three consecutive MVPs. Bird was the last to do it, in the 1980s.

Is Jokić the best basketball player in the NBA? Is he the best basketball player in the world? Most peers not on the Nuggets' roster did not think so at the time, and this was obvious during the All-Star weekend. Antetokounmpo and LeBron, All-Star team captains for the Eastern and Western conferences, respectively, drafted players for each team in front of a live televised audience an hour before the All-Star Game. Jokić was the second-to-last player chosen. He may have gone last had he not walked over to LeBron before he could announce his final pick. Some suggested that Jokić was selected so late because his fundamental style of play did not fit the up-tempo, athletic pace of the game. Most younger fans watch the All-Star Game to see the high-flying slam dunks and fancy plays. But his late selection could have also been a subliminal message to him and those eager to coronate him prematurely.

Although the Nuggets had the best record in the Western Conference the entire 2022–23 season, few NBA analysts and talk show hosts picked them to reach the finals. Many experts had them losing to the Lakers, who were awful and mired in chaos most of the season, if they met in the first round of the playoffs. Others picked the Golden State Warriors or the Phoenix Suns to eliminate them in the Western Conference playoffs. You seldom heard anyone doubt the ability of Jordan, Kobe, or LeBron to put a team on their back and carry them to victory in the playoffs. During the April 7 episode of NBA Radio's daily *Give and Go* series, host Rick Kamla, who is White, insinuated that Jokić should receive a pass if he could not carry Denver far in the playoffs. He was still an MVP-caliber player without the championship rings. His co-host, Antonio Daniels, a retired Black American NBA player, laughed and said it was ridiculous for Jokić to receive a pass not extended to Embiid, who also lacked playoff success.

In March, Gilbert Arenas, a retired NBA star turned controversial celebrity podcaster, appeared on the *Draymond Green Show*, a podcast hosted by polarizing Golden State forward Draymond Green. Arenas and Green, both Black Americans, called out what they saw as a double standard in the mainstream media regarding the European NBA players. Arenas said the following:

> So, when you have Luka, when you have Jokić, at the end of the day, it's like, "Yeah, they're good European players coming over, they're dominating, but do we hold them to the same standard, so it's like they get a free easy pass right?" They get a free, easy pass versus someone.... It might be the color of the skin a little bit.[85]

Months later, Arenas joked during a December 2023 podcast episode that the media is trying to "push these Euros on us," after Green was suspended indefinitely for slapping Phoenix's Bosnian center, Jusuf Nurkic, in a game.[86] Jason Johnson, a professor of political science at Morgan State University and an MSNBC contributor, bluntly stated that he found a double standard in Jokić's treatment during an appearance on the Peacock sports series *Brother from Another*. His gripe was with the NBA fining Jokić only $25,000 for pushing the Suns' governor, Matt Ishbia, during a playoff game that May. Johnson insinuated that a Black player would have been suspended at least one game and villainized by the press.

Analytics was a big part of the defense for Jokić's multiple MVPs and why many basketball analysts and media personalities already viewed him as the world's premier player. Bryan Kalbrosky, author of "With Nikola Jokic, NBA Analytics Aren't Bad Just Because You Don't Understand Them," used this argument to support Jokić's 2022–23 MVP run.[87] Andy Bailey made a similar argument based upon statistics in an article for *Bleacher Report* titled "Why Can't NBA Awards Voters See the Obvious MVP Front-runner?" Jokić leads the NBA in Basketball Reference's box plus/minus and FiveThirtyEight's RAPTOR (two of the internet's more popular catch-all metrics that endeavor to encapsulate all or most of a player's contributions into one number. The Nuggets score more (plus), and opponents score less (minus) when he plays.[88]

Brad Pitt's 2011 film *Moneyball* demonstrated how analytics determine how valuable players are based on efficiency and their contributions to winning. In the past decade, sports analytics has become a contentious subject. Statistical data and math have emphasized certain players deemed efficient and devalued others. For example, in his *CBS Sports* article "Efficiency vs. production: The layered tale of Kobe Bryant's statistical legacy," Matt Moore argued that Kobe was a very inefficient player throughout large chunks of his career. Consequently, Steve Nash (a White Canadian) was more deserving of the MVP awards in 2005 and 2006.[89] Shaquille O'Neal, who also lost an MVP to Nash, begs to differ. Bomani Jones shared his thoughts on analytics in a 2019 interview conducted by

The New Yorker. While Jones, who has two master's degrees in economics and was briefly enrolled in a doctoral program at UNC-Chapel Hill, saw value in analytics, he warned against becoming too dependent on the approach. "You could make the argument that the [earlier] version of Russell Westbrook was inefficient. But man, that Westbrook was so much fun to watch."[90]

Joel Embiid was awarded the 2022–23 MVP award on May 2, 2023. Rather than celebrate Embiid's accomplishment, FS1 host Colin Cowherd implied that the coronation felt like an anti-Jokić vote.[91] Cowherd made headlines two months later when he said, "Europe's best young players are now the world's best young players. Their guys will have titles. (American) guys will have clout." Daniels and Kamla addressed Cowherd's comments on *Give and Go*. Daniels said they sounded racially coded given that most European players, with notable exceptions like Antetokounmpo and Wembanyama, are White and most American stars are Black. Daniels also pointed out Cowherd's noticeable exclusion of African players when praising international stars' skills, coachability, and basketball IQ. In Cowherd's defense, Sam Mitchell, a retired Black NBA head coach who played in the league and in Europe, has said on his NBA Radio show, *NBA Weekend*, that European players receive better coaching and are taught fundamentally sound team basketball at a younger age than their American counterparts who are raised on more individualistic AAU basketball.[92]

Although analytics can be used to swiftly refute claims of racial basis toward Jokić's MVP candidacy or exceptions made for other European players like Luka, it is naive to dismiss the possibility of bias on the part of some white MVP voters, media members, or fans. While Whites have only won the award 10 times in the past 40 years, that is impressive because they only comprise 17 percent of the league's population. According to BasketballReference.com, at least one White player finished among the top five MVP vote-getters over the last 22 years. Sixty-five percent of MVP voters were White in 2023. There are no specific criteria for MVP voting available to the public, so many fans believe the voting is subjective. The League MVP has been rewarded since 1955. It was renamed the Michael Jordan trophy in 2022. Four White American players received the award before Bird's first MVP in 1984: Bob Pettit (1956 and 1959), Bob Cousy (1959), Dave Cowens (1973), and Bill Walton (1978). One would expect a much larger number, given the lack of media diversity at the time.[93]

Race is still a significant factor in American sports and how White and Black athletes are judged. The LSU-Iowa controversy that erupted during the final two weeks of the NBA's 2022–23 regular season provides a glaring example. Fans and media members condemned Louisiana State University's Black star player Angel Reese for taunting Caitlin Clark, the

University of Iowa's White superstar, while celebrating her team's victory in the national championship. Those same people cheered Clark for the same behavior two nights earlier.[94] It is also interesting that the game, televised on ABC and ESPN2 at 3:00 p.m. on Palm Sunday, broke every record for a women's basketball game. Astonishingly, 9.9 million viewers tuned in for Clark's anticipated coronation, shattering the 8.2 million record set in a 1992 semifinal game between Stanford and Virginia. This viewership was a 20 percent increase from the previous year's title game featuring former champions South Carolina and the University of Connecticut (UConn).[95] First Lady Dr. Jill Biden made things worse by suggesting that Iowa accompany LSU when they visit the White House. Since 1963, the president has only honored championship-winning teams at the White House. The LSU–Iowa game, televised on ABC on Palm Sunday, broke every record for a women's basketball game: 9.9 million viewers tuned in for Clark's anticipated victory.[96]

After the Indiana Fever made her the first pick in that spring's WNBA draft, nearly all their games sold out or were nationally televised and the ticket prices skyrocketed. She appeared on *Saturday Night Live* and signed a $28 million Nike deal. Clark received 700,000 fan votes to appear in the 2024 All-Star game, which equaled the combined number of the top 11 vote-getters in 2023. When she was fouled too hard in a game, it sparked a national discourse in the media and written think pieces. The same was true when she was excluded from the U.S. Women's Summer Olympics team roster in Paris. By the middle of the season, media members were projecting her to win the Rookie of the Year award and be the runner-up for league MVP behind the two-time MVP winner and WNBA's best player, A'Ja Wilson. After the Atlanta Dream eliminated the Fever from the playoffs, some fans posted racist comments about the Dream players online. Clark addressed her privilege in a majority Black league after being named Time's Athlete of the Year.[97]

While European players like Jokić and Luka may appear to receive some favoritism, they will never neatly fall into the Great White Hope category of a Bird, Bradley, or even Clark because they are not American. Their English is decent but not great, which hampers their marketing ability and the number of American endorsement deals. They prefer to spend their offseasons back home in Europe. I believe these players have the power to draw other White immigrants living in America and Europeans worldwide to the NBA. But they have not had the same sway as White Americans. Oklahoma City's Chet Holmgren was projected to be the league's next great White American star when drafted in 2022, but an injury sidelined him for his entire rookie season. Holmgren was the runner-up to Wembanyama in the Rookie of the Year voting the following season. Three American White college players were among the first 17 picks in the 2024 draft. University of Kentucky freshman Reed Sheppard was the third overall pick. Cooper Flagg, Duke University's ballyhooed freshman from Maine, is projected to be the number-one pick in the 2025 NBA draft. "The next white Blue Devils superstar may be about to break America," was the subtitle of a 2023 article published in *Slate*.[98]

David Aldridge, a prominent NBA writer for *The Athletic* and recipient of the Curt Gowdy Award by the Naismith Basketball Hall of Fame, was interviewed for the book. I asked him if globalization was to blame for the decline in American White players.

> *Oh, I don't know. That's kind of an unanswerable question. Do you consider Dirk Nowitzki White or German? Do you consider Pao Gasol White or Spanish? International players are coming from other countries, but what are we calling them? Is Luka White or Slovenian? There's not a box on the census that says Slovenian. How are we counting people? We kind of change how we count people all the time.*
>
> *I think in basketball, because there are fewer jobs available, it tends to be more of a meritocracy than other sports, but that's based on no data. Young White American men who played basketball (in the past) may be playing baseball or tennis now, or they are on skateboards, or they are not doing sports at all. The change in the racial makeup of NBA players occurred a long time ago. I don't know what all those people who played baseball in the forties, fifties, and sixties did after that. Were they still trying to play baseball, and they just got beaten out by better players? I wouldn't be able to answer that with any amount of intelligence.*
>
> *Economics certainly played a part in why there were more white players in the fifties, sixties, and even into the seventies. What was the saying: "You can play two Blacks on the road, three at home, and five when you're behind." There was a quota; you couldn't have more than four or five Blacks on your team because they thought it was bad for business. They came to an understanding that winning and losing was best for business, not the color of your team. But back to your original question, you can make the case that there are fewer African American players on rosters today because there are more internationally born players. I think it cuts both ways.*[99]

Jokić was awarded his third MVP on May 8, 2024. The Joker received 79 of 100 first-place votes and a total of 926 points. Each first-place vote is worth 10 points. Shai-Gilgeous Alexander, a Black Canadian, finished in second place with 640 points and 15 first-place votes. Luka was third with 566 points and four first-place votes.[100] European players continue to revolutionize the game of basketball. The best non–American professional leagues are in Europe. The increasing emphasis on finesse athletes capable of playing multiple positions is due to the European invasion. The new age of big men who dribble like guards and shoot threes rather than post up with their back to the basket is attributable to the European invasion. NBA players would not have moves like the "Euro step" had they not been popularized by Toni Kukoč and Manu Ginobili.[101] The early success of Schmidt, Sabonis, Raja, Kukoč, and Petrović opened the door for Ginobili, Gasol, and Nowitzki to win championships in the 2000s and 2010s. The current generation of Europeans not only carry that torch but are vying to redefine the game on their own terms.

Jokić proved Kendrick Perkins and all his doubters wrong with an incredible run through the 2022–23 playoffs. He was the first player in history to lead the league in points (500), rebounds (250), and assists (150) in a single postseason. His 53-point, 11-rebound outing against the Phoenix Suns in round two of the playoffs was legendary. He outplayed Lakers LeBron and Anthony Davis in the Western Conference finals, which Denver won in a four-game sweep. How could I forget to mention his 32 points, 21 rebounds, and 10 assists in game three of the NBA Finals? He is the first player in history to record a 30-20-10 triple-double. Denver eliminated Miami in game five of the NBA Finals, winning their first championship in franchise history. In his postgame interview with ESPN's Lisa Salters, the nonchalant Joker was more concerned with going back to Serbia to be with his family and his horses than being named finals MVP, validating anyone who called him the world's best player, or attending the massive parade being held in Denver three days later. "The job is done; we can go home now!"

5

Hoops Diplomacy

"You know, you know we love China. We love, you know, playing there ... we appreciate their support.... So you know, we love you."

—James Harden[1]

On February 19, 1948, one of the most critical games in NBA history was played at Chicago Stadium between the Minneapolis Lakers and the Harlem Globetrotters. Eighteen thousand fans packed the stadium to watch George Mikan and the Lakers, the league's marquee team, take on the Globetrotters, who entered the contest on an incredible 102-game winning streak. The game's attendance was twice the size of the most-attended game in history. The novelty of seeing an all-White professional team (the Lakers) play an all-Black professional team (the Globetrotters) for the first time was a driving force behind the crowd size. This friendly exhibition was supposed to be an easy win for the Lakers, but the Globetrotters must not have received that memo. The Lakers, led by Mikan in scoring, jumped out to a nine-point lead in the first half, but the Globetrotters held him to six points after halftime. The game was tied at 59 with 1:30 minutes left to play. Marques Haynes, the Globetrotters' ball-handling wizard, dribbled around the Lakers' defenders for the next 90 seconds before passing the ball to Ermer Robinson for the game-winning basket. The Globetrotters' 61–59 victory challenged racist notions about the ability of Blacks to compete against whites. The NBA integrated two years later.[2]

In 1926, the Savoy Ballroom in Chicago began hosting basketball games played by the Savoy Big Five to attract people to come dance once the games ended. Many of these players had attended Wendell Phillips High School on the Southside. They formed their own semiprofessional team after graduating. Abraham Saperstein, the son of Jewish immigrants, was a supervisor at a predominantly Black playground. Saperstein had hoped to play basketball for the University of Illinois, but his diminutive 5'3" stature deferred that lofty dream. He dropped out of school and took a job at the playground, where he met the Savoy Big Five players, who hired him as their manager. Saperstein was a shrewd businessman; after the team failed to pack the ballroom, he crafted a new strategy to rebrand and market them. He went to his father's tailor shop and asked him to design uniforms with the name *New York* across the front jersey. He believed the team would book more games if people thought they were from New York and traveled the world. The Harlem Globetrotters were born.[3]

Todd Boyd compares the Globetrotters' style of play with the "traditional" style of White players to classical music and jazz. White players were taught to make five passes and then shoot. If a player made four passes and then shot, he violated the structure of the offense. Black basketball was free. The rules and structure, like jazz, were about improvisation. By the early 1940s, the Globetrotters had moved out of small towns and were playing exhibitions against professional teams like the Original Celtics in arenas.[4] The Globetrotters were skilled players who would have been good enough to play in the NBA's precursor leagues were it not for Jim Crow. Part of the team's new success was the arrival of Reese "Goose" Tatum, a former Negro League baseball player from the Indianapolis Clowns (the team was famous for their hijinks on the baseball diamond). Tatum became the first "clown prince" of the Trotters. He pulled down the pants of his opponents, and he would smile with big bug eyes. Saperstein realized that he had struck gold. Whites were packing games to watch the Globetrotters "clown" on the basketball court to the rhythms of the 1925 jazz standard "Sweet Georgia Brown."[5] While the team was beloved by the Black community and provided one of the few professional opportunities for Black college athletes, their act did not play well with a faction of middle-class Blacks who saw Saperstein profiting from a new form of minstrelsy disguised as basketball.[6]

In 1952, Saperstein decided it was time to make good on the team's name. During their 25th anniversary, they set off on a five-month, 52,000-mile tour around the world. The response was overwhelming. Tens of thousands came to see them at Wembley Empire Stadium in London, Palais de Sport in Paris, and Foro Italico in Rome. Few places they visited had ever seen basketball. Even fewer had proper regulation-sized courts for them to play on. In Stuttgart, Germany, they played on a court elevated off the floor with beer barrels. They played in the middle of a cow pasture in Christchurch, New Zealand. They played at the bottom of an empty swimming pool in Cologne, Germany. When the team visited Barcelona, Spain, they used a bullring shortly after a bullfight ended.[7]

The Globetrotters were the first version of hoops diplomats. Diplomacy is maintaining peaceful relationships between nations, groups, and individuals. The U.S. State Department proclaimed the Globetrotters as ambassadors of goodwill to honor their diplomatic efforts. They sipped tea with Queen Elizabeth II and Prince Philip, ate caviar with Soviet premier Nikita Khrushchev, and enjoyed private audiences with Pope Pius XII and Pope John Paul II. In his article "Around the World: Problematizing the Harlem Globetrotters as Cold War Warriors," Damion Thomas discusses how the United States State Department used the team as goodwill ambassadors in a larger Cold War–era plot to demonstrate to the world that America was making progress in racial relations.[8] The government's use of the Globetrotters was the sports equivalent of the jazz diplomacy program, which sent the nation's greatest jazz musicians and luminaries, like Louis Armstrong and John "Dizzy" Gillespie, to Africa, Asia, and Europe to promote American values and positive race relations between 1954 and 1968.[9]

Sports have played an integral role in diplomacy and cultural exchange between nations since the first Olympic games of the modern era. My father is obsessed with the 1994 film *Forrest Gump*. He watches it whenever it comes on television. Fans of the film may remember the protagonist, Forrest (Tom Hanks), playing in a ping-pong (table tennis) tournament. Those scenes were based on ping-pong diplomacy in the early 1970s.[10] The U.S. exchanged ping-pong players with the communist People's Republic of China during the 1971 World Table Tennis Championships in Nagoya, Japan, to thaw the ice during the Cold War. This exchange resulted in President Richard Nixon's 1972 visit to Beijing, arguably his most significant foreign policy achievement.[11] The NBA currently sponsors PeacePlayers. This organization, founded in 2001, uses basketball to transform the lives of youth in South Africa, Northern Ireland, the Middle East, and the United States who have been impacted by political conflict and social inequality. The players in the program are taught peace education, conflict resolution, and leadership skills to become future global change agents.[12] PeacePlayers was awarded the Naismith Basketball Hall of Fame 2023 Mannie Jackson Basketball's Human Spirit Award.[13]

The Globetrotters were called on again in the 21st century to join an unlikely new sports ambassador to spread goodwill in arguably the most restrictive country on the planet: North Korea. The Globetrotters accompanied retired NBA "bad boy" Dennis Rodman for an exhibition for the country's dictator, Kim Jong-un. During the 1990s, Kim Jong-un became obsessed with Rodman's Chicago Bulls team. Consequently, Rodman was able to form a friendship with the dictator. The camaraderie led to Rodman making three more trips to North Korea, the release of an American political prisoner, and President Donald Trump's historic summit with Kim Jong-un in 2018. Rodman's controversial attempts to broker peace with North Korea and convince Russia to free imprisoned WNBA star Brittney Griner in 2022 could be viewed as positive effects of the

NBA's globalization. Likewise, the NBA's refusal to speak out against China's mistreatment of Hong Kong citizens in 2019 due to a hefty financial commitment to China, its largest foreign partner, is a sign of globalization's adverse effects. The NBA's silence and complicity in human rights violations for financial reasons contradicted the league's constant outspokenness on domestic civil rights issues involving Black Americans. This chapter will explore the NBA's role in diplomacy and geopolitics.

Sweet Georgia Brown

What if I told you a basketball game may have prevented nuclear war? *Vice* is a Canadian American magazine founded by Shane Smith in 1994 that publishes long-form essays dedicated to news, politics, culture, and lifestyle. An Emmy Award–winning televised docuseries based upon its reporting aired on HBO and Showtime between 2013 and 2023. Over the years, *Vice* has been fascinated with North Korea and its mercurial leader, Kim Jong Un. In 2012, *Vice* proposed a goodwill basketball game in order to get their cameras inside the "Hermit Kingdom" to see the people and how they interacted with their leader, who was relatively new and young at the time. Only a handful of Americans have met with the country's leaders since the Cold War. One of those visitors was Madeleine Albright, the first woman to serve as U.S. secretary of state. Albright visited North Korea in October 2000 to lay the groundwork for a potential visit by President Bill Clinton.[14] The president's trip would be canceled two months later after negotiations over the country's nuclear missile program failed to satisfy American demands.[15] During the trip, Albright gave then-leader Kim Jong Il (or Kim Jong II) a basketball signed by Michael Jordan. After Kim's son Kim Jong Un succeeded him in 2011, *Vice* hoped to exploit the family dynasty's love of the NBA to secure rare footage for a future news special.

The proposed goodwill game would be an exhibition between the North Korean national team and three current members of the Harlem Globetrotters: Anthony "Buckets" Blakes, Alex "Moose" Weeks, and William "Bull" Bullard. Dennis Rodman, a teammate of Michael Jordan in Chicago from 1995 to 1998, was asked to accompany the players. *Vice*'s Smith described the game as a foreign sports exchange program. North Korea accepted their offer of "basketball diplomacy." In December 2012, North Korea successfully launched a satellite into orbit. The rocket launch came seven months after the first botched attempt, Kwangmyŏngsŏng-3, exploded in the air after 90 seconds.[16] The U.S. and its allies saw this as a cover for testing deadly ballistic missiles and proof of the country's commitment to nuclear proliferation.[17] Ten years earlier, President George W. Bush, while making his State of the Union address, named North Korea, Iran, and Iraq as part of a terrorist-fueled "axis of evil" harboring hatred toward America and its allies.[18] With this as the backdrop, *Vice* and its merry band of hoops diplomats set off for Pyongyang, the capital city, in late February 2013. Rodman's agent, Darren Prince, told the press, "When I discussed with Dennis the invitation to go to North Korea … he knew it was a once-in-a-lifetime opportunity.… It would also give him the chance to speak directly to Kim. To tell him that the only way to go is … peace, not war."[19]

This would be like no other sports exhibition in history. "The second you land in North Korea, you realize you're no longer in control of anything," said Ryan Duffy, *Vice*'s correspondent and narrator for this trip.[20] Government officials instructed the Americans every step from landing at the airport. Upon arrival, Duffy, his camera crew, and the players were greeted by a motorcade waiting to transport them to their hotel. As they entered the hotel, they saw a banner hanging from the wall celebrating the country's most recent and third successful underground nuclear test. The television, controlled by the North Korean state media, was running news reports praising the nuclear scientists from the February 12 test, who happened to be staying at that same hotel, for their feat. Members of the North Korean secret police, who were often disguised as guides and translators, accompanied the Americans throughout their stay.

In addition to playing in the exhibition, the players agreed to host a basketball clinic. The players were told it was for a group of local high school kids in a gym. Instead, they were sent to a 10,000-seat stadium to train the country's best players under 18. The Globetrotters delivered most of the instruction, but Rodman did provide tips on his specialty: rebounding the basketball. One of the spectators in the gym was Ri Myung-hun, North Korea's most famous retired basketball player. Ri, who stands 7'9", was once the tallest man in the world. NBA scouts pursued him, but trade sanctions blocked all negotiations. Ri is an anomaly in a country where segments of the population have suffered severely from malnutrition.[21]

Following the clinic, the group took a state-sanctioned tour of the capital city. The first stop on the tour was the Sun Palace, the resting place for North Korea's last two deceased leaders, Kim Jong Il and his father, Kim Il Sung. Two large statues of the men stand side by side in the palace. The magnificent statues manifest how they were revered as gods in life and death. Duffy described the tour as one long propaganda stunt to tout the country's greatness and relatability. While he wanted to see the

Korean Demilitarized Zone (DMZ), the border barrier that has divided North and South Korea since the 1953 Korean Armistice Agreement, the tour bus took them to a dolphin show at a theme park reminiscent of America's SeaWorld. Oddly, the dolphin trainers took a moment to tell the bright-eyed children and their parents in the audience about the importance of the recent nuclear tests. Their next visit was to a fitness center and spa. The Globetrotters played ping-pong with the men in the center. They also visited an empty grocery store filled with food and drinks perfectly aligned on the shelves as if on display for an open house. Duffy sarcastically questioned why the city was so well-lit at night, given reports of electrical power outages. Were the night lights also part of the tour?

The following day, they took a three-hour drive to the International Friendship Exhibition, which featured a display of all the unique gifts North Korea received from other countries. Jordan's signed basketball was in a vault alongside gifts from Libyan dictator Muammar Gaddafi.[22] Afterward, they were taken to Kim Il-Sung University and the Grand People's Study House, Pyongyang's central library, where they received lessons on the country's nuclear accomplishments and openness to the rest of the world. While in the library, they saw a room full of people pretending to use the internet as they sat at keyboards without typing. One gentleman was staring at the Google search page the entire time. Duffy compared the tour to being in a live version of *The Truman Show*. This reference was to the 1998 film starring Jim Carrey as Truman Burbank, a man who discovers that his life is nothing more than a fictional television series populated with actors pretending to be his friends and family. "Everywhere we went, and everything we saw was designed to convey the opposite of what we know about North Korea," said Duffy.[23]

As strange as the first part of the trip may sound, the exhibition game and postgame festivities were even weirder. Minutes before the game began, everyone in the sold-out stadium stood to their feet and started clapping and cheering hysterically for nearly two minutes as Kim Jong Un and his wife, Ri Sol-Ju, entered the building. The first family took a seat next to Rodman in the stands. The two teams split up into a white and a red team with a mixture of American and North Korean players on both sides. This was the first time since the Korean War (1950–53) that Americans and North Koreans played on the same team in any athletic competition. The first half was relatively competitive and played like a traditional game. The halftime show included dancing chorus girls doing acrobatics and other performers. During the second half, the Globetrotters ramped up their routine hijinks and shenanigans to the delight of the crowd and Supreme Leader Kim Jong Un, who was grinning from ear to ear. One of the Globetrotters climbed atop a basket and kicked balls as opposing players shot into the hoop. Another player hung upside down from the rim and wiggled his body after he dunked. Despite all the clowning, the game's final quarter was surprisingly intense. The final score was 110–110.

At the game's conclusion, Dennis Rodman was given a microphone to address the crowd. He thanked the people for accepting him and his American "compadres" and apologized on behalf of the United States for the ongoing tension between the two countries. Rodman then looked in Kim Jong-un's direction and told him, "You have a friend for life."[24] The audience stood and applauded as the two men shook hands. The people chanted, "Live 10,000 years!" "Live 10,000 years!" "Live 10,000 years!" as their beloved leader exited the building with his entourage and new BFF, Rodman. This expression means that they are wishing his lifetime to last an eternity. Once the dignitaries left, the Globetrotters and Duffy, who played in the game, were sent to the locker room and told to change immediately. They were placed on a bus without being told where they were going next. All cameras were prohibited on the bus. Once they reached their secret destination, they were greeted by Kim Jong-un, other dignitaries, and the North Korean state media. A special dinner hosted by the Democratic People's Republic of Korea (DPRK) Olympic Committee had been planned to honor them. At that moment, they became the first Americans, excluding Rodman, to meet North Korea's new leader.[25]

Rodman—wearing a colorful bright pink tie, dark sunshades, a dark baseball cap, a black blazer, and a scarf that was long and untied—sat next to the first family at the dinner table. Duffy described the occasion as being in an alternative universe. After Kim Jong-un and Rodman gave the opening toasts, an all-woman band dressed in white blouses and cream skirts, sporting similar short hairstyles, came out playing the theme song to the 1976 American film *Rocky* on electric violins. The Globetrotters danced with some of the women as they performed. Before long, a drunken karaoke night broke out; Rodman took the microphone to sing Frank Sinatra's "My Way," and the Americans' designated interpreter accompanied him on the saxophone. Throughout the evening, Kim and other North Korean dignitaries repeatedly stated that they hoped this trip would ease tensions between the countries. Before the players departed North Korea, they entertained a group of schoolchildren in a playground. This was the only impromptu activity of their trip. "We realize that bringing a crew of basketball players to North Korea isn't going to lead to the country dismantling its nuclear program, shutting down its labor camps, or even toning down its anti–American rhetoric, but during our time there, we did accomplish something. Through basketball, we managed to bridge the divide, open a dialogue, and make a connection with real people. If only for a moment," stated Duffy.[26]

Bad as I Wanna Be

Dennis Rodman and Kim Jong-un are the quintessential examples of an odd couple. I will have more to say about Kim later, but first, who is Rodman, and how did he become America's most improbable goodwill ambassador? He was born on May 13, 1961, in Trenton, New Jersey, although he grew up in Dallas. In an interview, his mother, Shirley, described him as a clingy, shy child who barely spoke. "He was not outgoing at all. It took four of us to drag him on a bus just to go to the daycare; come on!"[27] His mother, who worked three jobs to make ends meet, was not very affectionate. Rodman's father, Philander, a Vietnam War veteran who served in the U.S. Air Force, abandoned the family when Rodman was three years old and relocated to the Philippines. The name Philander perfectly fit his father, who ended up fathering at least 28 other children with multiple women.[28] His father's absence devasted Rodman's self-confidence as a child, causing him to crave the attention of his younger sisters, Debra and Kim, who put makeup on him and dressed him in girls' attire to play "house."[29]

Rodman was an outcast for much of his childhood and adolescence. Other boys in the neighborhood bullied him because they thought he was queer. He did not possess artistic talent, make good grades, or have strong social skills. His athletic prowess developed later in life. He was cut twice from the high school football team and quit the basketball team. Dan Bickley, author of *No Bull: The Unauthorized Biography of Dennis Rodman* (1997), says Rodman's big protruding ears and skinny physique made him self-conscious of his appearance and triggered an inferiority complex.[30] The one thing he was good at was a pinball game at the local 7-Eleven, where he worked part-time. His mother nicknamed him "the worm" because of the way his body moved when he played.

Rodman had to attend summer school to graduate from high school. As he struggled to find his place in society, his sisters became college basketball stars. Since he lacked scholarship offers and did not want to enlist in the military, Rodman took a job as a janitor at Dallas Fort Worth International Airport. During the night shifts, he began using a broom to steal watches from a jewelry store in the airport. He managed to steal 50 watches before he was caught on the security camera and placed in the airport jail. Rodman says he stole the watches to give away as gifts to impress people. The court dropped all charges because he never sold any of the stolen merchandise. Rodman lost his job, spent the next two years unemployed, and lived at home with his mother before she kicked him out of the house. Homeless, with his life spiraling out of control on a dead-end street, he soon found a lifeline in the form of basketball. Rodman was only

5'8" when he graduated from South Oak Cliff High School. By age 20, he stood 6'7". His growth spurt inspired an obsession with playing basketball at a local recreation center. In 1982, he accepted an offer to play basketball at Cooke County College in Gainesville, Texas. Unfortunately, he flunked out in his freshman year and ended up back on the streets for the next six months.[31]

Rodman's second lifeline came from Lonn Reisman, an assistant men's basketball coach at Southeastern Oklahoma State University in Durant, Oklahoma. Coach Reisman came to his mother's home to recruit him. The awkwardly shy Rodman hid in his bedroom for almost two hours before he came out for the meeting. Reisman convinced the wayward 23-year-old to ride back to Oklahoma that same day. Rodman would be one of the few Black faces in rural Durant. He was frequently called a nigger, but it did not faze him because he was uncomfortable with his Blackness and more concerned with fitting in at all costs. His closest friendship was with Bryne Rich, a 13-year-old White boy he met while working as a counselor at the college's summer basketball camp. Rich, who had fatally shot his best friend in a hunting accident, had been in a state of depression and isolation before they met. Soon, the two were inseparable. Rodman could be found at Rich's parents' home when he was not on campus. At one point, Rodman asked the Rich family to adopt him, worsening relations with his biological mother. However, his relationship with the Riches was not perfect. Mrs. Rich scolded him for wanting to date White girls and even called him a nigger during an argument.

As for school, Rodman quickly made a name for himself on the court at the tiny Division II college. After Rodman scored 24 points and grabbed 19 rebounds, he asked his head coach if he was disappointed in his play after the first game. "Would you disappoint me every night this year?" his coach replied.[32] After an All-American career at Southeastern Oklahoma State, Rodman was drafted by the Detroit Pistons with the 27th pick in the 1986 draft. He was still very shy and innocent when he entered the NBA. Pistons coach Chuck Daly became a surrogate father figure to him. The Pistons provided another family for Rodman, who found his niche as the team's leading rebounder and defender. He bought wholeheartedly into the team's "Bad Boys" persona, making them the NBA's villains. For the first time in his life, he got to be the bully, picking fights with everyone from John Stockton to Michael Jordan. "He loved everything about that 'us against the world mentality' that the Pistons had," says Bickley.[33] Detroit won back-to-back NBA championships in 1989 and 1990. Rodman was named Defensive Player of the Year in 1990. Overcome by emotion and finally feeling accepted, he broke down in tears as he received the honor.

The good times in Detroit were only temporary. The team slowly crumbled after the Bulls swept them in the 1991 Eastern Conference finals. Some of his teammates were traded or retired. Coach Daly retired in 1992. Rodman, feeling abandoned again by his father figure and family, began lashing out. He had a tumultuous 82-day marriage to the White mother of his daughter. He was suspended five times in the 1992–93 season. On the night of February 11, 1993, he drove to the parking lot of the Pistons' home arena, where he fell asleep holding a rifle in his lap. Rumors circulated in the press the next day of a failed suicide attempt. Rodman says he put the gun to his head to metaphorically kill the old Dennis Rodman and birth a new version of himself. "When I left Detroit, my mentality became fuck the world," he says.[34]

Detroit traded Rodman to San Antonio that summer. He arrived for his first practice donning a bleached blond mohawk, a new hairstyle inspired by Wesley Snipes' character Simon Phoenix in the 1993 action film *Demolition Man*. While in San Antonio, he began experimenting with different hair colors, tattoos, and body piercings. He dated Madonna, a pop star known for her controversial, sexually charged music and persona. Rodman revealed in a May 1995 *Sports Illustrated* article that he fantasized about gay sex, frequented gay bars, and dressed in drag.[35] He found a new family in the LGBTQIA community. Critics thought it was just for shock value.[36]

Rodman's volatile behavior on and off the court forced the Spurs to trade him to Chicago at the end of the 1994–95 season. Bulls coach Phil Jackson believed his star players, Michael Jordan and Scottie Pippen, could manage Rodman's eccentric personality enough to get the best out of him. Despite an ugly head-butting incident with a referee that led to a six-game suspension, Rodman contributed to the Bulls' historic 72–10 regular season and their first of three consecutive NBA championships in his first season with Chicago. Jordan called Rodman the smartest teammate he ever had. Rodman studied players' shooting patterns to determine the angle the ball would bounce off the rim to grab rebounds. He averaged 14.9 rebounds a game. In the offseason, he rode down Manhattan's Fifth Avenue in a horse-drawn carriage wearing makeup, a pink wig, lipstick, and a white wedding gown to promote his autobiography, *As Bad as I Wanna Be*. Putting on a wedding dress transformed him into an international rock star who transcended sports. The book skyrocketed to the top of the *New York Times* bestseller list.

Believe it or not, Rodman competed with Jordan's celebrity in the late '90s. This newfound fame caused him to burn the candle at both ends. In the fourth episode of *The Last Dance*, Jordan shared a humorous story from the 1997–98 season. Rodman was working extra hard to help the Bulls recover from a losing record and the absence of disgruntled star Pippen. Once the Bulls began winning again, Rodman asked Coach Jackson if he could go to Las Vegas for 48 hours to unwind. His two-day excused absence morphed into a prolonged unexcused vacation. Jordan found where he was staying and went to his hotel to get him. He found Rodman in bed with Carmen Electra, a *Playboy* playmate and *Baywatch* actress, whom he married for nine days in 1998.[37] Rodman returned to the team to help Jordan capture his sixth championship ring.

After his glorious run with the Bulls ended, all the partying eventually caused Rodman to hit rock bottom. He had unsuccessful short stints with the Los Angeles Lakers and Dallas Mavericks. He drank himself out of a comeback attempt with the Denver Nuggets. Reality television offered him a modicum of fame once his playing career ended. He appeared on *Celebrity Mole*, *Celebrity Big Brother*, *Love Island* in the United Kingdom, and Donald Trump's *Celebrity Apprentice*. His time with Trump would come in handy years later. Rodman was inducted into the Naismith Memorial Hall of Fame in 2011. He thanked a mysterious woman named Peggy [Fulford] as he was making his acceptance speech. She was his *trusted* financial adviser. Unbeknownst to him, Peggy was mismanaging his bank accounts and stealing millions from him and other professional athletes.[38] It was around this time that Rodman, severely in need of money, received the invitation to North Korea. Peggy's son, Elkin King, who had become Rodman's hangout buddy in 2008, accompanied him on the trip. Rodman's agent did not even grasp the difference between North and South Korea when he signed the contract. The NBA did not sanction the trip, which an Irish gambling company sponsored.[39]

Dennis Rodman visited North Korea four times between February 2013 and January 2014. He knew more about Kim Jong Un than some CIA operatives. The final trip was to celebrate Kim Jong Un's birthday. A group of retired NBA players traveled with him. While drinking had been Rodman's pastime during previous visits, he was uncontrollably drunk throughout his final trip. His intoxication was apparent during a live televised interview with Chris Cuomo for CNN on January 7, 2014. The drunken ex-athlete began yelling at Cuomo after being asked questions about North Korea's human rights violations and the detainment of political prisoner Kenneth Bae, who was sentenced to 15 years for plotting to overthrow the government.[40] Rodman checked into rehab a week later. His foreign trips and budding friendship with the dictator made him toxic. He lost several financial opportunities and received death threats. He defended his travels by calling them basketball diplomacy akin to the ping-pong diplomacy of the 1970s. He also reminded the press that he was not a politician or official ambassador for the U.S. government. Ironically, when Kenneth Bae was released from prison on November 8, 2014, he thanked Rodman and credited his rant for his release.[41]

Little Rocket Man

Dennis Rodman's relationship with Kim Jong Un is not as improbable as it seems. Both men are eccentric characters whose backgrounds and family have shaped their lives. In Rodman's case, self-identity issues and a precarious relationship with his parents contributed to his becoming an enigmatic figure who always operated against the grain. As for Kim, the sins of his fathers led him down his current path as one of the world's most feared and misunderstood leaders. Like *The Godfather*'s Michael Corleone, he was predestined to be in the family business. Even his love for basketball can be attributed to his father. Kim was born on January 8, sometime between 1982 and 1984. His exact birth date is unknown to the public. This age discrepancy is another familial trait. Some scholars suggest that his birth year was changed to 1982 so that his birthday would symbolically fall 40 years after the birth of his father, Kim Jong Il, and 70 years after the birth of his grandfather, Kim Il Sung.[42]

Kim Jong Un's origin story dates to the early years of the Cold War. In 1948, Korea was divided between the democratic South and the communist North. The Soviet Union (USSR) appointed Kim Il Sung as North Korea's head of state. North Korea invaded South Korea on June 25, 1950, beginning a three-year civil war. American troops assisted South Korean military forces, while the USSR and China backed North Korea. At the war's conclusion, the Korean Demilitarized Zone (DMZ) was established to serve as a buffer zone between the divided countries.

Kim Il Sung ruled North Korea until his death in 1994. According to Calvin Sims, formerly of the Herbert W. Hoover Foundation, a propaganda-fueled cult of personality was formed around Kim Il Sung ("Great Leader") and his son ("Dear Leader"). The "Great Leader's" sudden death resulted in 10 days of national mourning. Hundreds of thousands attended his funeral. Kim Jong-il was given the country's highest post, chairman of the National Defense Commission, after his father's passing. This was the first time power was transferred from a father to a son in a communist nation. Once in power, Jong-il ruled with an iron fist. Amnesty International labeled North Korea "the last worst place on earth."[43] The government controlled the media and how much information citizens could be exposed to from the outside world. Political dissenters were detained in concentration camps, and then there was the famine in the late nineties. Amnesty International accused the government of starving people by unfairly distributing food resources to supporters and withholding it from dissenters. Hungry citizens could be publicly executed if caught stealing food.[44]

Jong Il adopted a military-first policy called Songun, which prioritized the Korean People's Army and designated resources to a nuclear program. As a result, military spending was 20 percent higher than the country's gross national product. Natural disasters in the mid–1990s contributed to the food shortage, but with resources dedicated to the military, things only worsened. This was one of the worst famines in the 20th century, which is why the 2014 *Vice* documentary emphasized their visit to a grocery store with shelves filled with food. Over a million people, 10 percent of the population, died during the famine. Although Jong-il signed an agreement with the U.S. to dismantle his nuclear weapons program in exchange for aid in 2003, the U.S. discovered that he was still secretly engaging in nuclear proliferation.[45]

North Korean propaganda portrayed their "Dear Leader" as a god. This tactic was reminiscent of the forced adoration of communist leaders Joseph Stalin (USSR) and Mao Zedong (China). According to propaganda, Jong Il was the greatest military strategist, urban developer, cinematographer, and furniture designer, as well as a genius at animal husbandry. When he suffered a fatal heart attack in 2011, a grand funeral was staged. As the funeral procession made its way down the street, 200,000 grief-stricken mourners, mostly dressed in military uniform, lined the road crying uncontrollably. Kim Jong Un walked in front of the hearse carrying his father's casket on its roof. After the national mourning period ceased, the 27-year-old was named his father's successor and appointed supreme commander of the Korean People's Army despite being the youngest of the family's three sons.[46]

By the 10th year of his rule, Kim had a growing arsenal of nuclear weapons and was the commander of the world's fourth-largest military. But he was torn between two worlds: the oppressive traditions of his forefathers and a personal desire to be viewed as a legitimate, modern leader on a global stage. Kim's childhood was atypical compared with other North Korean youth. He was nicknamed the little general but ordered to remain indoors until he was six. His earliest playmates were his 30-year-old bodyguards. Kim watched them shoot guns and do martial arts. Even now, he has bodyguards who inspect his food and carry a portable toilet for him to use to prevent foreign operatives from examining his feces and blood content. This behavior is rooted in his father's extreme paranoia.

Kim spent his teenage years in Bern, Switzerland, under the care of his maternal aunt, Ko Yong-suk, and her husband, Ri Gang. His parents sent him and his older brother Kim Jong Chol to live and attend a boarding school in Switzerland in 1996 when he was 12.[47] Kim's aunt and uncle provided a happy childhood for him and his brother. They took family trips to Euro Disney, now Disneyland Paris. They went skiing in the Swiss Alps, dined at Italian restaurants, and swam on the French Riviera.[48] When Kim was 14, his aunt and uncle defected from North Korea and settled in the

U.S. with the assistance of the Central Intelligence Agency (CIA), which paid them $200,000 for a home purchase.[49] They have lived anonymously since then, running a dry cleaners hours away from New York City. The couple vanished without saying goodbye to their nephews. Like Rodman, Kim suffered a sense of abandonment as a teen.

Globalization brought the NBA to North Korea. Kim's father, Kim Jong-il, became obsessed with Michael Jordan and the Bulls in the 1990s as they were making their dynastic run. He adored Jordan so much that he built a shrine in his honor and invited his Airness to Pyongyang. Jordan declined the invitation; however, Madeleine Albright delivered a basketball with his autograph when she visited the country in 2000.[50] Kim Jong-un adopted his father's passion for the NBA and Jordan's Bulls. "He started playing basketball, and he became obsessed with it. He used to sleep … with his basketball," says his Aunt Ko.[51] Despite his current stocky figure, Kim's classmate Nikola Kovacevic says he was a decent athlete. His routine outfit in school was a Bulls jersey or T-shirt, matching shorts, and a fresh pair of Air Jordan sneakers. Jordan was his favorite player, but he did own Rodman's number 99 Bulls jersey. Seth Rogan's controversial comedic film *The Interview* (2014), about a fictional interview with Kim (Randall Park) and an American journalist (James Franco) sent to Pyongyang to assassinate him, mocked the leader's love for hoops, depicting him aimlessly missing an alley-oop dunk on a lowered hoop. He was mocked again in a 2020 *Saturday Night Live* spoof of *The Last Dance* docuseries.

Kim enjoyed living like a rich kid in Europe. He attended NBA exhibition games in Paris. Perhaps he was in attendance when the Bulls won the 1997 McDonald's Open. His studies were interrupted when he was permanently brought back to North Korea at 17. Within the next decade, he took over the family business. Anna Fifield, the former Beijing bureau chief for the *Washington Post*, says Kim was seen as a potential reformer when he assumed office in 2011. He pledged to end hunger and modernize the country dubbed "The Hermit Kingdom." "In the early years of his rule, I saw this desire for his country … his people to be more worldly," says Jean H. Lee, former Pyongyang bureau chief for the *Associated Press*.[52] In 2012, he ordered the construction of ski resorts, amusement parks, shopping malls, restaurants, and luxury department stores throughout the country. He also brought the internet and social media influencers to the country. His younger celebrity wife, Ri Sol-ju, a famous singer in North Korea, assisted him in the country's rebranding. In 2018, he changed Ri's official title from comrade to first lady. Fifield described her as "the Kate Middleton of North Korea … there to humanize her husband."[53]

Jean H. Lee says Kim's attempts to modernize North Korea and present it as "a socialist fairyland" belie the problems that still exist under the surface. On February 13, 2017, Kim's older half brother, Kim Jong-Nam, died at Kuala Lumpur International Airport in Malaysia. After being overlooked for succession (like one of Logan Roy's incompetent kids), he moved to China for a quiet life.[54] The CIA persuaded Jong-Nam to become an informant and supply information on his brother. Hidden cameras videotaped him meeting with a CIA agent. On the day of his death, Doan Thi Huong, a 28-year-old Vietnamese woman, and Siti Aisyah, a 25-year-old Indonesian woman, were arrested at the airport. The women thought they were hired for a television show in which they would ambush unsuspecting individuals and smother their faces with baby oils and body lotions as a prank. As Jong-Nam approached the boarding station for his flight, they covered his face in what turned out to be a lethal VX nerve agent. He was immediately taken to the airport infirmary and pronounced dead 20 minutes later. The women were charged with the crime but spent only two years in prison. Kim was rumored to be responsible for the murder but denied culpability.[55]

Before President Obama left office, the U.S. imposed sanctions on North Korea in retaliation for ballistic missile testing. When President Donald Trump was elected months later, he made no qualms about his distaste for the Korean dictator. While speaking at a campaign rally in Alabama for Senator Luther Strange in September 2017, Trump derided Kim by referring to him as "little Rocket Man." Trump's "little Rocket Man" quip ignited an ongoing feud between the two men. It came as an inexplicable surprise when they agreed to meet for a summit in Singapore on June 12, 2018, months after trading threats of nuclear decimation.[56]

Another famous American was in Singapore on the day of the summit. Dennis Rodman was in town for moral support. As I mentioned, he was a cast member on Trump's *Celebrity Apprentice* reality series years earlier. Trump endorsed Rodman's international efforts when he was interviewed by Fox News in 2013. "Maybe Dennis is a lot better than what we have."[57] When Rodman visited North Korea in 2017, some analysts wondered if he was there to give Kim a message from the president. Was Rodman responsible for brokering a peace deal between the two leaders? Would he be involved in their meetings? No! Trey Yingst, the chief White House correspondent for the One America News Network, reported that Rodman was not involved and was solely going as a publicity stunt for Pot-Coin, a "community-based" cryptocurrency company for legalized marijuana sponsoring his trip.[58] Nevertheless, the summit was successful. An emotional Rodman wiped tears from his eyes as CNN's Chris Cuomo interviewed him while he was in Singapore. Wearing one of Trump's infamous "Make America Great Again" red baseball caps, he told Cuomo, "It's a great day. I am here to see it."[59] A year later, Trump became the first sitting U.S. president to visit North Korea. A journalist for the *South China Morning Post* credited Rodman for his diplomatic efforts and called him an unexpected hero.[60]

Despite all this goodwill, a 2021 *National Geographic* report claimed North Korea was still the oppressive state of old. While Kim presented himself as a progressive, friendly leader, his younger sister, Kim Yo-Jong, the Sweet Princess, continued to carry out the terror of past regimes. Yo-Jong became the deputy director of the publicity and information department of the Workers' Party of Korea in 2014. Six years later, Kim promoted her over his male generals to the highest level of the Politburo. Many view her as his likely successor. In June 2020, she ordered the bombing of a government complex in South Korea. The government claimed it was responding to defectors sending anti–North Korean propaganda over the border with balloons.[61] Later that month, she stated, "The USA should worry about receiving a Christmas gift from us."[62]

Free BG

Dennis Rodman volunteered his diplomatic and geopolitical *expertise* to the U.S. government in 2022 to bring WNBA star Brittney Griner home from a Russian prison. Griner, a 6'9" All-Star center for the Phoenix Mercury, is one of the world's best woman players. She has won a WNBA championship, NCAA Final Four, FIBA World Cup, and Olympic gold medal. Despite her lofty accomplishments, she earned only $227,900 from her WNBA salary in 2022–23. The women in the WNBA, as is the case for most professional American women's leagues, are grossly underpaid compared with their male counterparts. Many of these women supplement their salaries by playing overseas in the offseason. Griner's teammate Diana Taurasi and the recently retired legend Sue Bird played for Shabtai Kalmanovich, a Russian KGB spy turned billionaire businessman, for four years until his contract-style murder in 2009. They knew he had a checkered past, but he treated them like royalty and paid them as much as $1 million. At the time, the WNBA's annual salary was only $117,500. WNBA players can earn 10 times their salary playing abroad in Europe and Asia.[63]

Griner began playing for BC UMMC Ekaterinburg, a Russian women's basketball team in the Russian Premier League, in 2014. She helped the team win the EuroLeague championship in 2016, 2018, 2019, and 2021. Her annual earnings in Russia were $1 million. On February 17, 2022, she was detained in an airport and arrested on illegal drug smuggling charges. Russian customs officials found cartridges containing less than a gram of medically prescribed cannabis oil. Griner told officials she was tired and rushing to catch her flight, causing her to forget the cartridges were inside her luggage. Nevertheless, she was held in a Russian prison and not allowed to return home. On August 4, she received a nine-year prison sentence.[64]

Brittney Griner's arrest coincided with Russia's invasion of Ukraine on February 22. Many observers believed that she became a casualty of the Russo-Ukrainian War as the U.S. placed sanctions on Russia. Her ordeal became a dominant international news story thanks to the efforts of her WNBA family. The NBA also got involved in the fight to "Free BG." Commissioner Adam Silver told ESPN's Malika Andrews the league was working with the WNBA to bring Griner home during a televised interview in May before the draft lottery. Boston Celtics players wore black-and-orange shirts reading "We Are BG" as they practiced at the Chase Center in San Francisco, California, days before an NBA Finals matchup with the Golden State Warriors. During an episode of his talk show *The Shop: Uninterrupted*, formerly airing on HBO, LeBron James chastised the efforts of the U.S. government to bring her home. "I would be feeling like, 'Do I even want to go back to America?'"[65] Stephen Curry hosted the ESPYs, ESPN's annual sports award ceremony, in July. He joined WNBA stars Nneka Ogwumike and Skylar Diggins-Smith on stage to raise awareness. "She's one of us, the team of athletes in this room tonight and all over the world. A team that has nothing to do with politics or global conflict," said Curry.[66]

Griner's wife, Cherelle, asked Bill Richardson, a former United Nations ambassador and governor of New Mexico, to advocate for her. Richardson flew to Moscow to try to negotiate a deal to free Griner and Paul Whelan, an American citizen detained in Russia since December 2019 on alleged espionage charges.[67] Enter Dennis Rodman into the equation. The NBA's unofficial ambassador told an *NBC News* reporter at a Washington, D.C., restaurant he was planning to take a trip to Moscow. "I got permission to go to Russia to help that girl."[68] Rodman visited the Russian capital in 2014. At the time, he called Russian president Vladimir Putin, who is also viewed as a dictator and a threat to America, "cool" after they met. Rodman believed he could have the same luck in Russia as in North Korea. Once again, he was acting without the NBA's blessing.

The Biden administration was adamantly opposed to Rodman's pending rogue trip. State Department spokesperson Ned Price shared their feelings with the press. "We believe that anything other than negotiating further through the established channel is likely to complicate and hinder those release efforts." Price denied Rodman's claims that he "got permission" to meet with Putin.[69] At 8:30 a.m. on December 8, President Joe Biden announced the immediate release of Griner. Standing beside Vice

President Kamala Harris and Cherelle Griner, President Biden said, "She's safe. She's on a plane. She's on her way home."[70] Griner's release resulted from a prisoner swap for Viktor Bout, a dangerous Russian arms dealer. She landed in San Antonio the next day. Paul Whelan remained incarcerated until a prisoner swap occurred on August 1, 2024.[71] Dennis Rodman did not travel to Moscow or speak with Putin.

Selective Outrage

Perhaps Adam Silver should have used Dennis Rodman's diplomacy skills in 2019 to settle a conflict in Asia that placed their financial bottom line and public reputation in the crosshairs. On October 4, 2019, Houston Rockets general manager Daryl Morey tweeted, "FIGHT FOR FREEDOM STAND WITH HONG KONG."[72] Morey's tweet prompted swift backlash from the Chinese government and business partners who pulled their money from the Rockets. The team's governor, Tilman Fertitta, said Morey was not speaking on behalf of the organization. The NBA, which had spent years growing relations with China, declared Morey's tweet regrettable. LeBron called the tweet misinformed. "I do not believe there was any consideration for the consequences and ramifications of the tweet," LeBron tweeted.[73] Joseph Tsai, the Brooklyn Nets governor and a native of China, lobbied to have Morey fired for his remarks.[74] CCTV, China's state broadcaster, threatened to suspend broadcasts of the NBA's upcoming preseason games in Asia.

Morey deleted the tweet and posted an apology, saying, "I did not intend my tweet to cause any offense to Rockets fans and friends of mine in China."[75] The Rockets were in Tokyo for a two-game preseason series with the Toronto Raptors at the time of the controversy.[76] Houston shooting guard and 2017–18 league MVP James Harden addressed Morey's comments during a press conference with the Japanese media. "We apologize. You know, you know we love China. We love, you know, playing there.... They show us the most support and love."[77]

American politicians on both sides of the partisan aisle criticized the NBA for condemning Morey's tweet. Republican senator Ted Cruz called the NBA's behavior shameful. Democratic Representative Beto O'Rourke called the league an embarrassment. "The only thing the NBA should be apologizing for is their blatant prioritization of profits over human rights."[78] To understand the NBA's "selective outrage," to borrow the phrase popularized by Chris Rock's 2023 Netflix special, one must fully understand the Hong Kong protests and the league's relationship with China. It all started with a murder!

On February 8, 2018, a young couple, Chan Tong-kai and Poon

Hiu-wing, flew from Hong Kong to Taiwan for a vacation. Nine days later, only Chan returned to home. A month later, he confessed to killing Poon, who was carrying their unborn child. Hong Kong authorities could not charge him with a crime because it took place in Taiwan, and they could not extradite him because no such agreement existed between the countries. The following year, Hong Kong politicians proposed a new bill that would allow criminals to be deported and tried for their crimes in Taiwan. The proposed legislation would also enable extradition to mainland China. In China, there was no fair trial system, no fair penal system, and no separation of powers within the government. China and Hong Kong are vastly different administrative regions. However, this bill would give China more power and influence over Hong Kong, which is where things became complicated.[79]

Hong Kong is part of China but acts as a semiautonomous region. After China lost a series of wars to Great Britain in the late 1800s, it surrendered Hong Kong, which was a British colony until 1997. The British returned Hong Kong to China under a special agreement called "One Country, Two Systems." Hong Kong would become part of China, but the country would enjoy a high degree of autonomy and come directly under the Central People's Government. The citizens of Hong Kong would receive democratic freedoms such as voting, freedom of speech, press, and assembly. As a result, Hong Kong differed from the authoritarian mainland China, where citizens have few privileges and are harshly punished for speaking out against the government.[80] Hong Kong still has only a limited amount of freedom. Citizens cannot vote for their leader. The chief executive is selected by a small committee and approved by China. Laws are made at the Legislative Council Complex, or LegCo, which is predominantly occupied by political parties with business ties to China.

Under "One Country, Two Systems," Hong Kong will fully become part of China in 2047. However, China does not want to wait that long to assert its dominion over its neighbor.[81] In 2003, half a million Hong Kong citizens fought legislation that would have punished dissidents of the Chinese government. In 2014, tens of thousands of protestors occupied the city for weeks in reaction to China's influence on their country's elections. Five years later, on March 15, 2019, protestors staged a sit-in at the government headquarters. Then on June 9, hundreds of thousands gathered for a demonstration that led to a massive gathering outside the LegCo three days later to prevent the extradition bill's second reading. Another protest was staged on June 16 to fight the bill and raise awareness about the excessive use of force by the Hong Kong Police Force. Unlike previous protests, the 2019 demonstrations included lawyers and politicians for the first time. Generation Zers, the first Hong Kong citizens born under One Country, Two Systems, were at the forefront of the protests. They have the most to lose when the current system ends. In July, a military spokesman said China would mobilize troops to help restore order if necessary. President Trump commended China for its handling of the situation. The protests influenced the government to suspend the bill. Carrie Lam Cheng Yuet-ngor, Hong Kong's chief executive, withdrew the bill on September 4.[82]

If the NBA supported Daryl Morey and sided with Hong Kong, it would have ruined its biggest investments in its most important international market, China. On June 26, 2002, the Houston Rockets selected Yao Ming with the first overall pick. Ming, a native of Shanghai, China, began playing basketball when he was nine and joined the Shanghai Sharks junior team of the Chinese Basketball Association (CBA) when he was 13. His father and mother were 6'7" and 6'3", respectively. When he was a boy, doctors predicted that he could grow as tall as 7'3". The 7'6", 310-pound center was one of the largest men in NBA history. Ming was selected to eight All-Star teams, thanks mainly to the Chinese fan vote. His success made him a symbol for a new, modern China after the Cold War. On September 10, 2016, he was inducted into the Naismith Hall of Fame alongside his rival center Shaquille O'Neal and Allen Iverson. Ming is the only Chinese-born player in the Hall of Fame. Retirement did not end his affiliation with the sport. He served as the president of the CBA from 2017 to 2023.

Before Yao Ming, there was Song Tao, the first Chinese-born player to be drafted. The Atlanta Hawks selected him with the 67th pick in 1987. They discovered him when the Bulls played the Chinese National Men's Basketball team in a 1985 exhibition. Song raised more eyebrows by scoring 28 points and grabbing nine rebounds against Puerto Rico in the 1986 FIBA championship. The Hawks believed they had found a diamond in the rough; unfortunately, a career-ending knee injury ended Song's NBA career before it began. Ma Jian was the next Chinese athlete to attract the attention of NBA scouts. He received an offer to play at UCLA but failed his college exam due to the language barrier. He ended up playing for Utah Valley Community College and later the University of Utah. After college, Ma joined the NBA Summer League rosters for the Suns and the Clippers. He was among the last players cut from the Clippers' 1995–96 roster. Ma received a job as a commentator for Clippers' games on the Chinese radio station KAZN before returning to Asia to play professionally. The Mavericks drafted Wang ZhiZhi with the 36th overall pick in 1999. Wang became the first Chinese player to play in a regular season NBA game. Four other Chinese players joined the NBA after Yao Ming.[83] Jeremy Lin, the son of Taiwanese immigrants, became the most popular NBA player in the world for a brief period, known as "Linsanity," during his magical 2011–12 season with the Knicks.[84]

Basketball was popular in China long before the NBA came to the country. YMCA basketball missionaries introduced the sport to the country in 1894. Basketball and soccer were China's most popular sports by the mid-1930s. The sport flourished under the leadership of Mao Zedong. The People's Liberation Army used basketball to build solidarity.[85]

Yao Ming's success made the Rockets the unofficial home team of NBA fans in China. By 2017, the NBA had 60 million NBA fans in China and was the most popular sports league on Chinese social media. David Stern's lofty plan had finally come to fruition. When Stern became the league's commissioner in 1984, he envisioned it expanding internationally and conquering the Chinese market. Stern was more concerned with making money in China than diplomacy, goodwill, or scouting talent like Ming. The NBA secured a broadcasting rights contract with CCTV in 1990. The 1994 All-Star Game was the first NBA contest to air on CCTV. The league offered China free signals until 1998.[86] A 2005 NBA.com survey found that 40 percent of Chinese male basketball fans between 20 and 29 said basketball was their favorite sport. Eighty-three percent of males between ages 15 and 24 had watched at least one game. According to a survey conducted by TNT, by 2008, 75 percent of China's urban residents enjoyed watching and playing basketball.[87]

In 2015, the NBA signed an exclusive streaming contract with Tencent, a Chinese multinational technology and entertainment conglomerate. Before this arrangement, NBA fans in China were limited to two livestreams. Now, they can livestream almost every game. Tencent offered viewers free and paid content. For example, if 10 games were broadcast in one day, fans could stream two for free and pay to stream the others. During the 2015–16 season, the live-game audience exceeded 100 million. The number of Chinese NBA fans exceeded Yao Ming's playing days.[88] Before the Tencent deal, 20 local Chinese television stations contracted with the NBA to show their games. These local stations paid between $1,500 and $120,000 in copyright fees. Unsatisfied with the league's local television partnerships, Stern invested entirely in CCTV, which aired 96 games, including selected regular-season contests, the All-Star Game, and the playoff series in 2005–06. By 2018, CCTV-5, the CCTV sports channel, broadcast games five days a week and aired highlight video clips during daily sports news segments. Once CCTV took over, only a few local stations in Beijing, Shanghai, and Guangzhou carried games.[89]

As early as 2002, the NBA partnered with Sohu, one of China's most used websites, to create an official site for its Chinese fans. This was the first NBA news website with all the content written and spoken in Chinese. By 2005, NBA.com's Chinese affiliate exceeded three million clicks per day. On September 18, 2005, the Chinese website Xinchuankuanpin began carrying live games. Two years later, Xinchuan Sport and Hulianxingkong, China's NBA website, published an NBA livestream channel. Sohu Inc., a Chinese internet company, began replaying games during the 2005–06 season. Sohu established a blueprint for livestreaming games that was adopted by Sina, Sky website, PPLIVE, and eventually Tencent. In 2015, Tencent introduced the mobile app Tencent Sport to carry games. Most Chinese NBA fans use Tencent for NBA streaming and social media participation. Tencent charges subscribers a monthly membership fee of 30 yuan ($12) and a yearly fee of 298 yuan ($42) to access all live games, skip ads, change camera angles, and participate in special fan events.[90]

Yao Ming's 2011 retirement did little to diminish Chinese interest in NBA basketball. The following year, regular-season games received their second-highest ratings, with 585 million viewers. In the United States, 12.4 million viewers watched the 2022 NBA Finals between the Golden State Warriors and the Boston Celtics. Those numbers increase significantly when the viewership in China and other parts of the world is considered. CCTV banned NBA games for 18 months after Morey's tweet. By 2022, the fans' viewership was still lower than before the ban, but it was finally nearing those pre–Morey numbers. Viewership for the first seven games broadcast by CCTV that season rose by 80 percent compared with the former season.[91]

The Redeem Team was treated like the 1992 Dream Team when it came to Beijing for the 2008 Olympics. Three hundred seventy-eight million viewers watched the team play the Chinese men's national basketball team. The fanfare for the team's marquee star, Kobe Bryant, rivaled that of Michael Jordan in Barcelona. "Kobe's celebrity in China was like Michael Jackson about to go on tour. A girl fainted right in front of us trying to get to Kobe," said Olympic team member Carlos Boozer.[92] "It was thousands of fans waiting at the hotel to take pictures of our bus because they knew Kobe Bryant was on the bus," said Olympian Dwight Howard.[93] When Kobe and his daughter Gigi tragically died in a 2020 helicopter accident, the outpouring of grief in China was momentous.[94]

Kobe was one of many American-born NBA players embraced by the Chinese. His 2008 Olympic teammate Dwyane Wade left Jordan Brand in 2012 to sign an eight-year, $10 million deal with Li-Ning, a Chinese sportswear and sports equipment company founded by Chinese Olympic gymnast Li Ning. Wade's signature sneaker, Way of Wade (WOW), grossed $8 million in 2016, equaling the revenue of Nike's popular Kyrie Irving sneaker at the time. Wade's oldest son, Zaire, who plays professionally for the Cape Town Tigers of the Basketball Africa League (BAL), was given his own sneaker, "The Li-Ning Son of Flash."[95] Klay Thompson, a shooting guard who played for the Golden State Warriors before being traded to the Dallas Mavericks, is one the latest NBA stars to sign with Li-Ning. Thompson originally signed an $80 million sneaker deal with the Chinese company Anta, the world's third-largest sports manufacturing company behind Adidas and Nike. Kyrie Irving signed a five-year deal with Anta in 2023 after leaving Nike. As for Thompson, he has become a folk hero in China since his first visit in June 2017. "China Klay" became a popular internet meme exhibiting his hilarious exploits abroad, such as missing slam dunks and losing arm wrestling contests to young female fans.[96]

No NBA player, except for Ming and Kobe, is as beloved in China as Stephon Marbury. The former Coney Island high school prodigy was one of the league's most talented and exhilarating point guards for a time in the late 1990s and early 2000s. Failed stints with the Knicks and Celtics, a sexual encounter with a Knicks female intern, and bizarre viral videos showing him eating Vaseline and crying in a suicidal state ended his NBA career prematurely. Attempting to rebrand his image and make a comeback, Marbury signed with the Shanxi Brave Dragons of the CBA in 2010. He played for the Foshan Dralions, the Beijing Ducks, and the Beijing Royal Fighters between 2010 and 2018. Marbury's CBA career far exceeded his NBA years. His teams won the CBA championship in 2012, 2014, and 2015. He was a three-time CBA All-Star, the 2013 league MVP, and the MVP of the 2015 championship. Marbury starred in a 2017 autobiographical film called *My Other Home*, which focused on his leading the Beijing Ducks to the first CBA title in 2012.[97] He has been the head coach of the Beijing Royal Fighters since 2019.

A life-size bronze statue of Marbury was erected in Beijing to celebrate the Ducks' championship. His enormous success proved that former NBA stars could extend their playing careers and discover a new fanbase in China. One of the first NBA players embraced by the Chinese was New York City point legend Earl "The Pearl" Monroe, also known on the playgrounds as "Black Jesus." Monroe traveled to China in 1984 with a group of NBA All-Stars for exhibition games serving as diplomacy. He developed a following in China. Dwight Howard, an eight-time All-Star and 2020 champion with the Lakers, signed with the Taoyuan Leopards of the Taiwanese Men's Professional Basketball League (T1 League) in 2022. Howard, a 2008 Redeem Team member, went to Taiwan with hopes of returning to the NBA one day. There probably will not be a bronze statue of Howard anytime soon. He sparked anger across China by referring to Taiwan as "a country" in a promotional video with Taiwan's vice president, William Lai. Within days, the hashtag #HowardTaiwanindependence received 400 million views on the Chinese microblogging site Weibo. Beijing views Taiwan as an illegitimate "breakaway province" that is part of China's territory. Taiwan established a rival government in Taipei after a 1949 civil war between communist and nationalist factions. The U.S. recognizes only China as a country. Howard issued a statement to curb the controversy. "If I offended anyone in China, I apologize. It was not my intention to harm anyone."[98]

CREAM (Cash Rules Everything Around Me)

The NBA's kowtowing to China in 2019 over Daryl Morey's Hong Kong tweet made the league, unofficially branded "the wokest" (socially conscious) professional sports league, look incredibly hypocritical. The NBA has been at the forefront of social activism since the 2010s. In 2012, LeBron and his Miami Heat teammates posed for a viral photo wearing hoodies as a sign of support for the family of Trayvon Martin, an innocent Black teenager slain by a neighborhood watch captain while wearing a hoodie. Two years later, the NBA made headlines after V. Stiviano, the younger mistress of Los Angeles Clippers governor Donald Sterling, leaked a secret recording of Sterling making racist comments. "There's no room for Donald Sterling in the NBA," LeBron told reporters. Clipper players removed their warm-up jerseys before a game, turned them inside out to cover up the team logo, and threw them down at the midcourt. Commissioner Silver eventually issued Sterling a lifetime ban.[99]

The universal protest against Donald Sterling reignited a spirit of social activism and political consciousness that had been missing since the 1970s, when, as Theresa Runstedtler says in her book *Black Ball: Kareem Abdul-Jabbar, Spencer Haywood, and the Generation that Saved the Soul of the NBA*, a new generation of Black NBA players symbolized Black Power in a post–civil rights America.[100] Kobe and LeBron were among the countless NBA players wearing black "I Can't Breathe" T-shirts during pregame warm-ups to support Eric Gardner, an unarmed Black man who died from a police chokehold.

A week before the 2016 ESPY Awards, ESPN's annual athletes awards ceremony, two Black men, Alton Sterling and Philando Castile, were fatally shot by police officers. Neither Sterling nor Castile was violently resisting arrest when they were shot. LeBron, Carmelo Anthony, Chris Paul, and Dwyane Wade used the opening minutes of the internationally televised sports awards ceremony to speak out against police brutality and gun violence in Black communities. Paul declared they were carrying the torch of past Black athletes like Arthur Ashe, Jim Brown, Jackie Robinson, and Muhammad Ali, who used their platforms to fight injustice.[101] Days later, Commissioner Silver pulled the 2016 All-Star Game out of Charlotte, North Carolina, to protest a state law eliminating protection for gay, lesbian, and transgender individuals from discriminatory policies.[102]

5. Hoops Diplomacy

For the next three years, it became commonplace to see NBA players supporting domestic social justice issues in postgame interviews, on social media, and through public service announcements. Some players, like Celtics All-Star Jaylen Brown, attended marches after George Floyd's death in 2020. Brown drove 15 hours from Boston to Atlanta for a march.[103] Players did not hide their ill feelings toward President Donald Trump and his MAGA movement. The Golden State Warriors players and their head coach, Steve Kerr, refused to visit the White House after clinching the NBA championship. Kerr and Gregg Popovich, head coach of the San Antonio Spurs, frequently excoriated Trump in the press. After LeBron accused Trump of "not giving a fuck about the people," Fox News Channel host Laura Ingraham told him to "shut up and dribble."[104] In other words, stick to sports. The NBA went out of its way to promote Black Lives Matter, social justice initiatives, HBCUs, and voter registration drives in minority communities during its Covid-19 "Bubble" season in 2020.[105]

Silver and league governors supported the outspokenness of their players and coaches on these domestic issues. Consequently, the NBA's silence and pussyfooting around the Hong Kong–China controversy was bitterly disappointing. The league had already been called out for establishing a developmental academy for aspiring young players in Xinjiang, China. An ESPN report revealed countless cases of abuse of kids at the academy.[106] Enes Kanter Freedom, a Turkish-American former center for the Celtics, offered to educate LeBron on China's human rights violations.[107] China has been a thorn in LeBron's side for over a decade. Nike and David Stern expected LeBron to be their ambassador in Beijing during the 2008 Olympics. Human rights advocates and socially conscious celebrities like George Clooney were boycotting the Olympics because of China's role in the government-backed militia slaughter of hundreds of thousands of non–Arab Africans in Darfur, Sudan. Additionally, two million refugees were forced into camps in neighboring Chad.[108]

China's hosting of the Olympics could be viewed as an example of sportswashing, which occurs when governments and corporations use sports for propaganda to cover up corruption. Hitler's 1936 Berlin games were the first example of sportswashing. Qatar's hosting of the 2022 FIFA World Cup is a contemporary example.[109] Smith College professor Eric Reeves dubbed the Beijing Games the Genocide Olympics. Reeves was one of the loudest advocates for the people of Darfur despite being confined to a hospital bed with leukemia. LeBron's Cleveland Cavaliers teammate Ira Newble learned of Reeves's protest and threw his full support behind it. Newble reached out to Reeves to ask how he could help. Jill Savitt, a colleague of Reeves, asked Newble to write a letter to the Chinese government and get all his teammates to sign it. LeBron, who was 22 then, told Newble he would consider adding his signature, but he eventually declined. Newble believes he refused because it would have had dire consequences for NBA partner Nike, which was heavily invested in the Olympics. When LeBron arrived in Beijing for the Olympics, he and Kobe were asked to comment on the Darfur crisis. Kobe, another Nike spokesman, avoided the question. LeBron's response was as follows: "Basic human rights should always be protected. One thing you can't do is confuse sports and politics." Team USA coach Mike Krzyzewski asked reporters to respect his players' unwillingness to discuss geopolitical issues unrelated to basketball.[110]

Globalization has had positive and negative effects on the NBA. In the case of Dennis Rodman and North Korea, globalization has heightened the importance of basketball diplomacy in foreign policy, whether government officials admit it or not. The NBA's support for Brittney Griner helped to spotlight the plight of Americans unjustly detained in Russia and other oppressive countries. Regrettably, the Hong Kong Twitter (X) controversy and the Beijing Olympics demonstrated how the league's international business dealings could force it to ignore social justice issues that it would presumably refuse to stand for if they occurred in America.[111] The league was criticized for hosting two 2023 preseason games in Abu Dhabi, the capital of the United Arab Emirates, where homosexuality and transgender lifestyles are punishable by imprisonment, fines, castration, and death.[112]

The NBA is not the only American sports league to choose commerce over conscience. The 2023 merger between the Professional Golf Association (PGA) Tour and LIV Golf, a rival golf association financed by Saudi Arabia's sovereign wealth fund, is the most recent jarring example. Critics have accused Saudi Arabia of sportswashing away its countless human rights violations and involvement in 9/11. Fifteen of the 19 hijackers were Saudi, and the country funded al-Qaeda.[113] Commissioner Silver refused to condemn the PGA during an interview with *The Dan Patrick Show* on June 8, 2023. Perhaps this is because, in 2022, the NBA became the first American sports league to allow foreign sovereign wealth funds to buy 20 percent stakes in a team. This decision means that Saudi Arabia could probably purchase an NBA franchise in the future.[114] On June 22, 2023, it was announced that Qatar's sovereign wealth fund purchased a 5 percent stake in Monumental Sports and Entertainment, the parent company of the Washington Wizards (NBA) and the Washington Mystics (WNBA).[115]

David Aldridge shared his thoughts on the NBA's involvement with China and other foreign countries accused of human rights violations.

> *I think you'd be hard-pressed to find another business in the world that doesn't have to face the same issue that the NBA is facing. The question is, are you going to single out the NBA for criticism, whether it is deserved or not? If you are going*

> to say the NBA is wrong for doing business with China, I just hope you are not doing that on a computer or a phone that was probably produced in China by cheap labor. I hope you never fly because almost every major airline in the world has backed China's version of what the world should be in terms of identifying China and not identifying Taiwan. I hope you don't buy shoes or wear athletic shoes because they were probably made by Chinese people who receive less than a living wage. My point is we are all hypocrites on this. If you want to kill the NBA, you're entitled to it but look in the mirror because you are contributing to it by living in a consumer society.[116]
>
> I don't like sportswashing. I think it is terrible to take money from countries in which journalists were murdered. Golfers took the money. Ted Leonsis took the money.... I want to protest it. I think it's bad, but I think it's unrealistic to expect the NBA to be the one business in the world to stand on principle. Until Hollywood stops changing the plots of movies to be more sympathetic to China—then you cannot single the NBA out.[117]

Aldridge also had a message for public officials chastising NBA players for having sneaker deals with companies like Nike that do business with China.

> I remember Rick Scott, the senator from Florida, was one of the people criticizing LeBron. Rick Scott took money from a Chinese company during his campaign. What are we talking about? They were a Florida-based company, but their ownership was Chinese. When you say [LeBron's] wrong for doing this, and you are not looking at yourself, then I have a problem with that. I think it's a bit hypocritical.

The NBA is in a precarious position as a global brand. As new global conflicts and controversies arise, players and coaches will continue to find themselves on a proverbial hot seat. The most recent is the ongoing Israel-Hamas war between Israel and Hamas-led Palestinian militants from the Gaza Strip. The Minnesota Timberwolves played a preseason game against Maccabi Ra'nana from Israel 10 days after Hamas killed more than 1,400 Israelis and kidnapped 240 hostages in the surprise attack that launched the war. Maccabi players had "I Stand with Israel" written on their sneakers and the faces of hostages on their warm-up T-shirts. Timberwolves head coach Chris Finch shared his thoughts about the conflict and revealed his connection to Israel during a postgame interview.[118]

Coach Finch drew little fanfare for his comment; however, that was not the case for LeBron James. After LeBron tweeted support for Israel, the internet "came for him." Several social media users called out LeBron for siding with Israel rather than Palestine. "What part in Malcolm's autobiography told you it's okay to support oppression?"

That post referred to Malcolm X's support of Palestinians who felt oppressed and colonized since the State of Israel was established in 1948.

Danyel Reiche, a visiting professor at Georgetown University in Qatar, notes that a double standard exists in professional sports concerning public support for Israel or Palestine.[119] Historically, it has been safer for professional athletes to be pro–Israel. However, the war has caused many young people around the world, the NBA's target audience, to raise their voices in defense of Palestine.

It is not necessary for NBA players, coaches, or governors to speak on every domestic social and political issue, especially if they have limited knowledge of the subject. I feel the same way about events happening overseas. My doctorate in history does not qualify me to be an expert on every topic. Nor does making millions for dribbling a basketball qualify LeBron or any other player to speak on events in Asia or the Middle East. But if they share their opinions or make nonverbal gestures, they better be prepared for the backlash.

6

The Air Up There

> "...there's more Africans in the league.... It's more Africans in front offices and coaching. It's what Adam [Silver] is preaching on developing the game in Africa.... The next step for me is how do we form leagues? How do we build more facilities on the continent?"
>
> —Masai Ujiri[1]

The NBA's All-Star weekend has been one of my favorite pastimes since I was a kid in middle school. The event occurs every year in mid-February during the Presidents Day weekend. The weekend's current highlights include a celebrity game, a rising stars game, a three-point shooting contest, community service activities, an NBA Legends Brunch, the commissioner's State of the League address, a slam dunk contest, and the actual game. A who's who of celebrities typically sit courtside at the marquee events. The 2023 festivities were held in Salt Lake City, Utah, home of the Jazz. Despite an all-time outstanding performance by Mac McClung, an unknown 6'2" American White player from the Philadelphia 76ers, in the dunk contest and heartfelt reflections for the late Bill Russell at the Legends Brunch, the weekend was panned by most critics and sports talk show hosts. The lack of defense and effort exhibited by multiple players in Sunday night's 184–175 All-Star Game had the talking heads ready to abolish the weekend permanently.

While I am biased when it comes to All-Star weekend, the one thing the naysayers failed to recognize was the halftime show. Music has been integral to the NBA and this weekend since the 1976 ABA merger. Marvin Gaye's soulful rendition of "The Star-Spangled Banner" at the 1983 All-Star Game inspired Whitney Houston's timeless national anthem at Super Bowl XXV. Gaye's anthem was also the theme song for the 2008 Redeem Team at the Beijing Olympics. In 2011, 24-year-old Rihanna, just entering her prime, headlined an amazing All-Star Game halftime concert that featured unforgettable cameos from Drake and Kanye West (Ye). Three years later, in New Orleans, Earth, Wind & Fire; Janelle Monae; and

Trombone Shorty brought funk, soul, and jazz to television viewers worldwide. Music and fashion icon Pharrell Williams was also present to perform during the player introductions before the game. The 2023 All-Star halftime show may have been the most culturally significant musical performance in NBA history.

Pascal Siakam, a native of Cameroon and the Indiana Pacers All-Star power forward, introduced the evening's three performers. "Ladies and gentlemen, I am about to take you on a journey through Africa without even going on a plane," declared the first performer, Burna Boy (Damini Ebunoluwa Ogulu), one of the most popular artists in the world. Since his 2012 debut, the Nigerian performer has released multiple international hits and won the 2021 Grammy Award for Best World Music Album. His style combines Afrobeat, reggae, dancehall, and pop. Burna Boy is responsible for making Afrobeat a large part of today's mainstream pop music and hip-hop. Afrobeat, also known as Afro-pop, is a music genre that originated in Nigeria, Ghana, and the United Kingdom in the 2000s and 2010s.

Burna Boy performed his hits "It's Plenty" and "Alone" before passing the mic to fellow Nigerian Afrobeat singer and rapper Rema (Divine Ikubor). The 24-year-old rising star caught the world's attention with his 2022 single "Calm Down." The song's remix featuring Selena Gomez reached fourth place on the *Billboard* Hot 100 and was atop the U.S. Afrobeat Songs chart for 35 weeks. Rema, accompanied by a live band, singers, and dancers, performed "Calm Down" and his song "Holiday." The third performer was the marvelous Tems (Temilade Openiyi), a 28-year-old Nigerian Afrobeat and R&B singer who rose to prominence in 2020 with her duet on Wizkid's *Billboard* Hot 100 hit single "Essence." In addition to her Grammy for covering Bob Marley's "No Woman, No Cry," she received an Academy Award nomination for writing Rihanna's "Lift Me Up" for the *Black Panther: Wakanda Forever* soundtrack. Tems performed a medley including "Essence," "Free Mind," "Crazy Things," and "Higher," which was sampled by Future and Drake on their number-one *Billboard* single "Wait for U." Burna Boy ended the concert with his addictive dance track "Last Last."

During the 15-minute halftime performance, fans danced in front of the stage, waving green-and-white Nigerian flags. NBA all-stars Siakam, Edrice Femi "Bam" Adebayo, Giannis Antetokounmpo, and his brother Thanasis, who was not an All-Star, were on the floor dancing along with the fans.[2] Siakam danced to the soulful rhythms as he recorded the concert with his handheld camcorder. This was the first time any American professional sports league featured only African halftime performers for a major televised event. It was no coincidence that the cameras zoomed in on players who were either born in Africa or had African parents enjoying the concert. This historic moment epitomized the late Commissioner Stern's dream of globalization and the NBA's growing commitment to Africa.[3]

The NBA is invested in Africa in ways not seen in Europe or Asia. The league has established programs and academies on the continent to develop youth who dream of playing for American universities and in the NBA. In 2021, the NBA launched the Basketball Africa League (BAL), a joint effort between the league and FIBA with sponsorship from American corporations such as Nike, Pepsi, and Jordan Brand. ESPN and NBA TV provide television coverage of BAL games. While I genuinely want to root for the NBA's involvement in Africa, I wrestle with these questions: How much does Africa have to gain from this relationship? Are American corporations using basketball to attract new consumers and exploit Africa's resources—in this case, young athletic Black bodies—in the same vein as China exploiting the continent's other resources? This chapter will analyze these questions while spotlighting significant African NBA players and the evolution of the NBA on the continent.

Freaks Come Out at Night

As discussed in Chapter 4, the 2022–23 MVP competition was contentious. The three finalists were Serbian center Nikola Jokić, the media's pick for much of the season; African center Joel Embiid; and Giannis Antetokounmpo, who represents both Europe and Africa. Giannis's rise from obscurity to NBA stardom is something out of a Disney movie. In fact, Disney+ began streaming *Rise*, a biopic about him and his brothers Thanasis and Kostas, in 2022. Giannis is the son of Nigerians Charles and Veronica Antetokounmpo. His mother is Igbo, while his father is Yoruba. According to Dr. Chima J. Korieh, professor of African history at Marquette University, life in Nigeria from the 1980s to 1990s was extremely difficult due to an oil spillage that polluted the water and spread disease. Families were forced to seek better living conditions and work opportunities in Europe and overseas. In 1990, his parents left Lagos in search of opportunity in Greece.[4] They left their eldest son, Francis, in Nigeria with his grandmother. While in Greece, Charles and Veronica added four sons to the family: Thanasis, Giannis, Kostas, and Alexandros. All four of their boys would eventually play in the NBA. Francis, who reunited with the family in 2017, is currently a professional rapper in Greece.[5]

Giannis was born in Athens on December 6, 1994. His original surname, Adétòkunbọ̀, which means "the crown that returns from overseas" in Yoruba, was changed to Αντετοκούνμπο, the Greek transcription of Adetokunbo. It was then transliterated letter for letter and officially spelled on his Greek passport as Antetokounmpo. Neither Giannis nor his younger brothers were born with Greek citizenship due to nationality laws. In Greece, citizenship is determined by *jus sanguinis*, meaning citizenship is based on the parents' nationality.

When the Antetokounmpo family arrived in Greece, the country was dealing with rising immigration and bankruptcy. Natives often scapegoated these foreign newcomers for their financial problems. An extreme nationalist group called the Golden Dawn, masquerading as a political party with connections to Nazism, would routinely harass and assault immigrants in the streets and at the subway station.[6] Giannis and his brothers had to run home at night to avoid being attacked. "I was scared as fuck," said Giannis.[7] Scholar W.E.B. Du Bois famously said Black Americans experienced a double consciousness. They were torn between identifying as American and Black people of African roots. Growing up, Giannis often experienced a double consciousness of sorts. He was a man without a country because he grew up in Greece but did not have citizenship. At times, he felt like an outsider in Athens as a young Black boy in a predominantly White environment. Yet, he did not feel wholly Nigerian either because he never traveled to Africa or spoke his parents' native Yoruba and Igbo languages. He gained Greek citizenship in 2013 and received dual citizenship in Greece and Nigeria two years later.[8]

Giannis and his brothers were born on the lowest rung of Greek society. They lived in a tiny two-room apartment, sleeping three or four people in a bed, with barely enough food to keep their bellies full. His parents, Charles and Veronica, could not find steady work because they lacked immigration papers. As a result, the entire family lived in the shadows of the economy, pedaling sunglasses, watches, CDs, DVDs, and trinkets, hoping to make a measly $30 for the day, with the threat of incarceration always omnipresent.[9] When the boys were not outside hustling or at school, they were playing basketball at a local outdoor court. Eventually, Giannis and his brothers Thanasis and Kostas began walking five miles to play at the Filathlitikos gymnasium. They slept at the gym many nights rather than make that long trek back home. One day, Georgios Panou, a Greek sports agent, discovered Giannis playing at the gym. Giannis was a skinny 6'6" 15-year-old at the time. Panou videotaped him and sent the grainy footage to Alex Saratsis, his Greek business partner in America. Panou immediately recognized the youngster's potential and convinced his parents to adjust the boys' diets so they could gain more weight.[10]

In 2011, Giannis joined the senior men's team of Filathlitikos in the semipro Greek B Basket League. The following year, he signed a deal with the Spanish club CAL Zaragoza. The contract was for four years but included NBA buyouts at the end of each season so he could be drafted. That summer, Panou invited Jonathan Givony, ESPN's draft analyst, to Greece to watch Giannis play. According to Givony, European players at that time were typically discovered by NBA scouts through play in FIBA tournaments, the Nike Hoops Summit, or the NCAA. Giannis was not afforded any of those opportunities due to his lack of citizenship and a passport. Givony was impressed and began reporting about him. By 2013, Giannis's other agent, Saratsis, who worked at the Chicago office of the global sports agency Octagon, started receiving calls from six NBA scouts. Saratsis had less faith in Giannis's ability to make the NBA than Panou until that moment. He decided to fly to Greece to see what all the buzz was about.[11]

Giannis grew up playing the forward position due to his size, but he modeled his game after the speedy point guard Allen Iverson. He often mimicked Iverson's "killer crossover" move in games. Giannis admired Iverson so much that he cornrowed his hair just like him. His parents could not afford cable television, so he would pay $1 to watch highlights of Iverson and other NBA players for an hour at an internet café. Giannis says he made playing in the NBA his goal after he googled Kobe Bryant's salary and discovered that basketball paid enough to lift his family from poverty.[12] He did not officially meet Saratsis until the night before the 2013 NBA draft, and it was a struggle for Saratsis to convince him to fly to Brooklyn for the ceremony. For Giannis, this was only his second time leaving Greece, and he felt uncomfortable traveling without his family. He made the trip only because Saratsis was able to secure travel accommodations for Thanasis to accompany him.[13]

Giannis was still unknown to most American basketball fans when the Milwaukee Bucks drafted him with the 15th overall pick. Sports announcers and fans began referring to him as "The Greek Freak" because they could not pronounce his name. The 18-year-old rookie, who did not look a day over 14, averaged a modest 6.8 points and 4.4 rebounds. Giannis contemplated quitting and returning home because his family was denied visas three times before the Bucks' owner, Senator Herbert Kohl, reached out to Massachusetts senator and 2004 presidential nominee John Kerry to arrange for them to enter America. By his third season, Giannis quickly emerged as one of the league's most promising young talents. He signed a four-year, $100 million contract extension with the Bucks at the start of his fourth season. A sneaker deal with Nike came the next season, quite a feat for a young man who grew up sharing holey shoes with his brothers.

Giannis started in his first All-Star Game and was awarded Most Improved Player honors in 2016–17. First-team All-NBA honors and back-to-back league MVP awards soon followed. Before long, Giannis transformed the Bucks into perennial championship contenders. Thanasis, drafted by the Knicks in 2014, joined him in Milwaukee in 2019. After disappointing playoff eliminations between 2018 and 2020, the Bucks defeated the Phoenix Suns in the 2021 NBA Finals. Giannis was named finals MVP despite being hampered by a knee injury sustained in the Eastern Conference finals. He recorded 50 points, 14 rebounds, and five blocks in the series-clinching game-six victory. He celebrated by placing a 50-piece order of chicken nuggets at a Chick-fil-A drive-through window.[14] Giannis became the second player of Nigerian descent, after Hakeem Olajuwon, to win a league and finals MVP. He and Thanasis captured their championship rings a year after their brother Kostas won his ring with the Lakers.

The Bucks' success has boosted Milwaukee's economy. New apartments and restaurants have been constructed near the team's new $524 million Wisconsin Entertainment and Sports Center, which seats 17,000 fans. Saratsis calls it "the Giannis Effect." The Bucks clinched the top seed in the Eastern Conference in 2022–23 but were upset by Jimmy Butler and the miraculous Miami Heat in the first round of the playoffs. Despite having another brilliant season that rivaled his MVP years, Giannis finished third in MVP voting behind the runner-up Nikola Jokić and the winner Joel Embiid. In 2023, Giannis and his family launched the Charles Antetokounmpo Family Foundation (CAFF) in honor of his late father, who passed in 2017, to uplift immigrants in Greece and Nigeria.[15]

Joel Embiid is one of the ten best basketball players in the world. Philadelphia fans may argue that he is the world's best player. The 7'0", 280-pound center was born in Yaounde, Cameroon, on March 16, 1994. The son of a military officer, he grew up in a financially stable household. His family did not suffer the economic struggles experienced by the Antetokounmpos. As a child, he played soccer and dreamed of becoming a professional volleyball player in Europe. If sports did not work out, he wanted to be an astronaut. Embiid did not begin taking basketball seriously until he was 15. He fell in love with the game after watching the Lakers defeat the Celtics in the 2010 NBA Finals. Kobe Bryant, who clinched his fifth and final championship in that series, became his favorite player. Like Giannis, he was *discovered* by an older gentleman who also recognized his talent at a young age. Embiid attended a camp in Cameroon hosted by Luc Mbah a Moute. Embiid says he nearly missed this opportunity because he skipped the first day of camp. He did not believe he was good enough to compete because he lacked the experience of the other campers. Nevertheless, his raw talent was enough to capture Moute's attention. He was one of five boys selected to attend a more elite instructional camp called Basketball Without Borders in South Africa during the summer of 2011.[16]

Mbah a Moute migrated to the U.S. in 2001 to play high school and college basketball. He became the second player from Cameroon to earn a spot on an NBA roster when the Bucks drafted him in 2008.[17] Moute played with eight NBA teams between 2008 and 2020 before becoming a sports agent, with a focus on African talent, for Creative Artists Agency (CAA). He began mentoring Embiid and Pascal Siakam. He moved Embiid to the U.S. when he was 16 and enrolled him in his alma mater, Montverde Academy in Montverde, Florida.[18] After his first year, Embiid transferred to The Rock School in Gainesville, Florida. The team finished 33–4, winning a state championship in his senior year.

Embiid's collegiate career was short-lived. He declared for the NBA draft after one season at the University of Kansas, where he averaged 11.2 points and 8.1 rebounds. A debilitating stress fracture in his back caused him to slide in the 2014 draft. The Philadelphia 76ers chose him with the third pick, two spots behind his Kansas freshman teammate Andrew Wiggins from Canada. A broken navicular bone sidelined Embiid his first two seasons in Philadelphia. The Sixers selected Australian point guard Ben Simmons with the top draft pick in 2016. Simmons was projected to be the closest thing to LeBron James coming out of high school at Montverde Academy. Philadelphia general manager Sam Hinkie told fans to "trust the process" as they waited patiently for Embiid and Simmons to become Generation Z's version of Kobe and Shaq.[19]

Embiid finally made his long-awaited NBA debut on October 4, 2016, in a preseason game against the Celtics. An impressive first season resulted in a spot on the All-Rookie First Team. The next season, he became Philadelphia's first player since Allen Iverson to start in the All-Star Game. His elevated play caused the Sixers to sign him to a five-year, $148 million extension and raised the hopes of faithful Sixers fans seeking their first championship since 1983. The Sixers appeared poised to reach the NBA Finals in 2019. They took the Toronto Raptors to a decisive seventh game in the Eastern Conference semifinals. With the score tied at 90 and 4.2 seconds left to play, Kawhi Leonard dribbled the basketball to the far-right corner of the court and sank a series-ending three-point buzzer-beater. The two most memorable images from that frantic scene were Leonard falling into his teammate's arms in euphoric celebration and a tearful Embiid falling into his teammate's arms in agony. Two years later, Trae Young's upstart Atlanta Hawks squad robbed basketball fans of an anticipated conference finals matchup between Embiid and Giannis. Embiid's postgame comments about Simmons's lack of aggression permanently severed ties between the two All-Stars, who were seldom on good terms. The Sixers traded the disgruntled Aussie point guard, who missed all of 2021–22 with injuries and mental health issues, for James Harden the following season.

In the early years of his career, retired NBA players like Shaquille O'Neal and Charles Barkley criticized Embiid for being "too soft" on the court and not keeping his body in proper condition. By the start of the 2021–22 season, Embiid appeared to have heeded their advice. With Simmons away from the team, he fully embraced being the Sixers' alpha and omega. He won the first of two consecutive scoring titles, averaging 30.6 points per game. He was the first center since O'Neal to win the award and the first international player to receive that honor. He finished second to Jokić in MVP voting. The 2022–23 season was the best of his career. He challenged Jokić the entire season for MVP honors. In their only meeting, Embiid had 47 points, 18 rebounds, five assists, three steals, and two blocked shots. Most importantly, the Sixers defeated the Denver Nuggets 126–119.

As the regular season neared an end, ESPN basketball analysts Kendrick Perkins and JJ Redick helped launch a national debate about how race and ethnicity factored into whom voters would crown MVP. Embiid is Black and African. Jokić is White and European. After Embiid won the award, Andrew Lawrence published an article for *The Guardian* titled "Joel Embiid: the star who toppled critics and implicit bias to win NBA MVP."[20] Unfortunately, another second-round playoff loss, poor performances from Embiid and Harden, and Jokić's brilliance throughout the NBA Finals had many NBA analysts and fans on social media arguing that Embiid won his MVP only because of the controversy. Harden demanded and was granted a trade to the Clippers a week into the next season.

I Have a Dream

Joel Embiid modeled his game after Hakeem "The Dream" Olajuwon, the first African player drafted into the NBA.[21] The Houston Rockets made Olajuwon the first overall pick in a watershed 1984 draft class that included Charles Barkley, John Stockton, Oscar Schmidt, and a guy named Jordan. *USA Today* listed Olajuwon's black tuxedo and skinny red bow tie among the worst draft night outfits in NBA history. What he lacked in style he made up for on the court, leading the Rockets to back-to-back NBA championships in 1994 and 1995. His Rockets, nicknamed "Clutch City" for their ability to prevail when the odds were stacked against them, interrupted the Bulls' dynastic run of the nineties. The 12-time All-Star capped off an 18-year NBA career with a first-ballot Hall of Fame induction in 2008.

Akeem Olajuwon was born in Lagos, Nigeria, on January 21, 1963, the third eldest of his parents' eight children. He changed his name to Hakeem in 1991 after recommitting to his Islamic faith and becoming a devout

Muslim. Playing professional basketball was not a realistic dream for Nigerian boys when Olajuwon was coming of age. He played handball and excelled at soccer, playing the goaltender position. The speed, agility, and excellent footwork Olajuwon developed on the soccer field were a godsend when he shifted his focus to basketball. While the average NBA center in the 1980s and 1990s was slow and lumbering, he moved like a ballerina in the post, dizzying defenders with his fancy footwork and patented move, the Dream Shake.[22] With this move, he could catch the ball with his back to the basket, fake his defender in one direction, and then gracefully pivot in the opposite direction to score. He could also beat defenders with crossover dribbles and midrange jump shots.

Olajuwon began playing basketball when he was a 15-year-old student at Moslem Teachers College, a high school in Lagos. A basketball coach told him to stand in the middle of the court and block every shot that entered his airspace. He joined the Nigerian national basketball team and competed in the 1980 All-Africa Games.[23] A year later, Chris Pond, an American who coached a Central African Republic team, arranged for Olajuwon to take a college recruiting trip in the U.S. He visited Georgia Tech, Providence University, Oregon State University, the University of Houston, and St. John's University. His first stop was in New York City. When he arrived at the John F. Kennedy International Airport, the recruiter from St. John's that he was expecting to meet was absent. He had three other plane tickets in his bag for his exhibition. The weather in Queens, New York, was freezing that day. Once he stepped outside, a strong gust of cold wind slapped him in the face. He immediately went back inside the airport terminal, where he spotted a Nigerian baggage handler working. He asked the man which of his remaining destinations had weather akin to home. Houston, Texas, was his reply.[24] Mirin Fader, author of *Dream*, a 2024 biography on Olajuwon, says this never happened. Pond never had ties to Olajuwon, and he was always scheduled to visit the University of Houston. Fader says this myth has existed for years and was never debunked.[25]

Olajuwon's skills were unpolished coming out of Africa. "He didn't know how to post up. He had no power move to the basket; he had no turnaround shot. He could jump, but he didn't know when to jump or where to jump," said coach Lewis.[26] Nevertheless, Olajuwon was 7'0" and demonstrated enough potential for Lewis to take a chance on him. His parents did not have dreams of their son becoming a millionaire by playing American basketball. They wanted him to pursue a business degree and return home to run their cement company. "People in Nigeria dream of going to America to go to school. My parents don't know nothing about basketball. On the telephone, I talk to them only of education," said Olajuwon.[27]

The University of Houston Cougars were on the verge of competing with the blue bloods of college hoops when Olajuwon arrived. Coach Lewis made waves in the sixties when he signed Elvin Hayes and Don Chaney, the first Blacks to play at a Division 1 college in Texas. On January 20, 1968, the Cougars snapped UCLA's 27-game winning streak. The game, featuring future NBA legends Elvin Hayes and Lew Alcindor (Kareem Abdul-Jabbar), was played at the Astrodome, the first college game ever held in a dome. By the 1970s and early 1980s, critics accused Lewis of recruiting undisciplined players who played "streetball" and lacked defense. This was coded language for Black players. Olajuwon redshirted his freshman year because of a clearance issue with the NCAA. He joined the team as a sophomore in the 1981–82 season, although he was still considered a freshman based on his athletic eligibility, averaging 8.3 points, 6.2 rebounds, and 2.5 blocks off the bench. Houston reached the Final Four, losing in the semifinals to Michael Jordan and the eventual champion North Carolina Tarheels.

Olajuwon emerged as one of the best players in the country during his junior and senior seasons, to everyone's surprise. He had spent the summer training with Houston Rockets All-Star center Moses Malone. This tutelage was instrumental in his growth. Olajuwon anchored a team loaded with talent. Clyde Drexler, a future NBA Hall-of-Famer and member of the Dream Team, and the high-flying Benny Anders were the team's starting backcourt. In January 1983, Thomas Bonk, a reporter for the *Houston Post*, nicknamed the Cougars "Phi Slamma Jamma," college basketball's dunking fraternity, after witnessing them throw down 10 rim-rattling dunks in a 50-point blowout of Pacific University. A local disc jockey named DJ Captain Jack wrote a rap to honor the team, which became a regional anthem. Radio stations were playing the song four times an hour. The Cougars dunked the ball the way teams shoot three-pointers today. Ironically, a dunk at the buzzer allowed the underdog North Carolina State University Wolfpack to prevail over Houston in the 1983 national championship.[28] They lost to Georgetown in the 1984 national championship. Despite the loss, Olajuwon outplayed Final Four Most Outstanding Player award recipient Patrick Ewing, Georgetown's All-American center from Jamaica. He turned pro nearly three months later.[29]

Olajuwon was paired with the Rockets' promising young center Ralph Sampson at the start of his NBA career. The two seven-footers were dubbed "the Twin Towers." The Rockets defeated the defending champion Lakers in the Western Conference finals to play the Celtics for the NBA title in 1986. The Celtics, with five future Hall-of-Famers on their roster, won the series in six games. Sampson was traded to Golden State 19 games into the 1987–88 season. The once-promising Rockets struggled to win for the next few years. Olajuwon feuded with team management, coaches, and teammates. He says he was an angry young man until he rededicated his life to Allah.[30]

Michael Jordan's abrupt retirement to play baseball in October 1993 left a void in the NBA that Olajuwon and the Rockets filled. While MJ was chasing fastballs, Olajuwon won league MVP and became the world's best player. The Rockets beat the Knicks in seven grueling games in the NBA Finals. Olajuwon squared off with Ewing again for a championship. He was the victor this time when the confetti fell from the sky. He outplayed the 1994–95 MVP David Robinson in the next year's playoffs on his way to face a 23-year-old Shaquille O'Neal in the NBA Finals. The Rockets swept O'Neal's youthful Orlando Magic in four games to repeat as champions. Olajuwon won his second finals MVP award.[31]

The Rockets failed to win a third championship despite acquiring Charles Barkley and Scottie Pippen in 1998. Houston traded Olajuwon to Toronto for his final season in 2001–02. The Rockets drafted the Chinese center Yao Ming the following season. Olajuwon retired as one of the league's 10 greatest centers. In the summers of his postretirement years, he trained contemporary stars, notably Kobe and LeBron, in post moves and playing with their back to the basket. Gilbert Arenas created a buzz on his podcast by irreverently mocking the Dream for charging Giannis $50,000 to train with him. Ironically, Olajuwon does not have much of a relationship with Embiid. In a *Sports Illustrated* interview published on January 18, 2023, he praised Jokić and displayed faint enthusiasm for his fellow African. "He's got all the moves, but leveraging the moves is different. Why would he be shooting threes? [Shooting threes is] settling! You don't settle when you're trying to win."[32] Embiid responded to Olajuwon's critique:

> It's funny when you've got these old guys always talking about posting up, "you need to spend time in the paint," and all that stuff. You can't win this way anymore. It's not the fricking '90s or '80s like it used to be. So, they must not have any basketball IQ.[33]

Olajuwon was named the NBA's Ambassador to Africa in 2014. His job was to promote the development of basketball on the continent.[34] When he delivered his Naismith Memorial Basketball Hall of Fame acceptance speech in September 2008, he touched on the NBA's role in globalization.

> The NBA promotes the game on a global level. The last 15 years, I've seen the NBA grow tremendously where everywhere I travel, you see all the jerseys of the different teams everywhere in the world. The NBA is doing a fantastic job. Thank David Stern for his global vision and what he has accomplished.[35]

New Kids on the Block

Hakeem Olajuwon's success opened the door for other Africans entering the league in the 1980s and early 1990s. Manute Bol was the next to make an NBA roster. The 7'7" center shared the record for the tallest player in NBA history with former center Gheorghe Muresan, a Romanian. Bol's family, members of the Dinka tribe, was blessed with tall genes. His father and mother stood 6'8" and 6'10", respectively. His sister was 6'8". They were actually considered short compared with his great-grandfather, who stood 7'10". Bol looked like an oversize marathon runner due to his slim, barely 200-pound frame. He was born in South Sudan on October 16, 1962. Like Olajuwon, he grew up playing soccer, but his unstoppable growth spurt forced him to quit at 15 and try basketball. In 1982, Don Feeley, the former head coach at Fairleigh Dickinson University in New Jersey, was in Sudan holding basketball clinics for the country's national team when he met Bol. Feeley was responsible for Bol migrating to America to play college basketball.[36]

Bol attempted to enroll in Cleveland State University in Ohio but encountered numerous dilemmas. First, he could not provide his coach, Kevin Mackey, with a birth certificate. The university believed Bot was much older than the age listed. He could not speak or write English. Bol took classes at the Case Western Reserve University ESL Language Center to correct this deficiency; however, his English needed to be stronger to meet the university's standards.[37] Without ever suiting up for a game at Cleveland State, he declared for the 1983 draft. The San Diego Clippers drafted him with the 97th pick, a year before the Rockets selected Olajuwon. Once again, Bol encountered roadblocks concerning his eligibility. His passport listed him as being 19 years old and 5'2". The Clippers drafted him despite concerns about the language barrier because their coach, Jim Lynam, had a relationship with Don Feeley. However, the NBA ruled that he was ineligible to play because he missed the deadline to declare for the draft.[38]

Bol's unresolved eligibility issues prevented him from playing at another Division 1 college. He settled for admission to the University of Bridgeport, a Division II school in Connecticut noted for its strong English as a Second Language (ESL) program. After his first year at Bridgeport, Bol signed a contract to play with the Rhode Island Gulls of the United States Basketball League before declaring for the 1985 draft. Even though most scouts doubted he was ready, he needed the money to help his sister leave Sudan. The Washington Bullets drafted him in the second round. Two years later, Washington drafted Wake Forest University's 5'3" point guard, Tyrone "Mugsy" Bogues, the shortest man in the history of the NBA. The visually awkward pairing of Bol and Bogues made Washington more of a sideshow than a title contender. Bol's career spanned a decade with the Bullets, 76ers, Heat, and Warriors.[39]

Manute Bol's legacy will be his humanitarian efforts off the court. He regularly visited Sudanese refugee camps and founded the Ring True Foundation to raise money for refugees. He donated $3.5 million, most of his earnings, to help the cause. In 2002, Bol agreed to fight retired NFL player William "The Refrigerator" Perry on the Fox network's *Celebrity Boxing* series after the network agreed to display his foundation's phone number to take donations during the broadcast. Sadly, Bol resorted to other confounding stunts like this to secure money for Sudan. He signed a single-day contract with the Indianapolis Ice of the Central Hockey League and worked as a horse jockey for a day. In 2006, he participated in a three-week march from the headquarters of the United Nations in New York to the U.S. Capitol in Washington, D.C., to raise awareness about the genocide in Darfur.[40]

In 2002, the Sudanese government accused Bol of supporting the rebellious Sudan People's Liberation Army. The government would give him an exit visa only if he paid them. U.S. Senator Joseph Lieberman raised money to fly Bol and his family to Cairo, Egypt. The Bols remained in Egypt for six months until U.S. consulate officials granted them religious refugee status, allowing them to return to America.[41] Bol sacrificed his freedom, money, and life to improve his homeland's conditions. During a humanitarian trip, he contracted Stevens-Johnson syndrome, an allergic reaction to the drugs he needed to battle a kidney disease. Bol died from kidney failure on June 19, 2010, in Charlottesville, Virginia, and was laid to rest in Sudan. Sam Mellinger wrote the following in the *Kansas City Star* before he passed:

> Bol spent his entire basketball fortune and survived attacks on his life to save and improve lives in and around Sudan. He lost hundreds of family members in an ongoing war but saved or educated at least that many with peacemaking efforts that one author compared to Muhammad Ali.
>
> Ali is a legend, of course, while Bol is, at best, a cult hero and, at worst, a freak show. Maybe if Bol were a better player, we'd pay more attention. Maybe if he were doing his good deeds closer to *our* home instead of his, we'd help him more.[42]

Manute Bol is survived by 10 children from two marriages. His son Bol Bol was drafted by the Miami Heat in 2019. The Heat traded him to Denver on draft night. He currently plays for the Phoenix Suns. Manute Bol set a standard for humanitarian work that other African NBA players have followed. Four of those players are Dikembe Mutombo, Serge Ibaka, Pascal Siakam, and Bismack Biyombo.

Dikembe Mutombo Mpolondo Mukamba Jean-Jacques Wamutombo is a native of Kinshasa, Zaire (today the Democratic Republic of the Congo). He was attending a Jesuit-run Catholic high school and playing for Zaire's junior national basketball team when Herman Henning, a U.S. development officer, sent video footage of him playing to Georgetown, a Jesuit-run Catholic university in Washington, D.C. Mutombo received a USAID scholarship to attend Georgetown. He intended to study medicine and become a doctor. But John Thompson, the men's head basketball coach, had other plans for him. Thompson had a reputation for honing the skills of talented centers dating back to Patrick Ewing in the eighties and his predecessors in the seventies. The 7'2" Mutombo was paired alongside future NBA Hall-of-Famer Alonzo Mourning in Georgetown's frontcourt. Like Bol, he had to enroll in an ESL program to learn English. Mutombo made the best of his opportunities at Georgetown. He interned for the World Bank and the U.S. Congress during his summers. He graduated in 1991 with a bachelor's degree in linguistics and diplomacy.

The Denver Nuggets selected Mutombo as the fourth pick in the 1991 draft. He played 17 seasons in the NBA, scoring over 11,000 points and rebounds. The eight-time All-Star was a four-time winner of the Defensive Player of the Year award. He finished his career with the second most blocked shots in NBA history. His signature move was blocking an opponent's shot and waving his long, thin finger in his face. "No, No, No," he would say in his distinctive voice, reminiscent of *Sesame Street*'s Cookie Monster. 1994—when the Nuggets eliminated the 63–19 Seattle SuperSonics in the playoffs—was the first time an eighth seed upset a one seed in the NBA playoffs. Mutombo clinched the victory by lying on his back in the middle of the court and holding the ball over his head in unbridled jubilation. After spending the first decade of his career in Denver and Atlanta, he was traded to Philadelphia in the middle of the 2000–2001 season. With Mutombo and fellow Georgetown alumnus Allen Iverson, Philadelphia reached the NBA Finals, where Shaq and Kobe's Lakers defeated them.

Mutombo played his final five seasons alongside Chinese center Yao Ming in Houston. He was a member of the 2015 Hall of Fame class. Coach Thompson and NBA commissioner David Stern welcomed him into the Hall and sat on the stage as he delivered his acceptance speech. Mutombo recognized Stern for the NBA's commitment to improving conditions worldwide. He recognized retired players such as Olajuwon and current players traveling to South Africa to spread the game. "My life mission is to continue to change the living conditions of the people in Africa. I might not have won the championship, but I am a champion to so many people home," he stated in his final remarks.[43] Like Bol, Mutombo's legacy is his humanitarian work. He donated $10 million and oversaw the construction of a 300-bed hospital named in honor of his late mother, Biamba Marie Mutombo. The hospital opened in 2006 and was Kinshasa's first primary care facility in 40 years—a quarter of the city's 7.5 million residents lived in poverty. "I grew up poor, and I never forgot where I came from," he told medical students at Yale University.[44]

Mutombo also used his celebrity platform to find solutions to the spread of polio, AIDS, and malaria in Africa. He missed six weeks of the 2002–03 season because he contracted malaria during a trip to the continent. "Malaria is treatable, only in Africa they don't treat it well ... 5,000 Africans die every day from the disease," he told USA Today in 2002.[45] President Obama honored him at the "Let Freedom Ring" concert at the John F. Kennedy Center in 2010.[46] In 2011, he received the Goodermote Humanitarian Award from the Johns Hopkins Bloomberg School of Public Health.[47] Mutombo, 58, lost his fight with brain cancer on September 30, 2024. "It's a sad day, especially for us Africans," said Embiid.[48]

Serge Ibaka, Pascal Siakam, and Bismack Biyombo are currently playing in the NBA. Ibaka, a native of the Democratic Republic of the Congo, is the third youngest of 18 children. He played basketball in the Congo, France, and Spain before signing with the SuperSonics in 2008. Since then, he has played for five teams, including the 2019 NBA champion Toronto Raptors. Ibaka is UNICEF's ambassador in the Congo. The Serge Ibaka Foundation renovates boys' and girls' orphanages in the Congo. It confronts the lack of access to education. Millions of youths under the age of 17 are unable to attend school because of child labor and forced marriages. Ibaka's foundation distributed 80 tons of food to 8,000 poor families during the global pandemic in 2020.[49]

Pascal Siakam played with Ibaka on the 2019 Raptors. The Cameroonian native was one of the leading contributors to the team's only championship. He won the league's Most Improved Player award that season. He has made two All-Star teams and two All-NBA teams since the Raptors' title run. Less than two months after winning the championship, he returned to Cameroon. The 6'9" power forward bent down to be at eye level with the kids in SOS Children's Village Douala. Siakam was born and raised in Douala, the largest city in Cameroon. Douala is always at risk of flooding and landslides due to the annual 180 days of rain. Residents are susceptible to typhoid and malaria. Parents work long hours for low wages in the city's informal sector and have limited time to care for their children. SOS Children's Villages began working in Douala in 2007. Their mission is to provide people with childcare, health care, educational opportunities, and financial literacy. Siakam's role with SOS thus far has been more symbolic. He gives hope and is a shining example of what kids could aspire to be.[50]

Bismack Biyombo, a native of Lubumbashi, Zaire (Republic of the Congo), was drafted by the Sacramento Kings in 2011 and immediately traded to the Charlotte Bobcats (now the Hornets). He currently plays for the Oklahoma City Thunder. Biyombo has been a role player for most of his career. But he is an All-Star to the people in his native land. He has been donating money to Congo since entering the league. He established scholarships for youth to study in the U.S. Biyombo has helped to fund a new school building and basketball courts. In 2022, he donated his entire season's $1.3 million salary to build a hospital in honor of his father, who passed away from health complications after recovering from Covid-19 in 2021. "I wanted to make this year about my Dad because my Dad spent most of his life making his life about me, my brothers, my sisters, and servicing people," Biyombo told *Andscape*.[51]

Basketball Without Borders and the Birth of the BAL

Victor Wembanyanma is projected to be the NBA's best player within the next five years. The coveted top pick in the 2023 draft class was born and raised in France; however, there is an African connection to his backstory. Wembanyanma's father, Félix, migrated to France from the Democratic Republic of the Congo (DRC). Felix, a Black man, excelled in track and field, while his wife, Elodie de Fautereau, a White French woman, played and coached basketball. Although Wembanyanma identifies as European, it is vital to acknowledge his African roots. African media outlets such as africanews identify him as being French Congolese.

Seventy-seven players of African descent played in the NBA by the start of the 2021–22 season. Thirty players were born in Nigeria. The rest were from Senegal, Cameroon, and the DRC. The three most significant sources of the NBA's African talent pool are Basketball Without Borders, NBA Academy Africa, and the Basketball Africa League (BAL). In 2001, the NBA and FIBA initiated a series of summer camps called Basketball Without Borders (BWB). These camps have attracted over 2,300 boys under 18 from over 120 countries and 33 territories. BWB was founded to "promote friendship and understanding through sport." The first camp specifically focused on youth ages 12–14 impacted by the Yugoslav Wars (1991–2001). Basketball development for all youth became the primary focus in 2003. Today, camps are held in one of 20 cities for four days. Campers are selected by the FIBA, the NBA, or participating federations. Standout alumni include Jamal Murray, Josh Giddey, R.J. Barrett, Shai Gilgeous-Alexander, Joel Embiid, and Pascal Siakam. Embiid is the first BWB participant to win the MVP award.

BWB was introduced in Africa in 2003. At the time, Africa was described as "uncharted basketball territory," even though multiple players from the continent had already been drafted and experienced stellar careers. In 2015, BWB sponsored the inaugural NBA Africa Game in Johannesburg, South Africa. The game was played between Team Africa and Team World. Team Africa included Olajuwon, Mutombo, Ibaka, Biyombo, Giannis, and other current and retired players born in or with parents from Africa. Team World, which included players from different continents, won the game 101 to 97. NBA all-star Chris Paul and Luol Deng, a forward from South Sudan, won MVP honors for their respective teams. Mutombo was the official ambassador for the second game held two years later.[52]

The NBA launched another development initiative called NBA Academy in 2016. Academies were established in Australia, India, Mexico, and other Latin American countries. In 2017, the league partnered with three government-run academies in China. The NBA was forced to pull out of China after an ESPN investigation reported numerous violations. Two American coaches quit because they could no longer bear witness to the mistreatment of the kids at an academy in Xinjiang. Chinese coaches physically assaulted players who failed to perform to their standards. The players' academic achievement was disregarded. NBA deputy commissioner Mark Tatum, who oversees the league's foreign operations, told ESPN he was looking into the matter. The academy closed in 2019.[53]

NBA Academy Africa opened in Saly, Senegal, in 2017 to promote academics and basketball for 26 of the continent's most promising boys and girls between the ages of 14 and 20. It is a partnership between the NBA and SEED Project (Sports for Education and Economic Development), a Senegalese nonprofit organization. Prospective students are identified in multiple ways, including local selection camps. The academy has dormitories, two indoor courts, a pool, and a weight room. Days begin at 7:00 am with skill development and strength conditioning, followed by six hours of school. Most classes are held online, allowing students to work at their own pace. Afternoon practices last two hours. Over 35 former participants have committed to or attended NCAA Division I American universities. Three participants have signed NBA G League Ignite contracts, and one, Ulrich Chomche, has been drafted into the NBA.[54]

Adam Silver announced that the NBA and FIBA were partnering to form the BAL during his annual State of the League address at the 2019 All-Star weekend. Silver told reporters a tournament would be held later that year to determine the 12 teams that would represent the new league in its inaugural season. Six teams would play in the league's Sahara Conference, and the remaining six would be in the Nile Conference. After a five-game regular season, the top four teams per conference would advance to the playoffs. Unlike the NBA, which has a seven-game playoff series, the BAL would use the NCAA's March Madness format consisting of a single-game-elimination tournament. The champion received a trophy and $100,000. Monetary prizes of $75,000, $55,000, and $25,000 went to the top three runners-ups. Zamalek (from Egypt) beat U.S. Monsatir (from Tunisia) 76–63 in the first championship game.

BAL team rosters must have eight local players representing a particular country. Teams may sign four foreign players, but two must be from another African country. Sixteen countries have participated in the BAL's first three seasons. The Covid-19 pandemic canceled most of the league's inaugural season. Play was initially postponed on March 3, 2020, and resumed on May 16, 2021. It concluded on May 30, 2021, with the championship. Over three seasons of operation, live games have been broadcast in 215 countries and territories via ESPN, ESPN Africa, Tencent, NBA TV, NBA TV Canada, Voice of Africa Radio, social media, and radio stations in Egypt, Tunisia, Morocco, and the Middle East. Broadcasts have been translated into 14 languages. American hip-hop superstar J. Cole played three games with the Rwanda Patriots BBC in the inaugural season.[55] Zaire Wade, son of NBA legend Dwyane Wade, signed with the Cape Town Tigers in the league's third season.[56]

How is all this possible? The BAL has lucrative sponsorships with the NBA, Jordan Brand, Flutterwave, French Development Agency, New Fortress Energy, Nike, RwandaAir, and Wilson. On January 26, 2022, BAL and Hennessy introduced NBA Crossover, an invitation-only event exhibiting the synergy between NBA basketball and popular culture and technology. The French cognac brand Hennessy agreed to sponsor a celebrity basketball game in Nigeria featuring Nigerian musicians, artists, and media personalities. Hennessy and the BAL also agreed to donate a basketball court to the Lagos State Parks and Gardens Agency at Ikorodu Recreational Part. "We at Hennessy are thrilled to partner with NBA Africa…. Nigeria is such an important market for both Hennessy and the NBA," said the company's president and CEO, Laurent Boillot.[57] The league also boasts an impressive list of individual investors: Mutombo, Grant Hill, Joakim Noah, Luol Deng, Dambisa Moyo, and Academy Award winner Forest Whitaker, who is also a former goodwill ambassador for the United Nations Educational, Scientific and Cultural Organization (UNESCO).[58] Former U.S. president Barack Obama became a strategic partner in July 2021. Obama will hold a minority equity stake in the league. "His long-term vision is to fund Obama Foundation youth and leadership programs across Africa."[59]

6. The Air Up There

Amadou Gallo Fall serves as the BAL's commissioner. John Manyo-Plange is the vice president, and Victor Williams is the league CEO. Adam Silver is vested in their success and that of the league. The average salary for BAL players is $4,000–7,000 a month. The maximum monthly salary for the premier players is $35,000. Unlike the NBA, players are not drafted out of colleges, international leagues, or developmental leagues each summer. Most players already play for local club teams or are a part of the NBA Africa Academy. Usually, the premier talent does not stay in Africa to play in this league. Players like Embiid and Siakam go to America while young to play for college preparatory high schools like IMG Academy, Division 1 colleges, or the NBA's G League before getting drafted. The BAL provides players a platform to showcase their talent to NBA scouts who attend or watch the games on television or online. Thus far, the number of players joining the NBA is minimal. Anas Mahmoud, the star of BAL's 2021 champion, Zamalek, became the BAL's first player in the NBA when the Raptors signed him to their summer league roster in 2021. Evans Ganapamo, a player from South Africa's Cape Town Tigers, made the Bucks' summer league squad. Neither player signed an NBA regular-season contract.[60]

In 2022, the NBA Academy Africa collaborated with the Basketball Africa League on a new program called BAL Elevate. Each BAL team adds one academy player to their roster for the upcoming season. Mohab Yasser Abdallatif, a former BWB camper from Egypt, was the first academy alum to play in the BAL.

Need versus Greed

Africa is primed to become a breeding ground for NBA talent and an eager fan base over the next two decades. This was not the case in 1994 when the sports comedy film *The Air Up There* debuted in American theaters. Paul Michael Glaser, best known for playing Detective Dave Starsky in the 1970s television series *Starsky & Hutch*, directed this film about Jimmy Dolan (Kevin Bacon), a fictional assistant basketball coach at Saint Joseph's University. Dolan, a former star athlete at the school who failed to make the NBA because of an injury and his selfish ego, is in line to succeed the older head coach. During a university banquet, a video highlights a school the university sponsors in Kenya. Dolan is mesmerized by a short clip of a tall teenager playing basketball on a dusty playground. Immediately, he decides to buy a plane ticket to Kenya. The film is rife with stereotypes. Dolan arrives in the country's Northern Frontier District on a tiny bus with live chickens hanging from the ceiling. When he steps off the bus, everyone looks at him in amazement because of his White skin. He learns that he needs to take another bus to reach the recruit's village, but the last bus heading in that direction left in 1970.

When Dolan eventually reaches the village, two speechless, bared-chest young Black men wearing cloth wraps around their waists and beads around their necks lead him to Father O'Hara (Dennis Patrick). This White American priest runs the school sponsored by Saint Joseph's. Sister Susan (Yolanda Vazquez), a White nun who works with O'Hara at the school, informs him that the student he is recruiting is Saleh (Charles Gitonga Maina), the son of the village's chief, Urudu (Winston Ntshona). Dolan tells her he intends to "borrow" Saleh for the next four years, and then he can return home. Sister Susan sarcastically asks if the NBA will wish to "borrow" him afterward. When Dolan meets Saleh, he promises a trip to the NCAA Final Four if he is on the team. The 6'10" teenager is eager to commit but needs his father's blessing to leave. Dolan ignorantly tells Saleh all he needs to do is have a chicken dinner with his parents, and they will be on board. Saleh replies, "We don't eat chicken."[61]

After the chief rejects his first offer, Dolan tries to persuade him to have cows delivered to the village on behalf of his university. Saleh's parents still say no. They are skeptical of Dolan's motives and distrust his claims that he is truly giving back to their village and not exploiting their son. Dolan comes across as greedy and self-serving for much of the film. He begins to change as he grows closer to Saleh and the lovely Sister Susan. In the film's climax, he plays in a basketball game with Saleh and other villagers. Dolan paints his face, bares his chest, and dons the beads and cloth wrapping of the Kenyans. These actions symbolize his supposed adoption of the "Kenyan way" and respect for their culture. Although he says he is no longer concerned with recruiting his coveted African treasure, the film ends with Saleh being introduced in the starting lineup during Saint Joseph's first home game in the upcoming season. Dolan is presented as the team's new head coach.

The Air Up There does not compare with *Hoosiers*, *Friday Night Lights*, or *A League of Their Own* in the pantheon of classic sports cinema. It received a 21 percent rating out of 100 on Rotten Tomatoes.[62] Some critics panned it for following the cliché blueprint of numerous Disney films. Other critics attacked the film for much more severe reasons. A review in the *Austin Chronicle* called it an example of cultural imperialism. Keli Goff mentioned the film in an article she published in *The Daily Beast* 20 years later titled "Can 'Belle' End Hollywood's Obsession with the White Savior?"[63] I referenced this film because I wonder how many white recruiters envisioned a less sensationalized version of this experience when they first thought about recruiting African players in the 1980s.

The Air Up There raised questions for me as I pondered this topic. Is the NBA's relationship with Africa a positive effect of globalization or the sports equivalent of the neocolonialism that has been taking place in Africa in recent years? At the Berlin Conference of 1884–1885, representatives from 14 countries gathered in Germany, at the request of King Leopold II of Belgium, to set the parameters for colonialism in Africa.[64] These foreign powers defended their imperialistic "Scramble for Africa" by arguing that they were spreading the three C's (commerce, Christianity, and civilization) to the uncivilized heathens of this dark continent. By 1914, 90 percent of African territory was under the rule of seven European nations.[65] The U.S. participated in the conference but was among the seven countries not given possession of the continent.

Walter Rodney, a Guyanese scholar and activist, was among the preeminent intellectual critics of colonialism. Rodney's radicalism contributed to his deportation and later assassination in 1980. As a doctoral student at Howard University, I was introduced to his seminal publication, *How Europe Underdeveloped Africa* (1972). The students in my global affairs and world history courses have also become familiar with this book. Rodney's thesis states that Europe's rise as a world superpower in the 19th and 20th centuries resulted from its political and economic exploitation and decimation of Africa. The continent had once been home to many powerful empires. The decline of those empires and the transatlantic slave trade, which was responsible for selling 12.5 million able-bodied men, women, and children to the Americas, made Africa susceptible to European invasion. The seizure of land and commerce precipitated a development gap that left Africa financially reliant on its European colonizers. The necessity of a literate workforce contributed to maintaining a stable school system. However, the colonizers used schools and selected curricula to promote Western values and hostility toward traditional African mores.[66]

It was not until 1957, when Ghana gained its independence from Great Britain, that the constricting chains of colonialism began to break. Seventeen African nations achieved independence in 1960, known as the Year of Africa.[67] More countries would follow their lead throughout the sixties. Marvel's fictional African country, Wakanda, in the *Black Panther* series resonates with so many Black Americans because it reimagines what would have happened if Africa had never been colonized. Over the last 60 years, some African nations have thrived, while others have been plagued by political and economic strife, civil war, genocide, and disease. Neocolonialism, or the control of less developed countries by highly developed countries using globalization, economic and cultural imperialism, and forms of "soft power" such as conditional financial arrangements rather than military force, has dramatically impacted Africa in the 21st century.

The *Britannica* states, "Neocolonialism has been broadly understood as a further development of capitalism that enables capitalist powers to dominate subject nations through the operations of international capitalism."[68]

In 2019, the International Monetary Fund (IMF) called Africa the second-fastest-growing region in the world, with a projected $5 trillion economy forthcoming. The continent's 1.1 billion population is expected to double by 2050.[69] Lagos has more than 15.9 million residents and a population growth rate of 77 people per hour.[70] Africa and China formed a relationship in the Cold War era. Most foreign governments favored the Republic of China, the former government that became Taiwan, over the new Communist Party–controlled Chinese government. China found support from African nations in exchange for infrastructure projects. China began building hospitals, railroads, and universities throughout the continent. The U.S. and Europe initially borrowed money from the IMF and the World Bank to fund these projects as colonialism was ending in Africa. Once they began backing away from Africa in the 1970s, the door was left ajar for Chinese investors. In 1970, China began constructing the Tazara Railway, which links the Zambian town of Kapiri Mposhi and Dar es Salaam Port in Tanzania.[71]

Today, China is Africa's biggest trade partner, responsible for over 40 percent of all infrastructure investments. More than 10,000 Chinese-owned firms are operating in Africa. The value of their business is worth more than $2 trillion. "Right now, you could say that any big projects in African cities higher than three floors are most likely being engineered by the Chinese," said Daan Roggeveen, the founder of MORE Architecture.[72] China has invested over $340 billion in Africa. Its gross domestic product (GDP) has risen to second in the world.

The Trump administration nicknamed China's relationship with Africa "debt-trap diplomacy." *Bloomberg* claims that this "debt trap" myth has been used to villainize the Chinese and make Africans look incapable of handling their own affairs. Is there any validity to those claims? In 2015, 17 African countries were unable to repay their debts. Zambia owed China $8 billion in 2017.[73] Kenya's and Nigeria's debts are growing. The Chinese funded a $3.6 billion railway from Mombasa to Nairobi, Kenya. Export-Import Bank of China loaned Nigeria $1.3 billion for a 157-kilometer segment of the Lagos-Kano Railway. China financed $3 billion worth of infrastructure in the DRC, which is Africa's largest producer of copper and the world's biggest producer of cobalt.[74]

Africa has certainly not benefited from this relationship as much as China, bringing me back to my original questions about the NBA's African connection. A cynic might view this sudden interest and investment in Africa with a third eye open. Once again, you have outsiders solely interested in Africa for capitalist gain. When David Stern began expanding the NBA across international borders in the 1990s, he made it clear that his interest in growing the game was financially motivated. In the previous chapter, I discussed all the benefits the NBA has gained from its Chinese market. The league's corporate sponsors benefit from having their products marketed abroad. When Africans watch or attend BAL games, they see promotional material and products from American companies like Nike, Pepsi, and Jordan Brand. They taste the French cognac brand Hennessy.

During an interview with NBA Radio on August 10, 2024, Jim Boeheim, an assistant coach for the U.S. Olympic team (2008–2016), said Africa will be the primary hub for international NBA talent in the next 20 years. As the game continues to grow on the continent, you will see more players from the summer camps, the academy, and the BAL on NBA teams. Two players of African descent have won the league MVP since 2019. Real-life Jimmy Dolans will entice more young boys to enroll in American basketball factories masquerading as college prep high schools and universities as a path to the NBA. The earnings these players make will pale compared with the billions made by their NBA teams, mostly White corporate sponsors, and Western universities. While this is a small percentage of the continent's overall population, it still equals an increased foreign interest in young, able-bodied Black African males.

David Aldridge has a sharp opinion of individuals who accuse the NBA of exploiting Africa.

> *Of course they are doing it for money, but that doesn't mean it's disqualifying. We live in a capitalist society. The NBA is not an amateur basketball league. It's a league where people play for money, so if you accept that as your baseline, then I don't think you can be surprised if the NBA is looking at places around the world to be a potential benefactor. But it is not a bad thing that SEED and other programs in Africa are getting infrastructure from the NBA to make them run a little better and be the framework upon which something like the Basketball Africa League can grow and flourish.*
>
> *What's wrong with giving hundreds of kids in Africa the opportunity to develop their games to be drafted or go to American colleges? Other than the China Academy, there is no reporting that these academies are doing anything that is questionable.... I don't think people are selling these kids a pie-in-the-sky dream that if you come here, you will be an NBA player. But if it helps the kid get to an American college, what is wrong with that? I don't think they [the NBA] are going to save the world, but I don't think they're going to be the cause of its demise either.*[75]

Besides providing opportunities for a select group of young men and boys, how else is Africa benefiting from NBA globalization? The BAL is firmly committed to climate change and gender equality in Africa. The league's Green platform explores ways for players to help improve their environment. It has also partnered with the Green Great Wall Initiative, a program dedicated to creating 10 million green jobs by 2030 and restoring 100 million hectares of degraded land in the Sahel. Players can make a difference simply by shooting the basketball. The BAL has pledged to plant three trees for every three-point shot each player scores in a game. Thus far, more than 3,600 have been planted.[76] In November 2021, the BAL announced it was supporting the Center for Women's Global Leadership's "16 Days of Activism Against Gender-Based Violence Campaign," the world's longest-running campaign for women's rights. BAL teams began using their social media platforms to spotlight non-governmental organizations (NGOs) working in their countries to end discrimination against women. "The 16 Days of Activism campaign is a powerful reminder that we have a long way to go in elevating women to an equal place in all aspects of society, not just in Africa but around the world," said NBA Africa CEO Victor Williams.[77] "By investing in communities, promoting gender equality, and cultivating the love of the game of basketball, I believe that NBA Africa can make a difference for so many of Africa's young people," said President Obama.[78]

Africa benefits from the humanitarian efforts of native players like Mutombo, Bol, and Ibaka who use their celebrity, connections, and cash to make life better for those less fortunate. As the number of African players increases, there will be more millionaires with foundations giving scholarships for kids, not just promising student-athletes, to attend college and strengthen their career options. Africa also benefits from the individual investors involved in the BAL and these initiatives. Grant Hill and Forest Whitaker carry a substantial amount of clout. President Obama's connection to the league is invaluable. As the son of a Kenyan father, I doubt that he would be associated with anything that would exploit the people of Africa or its resources.

I would like to see Masai Ujiri take a leadership role in the BAL. If there is anyone dedicated to Africa's advancement, it is Ujiri. As detailed in Chapter 3, Ujiri is the former general manager and current president of the Toronto Raptors. He is responsible for Toronto's sole championship, in 2019. The Raptor's title run made him the first African to lead any American team in any major American sport to a championship. Once Ujiri finished celebrating with his players and staff, he flew back to his homeland in Zaria, Nigeria, to celebrate with the people and present his trophy to his childhood coach, Oliver Johnson. Despite his success in Canada, his most significant accomplishments are in Africa. In 2003, he launched Giants of Africa, a summer basketball camp in Nigeria for the country's best young prospects. When the Denver Nuggets offered him their general manager position in 2008, he told the team's president he would accept only if the salary increased by $50,000. He would use the extra pay to fund his camps in Africa. The president hung up the phone. Ujiri thought he blew it and feared having to tell his wife he did not get the job. Four minutes later, the president called back to accept his demands. The money allowed Ujiri to expand his camp throughout Nigeria and 14 other African countries.[79]

Today, Ujiri spends every August, his only time off during the year, in Africa, visiting each camp. He compares the talent on the continent to its natural resources, such as diamonds and gold. The average height in some tribes is 6'8". More than 100 campers have received scholarships to play college basketball in America. For some campers, like Daniel Teagan, receiving a scholarship is a matter of life or death. Teagan lives in Cameroon amid a deadly civil war. He travels eight hours in a heavily armed region, with the sound of gunshots and explosions going off around him, to reach the basketball court. Ujiri is passionate and dedicated to this venture because he sees himself in those kids. He shares his struggles with them, including how he became a scout and general manager after his NBA dreams were "deferred and dried up like a raisin in the sun."[80] Most campers will never make an NBA roster, but they can become future scouts, general managers, team presidents, and maybe team governors. He teaches his campers basketball and life skills to prepare them to become "Giants of Africa," meaning pillars and leaders of their communities. The kids recite the following mantra at each camp:

> I'm a giant. I'm a giant. I'm a leader. I'm a leader. I study hard. I study hard. I play hard. I play hard. I'm a giant. I'm a giant.[81]

In 2019, HBO's *Real Sports* television series profiled Ujiri. Reporters traveled with Ujiri to a camp in Cameroon and videotaped him at one of his finest teaching moments. At the last minute, he learned that the gym, which he had rented out exclusively for his campers months earlier, had also been rented out for a concert later that day. Ujiri was infuriated because he saw it as symbolic of the greed for money that causes Africans to cheat one another and not get ahead. He used this example to deliver a potent message to his campers. "You guys have to change that shit here and all over Africa 'cause it's bullshit…. We came here to play, be happy, learn basketball—and look at what we have to put up with. But you have to change it!"[82]

Adam Silver calls Ujiri the pied piper and the messiah for an entire continent. Silver was thoroughly impressed when he attended his Rwandan camp in 2019. "[Ujiri] has an incredible rolodex of relationships in Africa with leaders of countries, with sports ministers, with business leaders, and he has made many of those introductions for me. He's a leader in terms of pushing us all to believe in Africa," says Silver.[83] Ujiri has spoken publicly about the potential of the BAL to grow and produce more NBA talent over time. As for his own legacy, Ujiri says he will never be satisfied until he sees other Africans like him in similar executive positions. "If I'm in this position and nobody else comes after me, it's a failure."[84]

7

American Pastime

The NBA traditionally takes a back seat to college basketball for the NCAA tournament in March. But in the spring of 2023, the league had to share the spotlight with March Madness and Major League Baseball (MLB). The World Baseball Classic (WBC) was held March 8–21. The WBC, founded in 2005, is an international baseball tournament sanctioned by the International Baseball Federation, World Baseball Softball Confederation, Major League Baseball, and the Major League Baseball Players Association. A total of 6.5 million viewers watched the gold medal game between Japan and the U.S. With two outs in the top of the ninth inning, American slugger Mike Trout walked up to the plate to face Japanese pitcher Shohei Ohtani. The game's intensity and drama climaxed as these two MLB teammates from the Los Angeles Angels faced off with the gold and world supremacy on the line. Ohtani struck out Trout with an 87-mile-per-hour slider to secure a 3–2 victory and Japan's third WBC title.

Shohei Ohtani is baseball's equivalent of Victor Wembanyama. The game's future rests on his broad shoulders. Ohtani, a 30-year-old native of Iwate, Japan, arrived in America to play for the Angels in 2018 after four years of professional ball in his homeland. The All-Star pitcher and designated hitter/outfielder is the first player to record over 100 strikeouts, over 10 home runs, and over 20 stolen bases in a single season. Pitchers do not typically hit 44 homers in a season, as he did in 2023 before being shut down due to an oblique injury. His dual prowess frequently parallels the legendary George Herman "Babe" Ruth, who pitched for the Boston Red Sox before setting the home run record with the New York Yankees. Ohtani's presence brought the Angels millions in revenue from Asian sponsors. But is his dominance detrimental to baseball?

Some sports media members, notably NBA analyst Stephen A. Smith, questioned Ohtani's ability to captivate American audiences because he was born elsewhere. "I don't think it helps that the No.1 face is a dude that needs an interpreter so you can understand what the hell he's saying," said Smith.[1]

Ohtani is one of many current MLB players who speak English as a second or third language. I noticed this when I watched the 2023 Home Run Derby during the MLB All-Star activities. Many contestants had translators. Retired NBA star Yao Ming spoke only Mandarin Chinese and used an interpreter his first three seasons with the Houston Rockets. Ming was not the face of the league, but he was the NBA's most prominent non–American global ambassador at the time. The language barrier has not decreased Ohtani's popularity. He received the second-most fan votes for the 2023 MLB All-Star Game, has a sponsorship deal with American sports brand New Balance, and earns $40 million in endorsements. The Los Angeles Dodgers made the ultimate investment in Ohtani by signing him on December 9, 2023, to a jaw-dropping 10-year, $700 million contract. With the largest contract in American professional sports history, he could earn $70 million annually. Ohtani has already made history in a Dodgers uniform. On September 19, 2024, he became the first player to record 50 home runs and 50 stolen bases in a season. He led the Dodgers to their seventh World Series crown and unanimously won his third league MVP award in November.[2]

Baseball has been considered America's national pastime since the 19th century. Football surpassed baseball in domestic popularity in the 1970s, and in recent years, the NFL has steadily outpaced MLB and the NBA in domestic viewership and ticket sales. The NFL, despite several recent efforts, lags far behind both leagues in terms of globalization. By comparison, MLB has embraced globalization for decades, with Asia and Latin America, especially the Dominican Republic, becoming breeding grounds for potential talent. Over 28 percent of MLB players in 2022 were born outside the United States. According to MLB, 275 of 975 players on opening-day rosters were foreign-born. The 2024 MLB season opened in March with the Seoul Series in South Korea featuring Ohtani's Dodgers and the San Diego Padres. The following chapter compares the NBA's global influence with Major League Baseball and the National Football League. How beneficial is globalization to the NBA's leading competitors?

Buy Me Some Peanuts and Cracker Jack

Which professional American sports league is more relevant today? Baseball purists can point to data published in 2021 that rated MLB ahead of the NBA on a list of the world's most lucrative professional sports leagues. MLB had $10 billion in revenue compared with the NBA's $8 billion. Neither league matched the NFL's $16 billion in revenue.[3] During an episode of *First Take* in March 2022, Stephen A. Smith and his guest, Chris "Mad Dog" Russo, debated the popularity of Major League Baseball. "Baseball is in major, major trouble. Revenue is down, ratings are down, national ratings are down," declared the loquacious Smith.[4] The 2022 World Series between the Houston Astros and the Philadelphia Phillies, which averaged 11.8 million viewers per game, was the second-least-watched World Series in history. For comparison, that season's NBA Finals, featuring the Golden State Warriors and Boston Celtics, averaged 12.4 million viewers. However, the 2023 NBA Finals between the Denver Nuggets and Miami Heat declined to 11.6 million viewers.[5]

The NBA, which reigns supreme over MLB on social media, had over 70 million Instagram followers in 2022. That was more than the NFL, NHL, and MLB combined. MLB had just 8.9 million followers on Instagram. The NBA also surpassed MLB in followers on Facebook, Twitter (X), TikTok, and YouTube.[6] The NBA's social media dominance is mainly due to its younger fanbase. A 2017 Nielsen study found the median age of MLB viewers is 57 years old.[7] Regardless, the NBA's massive Instagram and TikTok followings will never earn it the title of America's pastime. Some individuals of a particular generation were raised to believe baseball is as American as apple pie. It is the oldest of the three major team sports in the U.S. The game's roots date back to two 18th-century English games: rounders and cricket. The rules for the modern game were drawn up by Alexander Joy Cartwright, a volunteer firefighter and bank clerk in New York City, in September 1845. The rule changes helped to differentiate the game from cricket. The New York Knickerbocker Baseball Club played the first official game a year later.[8]

America was torn apart during four bloody years of civil war between 1861 and 1865. When the young men representing the Northern Yankees and Southern Rebels were not in combat, they passed the quiet time playing baseball. From then on, the game became a popular staple associated with American culture and patriotism. In 1901, two wealthy Americans, William Hulbert and Ban Johnson, formed the National League and the American League, respectively. These leagues combined to create what we now know as the Major League. The Boston Americans defeated the Pittsburgh Pirates in the inaugural World Series played in 1903.

Two hundred and twenty-seven MLB players served in World War I, and over 500 fought in World War II. New York Yankees center fielder Joe DiMaggio was one of 37 future Hall-of-Famers to serve. He sacrificed three seasons to serve in the air force.[9] DiMaggio was among the earliest 20th-century athletes to cross into pop culture celebrity. Hollywood added to baseball's lore through timeless films like *Field of Dreams* (1989) and *A League of Their Own* (1992). Catchphrases from these iconic films, like "If you build it, they will come" and "There's no crying in baseball," became fixtures in the American lexicon.

When freedom and security were in peril after 9/11, Americans found solace in baseball. President George W. Bush threw out the first pitch at the Yankees' first home game after the terrorist attacks. Yankees shortstop Derek Jeter and his teammates went down to Ground Zero in New York City to comfort the families of the individuals killed in the World Trade Center. Likewise, David Ortiz and members of the Red Sox reminded Bostonians that Boston was their "fucking city" in the wake of a domestic terrorist attack at the 2013 Boston Marathon.[10] The Pentagon has spent millions to promote patriotic displays at MLB games since 2012.[11]

Professional baseball was an all-white American sport until Branch Rickey signed Jackie Robinson to play for the Brooklyn Dodgers in 1947. Robinson's success paved the way for more Blacks to integrate into the league over the next few decades. Diversity did not end with Black American players. Roberto Clemente, the first Caribbean and Latin American player enshrined into the National Baseball Hall of Fame, joined the Pittsburgh Pirates in 1955. Since then, the number of foreign-born players, especially from Latin America, has rivaled that of white Americans and surpassed Black Americans.

On the opening day of the 2023 MLB season, there were 269 international players on rosters, which composed 28.5 percent of the total MLB player population. These players represented 19 countries or territories outside the U.S. One hundred and four players hailed from the Dominican Republic. Venezuela, Cuba, and Puerto Rico produced 62, 21, and 19 players, respectively. The remaining countries and territories represented were Mexico, Canada, Japan, Colombia, Curaçao, Panama, South Korea, the Bahamas, Nicaragua, Aruba, Australia, Brazil, Germany, Honduras, and Taiwan. The 2022 World Series champion Houston Astros had 16, the most foreign-born players.[12]

MLB fans abroad have a few options to watch live games. Fox Sports, home of the MLB All-Star Game and World Series, airs live games in the Netherlands. Since 2020, ESPN Player has owned the rights to distribute games and the MLB Network in 96 countries throughout Europe and sub-Saharan Africa.[13] In 2021, Tencent agreed to stream live regular-season and playoff games in more than six Asian territories on its international over-the-top (OTT) platform, WeTV.[14] MLB signed a rights deal with China's Oriental Pearl Media, which lasted until 2023. Oriental Pearl New Media reached more than 100 million Chinese households and 31 regions in the country.[15]

The Birth of a Global Game

MLB globalization is not a 20th-century phenomenon ignited by a star-laden Dream Team or charismatic figure like Michael Jordan responsible for selling the game abroad. Globalization dates to the 19th century. The first Canadian Baseball League was established in 1877. The Canadian Professional Baseball Association debuted in 1911. Eighteen Canadian cities had professional baseball teams. The Montreal Royals, formed in 1928, joined the Syracuse minor league. Judge Kenesaw Mountain Landis, the commissioner of MLB from 1905 to 1922, attended the Royals' first game. Ten years later, the Brooklyn Dodgers purchased the Royals, giving MLB its first foreign farm team.[16] The Montreal Expos became MLB's first Canadian franchise in 1969. The Expos played in the National League East division until 2004, when they became the Washington Nationals. The Nationals won the 2019 World Series. MLB, like the NBA, lost one of its two Canadian teams to an American city.

The 1977 Major League Baseball expansion opened the door for the Toronto Blue Jays to join the American League. The Blue Jays debuted against the Chicago White Sox on April 7, 1977, on a field covered with snow from a minor storm. They won the game in front of 44,646 spectators. The Blue Jays finished their first season with 54 wins and 107 losses. They lost 102 and 109 games over the next two years. However, success eventually came north of the border, and Toronto captured its first American League title in 1985. Four years later, the team made history by making Cito Gaston MLB's first Black general manager. Under Gaston's leadership, Toronto won American League titles in 1990 and 1991. The stars finally aligned for the Blue Jays in 1992 and 1993. The team won back-to-back World Series championships. The most memorable moment from that championship run was Joe Carter's walk-off home run in game six of the 1993 World Series to clinch the title.

American baseball was introduced to continental Europe in 1874. Games were played in France, the Netherlands, and Sweden before World War I. Numerous exhibitions were staged in other European countries during World War II. The Yankees and Red Sox played in the inaugural London Series, a two-game regular-season series held in England, in June 2019. Baseball has never been as prominent in Europe as in Canada, Asia, the Caribbean, or Latin America. Only two players born in Europe (Germany and the Netherlands) appeared on opening-day rosters in 2022. MLB's European population dwindled to a single player at the start of the next season. The number of players born in Australia is as low.[17]

Unlike the NBA, which is flourishing in Africa, there were no African-born players on opening-day rosters in 2023. The continent did not produce a Major Leaguer until South African shortstop and second baseman Mpho' Gift Ngoepe played for the Pirates and Blue Jays in 2017. Baseball has thrived the most in South Africa. The country sent a national team to the 1974 Amateur World Series, the 2000 Summer Olympics, and the World Baseball Classic in 2006 and 2009.[18] In 1999, the sport was added to the All-Africa Games, a continental multisport event held every four years. There are currently 16 national baseball federations on the continent.

In 2002, Joseph A. Reaves published *Taking in a Game: A History of Baseball in Asia*. Reaves, a former journalist for the *Chicago Tribune*, is one of the leading American experts on baseball in Asia. According to Reaves, baseball appeared in China as early as the 1870s. The sport's introduction resulted from an education exchange program organized by Rong Hong, a Chinese native who was naturalized as an American citizen in 1852.[19] The game spread to the Philippines and was popular until World War II. Reaves argues that the decline in baseball's popularity overlapped with a growing interest in basketball.[20]

Baseball arrived in Korea in 1922. Twelve years later, an all-star team called the Reach All Stars featuring Babe Ruth put on an exhibition in Seoul. The presence of American soldiers during World War II contributed to the game's increasing popularity in the '40s. The Korean War divided the nation into two separate countries. Baseball remained relevant in South Korea, an American ally, but disappeared in North Korea. The Korean Baseball Organization was formed in 1981. A South Korean professional baseball league was established months later. The league attracted players from South Korea, the U.S., and Latin America who needed to improve to earn a Major League roster spot. The best homegrown players joined MLB or the Japanese professional leagues. In 1993, Chan Ho Park, a pitcher majoring in economics at Han Yang University, signed a $1.2 million contract with the Los Angeles Dodgers. He became a national hero and an inspiration for other aspiring players. Byung-Hyun Kim, a pitcher for the Arizona Diamondbacks and Boston Red Sox, was the only other Korean player to make the majors by the early 2000s.[21] Unfortunately, Kim is best remembered for giving up ninth-inning leads in games four and five of the 2001 World Series.

When baseball was introduced in Japan, the indigenous population applied a martial arts philosophy to how it should be played. Many regarded it as a "moral discipline" that required a "spiritual approach."[22] The baseball teams at Ichiko School and Meiji Gakuin School became bitter rivals in the early 1890s. The latter taught and played an American-influenced approach to the game. When Ichiko defeated the Yokohama Country Athletic Club, which included American players, in 1896, their "Japanese style" brand of baseball became the country's dominant style.

Japan's first professional league was organized in 1936. Bucky Harris was the first American player to play in the league, which disbanded following the 1941 bombing of Pearl Harbor. After Japan's defeat in World War II, baseball helped boost morale, especially among individuals from the working classes. By the 1950s, American baseball players and aspects of American popular culture began flooding the country.[23] We should also acknowledge that Black baseball players had something to do with the sport's growth in Japan. In 1927, the Philadelphia Royal Giants, members of the Negro Leagues, played a 24-game exhibition series, winning all but one game. Bob Kendrick, president of the Negro Leagues Baseball Museum and host of the *Black Diamonds* podcast series, credits this team with igniting the Japanese passion for American baseball.[24]

Pitcher Masanori Murakami was the first Japanese player in Major League Baseball. In 1964, his Japanese baseball club, the Nankai Hawks, agreed to let Murakami join the San Francisco Giants. The U.S. State Department played a role in negotiations to ensure no diplomatic problems arose between the two countries. The U.S. had recently entered the Vietnam War, which made the State Department sensitive to all Asian matters. Murakami made his MLB debut one day before the 19th anniversary of Japan's surrender to the U.S. in World War II.[25] He advanced from the Giants' farm system to their big-league roster after one season. "He had that 8 a.m.-to-4 p.m. curveball. He got to face the best players in baseball, and he proved he could compete with them," said Giants pitcher Gaylord Perry.[26] Murakami's contract stipulated that the Giants owned his rights only for the 1965 season, giving him the power to re-sign with San Francisco or return home at the season's conclusion. He chose to return to Japan. The contentious experience negotiating Murakami's contract made the Japanese League reluctant about sending other players to America.

Sixty-seven Japanese players have played in the majors. Ichiro Suzuki played for the Seattle Mariners from 2001 to 2012 and again from 2018 to 2019. He had previously played outfielder for the Orix BlueWave of Japan's Nippon Professional Baseball League. Suzuki won the American League Rookie of the Year and MVP awards in 2001. His 18-year MLB career included 10 Gold Glove awards, two batting championships, 10 All-Star nods, a league-leading stolen-base total, and an MLB record for the most hits (262) in a single season. A fan favorite in the U.S. and Asia, he earned $7 million in endorsements at his peak.

Suzuki left Seattle in 2012 to play alongside Derek Jeter and Alex Rodriguez on the Yankees. He spent three seasons in the Big Apple before finishing his career in Miami and Seattle. Suzuki was not the first Japanese player to don the classic blue Yankee fitted (ball cap) and pinstripes. Hideki Matsui, nicknamed Godzilla, signed with the Yankees in 2003 after 10 seasons with the Yomiuri Giants in Tokyo. Matsui earned two All-Star Game selections and was named MVP of the 2009 World Series. In 2005, the Yankees made him the highest-paid Japanese player in MLB history with a $52 million contract.

Major League Baseball and Latin America

Major League Baseball has made its greatest strides in Latin America. Nemesio and Ernesto Guillo established the Habana Base Ball Club in Cuba in 1868. Baseball was tied to Cuban politics from its inception. The island's full embrace of the game coincided with its fight for independence from Spain. As an American presence grew, partly due to an interest in sugar, Cubans turned to baseball instead of the Spanish sport of bullfighting. Cuba's lower classes were especially drawn to the American pastime. In 1872, Esteban Bellan, a Cuban national, made history as the first Latino on an MLB roster by signing with the New York Mutuals, a charter member of the National League.[27]

After Cuba gained its independence from Spain in 1898, it was occupied by the U.S. until 1902. Despite American occupation, Cubans continued to embrace baseball as a sign of resistance. They took great pride in beating the Americans in their own sport. A perfect example would be the Cuban select team defeating the Philadelphia Athletics, the 1911 World Series Champions, in a series of games. These international contests were responsible for the growth of baseball in Cuba. By the turn of the 20th century, "lassiez-faire business" practices made Cuba, and eventually the rest of Latin America, a breeding ground for Major League Baseball.

"The Latin American market was a new and cheaper option," writes Daniel Bloyce in his dissertation "The Globalization of Baseball."[28] MLB teams began scouting "White" Cuban players to sign. Jim Crow, which relegated American Blacks to the Negro Leagues in the 1920s, prohibited brown- and dark-skinned Latinos from playing in the majors. This shortsighted practice changed once Jackie Robinson successfully broke the color barrier with the Brooklyn Dodgers. By the late 1950s, 49 Cubans, including the dark-skinned third baseman Orestes "Minnie" Miñoso, were on MLB rosters. Miñoso, nicknamed the Cuban Jackie Robinson, migrated to the U.S. at the end of World War II to play for the New York Cubans in the Negro Leagues. Miñoso would eventually play for seven MLB teams, work as the first- and third-base coach for the Chicago White Sox, and be elected posthumously to the National Baseball Hall of Fame.[29]

The 1959 Cuban Revolution, resulting in the rise of Fidel Castro's reign, propelled the game to national pastime status. Cubans' love for baseball was further fueled by growing anti–American sentiment.[30] Castro, having severed ties with the U.S. to become a communist ally of the

Soviet Union (USSR), used baseball for political propaganda. Castro labeled Cuba's brand of amateur baseball *lea pelota libre* (free baseball). America's version of professional baseball was *la pelota esclava* (slave baseball). Castro's popularity among his people waned over the next 30 years as his regime became increasingly repressive. The collapse of the USSR in 1991 devastated the Cuban economy, which had become dependent on the Soviets, who bought their sugar at prices above market value.

President John F. Kennedy signed a trade embargo in 1962, ending all ties between the U.S. and Cuba. While the embargo prevented MLB teams from entering Cuba to scout more Cuban players, this did not prevent Cubans from entering the majors. In July 1991, Rene Arocha became the island's first player to defect from the national team. Arocha fled during a tournament held in Miami and eventually signed with the Saint Louis Cardinals.[31] Other defectors followed Arocha, but none of them had significant careers initially. To stop the best players from defecting to America, the Cuban government changed its laws in 1992 to allow retired players to coach overseas in countries other than the U.S. Players continued to defect despite the new laws. Liván Hernandez was the first elite player to defect to Major League Baseball successfully. After he joined the Florida Marlins in 1995, the Cuban government began allowing players over 30 to play and retire overseas.[32]

Baseball's most famous Cuban defector was Yasiel Puig, who made multiple unsuccessful attempts to defect beginning in 2009. The police stopped Puig's car the first time he tried to escape. His getaway "boat" never arrived on his second attempt. Police officers raided the safe house that was holding him another time. Puig's punishment was spending six days in police custody. On another occasion, the U.S. Coast Guard stopped a boat carrying him near Haiti. Desperate to reach America, he eventually sought the help of Los Zetas, a violent Mexican crime syndicate engaged in cocaine distribution and human smuggling. Puig took a 36-hour speedboat trip from Cuba to an island near Cancún, Mexico. He was accompanied by his girlfriend, a former Cuban boxer named Yunior Despaigne, and a *padrino*, a Spanish name for a lower cleric in the Afro-Catholic religion of Santeria. The cleric traveled with them for good luck. Raúl Pacheco, the Cuban American president of Miami-based T&P Metal and PY Recycling, promised to pay Puig's smugglers $250,000 upon his arrival in Mexico. When Pacheco failed to deliver the money, the smugglers held Puig and his travel companions for a $400,000 ransom.[33] Despaigne described the ordeal in an interview with *Los Angeles Magazine*:

> I don't know if you could call it a kidnapping because we had gone there voluntarily, but we also weren't free to leave.... If they didn't receive the money, they were saying that at any moment they might give [Puig] a machetazo [machete

blow], chop off an arm, a finger, whatever, and he would never play baseball again, not for anyone.[34]

A man identified as "El Rubio" (The Blonde) arrived and agreed to pay the ransom. Before paying the ransom, El Rubio helped Puig and the other men escape the compound where they were being detained in the middle of the night. A boat carried the men to Cancún. From there, they flew to Mexico City for a baseball showcase. The Dodgers signed Puig in 2012 to a seven-year, $42 million contract. His American dream was not always idyllic. He received death threats from the Los Zetas cartel because the smugglers never received their ransom money. A cartel member confronted him one night in Arizona while he was training with the team. Despaigne had a gun put to his head while in Hialeah, Florida.[35] Puig played in the right field for the Dodgers, Cincinnati Reds, and Cleveland Indians between 2013 and 2019. He was naturalized in 2019.

Baseball has been used to thaw icy relations between the U.S. and Cuba. On March 28, 1999, the Baltimore Orioles became the first American professional team to enter Cuba since the revolution when they played Equipo Cuba in Havana. A rematch was held in Baltimore weeks later on May 3. Cuba lost their home game but won in Baltimore, giving the Cubans bragging rights. Marcus F. Cuellar, author of "Runners Left on Base: Cuban Baseball Defection Experience and a Reevaluation of Baseball Diplomacy," describes these two exhibitions as a failed attempt at "soft diplomacy" because neither country's government was fully committed to easing tensions.[36] Baseball diplomacy would prove more instrumental in 2016 when the Tampa Bay Rays and the Cuban national team staged an exhibition game in front of 55,000 fans. The game coincided with President Barack Obama's 48-hour visit to the island.

President Obama attended the game with his wife, daughters, and mother-in-law. Rachel Robinson, the widow of Jackie Robinson, was among the dignitaries at the ballpark. Robinson played in Havana before signing with the Brooklyn Dodgers in 1947. Cuban President Raul Castro, Fidel's brother, sat with the Obamas. A week before the game, Obama announced that he was lifting a ban on American companies employing Cubans. The ban's removal meant that players like Puig no longer had to risk life and limb trying to defect. MLB teams could start signing players directly in Cuba. "They're not going to have those terms dictated to them. If the Obama administration or MLB pushes too hard to use baseball to open up Cuba, but only on US or MLB terms, that could suddenly raise big roadblocks with the Cubans," said Peter Bjarkman, author of *Cuba's Baseball Defectors: The Inside Story*.[37] At the start of the 2023 season, 18 Cubans were on Major League rosters.

Béisbol Has Been Very Good to Me!

On November 5, 2022, the Houston Astros defeated the Philadelphia Phillies to clinch their second World Series in five years. The Astros' victory was redemption for a cheating scandal that tainted their 2017 championship run. Johnnie B. "Dusty" Baker, Jr., the team's manager since 2020, became the third Black American manager to win a World Series. Baker's accomplishment was magnified because no American-born Black players were on either team. The last time this occurred was in 1950, three years after the start of integration.[38] Despite this egregious absence, there were countless Black faces on the field. Black players of Latin American and Caribbean descent, representing the African diaspora, have supplanted their Black American brethren for the last decade.[39] Most of these players were born in the Dominican Republic. The Astros had six Dominicans on their 2022 championship roster.

The Dominican Republic is as vital to Major League Baseball as Europe and Africa are to the NBA. In 2023, 10 percent of the players on all MLB rosters were Dominican. Baseball's connection to the Dominican Republic can be traced back to the 1860s when slave revolts forced Cuban sugar plantation owners to migrate to the island. Planters established sugar refineries in cities like San Pedro De Macoris and brought baseball with them. Soon, they began organizing games between their workers at the refineries. Planters promised their workers days off if their teams won to make the games more competitive. Passion for the game spread rapidly. The Dominican Republic national team's surprise defeat of Cuba in 1944 notified the rest of the world that Dominican baseball should be taken seriously. The Cuban Missile Crisis put Americans and Soviets on the verge of nuclear obliteration and severed all American ties with Cuba. President Kennedy's 1963 trade embargo on all exports to Cuba ended American relations with Cuba and extended to all professional sports. Now that Cuba was no longer a viable market for MLB, teams began seeking talent in the Dominican Republic that could be signed for less money than American-born players. The earliest Dominican signees were Ozzie Virgil; Juan Marichal; and brothers Felipe, Mateo, and Jesús Alou.[40]

If Michael Jordan had been the king of Chicago in 1998, a charismatic *brotha* from the Dominican named Sammy would have been the city's prince. Sammy Sosa grew up in abject poverty. He became a shoeshine boy when he was only eight to supplement his mother's meager income. Five years later, he met the man who changed his life forever. Bill Chase, an American businessman who regularly came to San Pedro to receive a shine, gifted him a blue baseball glove. "You might notice that Sosa only wears blue gloves," Chase noted in the 2000 autobiography *Sosa*.[41] With

Chase's help, Sosa arranged a deal with his boss to allow his younger brother to fill in for him when he left to play baseball. Sosa, like many Dominicans, found baseball to be a potential escape from poverty.[42] After being signed, at 16 years old, to the Texas Rangers' minor league system in 1985, he was promoted to Class A Gastonia, North Carolina, in the South Atlantic League in two years. Next, he played Class AA ball for Tulsa, Oklahoma, in the Texas League. Ironically, his Major League debut came on my birthday, June 16, 1989, against the Yankees at Bronx Stadium. Sosa hit his first home run a week later in Boston off Red Sox Cy Young Award–winning pitcher Roger Clemens.[43]

Sosa lasted slightly over a month in Texas before he was traded to the Chicago White Sox. His early years in the Windy City were hardly noteworthy. In 1990, he struck out 150 times, the fourth most in the American League. The White Sox shipped him off across town to the Cubs, the city's National League team and baseball fans' "loveable losers."[44] Sosa spent 12 years, the prime of his career, with the Cubs. He became a seven-time All-Star, a six-time Silver Slugger Award winner, and a two-time National League leader in home runs and runs batted in (RBI). His best season came in 1998 when he won the National League MVP. But his costarring role in the "Summer of Love" transformed him into one of sports' most unlikely and complicated heroes.

Baseball's "Summer of Love" was the pursuit of Roger Maris's single-season home run record of 61. Maris broke Babe Ruth's record of 60 home runs in 1961. The ordeal was so stressful for Maris that he lost substantial clumps of hair. Over the decades, this became the most revered record in all of American sports. Entering the 1998 season, Mark McGwire, a first baseman for the Saint Louis Cardinals, was the favorite to break the record. He hit a career-high 58 home runs the previous year. The 1998 season began on March 31. By the end of April, McGwire had already amassed 11 home runs, but he was not running away with the race. George Kenneth "Ken" Griffey, Jr., a Black American outfielder for the Seattle Mariners, was keeping things interesting. Griffey was arguably baseball's most famous athlete in America during the 1990s. Nike had Jordan for basketball and Griffey to market their baseball apparel. He tied McGwire with 15 home runs by May 15. McGwire hit 12 home runs over the next 13 games to take an eight-homer lead. Just as Griffey was fading, a new face entered the picture.[45]

Sammy Sosa recorded 36, 40, and 36 home runs between 1995 and 1997. No one expected the 29-year-old slugger to be a legitimate contender to break Maris's record, but something was different about the summer of '98. Sosa set a record for the most home runs in a month, which still stands. His 20 home runs in June tied him with Griffey and silenced the critics who did not think he was worth the $42.5 million contract he received the previous year. Some folks thought an adjustment to his hitting mechanics was the reason for his unexpected hitting streak. Sosa and Griffey each had 33 home runs heading into July. McGwire was still leading with 37. By the end of the month, Sosa and McGwire were tied at 55. Griffey finished the season with 56.

On September 7, McGwire tied Maris. The historic feat happened on the 61st birthday of McGwire's father, John. He hit number 62 off a pitch from Sosa teammate Steve Trachsel in the fourth inning the next day. "There it is! 62! Touch first, Mark! You are the new single-season home run king!" said Cardinals announcer Joe Buck.[46] The game came to a halt. As the entire Busch Stadium in Saint Louis erupted into raucous applause, McGuire raised his 10-year-old son, Matthew, dressed in a Cardinals uniform, in the sky and kissed him on the mouth. Sosa walked over from right field to congratulate him. The two competitors embraced as McGwire raised Sosa in the air. They blew kisses at each other and embraced again. McGwire walked over to the Maris family, sitting near the dugout, and hugged each of them. The young man who caught McGwire's ball brought it to him. He could have made millions by selling it but said returning it was the noble thing to do. President Clinton called McGwire after the game to express his well-wishes.

Mark McGwire made history first, but Sosa was not ready to concede. His 64th and 65th home runs tied McGwire on September 23. He hit another to take the lead on September 25. McGwire tallied his 66th home run 45 minutes later that day. Sosa did not hit another home run that season. McGwire was ready to sit out the final regular-season games, but his manager, Tony La Russa, thought he owed it to the fans to play. McGwire hit home runs in the last two games of the regular season. His home run record of 70 stood until San Francisco Giants left fielder Barry Bonds hit 73 home runs in 2001. McGwire versus Sosa was many things. It was David versus Goliath. Standing 6'5" and 245 pounds, McGwire was baseball's version of Paul Bunyan, the giant lumberjack popularized in North American folklore in the 20th century. In 1998, "Big Mac," as he was nicknamed, towered over the six-foot, 165-poound Sosa.[47] To use a basketball analogy, this was Bird versus Magic. The charismatic Sosa was the perfect counter to the stoic McGwire. It was said that Sosa would allow a ham sandwich to interview him. As the race grew closer to 61, they began conducting joint interviews. Television networks, not solely ESPN, broke into national programming to cover each at bat until the record was broken.

The Bird-Magic rivalry had an underlying racial component. Race, ethnicity, and nationality also factored into the coverage of McGwire-Sosa. In her dissertation "Exertions: Acts of Citizenship in the Globalization of

Major League Beisbol," Lara D. Nielsen described the Saint Louis slugger as the All-American White hero. McGwire grew up in the middle class in Pomona, California. His first hit in Little League was a home run. He was a pitcher at the University of Southern California. He won a World Series ring with the Oakland Athletics in 1989. His red hair and massive muscles made him the ideal poster boy for baseball's popular "chicks dig the long ball" commercials. The cameras focused on his son running into his arms after games as he set these milestones. The Maris family embraced him as one of their own. When Sosa was close to the record, neither the Maris family nor MLB commissioner Alan Huber "Bud" Selig appeared at his games.[48]

Mark McGwire barely knew who Sammy Sosa was until that June. "He was the golden boy," said Sosa in the 2020 ESPN 30 for 30 film *Long Gone Summer*.[49] I remember that summer vividly. Despite my love for the NBA, I follow baseball too. Sosa was grinning too much in interviews and being overly gracious toward McGwire. He would say things in his thick Caribbean accent like, "He is the man in the United States. I am the man in the Dominican Republic. Hehehe." Another one of his famous sayings was, "Baseball has been very good to me" (invoking *SNL*'s Garrett Morris as Chico Escuela). The pursuit of the record made Sosa a household name in America. When Michael Jordan declined an invitation to sit beside First Lady Hillary Clinton at President Clinton's State of the Union Address, Sosa filled in. The mainstream media and fans loved "Slamming Sammy," but it was always evident throughout the summer who was favored to win.[50]

In his 2007 article "Race in 'the Race,'" M.L. Butterworth described the racial optics in the media's coverage of the home run race.

> The media portrayed McGwire to be a mythic hero because of his whiteness.... McGwire was consistently described by his strength through statistical measurements.... Even *Time* magazine labeled McGwire as the "Hero of the Year" in 1998.... Sosa never received attention as a mythical figure. Instead, most of the comments made were about his Dominican heritage that reinforced Latino and dark-skinned stereotypes while also portraying him as an intruder in the way of McGwire's record.[51]

Many sportswriters say the home run race resurrected baseball in America. MLB ratings had declined after the 1994–95 strike, the longest work stoppage in league history. The World Series was canceled for the first time. No American professional sports league has ever missed an entire postseason. Michael Jordan ended his brief stint in Minor League Baseball during the lockout and returned to playing basketball. McGwire and Sosa brought fans back to the ballparks and reestablished baseball's place as the national pastime. Unfortunately, those good tidings of great joy were ruined by a cheating scandal. McGwire and Sosa, along with other notable players, were accused of taking performance-enhancing drugs (PEDs) to hit all those home runs. They both denied the accusations during a nationally televised 11-hour congressional hearing on March 17, 2005. Sosa brought an interpreter, claiming he had difficulty understanding English because he was from the Dominican Republic.[52]

McGwire finally admitted to taking steroids in 2010.[53] After a few years as an outcast, he returned to baseball as a hitting coach for the Cardinals, Dodgers, and Padres. Sosa still denies knowingly using PEDs. Once a beloved superhero in Chicago, he is now a pariah. He has not been welcomed at Wrigley Field, the Cubs' home, since 2004. Making matters worse, the once dark-skinned Sosa now resembles the late pop singer Michael Jackson. Many people believe he is bleaching his skin, a widespread practice among darker Blacks in the Caribbean and Africa. Sosa refutes those claims.[54] Baseball writers have refused to vote for either McGwire or Sosa on the Hall of Fame ballot because of their PED use.

Sammy Sosa was the most popular Dominican MLB player until the PED allegations sullied his reputation in the early 2000s. Around that time, other Dominicans emerged as the league's most popular players. The Red Sox were an inning away from being swept by the Yankees in the 2004 American League Championship Series (ALCS). All-Star Yankees relief pitcher Mariano Rivera, from Panama, blew a one-run lead in the ninth inning. The Red Sox won that game and the next three. They were the first team in professional American sports to accomplish this remarkable feat. Dominicans Pedro Martínez and David "Big Papi" Ortiz were primarily responsible for this historic comeback. Martinez was the winning pitcher in game five and the relief pitcher for an inning in the decisive seventh game. Ortiz hit three home runs and 11 RBIs on his way to an ALCS MVP trophy. The Red Sox defeated the Cardinals in the World Series, ending the "Curse of the Bambino," Boston's 86-year championship drought since trading Babe Ruth to the Yankees in 1918. Today, both players are first-ballot inductees in the Baseball Hall of Fame and highly visible sports media figures. Ortiz, a figure as charismatic as Sosa, is a member of Fox's pre- and post-game shows during the playoffs, World Series, All-Star Game, and World Baseball Classic.

The Dominican Dream

In Chapter 5, I questioned if the NBA's dealings in Africa had a hint of neocolonialism and exploitation. Respected scholars have raised similar questions about MLB's investment in the Dominican Republic. I focused on MLB's academy system and Big League Advance to address this subject.

Once MLB turned its sights toward the Dominican Republic, it needed a way to find and nurture talent. Epy Guerrero and Ralph Avila developed a solution. Guerrero, a Dominican native and a scout for the Blue Jays, saw a wealth of talent in his homeland. In 1973, he convinced the Blue Jays to construct an academy in the Dominican Republic to serve as a training facility for teenage baseball players. It was equipped with baseball fields, dining rooms, and housing for the players. In 1987, Ralph Avila, a Cuban native and a part-time scout for the Dodgers, oversaw the creation of Campo Las Palmas, the team's baseball academy in the Dominican Republic. The Dodgers invested millions into the academy.[55]

The academies created the first formal process for Dominican talent to reach MLB rosters. There are currently 30 academies representing all 30 MLB teams in the Dominican Republic. Once scouts identify talent, tryouts are held. The standout players receive contracts to train at an academy. Most Caribbean and Latin American prospects, except Puerto Ricans and Cubans, are sent to an academy. (Puerto Ricans can be selected in the MLB draft because the island is a U.S. territory.) Players become eligible to sign a contract with an academy, beginning on the second day in July, once they turn 16. In the Dominican Republic, there are local scouts called *buscónes*, which comes from the Spanish word *buscar*, meaning "to search" or "to look for." The *buscónes*, working as middlemen for MLB teams, begin scouting players from a very young age. Over the years, these scouts have been accused of preying on and exploiting kids.[56]

Life in the Dominican Republic is far from ideal. As of 2018, more than 30 percent of the population lived below the poverty line. Sadly, this was an improvement over previous years. The poverty rate was 50 percent between 2000 and 2010. The average annual income was $5,000 throughout the 2000s. Five million residents earned less than $1.25 a day.[57] USAID states the national unemployment rate has been 5.5 percent for the past decade. Eighteen percent of male youth were unemployed, not attending school, or not enrolled in training programs for a trade. A UNESCO report found that 94 percent of the population was literate, but the country still suffered from poor education rates.[58] Eighty percent of Dominicans did not have a high school diploma, the highest dropout rate in Latin America.[59]

When the late rapper The Notorious B.I.G. recited the lyrics "Either you are slingin' crack rock, or you got a wicked jump shot" on his 1994 album *Ready to Die*, he was reporting on an uncomfortable truth in many American inner cities.[60] Basketball was the alternative to selling drugs for poor Black males hungry for a piece of the American Dream's apple pie. The 1994 documentary *Hoop Dreams* brilliantly captured the lifelong aspirations and struggles of two inner-city Chicago youths, William Gates and Arthur Agee, trying to make the NBA. Parallels can be drawn between these Black American youth and their Black and brown counterparts in the Caribbean striving for the riches of a Major League career. Call it the Dominican Dream.

Unlike the NBA, where players are drafted and immediately begin playing and earning a significant salary, the process in baseball is much longer. If a player is selected to train at an academy, he must play Low- or Single-A, High-A, AA, and finally AAA Minor League ball before getting called to a Major League roster. Even though the best players can reach the "Big Leagues" quickly, only 25 percent of academy participants get promoted to the Low-A level. Two to 5 percent of participants get signed to Major League rosters. Players are separated from their families for six months during their stays at the academies. Most Dominicans are willing to sacrifice everything despite such low odds to achieve their ultimate dream because it is better than their current reality. Many prospective players come from families where four people share a one-room living space. The money they receive from an academy contract is life-changing enough to help them buy their parents a home, purchase a car, or start a business.[61] Alvin Guzman received a $2 million contract from the Arizona Diamondbacks when he was 16 to play for their Minor League teams. He became the family's breadwinner before he was old enough to vote in America.

After agriculture and tourism, baseball has become the Dominican Republic's third-leading source of revenue. American baseball brings in $75–80 million annually. However, there is a dark side to the academies and MLB's expansion into the country. Kids train nine hours a day, which leaves little time for education. Trainers give players vitamin B shots to help them play better or recover faster from injuries. In some cases, kids receive steroids and dangerous drugs from trainers without their knowledge. There is the tragic story of one 18-year-old named Ponciano who had half of his right leg amputated after he was injected with dangerous doses of steroids.[62] Some players fail to achieve success because of language barriers. Players who cannot learn English have struggled to communicate with coaches and trainers. Miscommunication can have dangerous effects. For example, some players dealing with injuries chose not to disclose that information because they did not know how to express themselves appropriately and feared being sent home. Miscommunication can cause owners or coaches to mislabel players as "lazy."[63]

Patrick Gentile argues in his master's thesis, "MLB 's Neocolonial Practices in the Dominican Republic Academy System," that MLB's dominance in the country is a form of neocolonialism:

> MLB academies illustrate how neocolonialism is "a continuation of western colonialism without the traditional mechanism of expanding frontiers and territorial control but with elements of political, economic and cultural

control." For neocolonialism to occur, there must be a history of past successful colonialism, which the United States has exhibited in the Dominican Republic. Between 1870 and 1900, Americans became the most potent international influence in the Dominican Republic because they invested heavily in the sugar industry. The United States also invaded the country in the early 20th century, further colonizing the Dominican Republic.[64]

Alan Klein, a professor of sociology-anthropology at Northeastern University and the author of *Dominican Baseball: New Pride, Old Prejudice*, has devoted much scholarship to the relationship between Major League Baseball and Latin America. Klein says MLB's entrance into the Dominican Republic in the sixties was an extension of neocolonists' practices. He acknowledges the mutual benefits for both parties. The academies provide financial and educational opportunities the players would not have received otherwise. The Dominican Republic gets $50–75 million in annual revenue from MLB's investment. By comparison, MLB earns $7 billion annually from this cheap labor supply. Despite this unequal partnership, rooted in American prejudice, Klein argues that Dominicans have developed a "new pride" to fight this exploitation and even the playing field economically by regaining control over their valuable natural resource: young baseball players.[65]

When 22-year-old Dominican shortstop Fernando Tatis, Jr., signed a 14-year, $340 contract extension with the San Diego Padres, $30 million of his new contract went to Big League Advance (BLA). This organization is a unique alternative to the traditional academy system. How does it work? BLA invests money into prospective baseball players at a young age. Players receive seed money to launch their careers. Players do not make much in the minor leagues. At Triple-A ball, the level just below the majors, the salary for a five-month, 144-game season is $14,700. At Single-A, the lowest rung on the ladder, they earn just over $10,000 to play 132 times. BLA clients like Dominican Francisco Mejia can earn as much as $360,000.[66]

BLA's goal is to project who will go bust versus boom. It uses analytics to predict the players' future earnings. It is like investing in publicly traded companies on the stock market, except BLA investors are gambling on human stock. BLA was founded in 2016 by Michael Schwimer, a former relief pitcher who played 47 games with the Philadelphia Phillies before injuries cut his career short at 27. He claims that he started BLA to benefit young players struggling to make ends meet while in the minors. BLA makes money only if their clients advance beyond the minor leagues.

One must use a third eye when carefully reviewing BLA's business motives. Schwimer lives in a mansion equipped with a basketball court, automatic rebounding machine, home gym, and golf simulator, allowing him to play on any course in the world. Scott Boras, the top sports agent in baseball for the past 20 years, accuses Schwimer of preying on poor, less educated kids in Latin American countries like the Dominican Republic. Boras says BLA uses devious tactics like promising players $800,000 signing bonuses in exchange for 15 percent of all their future earnings in the majors. Tatis is paying BLA $30 million for a $500,000 loan. Schwimer, who is white, defends BLA by telling his critics he provides these kids and fledgling young men a safer option than the illegal street agents who have been exploiting them for years. He talks about a former BLA client who never made a Major League roster but used his seed money to pay for graduate school. But despite this one success story, many players do not advance to the majors and run into IRS problems with their seed money due to financial illiteracy.[67]

Is globalization good for Major League Baseball? Yes. The sport of baseball and the MLB brand have grown exponentially over the past few decades. Globalization is responsible for many of the league's best players and brightest stars since Sammy Sosa helped rescue baseball with the 1998 home run race. MLB is a multibillion-dollar industry with games, livestreaming, and merchandise sold everywhere from Europe to Asia. Globalization has allowed baseball to play a role in geopolitics. Yet, we should not ignore the downside of globalization, which is the exploitation of young players and neocolonial practices in the Dominican Republic. As a strong proponent of social justice issues, I consider this highly problematic. I have the same critique of the NBA's partnership with China and possible future partnerships with Saudi Arabian investment groups. Globalization has also given MLB an excuse not to do more to nurture talent in America's Black communities as it did in past decades. More dark bodies from Latin America entering the game equals fewer Black American faces on rosters. It is a phenomenon akin to the disappearing White American ballplayer on NBA rosters.

Are You Ready for Some Football?

A 1972 Gallup poll gave baseball fans a bitter dose of reality. Americans voted football ahead of baseball as their favorite sport for the first time. Six years later, NFL Films called the Dallas Cowboys "America's Team" and their quarterback, Roger Staubach, "Captain America." The NFL began challenging MLB for the nation's attention a decade earlier. In 1966, the National Football League merged with its rival, the American Football League (AFL), to form the NFL as we know it today. This union preceded the NBA-ABA merger. The first AFL-NFL World Championship Game was played at the Los Angeles Memorial Coliseum on January

15, 1967, between the NFL's Green Bay Packers and the AFL's Kansas City Chiefs. Broadway Joe Willie Namath's New York Jets upset the favored Baltimore Colts in the first official Super Bowl two years later.[68]

The NFL had 82 of the 100 most-watched domestic broadcasts in 2022.[69] Super Bowl LVII, played on February 12, 2023, between the Kansas City Chiefs and the Philadelphia Eagles, amassed over 115 million viewers, making it the most-watched program in American television history.[70] Super Bowl LVIII topped that number a year later with 123.7 million viewers, thanks in part to countless Taylor Swift fans tuning in to watch the pop icon cheer for her boyfriend, Kansas City Chiefs tight end Travis Kelce, on the field. Thirty million viewers tuned in to watch Usher's halftime concert extravaganza.[71] The NFL is the only professional sports league to receive television coverage on all four major American networks. Fans can also view games on ESPN, the NFL Network, Nickelodeon, and two digital streaming platforms (Amazon Prime and Peacock). The NFL dominates chatter and sports headlines much of the year, even though the season lasts barely six months. As for social media, the league's official TikTok, Instagram, and Twitter accounts have 70.6 million followers combined. Fantasy football and the legalization of sports betting have only tightened the league's grip on American hearts and minds.

The NFL had six of the 10 of the world's most lucrative sports franchises in 2023. The Cowboys topped the list with a value of $8 billion.[72] Only two NBA teams were on the list. The Golden State Warriors were ranked eighth at $5.6 billion, and the Los Angeles Lakers were ranked 10th at $5.5 billion.[73] NFL commissioner Roger Goodell's annual $64 million salary dwarfs NBA commissioner Adam Silver's $10 million salary and MLB commissioner Rob Manfred's $17.5 million salary.[74]

Football fans outside U.S. markets can enjoy the game using NFL Game Pass, which provides access to all regular-season games, the playoffs, and the Super Bowl. NFL Game Pass Season Pro allows fans to livestream games, watch past games on demand, and watch highlights using multiple digital devices. Fans can also view related programming from the NFL Network and HBO. The league does not partner with Tencent like the NBA or MLB in China. A total of 103,467 spectators attended the NFL's first international game in 1994 when the Cowboys played the Houston Oilers at Mexico City's Estadio Azteca. The Buffalo Bills played in Toronto every year from 2008 until 2012. Thirteen preseason games were held in Tokyo between 1989 and 2005. The league failed to play a preseason game in China in 2007 and 2009.[75]

Even though the NFL is still playing catch-up when it comes to globalization, it is diligent in making progress. When the NFL released its schedule for the upcoming 2023 season, promoted by hourlong television specials on ESPN and the NFL Network, its five international games were spotlighted. Three games would be played in London, while Patrick Mahomes, Travis Kelce, and the defending Super Bowl champion Chiefs played in one of two games in Germany. The NFL hosted games in these locations and Mexico City the previous season. The league hosted its first game in Sao Paulo, Brazil, in the 2024 season.

Roger Goodell has publicly expressed his desire to hold two games in London's Wembley Stadium each season and eventually place a team in London. The NFL has been fascinated with European expansion for decades. The plan for European football was first announced in 1974. The Intercontinental Football League (IFL), proposed to launch in 1975, planned to include teams in Barcelona, Berlin, Istanbul, Munich, and Vienna. Unfortunately, geopolitical strife in Europe, political assassinations, and kidnappings persuaded the State Department to warn NFL commissioner Pete Rozelle against further pursuing globalization. The IFL was disbanded before a game was played.

The World Football League (WFL), which debuted in 1974 without any affiliation to the NFL, was hardly an example of globalization. Hawaii was the farthest location for a franchise. The upstart league emerged as the NFL was undergoing a players' strike. The WFL tried to poach disgruntled NFL players by offering them more money. The NFL paid its players less than the other major American team sports at the time. Cowboys running back Calvin Hill, father of NBA Hall-of-Famer and current USA Basketball director Grant Hill, signed a contract with the Hawaii Hawaiians. Nearly 60 NFL players defected to the WFL before it ceased operations after one season. In 1989, the World League of American Football (WLAF) was introduced to promote American football overseas. Twenty-six of the NFL's 28 teams invested $50,000 to cover the startup cost for this new spring football league. The WLAF had 10 teams, seven in North America and three in Europe. NFL commissioner Paul Tagliabue viewed this experiment as a developmental minor league for prospective NFL players.

The WLAF was renamed NFL Europe in 1998. Future Super Bowl XXXIV MVP Kurt Warner played quarterback for the Amsterdam Admirals. Jake Delhomme, the Carolina starting quarterback in Super Bowl XXXVIII, was Warner's backup on the Admirals. Oliver Luck, father of 2012 number-one NFL draft pick Andrew Luck, was the league's president. NFL Europe rebranded itself as NFL Europa in 2006 to reflect Europe's name in most languages. The name change did little to prevent this international experiment from failing. NFL Europa was losing $30 million a season. American football did not match futbol (soccer), Europe's most popular sport. The league closed for business in 2007.

International players have appeared on NFL rosters since the inaugural 1920 season. Brothers John and Phil Nesser represented Germany on the Columbus Panhandles. Tommy Hughitt was the first Canadian NFL player. Ignacio Saturnino "Lou" Molinet was the first Latin American player. The Cuban native joined the Frankford Yellow Jackets in 1927. Jon Lee was the NFL's first Asian player. Lee was a native of Seoul, South Korea, the birthplace of Pittsburgh Steelers wide receiver and Super Bowl XL MVP Hines Ward. At least eight punters were born in Australia.

The Pro Football Hall of Fame has enshrined nine international players. Danish placekicker Morten Andersen received his bust in Canton, Ohio, the site of the Hall of Fame, in 2017. Andersen played for six teams between 1982 and 2007. He holds the record for the most NFL games played at 382 and is the highest scorer in league history based on his number of successfully made field goals. Twelve international players were drafted in 2015, an NFL record. Two years after this historic draft, the league introduced its International Player Pathway (IPP) program, which allows foreign-born athletes to make the NFL by hosting scouting combines (weeklong player showcases) in England and Mexico. Fifty-six players representing 16 countries participated in the 2021 program. Some of the program's notable alumni include German fullback Jakob Johnson (Las Vegas Raiders), Australian tackle Jordan Mailata (Philadelphia Eagles), English defensive end Efe Obada (Washington Commanders), and Chilean tight end Sammis Reyes (Jacksonville Jaguars).[76]

Much like the NBA, the NFL is making inroads in Africa. Currently, more international players are hailing from Africa (100) than any other continent.[77] The Tampa Bay Buccaneers signed the first African player, Obed Ariri, in 1984. The Nigerian placekicker was initially drafted by the Baltimore Colts in 1981 but failed to make the final roster. Obed was cut by Tampa Bay at the end of the preseason. He had a brief stint with the Washington Redskins during the players' strike in 1987. That same year, the Kansas City Chiefs drafted a 260-pound Nigerian running back named Christian Okoye. Nicknamed the Nigerian Nightmare, Okoye transitioned to football after a collegiate track and field career failed to blossom into a spot on the Olympic team. Okoye played five seasons in Kansas City, leading the league in rushing yards in 1989 and receiving All-Pro selections in 1989 and 1991.[78]

The New York Giants drafted British-Nigerian defensive end Ositadimma "Osi" Umenyiora. Osi was a pivotal member of two Super Bowl championship teams, including the 2007–2008 Giants squad that upset Tom Brady's 16–0 New England Patriots on the verge of a perfect season. Today, the retired champion is busy serving as the league's official ambassador in Africa. In 2020, he and former NBA player Ejike Ugboaja established Uprise, a developmental camp for young Africans with dreams of playing professional football. Three Nigerian players affiliated with Uprise were signed to NFL rosters in 2021. The following year, NFL Africa, the league's official platform to highlight players on the continent, held its first official training camp. Scouts from various teams attended the event in search of talent for the league's International Player Pathway. Osi predicts that it is only a matter of time before the first NFL game is played in Africa.[79] NFL Network's *NFL 360* series presented a special report on Osi's work in Africa during Black History Month in 2024. It documented his bringing African-born and Black American NFL players back to the continent to work with the native people and the youth. They also visited the Cape Coast Slave Castle in Ghana to better understand the impact of the transatlantic slave trade on West Africa. Osi and the other men stood inside the dungeons where enslaved men and women slept, ate, defecated, and died.

Africans are also making inroads in the NFL at the administrative level. The Minnesota Vikings hired Kwesi Adofo-Mensah as their general manager in 2022. The Ivy League–educated son of Ghanaian immigrants was a trader on Wall Street and the vice president of football operations for the Cleveland Browns before taking the job.[80] Adofo-Mensah, like the NBA's Masai Ujiri, hopes to use his platform to inspire other individuals of African descent to secure leadership positions in professional sports.[81]

The NFL is the last truly American professional sports league in the U.S. It has the fewest international players, coaches, and executives of the big three leagues. The NFL has embraced American patriotism more than any of its competitors. Howard Bryant details the league's ties to the military in his book *The Heritage: Black Athletes, a Divided America, and the Politics of Patriotism*. As I discussed in Chapter 2, Bryant documents the millions of dollars the league made with the military after 9/11 to honor soldiers, promote the war effort, and uplift patriotism.[82] I grew up in the Washington, D.C., area. Our local NFL team, the Redskins, was engrossed in a naming controversy for decades. Many social activists and media members called the team's name and logo racially offensive to the Native American community. After a temporary name change to the Washington Football Team, they rebranded themselves as the Commanders in 2022. The name is supposed to represent the city's rich military history. At the 2023 Hall of Fame ceremony, Zach Thomas and Jamael Orondé "Ronde" Barber ended their induction speeches honoring God and country. "Thank you. God bless our troops. And God bless America," said Thomas.[83]

The NFL might be the only professional sports league that does not need globalization. In recent years, there have been cracks in the league's shield, notably safety concerns about chronic traumatic encephalopathy (CTE) caused by head trauma and concussions. Thus far, those concerns have not been magnified enough to turn American youth away from playing and viewers from tuning in to games. Political protests and domestic violence cases have cost the league some fans, but not enough to factor in significantly. The NFL dominates television ratings without the global market that the NBA and MLB partly depend on.

The NFL does not need globalization because it already has the best farm system for training cheap labor in its own backyard. Division I college football, the second-most-popular sport in America, is the league's equivalent of the NBA's academies in Africa and MLB's academies in the Dominican Republic. For decades, colleges hid behind the "student-athlete" model designed by Walter Byers, the first executive director of the NCAA, to avoid having to pay players on scholarship and prevent them from unionizing.[84] The U.S. Supreme Court finally ruled that college athletes could be compensated for their name, image, and likeness (NIL) in 2021. Collegiate standouts in 2023, like University of Southern California quarterback Caleb Williams, were already appearing in nationally televised commercials and earning over $1 million from lucrative NIL deals.[85] Now collegiate football players can earn a salary like Minor League Baseball players before signing professional contracts.

In conclusion, the data shows that the NBA and MLB currently benefit the most from globalization. Major League Baseball has a strong international presence but trails the NBA and NFL in viewership and social media followers. NBA players are more popular domestically and globally than their baseball counterparts. Thus far, the NBA has connected more effectively with the world's youth than Major League Baseball. The NBA lacks the blatant examples of exploitation found in baseball's recruitment of poor Dominican players. While the NFL does not need globalization to survive as much as its competitors, this will not halt efforts to grow the game beyond American borders. As the NFL continues to expand internationally, it will be fascinating to see if it can ever surpass the NBA's global reach in future generations.

Epilogue

In mid–February 2024, I traveled on Delta Airlines flight 5839, sitting beside a young Black woman from the Cayman Islands. Her boyfriend, a young White high school principal in Ontario, Canada, was seated in the aisle across from us. She had bought tickets to the NBA's All-Star weekend in Indianapolis, Indiana, for his birthday. They were flying back home to Ontario after the long weekend. It was their first time experiencing All-Star weekend and also my first time attending the event. Neither the four-inch snowstorm on my first day in town nor the 15-degree weather could stop me from fulfilling a childhood aspiration to experience this event. Although sports pundits and talk show hosts took turns criticizing the event for nearly a week after it was over because of lackluster performances by the players in the All-Star Game and the events preceding it the night before, I found a lot to appreciate.

First, the league's popularity appears strong among millennials, Generation Z, and Generation Alpha (individuals born between 2010 and 2024). I saw young people of all races and ethnicities in groups and with their parents. The couple I met on my flight was an example of the global representation present in Indianapolis. In addition to foreign fans and media members, attendees included Zedd, the German record producer and DJ, who performed with hip-hop star T-Pain for the Friday night concert at the Indiana Convention Center to kick off the weekend. Viola Brand, a world-champion artistic cyclist from Germany, wowed crowds with her bicycle at the All-Star practice and All-Star Saturday Night festivities. I spotted Toronto Raptors superfan Nav Bhatia at multiple events. Twelve current and former international players, including Victor Wembanyama, Nikola Jokić, Luka Dončić, and 2023 Hall of Fame inductee Pau Gasol, participated in some events during the weekend. In 2023, Commissioner Adam Silver revealed that he was exploring the possibility of American-born all-stars playing their international counterparts in a future game to increase competition.[1]

When I began researching this topic, I aimed to answer the following questions: What does the NBA's ascension to a billion-dollar global empire teach us about the globalization of American sports and culture since the end of the Cold War and the dawn of the millennium? How beneficial is globalization for the NBA? Is globalization necessary for the NBA and rival professional sports leagues to thrive in the 21st century? Has globalization made American-born NBA players replaceable? Globalization has impacted nearly every aspect of life in America. It was only a matter of time before globalization would affect the NBA. The league was experimenting with globalization as early as the 1970s with exhibitions and coaching clinics. While it would be easy to give the late Commissioner David Stern all the credit for being forward-thinking, that would be disingenuous. Stern initially opposed globalization, and if it had not been for FIBA's Boris Stanković and Dave Gavitt, there would not have been a Dream Team at the 1992 Barcelona Summer Olympics. The NBA got lucky in 1992, and the dominance of Michael Jordan's Bulls teams only heightened the league's popularity worldwide. The NBA benefited from the emergence of transnational corporations such as Nike, which was able to market its brand globally. In turn, the NBA, especially Jordan, helped to boost Nike's sales globally. The NBA also benefited from the growth of cable television and the internet at the end of the 20th century. Now fans across the globe can experience its product. The NBA's international growth was symbolic of American culture, in general, becoming global. American fashion, music, film, and sports spread internationally, and international influences also shaped them.

How beneficial is globalization for the NBA? Four of the league's 10 best current players are foreign-born. Nikola Jokić captured his third MVP award in four years on May 8, 2024. The top three runners-up were Shai Gilgeous-Alexander, Luka Dončić, and Giannis Antetokounmpo, respectively. Domantas Sabonis finished eighth in MVP voting. Victor Wembanyama already appears to be on track to become the face of the league as reigning superstars LeBron James and Stephen Curry near the twilight of their playing careers. Wemby beat out Chet Holmgrem for Rookie of the Year. He was the runner-up for the Hakeem Olajuwon Defensive Player of the Year award, which went to fellow Frenchman Rudy Gobert for the fourth time since 2018.[2]

The success of these international players is likely to continue the trend of teams looking abroad to find the next unicorn. Six of the first 12 selections in the 2024 draft were international. Three of those players, including the top two picks, Zacchaire Risacher and Alex Sarr, were French. This was the most players from the same foreign country selected within the first ten picks. Risacher is the fourth foreign-born overall top draft pick since 2002.[3]

While you could call it "The Wemby Effect," NBA analyst Fran Franschilla says this French revolution has been building since 2004. Franschilla credits exemplary youth coaching and African immigration for France's success. Retired NBA star Tony Parker opened a basketball academy in Lyon, France, in 2019 to train high school students.[4] Wemby and France pushed a stacked U.S. team in the 2024 Olympics gold medal game. The next day the French women came up two points shy of ruining the American women's 61-game Olympic winning streak.[5]

The Memphis Grizzlies made Ulrich Chomche the first draft pick from NBA Academy Africa. Johnny Furphy, an alumnus of NBA Academy Australia, was the 35th draft pick. Furphy will join Wembanyama in San Antonio. Twenty of the 58 draftees were born abroad. ESPN's draft broadcasting crew expressed concern with the decline in American draftees. Stephen A. Smith said this is a warning for Black American kids to let them know they are replaceable. Could the NBA's demographics end up like MLB in a generation?[6]

Globalization has opened new markets for the league to broadcast games, hold exhibitions, and find new fanbases to buy its merchandise. The league's corporate sponsors benefit by finding new markets to sell NBA-related products. Globalization has also helped the league to promote social issues internationally. Social media enabled the Black Lives Matter movement to reach the masses abroad during the 2020 George Floyd protests. The league and its players played a part in raising awareness via social media and having Black Lives Matter logos on their courts whenever games were televised and livestreamed. The league also raised awareness for political prisoners in Russia during Brittney Griner's 10-month ordeal. Furthermore, training academies, summer camps, and programs like Basketball Without Borders have provided opportunities for impoverished kids in Africa and their peers in war-torn European countries to achieve a better life, attend American universities, and create generational wealth for their families if they turn pro.

I do not intend to paint the NBA as a humanitarian nonprofit organization. David Stern made it painfully clear that his objectives for globalization were to make money. I have already discussed Jordan's refusal to display the logo of Nike's rival Reebok on his warm-up jacket at the 1992 Olympics. The NBA is not in Africa out of the goodness of their hearts or in the spirit of missionary work. They are there to groom future talent, grow the NBA brand, and make money. The league is always motivated by capitalistic ambitions. In this case, it is no different from any other transnational corporation. The NFL and MLB are doing the same thing. Professional sports are a microcosm of big business in the post–Cold War era and millennium.

The NBA has experienced the pros and cons of globalization. Globalization has allowed it to promote patriotism through Olympic and FIBA competitions during the war. This was the case with Coach K and the 2008 Redeem Team. The league can indirectly take credit for some of Dennis Rodman's diplomatic work in North Korea. Colin Cowherd insinuated that the focus on global talent has decreased domestic television viewership. Similar arguments have been made about declining interest in MLB and men's tennis; however, there is no data to prove this. The league's relationship with China and refusal to support Hong Kong are the most glaring examples of the cons. Some social justice activists and scholars might question the league's motives in Africa and accuse it of exploitation. MLB has experienced this because of its involvement in the Dominican Republic. The NBA has already suffered a black eye recently because of the mistreatment and lack of academic preparation for the students at its academy in China. As Saudi investment groups are making inroads in golf and other American professional sports now, NBA governors must contend with sportswashing and more international human rights violations. Now, NBA players are asked about and expected to have opinions on geopolitical matters that many Americans are unfamiliar with.

Is globalization necessary for the NBA and rival professional sports leagues to thrive in the 21st century? While the NFL has been highly successful with a primarily American product, it now embraces globalization. The NFL's International Players Pathway program, African academies, and games abroad are an attempt to compete with soccer as the world's most popular sport. Major League Baseball has been heavily invested globally since the early 20th century. MLB's brightest star is Shohei Ohtani, a native of Japan. Ohtani, a member of the 2024 World Series champion Los Angeles Dodgers, plays in one of the largest American television markets. This will only increase his visibility and that of the MLB domestically and internationally. The NHL and PGA have also been expanding abroad since the last century.

Ironically, the WNBA lags in globalization. Only 25 international players were on WNBA rosters in 2022. Perhaps the creation of the NBA Academy Women's Program in 2018 will make a difference. In 2019, Han Xu (China) became the Academy's first alumna to be drafted into the WNBA. The Washington Mystics selected Aaliyah Edwards (Canada), another alumna, with the sixth pick in the 2024 draft.[7]

This book addresses an important topic that scholars still need to research thoroughly. The NBA is a multibillion-dollar global corporation that impacts professional and collegiate sports, the fashion industry, music, social media, politics, secondary education, discussions on race and gender, and social justice issues. Faculty should address this subject in their classrooms. Likewise, casual sports fans need to understand the magnitude of what they are experiencing when they watch or attend an NBA game. Hopefully, this book can serve as a starting point for in-depth research conducted by current and future scholars. I would like to see those scholars fill in the gaps in my research. I could not spend time on the NBA's impact in Australia, Latin America, and the Middle East. My discussion of Asia was limited to China and Korea. Research is needed on lesser-known African, Canadian, and European players and administrators, which I could not cover in this publication.

One limitation I faced was not being able to visit some of the countries I discussed while writing this book. I encourage future researchers to apply for grants to fund their travel. Also, I could not interview NBA players, league officials, and many of the sports journalists covering the NBA. Future researchers should know that these interviews are difficult to secure and usually take months to arrange. Many of these individuals will not grant interviews during the season. Although you will have a better chance in the offseason, it is still challenging to go through various agents, publicists, and team representatives to get a hold of the players. In other cases, people may talk only with inquirers affiliated with a major entity such as ESPN, NPR, or Random House. Some ideal interviewees might be skeptical about participating in a project that could paint the NBA negatively. I am grateful for David Aldridge's and Roland Houston's willingness to participate. Houston serves as a technical director at NBA Academy Africa.

There are several implications for future research. What steps is the NBA taking to grow the game further in Australia, Latin America, and the Caribbean? Are efforts being made to ensure that American athletes stay relevant? What is the NBA doing to ensure that the WNBA can grow internationally? Researchers abroad could check for bias in their country's coverage of native-born NBA players versus those from America and other countries.

I am excited to see future books, journal articles, dissertations, podcasts, and documentaries on this subject. I am eager to see if Wemby can live up to the oversized hype. How many championships and MVP awards can the Joker (Nikola Jokić) win? Will Luka (Dončić) break Kobe's 81-point record? Will he break Wilt's 100-point record? Will the next MJ or LeBron hail from Canada, China, Egypt, Puerto Rico, or the United Kingdom? Will American sports fans accept an international player as the face of the NBA and the nation's most popular athlete? Only time will tell!

Chapter Notes

Preface

1. Arthur Pincus, "Butch Lee's Road Winds to the Pros," *New York Times*, March 11, 1978, accessed on January 10, 2024, https://www.nytimes.com/1978/03/11/archives/butch-lees-road-winds-to-the-pros-al-rode-him-pretty-hard-ncaa.html.
2. Natalie La Roche Pietre, "Al Horford's Celtics win kindles Dominican pride locally," *Boston Globe*, June 18, 2024, https://www.bostonglobe.com/2024/06/18/sports/al-horford-first-dominican-champion/.

Introduction

1. Curtis "50 Cent" Jackson is a media mogul who was among the world's best-selling rappers in the early 2000s. He threw out the first pitch at a New York Mets game on May 27, 2014. Many sports fans consider this one of the worst ceremonial pitches in Major League Baseball history.
2. Victor Wembanyama is the son of a Black father from the Democratic Republic of the Congo and a white mother from France.
3. "Stephen Curry about Wembanyama: 'He's like the NBA 2K create-a-player,'" *Basketball News*, October 7, 2022, accessed on October 10, 2022, https://basketnews.com/news-178960-stephen-curry-about-wembanyama-hes-like-the-nba-2k-create-a-player.html.
4. Brian Wacker, "Adam Silver issues tanking warning for teen phenom Victor Wembanyama," *New York Post*, October 6, 2022, accessed on October 10, 2022, https://nypost.com/2022/10/06/adam-silver-warns-nba-teams-tanking-for-victor-wembanyama/.
5. Erin Walsh, "Woj: Victor Wembanyama, Could Add $500M in Value to a Franchise, Says Team President," *Bleacher Report*, October 6, 2022, accessed on October 10, 2022, https://bleacherreport.com/articles/10051541-woj-victor-wembanyama-could-add-500m-in-value-to-a-franchise-says-team-president.
6. The San Antonio Spurs have a strong track record with French players. They drafted four-time champion Tony Parker in 2001. Boris Diaw helped the team win the NBA championship in 2014.
7. Nicholas Rice, "Britney Spears Says Her Reaction to Victor Wembanyama Security Scuffle Was a 'Cry Out on All Levels,'" *People*, July 8, 2023, accessed on July 9, 2023, https://people.com/britney-spears-on-her-reaction-to-victor-wembanyama-security-scuffle-7558276.
8. "NBArank 2023: Player rankings for 2023–23, from 10 to 1," *ESPN*, October 12, 2023, accessed on November 14, 2023, https://www.espn.com/nba/story/_/id/38633041/nbarank-2023-player-rankings-2023-24-10-1.
9. Institute for Immigration Research at George Mason University, https://iir.gmu.edu/immigrants-athletes-and-inclusion/in_sports/players-in-the-national-basketball-association-nba
10. Monte Poole, "Race in America: A Candid Conversation," *NBC Sports*, September 11, 2020, accessed on October 11, 2022, https://www.nbcsports.com/bayarea/kings/kings-vivek-ranadive-recalls-prevalence-racism-fear-after-911.

11. Alibaba is a Chinese multinational technology company regarded as one of the world's largest e-commerce retailers.

12. "Joseph Tsai to buy rest of Nets from Mikhail Prokhorov," *NBA.com*, April 16, 2019, accessed on October 11, 2022, https://www.nba.com/news/report-joseph-tsai-buy-nets-23-billion.

13. Michael Kaskey-Blomain, "Adam Silver on NBA using 'Governor' in place of 'owner' title: 'We moved away from that term years ago,'" *CBS Sports*, June 24, 2019, accessed on October 11, 2022, https://www.cbssports.com/nba/news/adam-silver-on-nba-using-governor-in-place-of-owner-title-we-moved-away-from-that-term-years-ago/.

14. Pietra Rivoli, *The Travels of a T-Shirt in the Global Economy: An Economist Examines the Markets, Power, and Politics of World Trade* (Hoboken, New Jersey: Wiley, 2014).

15. Mark Juergensmeyer, *Thinking Globally: A Global Studies Reader* (University of California Press, 2014), xiv and 6.

16. *Ibid.*, 7.

17. Lael Brainard, "Globalization in the Aftermath: Target, Casualty, Callous Bystander?" *Brookings*, November 28, 2001, October 13, 2022, https://www.brookings.edu/research/globalization-in-the-aftermath-target-casualty-callous-bystander/.

18. FIFA is an acronym for The Fédération internationale de football association.

19. Alen Bairner, "Globalization and Sport: The Nation Strikes Back," *Phi Kapp Phi Forum* 83, no. 4 (Fall 2003): 34.

20. Mike Cronin, "The Globalization of Sport," *History Today* 53, no. 7 (July 2003): 26.

21. Puff Daddy (featuring The Notorious BIG and Ma$e), "Been Around the World," *No Way Out*, Arista/Bad Boy, 1997.

22. The Air Jordan 13s were the 13th model in Nike's Air Jordan sneaker line. The white-and-black colorway, released in 1997, was famously worn by Denzel Washington's character, Jake Shuttlesworth, in the 1998 Spike Lee basketball film *He Got Game*.

23. Murray Crnogai, "The Bulls didn't win just any international exhibition tournament—they won the 1997 McDonald's Open Championship!" April 21, 2020, accessed on October 4, 2022, https://www.basketballnetwork.net/old-school/the-bulls-didnt-win-just-any-international-exhibition-tournament-they-won-the-1997-mcdonalds-open-championship.

24. William Claiborne, "Bullets Pilgrims in Jerusalem," *Washington Post*, September 7, 1978: G1.

25. Josh Parker, "This Day in History: First NBA Team Plays in China,"*thatsmags.com*, August 24, 2018, accessed on October 9, 2022, http://www.thatsmags.com/beijing/post/20352/this-day-in-history-washington-bullets-visit-china.

26. Kevin Scheitrum, "History of the NBA Global Games," *NBA.com*, n.d., accessed on October 9, 2022, https://www.na.com/global/games2013/all-time-international-game-list.html.

27. Tim MacMahon, "How the NBL's Adelaide made their mark during a historic NBA preseason voyage," *ESPN*, October 6, 2022, accessed on October 8, 2022, https://www.cbssports.com/nba/news/phoenix-suns-stunned-by-australian-club-adelaide-36ers-in-preseason-loss/.

28. Chris Milholen, *Basketball Beyond Borders: The Globalization of the NBA* (Washington, D.C.: Amazon Kindle Direct Publishing, 2019), 17–25.

29. Pu Haozhou, "From 'Ping-Pong Diplomacy' to 'Hoop Diplomacy': Yao Ming, Globalization, and the Cultural Politics of U.S.-China Relationships" (Thesis, Florida State University 2012), 16.

30. Jeff Zillgitt, "How 1992 Dream Team shaped Dirk Nowitzki, Pau Gasol and Tony Parker on way to Hall of Fame," *USA Today*, August 10, 2023, accessed on August 11, 2023, https://www.usatoday.com/story/sports/nba/2023/08/10/dirk-nowitzki-pau-gasol-tony-parker-basketball-hall-of-fame/70546505007/.

31. Michael C. Wright, "What to know as Nets, Cavs meet in NBA Paris Game 2024," *NBA.com*, January 11, 2024, accessed on January 11, 2024, https://www.nba.com/news/nets-cavs-nba-paris-game-2024. Cam Cobey, "Looking back at the history of NBA Mexico Games," *NBA.com*, https://www.nba.com/news/looking-back-at-the-history-of-nba-mexico-games.

32. Richard Sutcliffe, "How NBA's new tournament takes inspiration from soccer's oldest cup competition," *The Athletic*, November 1, 2023, accessed on December

7, 2023, https://theathletic.com/5016386/2023/11/02/nba-in-play-tournament-fa-c up/.

Chapter 1

1. *The Dream Team*, directed by Zak Levitt, aired June 13, 2012, NBA TV.
2. Ibid.
3. David Clay Large, *Munich 1972: Tragedy, Terror, and Triumph at the Olympic Games* (Washington, D.C.: Rowman & Littlefield Publishers, 2012).
4. Yuri Brokhin, *The Big Red Machine: The Rise and Fall of Soviet Olympic Champions* (New York: Random House, 1978), 136.
5. Carson Cunningham, "American Hoops: The History of United States Basketball from Berlin to Barcelona" (thesis, Purdue University 2006), 301–310.
6. The Most Controversial Basketball Game, May 17, 2018, video https://www.youtube.com/watch?v=8DG69GH4OXo.
7. Cunningham, 313–314.
8. Gary Smith, "A Few Pieces of Silver," *Sports Illustrated*, June 15, 1992, accessed on November 8, 2022, https://vault.si.com/vault/1992/06/15/robbed-of-gold-medals-in-munich-the-72-us-olympic-basketball-team-will-not-betray-its-principles-for-a-few-pieces-of-silver.
9. Ibid.
10. Howard Berkes, "Nazi Olympics Tangled Politics and Sport," *NPR*, June 7, 2008, accessed on November 10, 2022, https://www.npr.org/2008/06/07/91246674/nazi-olympics-tangled-politics-and-sport.
11. William J. Baker, *Sports in the Western World* (Champaign: University of Illinois Press, 1988), 269.
12. Joshua K. Wright, "Coach John Thompson, Jr., in Retrospect," *Diverse*, September 8, 2020, accessed November 11, 2022, https://www.diverseeducation.com/sports/article/15107716/coach-john-thompson-jr-in-retrospect.
13. *The Dream Team*.
14. Jack McCallum, *The Dream Team: How Michael, Larry, Charles, and the Greatest Team of All Time Conquered the World and Changed the Game of Basketball Forever* (New York: Ballantine Books, 2013), 5–9.

15. "Boys to Men," *The Dream Team Tapes*, season one, episode two, podcast audio, May 18, 2020.
16. Richard Goldstein, "Dave Gavitt, Founding Force of the Big East Conference, Dies at 73," *New York Times*, September 17, 2011, accessed on November 16, 2022, https://www.nytimes.com/2011/09/18/sports/ncaabasketball/dave-gavitt-the-big-easts-founder-dies-at-73.html.
17. Ibid.
18. "The Future King and the Greek Tragedy," *The Dream Team Tapes*, season one, episode three, podcast audio, May 25, 2020.
19. During his 13 years as the Detroit Pistons general manager, McCloskey traded over 30 players in an attempt to make the team NBA champions.
20. *Bad Boys*, directed by Zak Levitt, aired April 17, 2014, ESPN.
21. Ibid.
22. *The Dream Team*.
23. Daddy Rich was a fictional, flashy character played by Richard Pryor in the 1976 comedy movie *Car Wash*.
24. *The Dream Team*.
25. Earvin "Magic" Johnson and William Novak, *My Life* (New York: Random House, 1992).
26. *They Call Me Magic*, "Junebug," written and directed by Rick Famuyiwa, aired April 22, 2022, Apple TV+.
27. *Legacy: The True Story of the LA Lakers*, "Episode 1," written and directed by Antione Fuqua, aired April 15, 2022, Hulu.
28. Scott DeCamp, "NCAA tournament final ratings up, but still a far cry from Magic–Bird in 1979," *MLive.com*, April 6, 2017, December 24, 2022, https://www.mlive.com/spartans/2017/04/ncaa_tournament_final_ratings.html.
29. *Magic & Bird: A Courtship of Rivals*, directed by Ezra Edelman, aired March 10, 2010, HBO.
30. Jackie Macmullan, *When the Game Was Ours* (Columbia, Maryland: Houghton Mifflin Harcourt, 2009).
31. *Magic & Bird*.
32. Kenneth A. Harris and Tim Povtak, "Barkley Throws Man Through Bar Window," *Orlando Sentinel*, October 27, 1997, accessed on December 7, 2022, https://www.sun-sentinel.com/news/fl-xpm-1997-10-27-9710270306-story.html.

33. *Let's Go*, podcast audio, November 21, 2022.
34. Roy S. Johnson, "Thomas Explains Comments on Bird," *New York Times*, June 5, 1987, accessed on November 25, 2022, https://www.nytimes.com/1987/06/05/sports/thomas-explains-comments-on-bird.html.
35. "The Cool Kids Don't Include Isiah," *The Dream Team Tapes*, season one, episode three, podcast audio, May 25, 2020.
36. Todd Boyd, *Young, Black, Rich, and Famous: The Rise of the NBA, The Hip Hop Invasion, and the Transformation of American Culture* (Lincoln, Nebraska: Bison Books, 2008), 107–108.
37. American sprinters John Carlos and Tommie Smith were stripped of their Olympic medals for making a public demonstration against racism and poverty while standing on the award stand at the 1968 Summer Olympics.
38. Joshua K. Wright, *Wake Up, Mr. West: Kanye West and the Double Consciousness of Black Celebrity* (Jefferson, North Carolina: McFarland, 2022), 141.
39. Booker T. Washington, *Up from Slavery* (Garden City, New Jersey: Dover Publications, 1995).
40. Wright, 3.
41. *Ibid.*, 5.
42. *The Last Dance*, "Episode I," written and directed by Jason Hehir, aired April 19, 2020, ESPN/Netflix.
43. *Ibid.*
44. Mary Genevieve McDonald, "Clean Air: Representing Michael Jordan in the Reagan-Bush Era" (PhD diss., University of Iowa, 1995), 80.
45. David Halberstam, *Playing for Keeps: Michael Jordan and the World He Made* (New York: Crown, 1991), 81.
46. *Ibid.*, 81.
47. *The Dream Team*.
48. *Ibid.*
49. The Fab Five was the nickname given to the five freshmen who started and led the University of Michigan men's basketball team to the NCAA Final Four in 1992. The players were a cultural phenomenon for college sports and hip-hop.
50. *The Dream Team*.
51. *Ibid.*
52. Trophy Room is a sneaker boutique in Orlando, Florida, owned by Michael Jordan's youngest son, Marcus Jordan.
53. Information provided by Trophy Room with the release of the Air Jordan 7s on November 4, 2022.
54. *The Dream Team*.
55. Phil Jasner, "Will Barkley listen, or play the Ugly American role?" *Baltimore Sun*, July 27, 1992, accessed on August 16, 2023, https://www.baltimoresun.com/news/bs-xpm-1992-07-27-1992209182-story.html.
56. Martha Sherrill, "The Olympic Lip," *Washington Post*, July 29, 1992, accessed on August 16, 2023, https://www.washingtonpost.com/archive/lifestyle/1992/07/29/the-olympic-lip/d6fb3fae-e48c-4b7a-a72c-60c31223777b/.
57. Scottie Pippen, *Unguarded* (New York: Atria Books, 2021), 147–148.
58. *Ibid.*
59. McCallum, 251–257.
60. "The Once and Future King," *The Dream Team Tapes*, season one, episode five, podcast audio, June 8, 2020.
61. *The Last Dance*, "Episode V," written and directed by Jason Hehir, aired May 3, 2020, ESPN/Netflix.
62. George Bush, *A World Transformed* (New York: Knopf, 1998), 362–364 and 370.
63. *The Nineties*, "New World Order," written and directed by Laurens Grant, aired July 30, 2017, CNN.
64. "Persian Gulf War," *History.com*, November 9, 2009, accessed on December 8, 2022, https://www.history.com/topics/middle-east/persian-gulf-war.
65. Russel Dinallo, dir., *E:60*, season 15, episode 7, "Whitney's Anthem," aired on February 11, 2022, on ESPN.
66. Vive Barcelona, *The Dream Team Tapes*, season one, episode seven, podcast audio, June 27, 2020.
67. Author source missing.
68. Walter LaFeber, *Michael Jordan and the New Global Capitalism* (New York: W.W. Norton & Company, 2002), 58–60.
69. *UnBanned: The Legend of the AJ1*, directed and written by Dexton Deboree, aired February 14, 2019, Hulu.
70. Roland Lazenby, *Michael Jordan: The Life* (New York: Back Bay Books, 2015), 242–244.
71. *Sole Man*, directed by Dan Marks and Jon Weinbach, aired April 16, 2015, ESPN.

72. Nike Air Jordan "Banned!" advertisement aired February 1985, 30 seconds.
73. *UnBanned*.
74. Elizabeth Semmelhack, *Out of the Box: The Rise of Sneaker Culture* (New York: Rizzoli Electa, 2015).
75. *UnBanned*.
76. Rick Telander, "Senseless. In America's cities, kids are killing kids over sneakers and other sports apparel favored by drug dealers. Who's to blame?" *Sports Illustrated*. May 14, 1990, accessed on December 9, 2022, https://vault.si.com/vault/1990/05/14/senseless-in-americas-cities-kids-are-killing-kids-over-sneakers-and-other-sports-apparel-favored-by-drug-dealers-whos-to-blame.
77. LaFeber, 65–67 and 79–83.
78. Adam Howard, "Kareem Abdul-Jabbar: Michael Jordan chose 'commerce over conscience,'" *MSNBC*, November 5, 2015, accessed on December 9, 2022, https://www.msnbc.com/msnbc/kareem-abdul-jabbar-michael-jordan-chose-commerce-over-conscience-msna717846.
79. Dave Zirin, *What's my name, fool? Sports and resistance in the United States* (Chicago, Illinois: Haymarket Books, 2005), 79.
80. *The Last Dance*, "Episode V," written and directed by Jason Hehir, aired. May 3, 2020, Netflix.
81. *Ibid*.
82. *Ibid*.
83. *The Redeem Team*, directed by Jon Weinbach, aired October 7, 2022, Netflix.
84. *Ibid*.
85. Lazenby, 444–450.
86. *Ibid*., 481–486.
87. LaFeber, 135.
88. David Smith, "'Michael Jordan changed the world': the true story behind Nike movie Air," *The Guardian*, April 5, 2023, accessed on October 9, 2023, https://www.theguardian.com/film/2023/apr/05/michael-jordan-changed-the-world-the-true-story-behind-nike-movie-air.

Chapter 2

1. Paul Peszko, "Kobe Bryant: A Gold Medal More Important Than NBA Title," *Bleacher Report*, July 24, 2008, accessed on December 10, 2022, https://bleacherreport.com/articles/40683-kobe-bryant-a-gold-medal-more-important-than-nba-title.
2. Rebecca Schuman, "Kerri Strug Shouldn't Have Been Force to Do That Vault," *Slate*, July 31, 2021, accessed on December 10, 2022, https://slate.com/culture/2021/07/kerri-strug-simone-biles-vault-atlanta-legacy-injuries.html.
3. Marie Brenner, "American Nightmare: The Ballad of Richard Jewell," *Vanity Fair*, February 1997, accessed on December 11, 2022, https://archive.vanityfair.com/article/share/1fd2d7ae-10d8-474b-9bf1-d1558af697be.
4. *As We Rise: 25 Years of the WNBA*, aired May 14, 2022, NBA TV.
5. *Dream* On, directed by Kristen Lappas, aired June 15, 2022, ESPN.
6. On Top of the World, *The Dream Team Tapes*, season two, episode one, podcast audio, February 23, 2021.
7. "The Once and Future King," *The Dream Team Tapes*, season one, episode five, podcast audio, June 8, 2020.
8. "Bush v. Gore," *Oyez*, accessed July 7, 2023, https://www.oyez.org/cases/2000/00-949.
9. The dot-com bubble refers to the stock market bubble in the late 1990s caused by the rapid and uncontrollable growth of the internet and new web-based startup companies. Several people became millionaires overnight. However, the success and existence of many of these companies was short-lived. Cisco Systems, for example, lost 80 percent of its stock value.
10. Afsin Yurdakul, "He told Bush that 'America is under attack,'" *NBC News*, September 10, 2009, accessed on December 12, 2022, https://www.nbcnews.com/id/wbna32782623.
11. *Nothing Was the Same* (2013) is the third studio album from hip-hop superstar Drake.
12. Garrett M. Graff, *Only Plane in the Sky: An Oral History of 9/11* (New York: Avid Reader Press, 2020).
13. Pu Haozhou, "From 'Ping-Pong Diplomacy' to 'Hoop Diplomacy:' Yao Ming, Globalization, and the Cultural Politics of U.S.-China Relations" (Master's thesis, Florida State University, 2012).
14. Quotes from the White House and the George W. Bush Library's exhibit "9/11: The Steel of American Resolve," accessed on December 13, 2022,

https://georgewbush-whitehouse.archives.gov/news/releases/2001/09/20010920-8.html, and https://www.georgewbushlibrary.gov/explore/exhibits/911-steel-american-resolve.

15. *Ibid.*

16. David Zucchino, "The U.S. War in Afghanistan: How It Started, and How It Ended," *The New York Times*, October 7, 2021, accessed on December 13, 2022, https://www.nytimes.com/article/afghanistan-war-us.html.

17. "Mushroom Clouds," *Slow Burn*, season eight, episode three, podcast audio, May 5, 2021.

18. Text of President Bush's Mission Accomplished speech, May 1, 2003, accessed on December 13, 2022, https://www.cbsnews.com/news/text-of-bush-speech-01-05-2003/.

19. Nicolas Anastacio and Mark Murray, "The Iraq War—by the numbers," *NBC News*, March 20, 2023, https://www.nbcnews.com/meet-the-press/meetthepressblog/iraq-war-numbers-rcna75762.

20. Steve Popper, "BASKETBALL: ROUNDUP; Last 5 Players Named to U.S. Olympic Team," July 9, 2004, accessed on December 14, 2022, https://www.nytimes.com/2004/07/09/sports/basketball-roundup-last-5-players-named-to-us-olympic-team.html.

21. *The Redeem Team*, directed by Jon Weinbach, aired October 7, 2022, Netflix.

22. Diane Pucin, "Ship of Dream Teams," *Los Angeles Times*, August 26, 2004, accessed on December 14, 2022, https://www.latimes.com/archives/la-xpm-2004-aug-26-sp-olyluxury26-story.html.

23. *The Redeem Team*, 2022.

24. "On this day 16 years ago: Puerto Rico shocked the USA at the Athens Olympics," *Fiba Basketball*, August 15, 2020, accessed on December 14, 2022, https://www.fiba.basketball/news/on-this-day-16-years-ago-puerto-rico-shocked-the-usa-at-the-athens-olympics.

25. *The Redeem Team*, 2022.

26. *Ibid.*

27. Jadakiss, "Why," *The Kiss of Death*, Ruff Ryders/Interscope, 2004.

28. "Kobe's 1st Quarter," *The Dream Team Tapes*, season two, episode two, podcast audio, February 23, 2021.

29. Bakari Kitwana, *The Hip-Hop Generation* (New York: Civitas Books, 2002), 121–128.

30. *A Kid from Coney Island*, directed by Chike Ozah and Coodie Simmons, aired April 6, 2020, Netflix.

31. David Nakamura, "Wilder Releases VA. Prep Star Iverson from Jail," *Washington Post*, December 31, 1993, accessed on December 14, 2022, https://www.washingtonpost.com/archive/sports/1993/12/31/wilder-releases-va-prep-star-iverson-from-jail/bb62aa7e-5138-4482-b7f0-41f49ffd0107/.

32. Todd Boyd, *Young, Black, Rich, and Famous: The Rise of the NBA, the Hip Hop Invasion, and the Transformation of American Culture* (Lincoln, Nebraska: Bison Books, 2008), 150–160.

33. "The Future King and the Greek Tragedy," *The Dream Team Tapes*, season two, episode three, March 2, 2021.

34. Drew Silverman, "Jerry Colangelo, Long-Time Architect of USA Basketball, Reflects on a Golden Career," July 29, 2021, *USAB.com*, accessed on December 15, 2022, https://www.usab.com/news-events/news/2021/07/jerry-colangelo-feature.aspx.

35. The Godfather, *The Dream Team Tapes*, season two, episode four, podcast audio, March 9, 2021.

36. Silverman.

37. "The Godfather," *The Dream Team Tapes*, season two, episode four, podcast audio, March 9, 2021.

38. *The Redeem Team*, 2022.

39. "Coach K's Ways," *The Dream Team Tapes*, season two, episode four, podcast audio, March 16, 2021.

40. Coach Bobby Knight won three NCAA championships at Indiana University and coached the 1984 Olympic team to a gold medal.

41. Ian O'Connor, *Coach K: The Rise and Reign of Mike Krzyzewski* (Boston: Mariner Books, 2022).

42. A referee calls a charge when an offensive player makes physical contact with a defender on the opposing team that has an established position on the court.

43. "Coach K's Ways," *The Dream Team Tapes*, season two, episode four, podcast audio, March 16, 2021.

44. *The Redeem Team*, 2022.

45. Gabriel Sherman, *The Loudest Voice*

in the Room: How the Brilliant, Bombastic Roger Ailes Built Fox News—and Divided a Country (New York: Random House, 2014), 257–267.

46. Howard Bryant, *Full Dissidence: Notes from an Uneven Playing Field* (Boston: Beacon Press, 2021).

47. Eyder Peralta, "Pentagon Paid Sports Teams Millions for 'Paid Patriotism' Events," *NPR*, November 5, 2015, accessed on December 16, 2022, https://www.npr.org/sections/thetwo-way/2015/11/05/454834662/pentagon-paid-sports-teams-millions-for-paid-patriotism-events.

48. Terry Pluto and Brian Windhorst, *Lebron James: The Making of an MVP* (Cleveland, Ohio: Gray & Company, Publishers, 2009).

49. Jeff Benedict, *LeBron* (Chestertown, Maryland: Avid Reader Press, 2023), 19–21 and 25–27.

50. Charles McGrath, "N.B.A. Star, Now Memoirist, on Hometown Court," *New York Times*, September 4, 2009, accessed on March 15, 2024, https://www.nytimes.com/2009/09/05/books/05lebron.html.

51. Tim Graham, "LBJ and NFL: A fantasy based in reality," *ESPN*, July 7, 2010, accessed on December 17, 2022, https://www.espn.com/nfl/news/story?id=5360552.

52. Matt Babcock, "ABCD Camp: The mecca of high school basketball circa 2001," *Basketballnews.com*, May 12, 2022, accessed on December 17, 2022, https://www.basketballnews.com/stories/abcd-camp-the-mecca-of-high-school-basketball-circa-2001.

53. Grant Wahl, "Ahead of his class," *Sports Illustrated*, February 18, 2002, accessed on December 18, 2022, https://vault.si.com/vault/2002/02/18/ahead-of-his-class-ohio-high-school-junior-lebron-james-is-so-good-that-hes-already-being-mentioned-as-the-heir-to-air-jordan.

54. GOAT is an acronym for greatest of all time.

55. *Ibid*.

56. Mike Sielski, *The Rise: Kobe Bryant and the Pursuit of Immortality* (New York: St. Martin's Press, 2022).

57. Gavin Newsham, "How growing up in Italy for 7 years turned Kobe Bryant into a star," January 8, 2022, accessed on December 19, 2022, https://nypost.com/2022/01/08/how-kobe-bryants-childhood-in-italy-turned-him-into-a-star/.

58. "A Young Man in Lower Merion," *I Am Kobe*, season one, episode three, podcast audio, November 23, 2021.

59. *Kobe Bryant's Muse*, directed by Gotham Chopra (Newport Beach, CA: Granity Studios, 2015).

60. WPVI-TV, a.k.a. 6 ABC in Philadelphia, Pennsylvania, provided footage of Kobe Bryant's 1996 announcement.

61. *Ready or Not: The 96 Draft*, aired April 11, 2021, NBA TV, https://www.youtube.com/watch?v=WCplazTFR0Q&t=4265s.

62. *Shaq*, "The Fall," directed by Robert Alexander, aired December 7, 2022, HBO Max.

63. Historically, Black men in America have been imprisoned and lynched because of rape accusations involving white women. During the early 20th century, many Black men were falsely accused of sexually assaulting white women who feared the repercussions of being found intimate with someone who was not white. Was Kobe another victim of this racist scapegoating or excused because of his celebrity and likeability? Tracey Owens Patton and Julie Snyder-Yuly, "Any Four Black Men Will Do: Rape, Race, and the Ultimate Scapegoat," *Journal of Black Studies* 17, no. 6 (July 2007): 859–895.

64. Marlow Stern, "Kobe Bryant's Disturbing Rape Case: The DNA Evidence, the Accuser's Story, and the Half-Confession," *The Daily Beast*, April 11, 2016, accessed on December 20, 2022, https://www.thedailybeast.com/kobe-bryants-disturbing-rape-case-the-dna-evidence-the-accusers-story-and-the-half-confession?ref=scroll.

65. Kurt Badenhausen, "Kobe Bryant's Sponsorship Will Rebound," *Forbes*, September 3, 2004, December 20, 2022, https://www.forbes.com/2004/09/03/cz_kb_0903kobe.html?sh=666f208827c6.

66. Kobe Bryant's 81 points are the second-most points scored in an NBA game. Wilt Chamberlain, a center for the Philadelphia Warriors, scored 100 points against the New York Knicks on March 2, 1962.

67. Phil Jackson, *The Last Season: A*

Team in Search of Its Soul (New York: Penguin Books, 2005).

68. *The Redeem Team.*

69. Marvin Gaye's rendition of the national anthem is next to Whitney Houston's as the most memorable live performance. Justin Tinsley, "The players' anthem: when Marvin Gaye sang 'The Star-Spangled Banner' at the 1983 All-Star Game," Andscape, February 13, 2008, accessed on December 22, 2022, https://andscape.com/features/marvin-gaye-the-star-spangled-banner-1983-nba-all-star-game-players-anthem/.

70. *The Redeem Team.*

71. Ibid.

72. Ibid.

73. MAGA is an acronym for Make America Great Again.

74. *Woke* is a term popularized in the late 2010s for socially conscious and active people in America. It was commonly associated with Blacks, other minorities, and their white liberal allies.

75. "La Busqueda Para El Oro," *The Dream Team Tapes*, season two, episode 10, podcast audio, April 20, 2021.

76. Cleveland fans like Scott Raab lambasted LeBron James for his "disloyalty" when he chose to play in Miami, Florida, for the Heat. Scott Raab, *The Whore of Akron: One Man's Search for the Soul of LeBron James* (New York: Harper Perennial, 2012).

77. Chase Peterson-Withorn, "LeBron James Is Officially A Billionaire," *Forbes*, June 2, 2022, accessed on December 22, 2022, https://www.forbes.com/sites/chasewithorn/2022/06/02/lebron-james-is-officially-a-billionaire/?sh=5e4981b3453e.

78. "Dwyane Wade Signs Lifetime Deal with Li-Ning Way of Wade," *Bleacher Report*, July 19, 2018, accessed on December 22, 2022, https://bleacherreport.com/articles/2786663-dwyane-wade-signs-lifetime-deal-with-li-ning-way-of-wade.

79. Father Don Bosco Onyalla, "African Clergy, Religious, Laity Pay Tribute to Basketball Superstar Kobe Bryant," *ACI Africa*, January 28, 2020, accessed on December 22, 2022, https://www.aciafrica.org/news/730/african-clergy-religious-laity-pay-tribute-to-basketball-superstar-kobe-bryant.

80. Paolo Songco, "The biggest Kobe Bryant mural in Europe was just completed," *Cluth Points*, June 5, 2020, accessed on December 22, 2022, https://clutchpoints.com/lakers-news-the-biggest-kobe-bryant-mural-europe-was-just-completed.

81. Sopan Deb, "How Kobe Bryant Helped the NBA Conquer the World," *New York Times*, January 28, 2020, accessed on December 23, 2022, https://www.nytimes.com/2020/01/28/sports/basketball/kobe-NBA-global.html.

82. Ibid.

83. Kurt Helin, "Canada beats USA in overtime to win bronze medal behind 39 from Dillon Brooks," *NBC Sports*, September 10, 2023, accessed on October 11, 2023, https://www.nbcsports.com/nba/news/canada-beats-usa-in-overtime-to-win-bronze-medal-behind-39-from-dillon-brooks.

84. Ben Golliver, "With Olympic gold on the line, Steph Curry, LeBron James deliver for U.S.," *The Washington Post*, August 10, 2024, https://www.washingtonpost.com/sports/olympics/2024/08/10/usa-france-olympic-basketball-gold-medal-steph-curry/.

Chapter 3

1. Drake, "Weston Road Flows," *Views*, Cash Money/Young Money/Republic, 2016.

2. Arash Markazi, "Oral History: Night Kobe scored 81 points," *ESPN.com*, January 21, 2016, accessed on December 29, 2022, https://www.espn.com/espn/feature/story/_/id/14609380/how-los-angeles-lakers-kobe-bryant-made-history-81-point-game.

3. Jon Krawczynski, "Sam Mitchell reflects on Kobe's 81: 'I don't think too many were volunteering to guard him that night,'" *The Athletic*, December 18, 2017, accessed on December 29, 2022, https://theathletic.com/188438/2017/12/18/sam-mitchell-kobe-bryant-81-point-game-i-dont-think-too-many-were-volunteering-to-guard-him-that-night/.

4. Markazi.

5. John Melady, *Breakthrough! Canada's Greatest Inventions and Innovations* (Toronto: Dundurn, 2013), 58–60.

6. Kat Eschnar, "The YMCA First

Opened Gyms to Train Stronger Christians," *Smithsonian Magazine,* December 29, 2017, accessed on December 30, 2022, https://www.smithsonianmag.com/smart-news/ymca-first-opened-gyms-train-stronger-christians-180967665/.

7. James Naismith's 13 original rules of basketball were published on January 15, 1891, in *The Triangle,* the Springfield College school newspaper.

8. Walter LaFeber, *Michael Jordan and the New Global Capitalism* (New York: W.W. Norton & Company, 2002), 33–34.

9. "First basketball game played," *History.com,* November 8, 2021, accessed on December 29, 2022, https://www.history.com/this-day-in-history/basketball-invention-james-naismith.

10. David Hollander, *How Basketball Can Save the World: 13 Guiding Principles for Reimagining What's Possible* (New York: Harmony, 2023), 116–117.

11. Chris Milholen, *Basketball Beyond Borders: The Globalization of the NBA* (Washington, D.C.: Amazon Kindle Direct Publishing, 2019), 21.

12. Ibid., 25.

13. "Toronto's Big Bang," Dunkumentaries season one episode four, podcast audio, April 4, 2016.

14. John Banks, "Who Invented Hockey?" *History.com,* April 22, 2022, accessed on January 3, 2023, https://www.history.com/news/who-invented-hockey-origins-canada.

15. The NBA does currently host an annual exhibition game in Mexico.

16. The Toronto Raptors and Vancouver Grizzlies were the 28th and 29th teams to join the league, respectively.

17. The Vancouver Grizzlies were the first NBA franchise to have a website.

18. Clifton Brown, "1995 NBA Playoffs; Anthony Could Go in the Expansion Draft," *New York Times,* June 14, 1995, accessed on January 2, 2023, https://www.nytimes.com/1995/06/14/sports/1995-nba-playoffs-anthony-could-go-in-the-expansion-draft.html.

19. Gerald Narciso, "Here Today, Gone Forever? Whatever Happened to Bryant 'Big Country' Reeves?" *Bleacher Report,* September 26, 2018, accessed on January 3, 2023, https://bleacherreport.com/articles/2796045-here-today-gone-forever-whatever-happened-to-bryant-big-country-reeves.

20. The Naismith Cup was an annual preseason exhibition between the Vancouver Grizzlies and the Toronto Raptors from 1995 until 2000.

21. Jeff Zillgitt, "It looks as if the NBA is headed for a lockout," *The Sporting News,* June 29, 1998, accessed on January 4, 2023.

22. Steve Francis, "I Got a Story to Tell," *Players' Tribune,* March 8, 2018, accessed on January 4, 2023, https://www.theplayerstribune.com/articles/steve-francis-i-got-a-story-to-tell.

23. Jerry Bembry, "Francis gets boot to Houston; In an 11-player deal, Grizzlies part with disgruntled top pick; Trade NBA's largest ever; at last moment, Orlando joins mix," *Baltimore Sun,* August 28, 1999, accessed on January 4, 2023, https://www.baltimoresun.com/news/bs-xpm-1999-08-28-9908280022-story.html.

24. Mike Beamish, "NBA Grizzlies, 10 years later: Still in hibernation," *Vancouver Sun,* February 19, 2011, accessed on September 16, 2023, https://vancouversun.com/news/nba-grizzlies-10-years-later-still-in-hibernation.

25. Stephen Dyell, "Oh Canada: The Next NBA Destination?" *Bleacher Report,* August 26, 2009, accessed on January 4, 2023, https://bleacherreport.com/articles/243151-oh-canada-the-next-nba-destination.

26. Milholen, 168.

27. De-extinction is the genetic process of creating organisms that resemble extinct species.

28. Scott Mendelson, "The Box Office Legacy of 'Jurassic Park,' 20 Years Later, *Forbes,* April 5, 2013, accessed on January 7, 2023.

29. Adam Francis, "Toronto Raptors," *The Canadian Encyclopedia,* June 14, 2019, accessed on January 7, 2023, https://www.thecanadianencyclopedia.ca/en/article/toronto-raptors.

30. The Toronto Raptors have had nine head coaches since their founding.

31. Sam Holako, "A Look Back at the 96 Draft—Raptors Take Marcus Camby With the 2nd Pick," *Raptors Republic,* May 17, 2022, accessed on January 7, 2023, https://www.raptorsrepublic.com/2022/05/17/a-look-back-at-the-96-draft-raptors-take-marcus-camby-with-the-2nd-pick/.

32. Doug Smith, *We The North: 25 Years of the Toronto Raptors* (New York: Viking Press, 2020), 30.
33. Sam Borden, "For Frederic Weis, Knicks' Infamous Pick, Boos Began a Greater Struggle," *New York Times*, July 14, 2015, accessed on January 9, 2023, https://www.nytimes.com/2015/07/15/sports/basketball/for-frederic-weis-knicks-99-draft-choice-boos-marked-start-of-a-greater-struggle.html.
34. Borden.
35. Rachel Alex, "A Musician Who Can Jam," *Washington Post*, December 16, 1999, accessed on January 13, 2023, https://www.washingtonpost.com/archive/sports/1999/12/16/a-musician-who-can-jam/56568bdf-4671-4ad3-8eac-e3aa7b78f75f/.
36. Borden.
37. Sonny Vaccaro secured McGrady a $12 million sneaker deal with Adidas. The deal also paid McGrady's high school coach $150,000 annually for the first six years of his professional career.
38. Vince Carter and Tracy McGrady shared their story of learning about their family connection during a 2016 interview with Rachel Nichols on ESPN's former basketball series *The Jump*.
39. Chris Young, *Drive: How Vince Carter Conquered the NBA* (Toronto: Doubleday Canada, 2001).
40. Zaron Burnett III, "Why did the NCAA Ban the Slam Dunk for Nine Years?" *Mel*, accessed on January 23, 2023, https://melmagazine.com/en-us/story/why-was-the-slam-dunk-banned.
41. Jason Buckland, "Rise of Vinsanity: The Story of the 2000 Dunk Contest," *ESPN*, June 25, 2020, January 15, 2023, https://www.espn.com/nba/allstar2014/story/_/page/dunk-2000/oral-history-2000-nba-slam-dunk-contest.
42. Ibid.
43. Ibid.
44. "Vince Carter interview: on NBA TV's The Interview," interview by Steve Smith, February 15, 2016, video, 45:45, https://www.youtube.com/watch?v=SdD06cKu6eY&t=13s.
45. Buckland.
46. "Carter criticized after loss," *CBC*, May 21, 2001, January 16, 2023, https://www.cbc.ca/sports/basketball/carter-criticized-after-loss-1.284617.
47. *The Carter Effect*, directed by Sean Menard (Akron, Ohio: Uninterrupted, 2017).
48. Ibid.
49. Ibid.
50. Ibid.
51. Mabel F. Timlin, "Canada's Immigration Policy, 1896–1910," *Canadian Journal of Economics and Political Science*, XXVI, no. 4 (November 1960): 88.
52. These are visible minority and population groups by generation status in Canada's provinces and territories, census metropolitan areas, and census agglomerations with parts.
53. Neamen Baatai, "How a former NBA Superstar is making a unique impact in STEM," *Jaro4me*, September 26, 2021, accessed on January 20, 2023, https://jaro4me.com/technology/how-a-former-nba-superstar-is-making-a-unique-impact-in-stem/.
54. Chris Bosh, *Letters to a Young Athlete* (New York: Penguin Press, 2021).
55. Smith, 124.
56. *Real Sports*, season 25, episode 10, first broadcast October 22, 2019, by HBO.
57. Masai Ujiri became Toronto's president of basketball operations in 2016. Jeff Weltman replaced him as the team's general manager.
58. John Gonzalez, "An Oral History of the Shot That Changed Toronto and Kawhi Leonard Forever," *The Ringer*, December 10, 2019, accessed on October 18, 2023, https://www.theringer.com/nba/2019/12/10/21003385/oral-history-the-shot-kawhi-leonard-toronto-raptors-philadelphia-sixers.
59. "Raptors superfan Nav Bhatia to miss first-ever home game Friday," *Sportsnet*, December 21, 2021, accessed on January 24, 2023, https://www.sportsnet.ca/nba/article/raptors-superfan-nav-bhatia-miss-first-ever-home-game-friday/.
60. Hattie Collins, "How Did Drake Become The World's Biggest Pop Star?" *British Vogue*, May 15, 2020, accessed On January 24, 2023, https://www.vogue.co.uk/arts-and-lifestyle/article/drake-worlds-biggest-pop-star.
61. *The Carter Effect*.
62. Toronto is called the 6ix (Six) because of the six municipalities that were integrated into Toronto City proper in 1988. The number six is also prominent

in the city's telephone area codes: 416 and 647.

63. "Drake the ultimate team fanboy," *Bay of Plenty Times*, Tauranga, New Zealand, May 30, 2019.

64. Doug Smith, "Raptors crowned NBA champions for first time in team history," *Toronto Star*, June 13, 2019, accessed on September 16, 2023, https://www.thestar.com/sports/raptors/raptors-crowned-nba-champions-for-first-time-in-team-history/article_e90bdfa3-4381-5607-a5ba-a532916ebb39.html.

65. In 2021, the Raptors revealed their OVO edition jerseys, which featured an owl logo. The owl is the official logo of Drake's OVO (October's Very Own) record label, which is distributed by Warner Music Group.

66. The Las Vegas Aces won the WNBA championship in 2022 and 2023.

67. "Toronto awarded WNBA's 1st Team outside U.S., to play in '26," *ESPN*, May 23, 2024, https://www.espn.com/wnba/story/_/id/40202150/toronto-awarded-wnba-1st-team-us-play-26

Chapter 4

1. Colin Cowherd shared his feelings about the growing dominance of European basketball players in the NBA during an episode of his daily television series, *The Herd with Colin Cowherd*, on FS1.

2. Thomas Beller, "The Jokic Files: My quest to understand the oddest player in the NBA," *Slate*, November 14, 2022, accessed on April 8, 2023, https://slate.com/culture/2022/11/nikola-jokic-denver-nuggets-history-profile-record.html.

3. Handles is a slang term for dribbling and ball-handling skills in basketball.

4. *First Take*, season 17, aired on March 7, 2023, ESPN.

5. Nikola Jokic finished sixth in scoring, averaging 27.1 points per game, during the 2021-22 season when he captured his second consecutive MVP. He was 12th in scoring the previous season and 20th in the 2022-23 season.

6. *Game Theory with Bomani Jones*, season two, episode seven, aired on March 10, 2023, HBO.

7. Bomani Jones, Twitter post, March 7, 2023, 10:00 a.m.

8. Kevin Lloyd, interviewed by Joshua K. Wright, January 15, 2019. Story of the Virginia Interscholastic Association (VIA), Washington, D.C., https://viastory.org/oral-history.

9. Steve Achburner, "How a trio of pioneers gave rise to racial integration in the NBA," *NBA.com*, March 31, 2022, accessed on March 15, 2023, https://www.nba.com/news/how-chuck-cooper-nat-clifton-earl-lloyd-changed-nba-racial-integration.

10. *Bill Russell: Legend*, written and directed by Sam Pollard, aired February 8, 2023, Netflix.

11. William C. Rhoden, *Forty Million Dollar Slaves: The Rise, Fall, and Redemption of the Black Athlete* (Largo, Maryland: Crown, 2007), 63-75.

12. Claude Johnson, *Black Fives: The Alpha Physical Culture Club's Pioneering African American Basketball Team, 1904-1923*, volume one (Greenwich, Connecticut: Black Fives Publishing, 2012).

13. During a game against the St. Louis Hawks on December 26, 1964, the Boston Celtics became the first NBA to start five Black players in a game.

14. *Bill Russell: Legend*

15. During the 1970s, Boston, Massachusetts, became the epicenter of racial strife when white Bostonians reacted violently to a court order mandating compulsory busing to desegregate schools. A picture went out around the world showing a white teenager attempting to stab a Black man, Ted Landsmark, in the heart with the sharp point of a flagpole with an American flag attached.

16. Bill Russell used his platform as a professional athlete to become a leading celebrity advocate for the Civil Rights Movement in the 1950s and 1960s.

17. William F. Russell, *Second Wind: The Memoirs of an Opinionated Man* (New York: Random House, 1979).

18. James Dafor, "The NBA logo's complicated history, explained," *SB Nation*, February 25, 2021, accessed on March 17, 2023, https://www.sbnation.com/nba/22300942/nba-logo-history-jerry-west-kobe-bryant.

19. Jerry West, *West by West: My Charmed, Tormented Life* (Boston: Back Bay Books, 2012).

20. *When the Garden Was Eden*, directed by Michael Rapaport, aired April 14, 2014, ESPN.

21. Adam J. Criblez, "White Men Playing a Black Man's Game: Basketball's Great White Hopes of the 1970s," *Journal of Sports History* 42 (2015): 371–382.

22. Andrew John Lindsay, "Has the Great White Hope left the building? White attitudes and Black opportunity in American heavyweight boxing, 1949–1983" (PhD diss., University of Toledo, 2002).

23. Joshua K. Wright, *Wake Up, Mr. West*: *Kanye West and the Double Consciousness of Black Celebrity* (Jefferson, North Carolina: McFarland, 2022), 62.

24. Theresa Runstedtler, *Jack Johnson, Rebel Sojourner: Boxing in the Shadow of the Global Color Line* (Oakland: University of California Press, 2013).

25. Ibid., 62.

26. Ibid., 63.

27. Ibid., 64.

28. Geoffrey C. Ward, *Unforgivable Blackness: The Rise and Fall of Jack Johnson* (New York: Vintage, 2006).

29. Ron Briley, "Basketball's Great White Hope and Ronald Reagan's America: *Hoosiers* (1986)." *Film & History: An Interdisciplinary Journal of Film and Television Studies* 35, no.1 (Fall 2005).

30. In the 2023 ESPN docuseries *The Luckiest Guy in the World*, Bill Walton's NBA teammates in Portland revealed that some fans and media treated him like a Great White Hope. Walton objected to that treatment.

31. Dave Zirin and Frank Guridy, "Bill Walton Was Once a Trailblazing Radical," *The Nation*, September 6, 2023, accessed on October 18, 2023, https://www.thenation.com/article/society/bill-walton-activism/.

32. Harry Potter is a fictional wizard in a series of fantasy novels for kids and teens written by British author J.K. Rowling between 1997 and 2007.

33. The goaltending rule prevents players on the opposing team from interfering with the basketball while it is on its way into the basket.

34. Michael Schumacher, *Mr. Basketball: George Mikan, the Minneapolis Lakers, and the Birth of the NBA* (Minneapolis: University of Minnesota Press, 2008).

35. "The Invisible Revolution," *Death at the Wing*, season one, episode one, podcast audio, March 21, 2021.

36. Jackie MacMullan, Rafe Bartholomew, and Dan Klores, *Basketball: A Love Story* (New York: Crown, 2019).

37. Scott Ostler, "Ex-Laker Haywood Tells of Plan He Had to Kill Westhead," *Los Angeles Times*, June 5, 1988, accessed on March 21, 2023, https://www.latimes.com/archives/la-xpm-1988-06-05-sp-6828-story.html.

38. Keith Harriston and Sally Jenkins, "Maryland Basketball Star Len Bias is Dead at 22," *Washington Post*, June 20, 1986, accessed on March 21, 2023, https://www.washingtonpost.com/wp-srv/sports/longterm/memories/bias/launch/bias1.htm.

39. *Magic & Bird: A Courtship of Rivals*, directed by Ezra Edelman, aired March 10, 2010, HBO. *When the Garden Was Eden*, directed by Michael Rapaport, aired April 14, 2014, ESPN.

40. Theresa Runstedler, *Black Ball: Kareem Abdul-Jabbar, Spencer Haywood and the Generation that Saved the Soul of the NBA* (New York: Bold Type Books, 2003).

41. Dave Zirin, Twitter post, March 8, 2023, 9:30 p.m.

42. Jackie MacMullan, *When the Game Was Ours* (Boston: Mariner Books, 2010).

43. Gucci Row refers to the courtside seats at the Forum, home to the Lakers from 1967 to 1999. Celebrities and the wealthy began sitting there in the 1980s when Magic Johnson's teams won five championships.

44. *A Courtship of Rivals*.

45. Ibid.

46. Roy S. Johnson, "Thomas Explains Comments on Bird," *New York Times*, June 5, 1987, accessed on March 24, 2023, https://www.nytimes.com/1987/06/05/sports/thomas-explains-comments-on-bird.html.

47. Elvis Presley, dubbed the King of Rock & Roll, was accused of stealing his dance moves and singing style from uncredited Black blues singers.

48. Bird revealed to Reggie Miller and Isiah Thomas during a 2024 episode of *NBA Stories: Indiana Glory* that he made the comment in jest to relax the other competitors in the locker room. But no one got the joke.

49. *I Hate Christian Laettner*, directed by Rory Karpf, aired March 15, 2015, ESPN.

50. *Untold: Malice at the Palace*, directed by Floyd Russ, aired August 10, 2021, Netflix.
51. "Bird Says League Needs More White Superstars," *Buffalo News*, June 10, 2004, accessed on March 24, 2023, https://buffalonews.com/news/bird-says-league-needs-more-white-superstars/article_f6ac08e5-b07b-538b-a501-5789992cdf7a.html.
52. Captain Ahab is the fictional protagonist in the 1851 novel *Moby Dick*. Ahab is a captain obsessed with finding the great white whale Moby Dick that bit his leg off on a previous voyage.
53. "The Triangulation of Phil Jackson," *Shattered: Hope, Heartbreak, and the New York Knicks*, season one, episode six, podcast audio, March 18, 2021.
54. Noel Ignatiev, *How the Irish Became White* (Routledge: New York, 1995).
55. Information provided by the Naismith Memorial Basketball Hall of Fame, https://www.hoophall.com/hall-of-famers/oscar-schmidt/.
56. During the 2011 season, Kobe Bryant challenged his Lakers teammate Pao Gasol to stop playing like the "white swan" and be more like the "black swan." Kobe used a reference to the 2010 film *The Black Swan*, starring Natalie Portman as a soft, timid ballerina (the white swan) who loses her mind in an attempt to compete with an aggressive, sensual, and cutthroat new rival played by Mila Kunis (the black swan). He advised Gasol to stop playing soft and be more assertive like himself. Eddie Johnson, a retired NBA player and current media member who played overseas, says that the "soft" label was a myth created to elevate American players above their European counterparts.
57. The Pan American Games (or Pan Am Games) is a continental multisport event in the Americas held every four years in the summer before the Summer Olympics.
58. *The 1984 Draft*.
59. The EuroBasket, or the European Basketball Championship, is an international tournament held every four years. The senior men's national teams in Europe compete against each other.
60. Miholen, 119–121.
61. Todd Spehr, *The Mozart of Basketball: The Remarkable Life and Legacy of Dražen Petrović* (Champaign, Illinois: Sports Publishing, 2016), 5.
62. Ibid., 67–69.
63. Ibid., 72–94.
64. Ibid., 120–125.
65. Ibid., 162.
66. Alan Taylor, "20 Years Since the Bosnian War," *The Atlantic*, April 13, 2012, accessed on April 1, 2023, https://www.theatlantic.com/photo/2012/04/20-years-since-the-bosnian-war/100278/.
67. "Drazen Petrovic and Basketball's Cold War," *Death at the Wing*, season one, episode six, podcast audio, June 10, 2022.
68. Harvey Araton, "Petrovic Carried Torch for European Players," *New York Times*, June 10, 1993, B15.
69. John Nizinski, "Drazen Petrovic: Remembering the Star That Didn't Get to Shine," *Bleacher Report*, January 17, 2012, accessed on April 2, 2023, https://bleacherreport.com/articles/1020997-drazen-petrovic-remembering-the-star-that-didnt-get-to-shine.
70. The Backstreet Boys were one of America's most successful teenage pop groups from the mid-1990s to the early 2000s.
71. Thomas Pletzinger, *The Great Nowitzki: Basketball and the Meaning of Life* (New York: W.W. Norton & Company, 2019), 68–72.
72. Ibid., 123 and 131.
73. Pletzinger, 88–91.
74. James Herbert, "The Dirk Nowitzki Stories: An oral history of the Dallas Mavericks legend," *CBS Sports*, April 9, 2019, accessed on October 18, 2023, https://www.cbssports.com/nba/news/the-dirk-nowitzki-stories-an-oral-history-of-the-dallas-mavericks-legend/.
75. Ibid., 177–178.
76. Heat Culture is a popular catch-phrase used to describe the Miami Heat's winning ways and professional attitude.
77. Ibid., 63.
78. Hunter Felt, "Is Dirk Nowitzki the most important European player ever?" *The Guardian*, March 21, 2019, accessed on February 10, 2024. https://www.theguardian.com/sport/2019/mar/21/is-dirk-nowitzki-the-most-important-european-player-ever.
79. Pletzinger, 65.
80. "Luka Dončić's 60-point, 21-rebound triple-double stuns NBA Twitter," *ESPN*.

com, December 27, 2022, accessed on April 6, 2023, https://www.espn.com/nba/story/_/id/35332269/luka-doncic-60-point-triple-double-stuns-nba-twitter.

81. "LeBron James: 'Luka Doncic reminds me of the way I play the game,'" *MARCA*, February 19, 2022, accessed on July 28, 2023, https://www.marca.com/en/basketball/nba/2022/02/20/6211d00146163f836a8b45e3.html.

82. Jack Baer, "Luka Doncic scores 73 points vs. Hawks, tied for fourth-most in NBA history," *Yahoo Sports*, January 26, 2024, accessed on January 27, 2024, https://sports.yahoo.com/luka-doncic-scores-73-points-vs-hawks-tied-for-fourth-most-in-nba-history-023607554.html.

83. Henry McKenna, "Jay Williams calls out Montrezl Harrell over exchange with Luka Doncic," *USA Today*, August 23, 2020, accessed on April 6, 2023, https://ftw.usatoday.com/2020/08/jay-williams-ripsmontrezl-harrell-luka-doncic-whiteboy.

84. Grant Afseth, "'Why Not Give James Harden His Love?' Jamal Crawford Claims Luka Doncic Hypocrisy," *Sports Illustrated*, February 1, 2023, accessed on April 8, 2023, https://www.si.com/nba/mavericks/news/dallas-mavs-luka-doncic-james-harden-houston-rockets-jamal-crawford-claims-hypocrisy.

85. *The Draymond Green Show*, season two, podcast audio, March 2, 2023.

86. Gilbert Arenas, X Post, December 13, 2023, 3:28 p.m.

87. Bryan Kalbrosky, "With Nikola Jokic, NBA analytics aren't bad just because you don't understand them," *USA Today*, April 12, 2022, https://ftw.usatoday.com/2022/04/nba-mvp-nikola-jokic-advanced-analytics-stats-joel-embiid.

88. Andy Bailey, "Why Can't NBA Awards Voters See the Obvious MVP Front-runner?" *Bleacher Report*, December 19, 2022, accessed on April 11, 2023, https://bleacherreport.com/articles/10059103-why-cant-nba-awards-voters-see-the-obvious-mvp-front-runner.

89. Matt Moore, "Efficiency vs. production: The layered tale of Kobe Bryant's statistical legacy," *CBS Sports*, April 7, 2016, accessed on April 10, 2023, https://www.cbssports.com/nba/news/efficiency-vs-production-the-layered-tale-of-kobe-bryants-statistical-legacy/.

90. Isaac Chotiner, "Bomani Jones on the NBA, Analytics, and Race," *The New Yorker*, June 17, 2019, accessed on April 11, 2023, https://www.newyorker.com/news/q-and-a/bomani-jones-on-the-nba-analytics-and-race.

91. https://flipboard.com/@FoxSportsRadio/colin-cowherd-on-joel-embiid-winning-mvp-it-was-anti-nikola-jokic-vote/a-R6vjstqkSr6oMZK0V69cog%3Aa%3A2598408595-8dd5b80dd4%2Fiheart.com.

92. Sam Mitchell expressed his disdain for the training of American youth at the AAU level during an episode of NBA Radio's *NBA Weekend* on December 2, 2023.

93. https://www.espn.com/nba/history/awards/_/id/33.

94. William C. Rhoden, "LSU's Angel Reese, Iowa's Caitlin Clark and the double standards of race in sports," *Andscape*, April 3, 2003, accessed on April 17, 2023, https://andscape.com/features/lsus-angel-reese-iowas-caitlin-clark-and-the-double-standards-of-race-in-sports/.

95. Remy Tumin, "NCAA Women's Tournament Shatters Ratings Record in Final," *New York Times*, April 3, 2023, accessed on April 13, 2023, https://www.nytimes.com/2023/04/03/sports/ncaabasketball/lsu-iowa-womens-tournament-ratings-record.html.

96. Remy Tumin, "NCAA Women's Tournament Shatters Ratings Record in Final," *New York Times*, April 3, 2023, accessed on April 13, 2023, https://www.nytimes.com/2023/04/03/sports/ncaabasketball/lsu-iowa-womens-tournament-ratings-record.html.

97. "Caitlin Clark calls out racist 'trolls' spreading hate toward WNBA players," *The Guardian*, September 28, 2024, accessed on September 29, 2024, https://www.theguardian.com/sport/2024/sep/28/caitlin-clark-response-wnba-trolls-online-hate.

98. Luke Winkie, "The Dukeman Cometh," *Slate*, October 31, 2023, accessed on November 2, 2023, https://slate.com/culture/2023/10/cooper-flagg-duke-basketball-race-oh-no.html.

99. David Aldridge, interviewed by Joshua K. Wright, January 5, 2024.

100. "Voting results: 2023-24 NBA regular-season awards," *NBA.com*, May 23,

2024, https://pr.nba.com/voting-results-2023-24-nba-regular-season-awards/.

101. The Euro step is a basketball move in which an offensive player picks up their dribble, takes a step in one direction, and then quickly takes a second step in another direction.

Chapter 5

1. James Harden issued a public apology to China and Chinese NBA fans on behalf of the league following a controversial tweet posted by his general manager, Daryl Morey, that was critical of the country.

2. Avery Yang, "Black History Month: The Harlem Globetrotters' 1948 Win Over the Lakers Changed Basketball," *Sports Illustrated*, February 19, 2020, accessed on May 5, 2023, https://www.si.com/nba/2020/02/19/black-history-month-harlem-globetrotters-lakers.

3. *Biography*. "The Harlem Globetrotters: America's Court Jesters," directed by Greg Weinstein (1999, New York: A&E Television Networks), DVD.

4. LaFeber, 37.

5. Ben Lombardo, "The Harlem Globetrotters and the Perpetuation of the Black Stereotype," *Physical Educator*, 35, no. 2 (1978): 60.

6. Minstrelsy was the earliest form of popular entertainment in America. White performers, attempting to portray Black characters, darkened their faces with burnt cork, dressed in tattered clothing, spoke in broken English, and sang Negro spirituals. These antics amounted to a less-than-flattering effort to mimic Blackness through grotesque forms of cultural appropriation and racial cross-dressing.

7. *Biography*. "The Harlem Globetrotters."

8. Damion Thomas, "Around the World: Problematizing the Harlem Globetrotters as Cold War Warriors," *Cultures, Commerce, Media, Politics* 14, no. 6 (2011): 778–791.

9. Lisa Davenport, *Jazz Diplomacy: Promoting America in the Cold War Era* (Jackson: University Press of Mississippi, 2013).

10. Pu Haozhou, "From 'Ping-Pong Diplomacy' to 'Hoop Diplomacy': Yao Ming, Globalization, and the Cultural Politics of U.S.-China Relations" (Master's thesis, Florida State University 2012).

11. Evan Andrews, "How Ping-Pong Diplomacy Thawed the Cold War," *History*, April 8, 2016, accessed on May 5, 2023, https://www.history.com/news/ping-pong-diplomacy.

12. https://peaceplayers.org/.

13. Basketball HOF. Twitter Post. August 11, 2023, 11:37 p.m.

14. "Albright makes a historic visit to North Korea," *The Guardian*, October 23, 2000, accessed on May 6, 2023, https://www.theguardian.com/world/2000/oct/23/northkorea.

15. "Clinton won't travel to North Korea," *CNN*, December 29, 2000, accessed on May 6, 2023, https://www.cnn.com/2000/ASIANOW/east/12/28/clinton.nkorea/index.html.

16. Jethro Mullen and Paul Armstrong, "North Korea carries out a controversial rocket launch," *CNN*, December 12, 2012, accessed on May 6, 2023, https://www.cnn.com/2012/12/11/world/asia/north-korea-rocket-launch/index.html.

17. Nuclear proliferation is the spread and acquisition of nuclear weapons and technology, often for warfare.

18. "Text of President Bush's 2002 State of the Union Address," *Washington Post*, January 29, 2002, accessed on May 6, 2023, https://www.washingtonpost.com/wp-srv/onpolitics/transcripts/sou012902.htm.

19. Michael Dulka, "Dennis Rodman Joins Group of Harlem Globetrotters to Film Show in North Korea," *Bleacher Report*, February 26, 2013, accessed on May 6, 2023, https://bleacherreport.com/articles/1544461-dennis-rodman-joins-group-of-harlem-globetrotters-to-film-tv-show-in-north-korea.

20. *Vice*, "Basketball Diplomacy," episode 10, June 14, 2013, HBO.

21. Frank Smith, "Reports of people 'starving' as N Korea Struggles to feed itself," *Al Jazeera*, July 1, 2021, accessed May 7, 2023,. https://www.aljazeera.com/news/2021/7/1/humanitarian-disaster-looms-in-north-korea.

22. *Vice*, "Basketball Diplomacy."

23. Ibid.

24. Helena Andrews-Dyer, "A brief guide to Dennis Rodman's long, weird history with North Korea," *Washington Post*, June 12, 2018, accessed on May 9,

2023, https://www.washingtonpost.com/news/reliable-source/wp/2018/06/12/a-brief-guide-to-dennis-rodmans-long-weird-history-with-north-korea/.
25. Vice, "Basketball Diplomacy."
26. Ibid.
27. *Rodman: For Better or Worse*, directed by Todd Kapostasy, aired September 10, 2019, ESPN.
28. A philander is a man who engages in casual sexual relationships with several women.
29. Dennis Rodman and Tim Keown, *Bad as I Wanna Be* (Delacorte Press, 1996).
30. Dan Bickley, *No Bull: The Unauthorized Biography of Dennis Rodman* (New York: St. Martin's Press, 1997).
31. Rodman and Keown.
32. *Rodman: For Better or Worse*.
33. Ibid.
34. Ibid.
35. Michael Silver, "Rodman unchained. The Spurs' no holds-barred forward gives new meaning to the running game," *Sports Illustrated*, May 29, 1995, accessed on May 10, 2023, https://vault.si.com/vault/1995/05/29/rodman-unchained-the-spurs-no-holds-barred-forward-gives-new-meaning-to-the-running-game.
36. Eva Boesenberg, "Who's Afraid of Shaq Attaq? Constructions of Black Masculinity and the NBA," *Engendering Manhood*, 43, no. 4 (1998): 689.
37. *The Last Dance*, "Episode IV," written and directed by Jason Hehir, aired April 26, 2020, ESPN/Netflix.
38. Alex Prewitt, "She Won Athletes' Hearts. And Robbed Them Blind," *Sports Illustrated*, September 19, 2019, accessed on May 12, 2023, https://www.si.com/nba/2019/09/19/athete-financial-advisor-embezzlement-fraud-scandal-peggy-ann-fulford.
39. *The Rich and Shameless*, "Stolen Millions," episode 8, written and directed by Jessica Burgess, aired May 7, 2023, TNT.
40. Lucy McCalmont, "Rodman yells at CNN's Cuomo," *Politico*, January 7, 2014, accessed on May 13, 2023, https://www.politico.com/story/2014/01/dennis-rodman-north-korea-basketball-101825.
41. Rishi Iyengar, "Dennis Rodman Says He Helped Secure Kenneth Bae's Release from North Korea," *Time*, November 9, 2014, accessed on May 14,
2023, https://time.com/3575237/dennis-rodman-north-korea-prisoner-kenneth-bae-kim-jong-un/.
42. Paul Szoldra and Veronka Bondranenko, "How North Korean leader Kim Jong-Un became one of the world's scariest dictators," *The Independent*, June 15, 2018, accessed on May 15, 2023.
43. Jonathan Watts, "North Korea 'using food as a weapon,'" *The Guardian*, January 20, 2004, accessed on May 15, 2023, https://www.theguardian.com/world/2004/jan/21/northkorea.
44. Stephen Haggard and Marcus Noland, *Famine in North Korea: Markets, Aid, and Reform* (New York: Columbia University Press, 2007).
45. "North Korea conducts nuclear test," *BBC*, May 25, 2009, accessed on May 14, 2023, http://news.bbc.co.uk/2/hi/asia-pacific/8066615.stm.
46. Justin McCurry, "North Korea holds funeral for Kim Jong-il," *The Guardian*, December 27, 2011, accessed on May 15, 2023, https://www.theguardian.com/world/2011/dec/28/kim-jong-il-funeral-north-korea.
47. Anna Fifield, "The secret life of Kim Jong Un's aunt, who has lived in the U.S. since 1998," *Washington Post*, May 27, 2016, accessed on May 16, 2023, -https://www.washingtonpost.com/world/asia_pacific/the-secret-life-of-kim-jong-uns-aunt-who-has-lived-in-the-us-since-1998/2016/05/26/522e4ec8-12d7-11e6-a9b5-bf703a5a7191_story.html.
48. Ibid.
49. Kim Jong-un's aunt and uncle fled North Korea because his mother had terminal cancer. They feared losing their privileged status once she passed away and Kim Jong-un graduated from high school.
50. Bob Garcia IV, "Kim Jong-il Once Built a Michael Jordan Shrine Next to a Crocodile Handbag from Fidel Castro," *Sportscasting*, December 29, 2020, May 16, 2023, https://www.sportscasting.com/kim-jong-ii-once-built-a-michael-jordan-shrine-next-to-a-crocodile-handbag-from-fidel-castro/.
51. Fifield.
52. *National Geographic*, "North Korea: Inside the Mind of a Dictator," aired February 15, 2021.
53. Ibid.
54. Logan Roy is the fictional patriarch

and CEO of the global media conglomerate Waystar RoyCo on the HBO series *Succession* (2018–2023).

55. Scott Neuman, "North Korean Leader's Slain Brother Was Reportedly Working with the CIA," *NPR*, June 11, 2019, accessed May 16, 2023, https://www.npr.org/2019/06/11/731539543/north-korean-leaders-slain-brother-was-reportedly-working-with-the-cia.

56. Trixia Carungcong Ferguson, "Trump-Kim Summit: U.S. willing to offer North Korea 'unique' security guarantees in exchange for denuclearization, says Pompeo," *The Straits Times*, June 12, 2018, accessed on May 16, 2023, https://www.straitstimes.com/singapore/complete-verifiable-denuclearisation-is-only-outcome-us-will-accept-at-trump-kim-summit.

57. Austin Ramzy, "Dennis Rodman, Frequent Visitor to North Korea, Is Back," *New York Times*, June 13, 2017, accessed on May 16, 2023, https://www.nytimes.com/2017/06/13/world/asia/dennis-rodman-north-korea.html.

58. Des Bieler, "Dennis Rodman eyeing trip to Singapore for Trump's summit with Kim Jong Un," *Washington Post*, June 5, 2018, accessed on May 16, 2023, https://www.washingtonpost.com/news/early-lead/wp/2018/06/05/dennis-rodman-eyeing-trip-to-singapore-for-trumps-summit-with-kim-jong-un/.

59. Steve George, "Dennis Rodman gets emotional discussing Trump and Kim," *CNN*, June 12, 2018, accessed on May 16, 2023, https://www.cnn.com/2018/06/11/asia/rodman-trump-kim-summit-intl/index.html.

60. Jonathan White, "Dennis Rodman's North Korea trips brought scorn and ridicule, but he deserves credit," *South China Morning Post*, May 12, 2020, accessed on May 16, 2023, https://www.scmp.com/sport/basketball/article/3083842/dennis-rodmans-north-korea-trips-brought-scorn-and-ridicule-he.

61. Debra Killalea, "North Korea's Kim Yo-jong makes her debut on the world stage by blowing up a liaison office," *Australian Broadcasting Corporation*, June 17, 2020, accessed on May 16, 2023, -https://www.abc.net.au/news/2020-06-18/north-korea-blows-up-building-as-kim-yo-jongs-power-grows/12363650.

62. Jeremy Diamond and Kevin Liptak, "Biden's North Korea strategy is a long way from Trump's showy diplomacy," *CNN*, May 16, 2022, accessed May 21, 2022. https://www.cnn.com/2022/05/21/politics/joe-biden-north-korea-south-korea/index.html.

63. *The Spy Who Signed Me*, 30 for 30, season six, episode one, podcast audio, September 6, 2022.

64. Joe Morgan, "Brittney Griner sentencing: How the WNBA star's salary compares to her Russian earnings." *Fox Business*, August 4, 2022, accessed on May 17, 2023, https://www.foxbusiness.com/sports/brittney-griner-sentencing-how-the-wnba-stars-salary-compares-to-her-russian-earnings.

65. *The Shop: Uninterrupted*, "Episode 18," directed by Robert Alexander, written by Paul Rivera, HBO, July 15, 2022.

66. Madison Williams, "Steph Curry Leads Powerful Message About Brittney Griner at the ESPYs," *Sports Illustrated*, July 20, 2022, accessed on May 17, 2023, https://www.si.com/wnba/2022/07/21/steph-curry-leads-powerful-message-about-brittney-griner-at-the-espys-video.

67. Natasha Dye, "Former UN Ambassador Bill Richardson Meeting with Russian Leadership to Discuss Brittney Griner," *People*, September 15, 2022, accessed on May 17, 2023, https://people.com/sports/bill-richardson-former-un-ambassador-in-moscow-to-discuss-brittney-griner/.

68. Jonathan Allen, "Dennis Rodman says he's going to Russia to seek release of Brittney Griner," *NBC News*, August 21, 2022, accessed on May 17, 2023, https://www.nbcnews.com/news/dennis-rodman-says-going-russia-seek-release-brittney-griner-rcna44106.

69. Jelani Scott, "Biden Administration Responds to Rodman's Brittney Griner Plan," *Sports Illustrated*, August 22, 2022, accessed on May 17, 2023, https://www.si.com/wnba/2022/08/22/biden-administration-responds-dennis-rodman-brittney-griner.

70. "Remarks by President Biden on the Release of Brittney Griner," December 8, 2022, accessed on May 17, 2023, https://www.whitehouse.gov/briefing-room/speeches-remarks/2022/12/08/remarks-by-president-biden-on-the-release-of-brittney-griner/.

71. Michael D. Shear and Peter Baker, "Inside the Prisoner Swap That Freed Brittney Griner," *New York Times*, December 9, 2022, accessed on May 17, 2023, https://www.nytimes.com/2022/12/09/us/politics/brittney-griner-prisoner-swap.html.
72. Daryl Morey, Twitter post, October 4, 2019, 9:41 p.m.
73. LeBron James, Twitter post, October 14, 2019, 10:35 p.m.
74. Ariel Zibler, "Nets owner Joe Tsai reportedly tried to get Daryl Morey fired over tweet," *New York Post*, April 15, 2022, accessed on May 18, 2023, https://nypost.com/2022/04/15/nets-owner-joe-tsai-reportedly-tried-to-get-daryl-morey-fired/.
75. Daryl Morey, Twitter post, October 7, 2019.
76. Ed O'Deven, "Raptors and Rockets reflect on Tuesday's NBA Japan Games opener," *Japan Times*, October 9, 2019, accessed on May 18, 2023, https://www.japantimes.co.jp/sports/2019/10/09/basketball/nba/raptors-rockets-reflect-tuesdays-nba-japan-games-opener/.
77. Daniel Victor, "Hong Kong Protests Put N.B.A. on Edge in China," *New York Times*, October 7, 2019, accessed on May 18, 2023, https://www.nytimes.com/2019/10/07/sports/basketball/nba-china-hong-kong.html.
78. Beto O'Rourke, Twitter post, October 6, 2019, 11:22 p.m.
79. Christy Leung, "Extradition bill not made to measure to mainland China and won't be abandoned, Hong Kong leader Carrie Lam says," *South China Morning Post*, April 1, 2019, accessed on May 19, 2023, https://www.scmp.com/news/hong-kong/politics/article/3004067/extradition-bill-not-made-measure-mainland-china-and-wont.
80. Mainland China is a geopolitical term defined as the territory governed by the People's Republic of China and other territories within Greater China.
81. "Hong Kong Protests Explained," *Amnesty International*, September 2019, accessed on May 19, 2023, https://www.amnesty.org/en/latest/news/2019/09/hong-kong-protests-explained/.
82. Siobhan O'Grady, Ruby Mellen, and Miriam Berger, "What's happening in Hong Kong? Some key questions, answered," *Washington Post*, November 14, 2019, accessed on May 19, 2023, https://www.washingtonpost.com/world/2019/08/09/airport-sit-ins-citywide-strikes-street-protests-whats-happening-hong-kong/.
83. Xingda Tong, "The Impact of the NBA-Tencent Exclusive Streaming Agreement on Chinese Basketball Viewers" (Master's thesis, Drexel University, 2018), 14.
84. Jeremy Lin was a cultural icon who challenged stereotypes about Asian men and masculinity.
85. David Hollander, *How Basketball Can Save the World* (New York, NY: Harmony, 2023), 125–127.
86. Tong, 15.
87. *Ibid.*, 16
88. *Ibid.*, 17.
89. *Ibid.*, 18.
90. Tong, 23.
91. Rory Carroll, "NBA-China's NBA viewership approaching pre-ban levels—source," *Reuters*, December 8, 2022, accessed on May 22, 2023, https://www.reuters.com/lifestyle/sports/nba-chinas-nba-viewership-approaching-pre-ban-levels-source-2022-12-08/.
92. *The Redeem Team*, directed by Jon Weinbach, aired October 7, 2022, Netflix.
93. *Ibid*.
94. Sopan Deb, "How Kobe Bryant Helped the NBA Conquer the World," *New York Times*, January 28, 2020, accessed on December 23, 2022 https://www.nytimes.com/2020/01/28/sports/basketball/kobe-NBA-global.html.
95. Shandel Richardson, "Dwyane Wade's Son Get His First Signature Shoe," *Sports Illustrated*, February 13, 2023, accessed on May 23, 2023, https://www.si.com/nba/heat/miami-news/dwyane-wades-son-gets-his-first-signature-shoe.
96. Paolo Uggetti, "Klay Thompson Is Having the Time of His Life in China," *The Ringer*, June 30, 2017, accessed on May 23, 2023, https://www.theringer.com/2017/6/30/16044484/nba-klay-thompson-having-fun-in-china-golden-state-warriors-fdf2c4408f2d.
97. *A Kid from Coney Island*, directed by Chike Ozah and Coodie Simmons, aired April 6, 2020, Netflix.
98. Brigitte Pu, "Ex-NBA star Dwight Howard sparks anger in China by calling

Taiwan a 'country,'" *NBC News*, May 12, 2023, accessed on May 23, 2023, https://www.nbcnews.com/news/world/ex-nba-star-dwight-howard-sparks-anger-china-calling-taiwan-country-rcna84097.

99. Ramona Shelburne, "When the Donald Sterling sage rocked the NBA—and changed it forever," *ESPN*, August 20, 2019, accessed on May 23, 2023, https://www.espn.com/nba/story/_/id/27414482/when-donald-sterling-saga-rocked-nba-changed-forever.

100. Theresa Runstedtler, *Black Ball: Kareem Abdul-Jabbar, Spencer Haywood, and the Generation that Saved the Soul of the NBA* (New York: Bold Type Books, 2003).

101. Melissa Chan, "Read LeBron James and Carmelo Anthony's Powerful Speech on Race at the ESPYs Awards," *Time*, July 14, 2016, accessed on May 24, 2023, https://time.com/4406289/lebron-james-carmelo-anthony-espy-awards-transcript/.

102. Scott Cacciola and Alan Blinder, "NBA to Move All-Star Game From North Carolina," *New York Times*, July 21, 2016, accessed on December 3, 2023, https://www.nytimes.com/2016/07/22/sports/basketball/nba-all-star-game-moves-charlotte-transgender-bathroom-law.html.

103. Jack Maloney, "George Floyd Death: Celtics' Jaylen Brown drove 15 hours from Boston to Atlanta to lead peaceful protest," *CBS Sports*, June 1, 2020, accessed on December 4, 2023, https://www.cbssports.com/nba/news/george-floyd-death-celtics-jaylen-brown-drove-15-hours-from-boston-to-atlanta-to-lead-peaceful-protest/.

104. Joshua K. Wright, *Wake Up, Mr. West: Kanye West and the Double Consciousness of Black Celebrity* (Jefferson, North Carolina: McFarland, 2022), 211–214.

105. In March 2020, the NBA and other American sports leagues suspended play for safety precautions associated with the Covid-19 pandemic. The NBA resumed its season in a bio-secure bubble at Walt Disney World in Orlando, Florida. NBA players wore T-shirts with pro–Black Lives Matter and social justice logos. Courts had social justice messages written on them in large letters.

106. Steve Fainaru and Mark Fainaru-Wada, "ESPN investigation finds coaches at NBA China academies complained of player abuse, lack of schooling," *ESPN*, July 29, 2020, accessed on July 13, 2024, https://www.espn.com/nba/story/_/id/29553829/espn-investigation-finds-coaches-nba-china-academies-complained-player-abuse-lack-schooling.

107. George Packer, "We Are All Realists Now," *The Atlantic*, February 16, 2022, accessed on May 24, 2023, https://www.theatlantic.com/ideas/archive/2022/02/who-cares-human-rights-enes-kanter-freedom/622812/.

108. Jeff Benedict, *LeBron* (Chestertown, Maryland: Avid Reader Press, 2023), 252.

109. Tom McTague, "The Qatar World Cup Exposes Soccer's Shame," *The Atlantic*, November 19, 2022, accessed on June 6, 2023 https://www.theatlantic.com/international/archive/2022/11/qatar-hosting-fifa-world-cup-soccer/672171/.

110. Ibid., 264–265 and 309–310.

111. Twitter was rebranded as X in July 2023.

112. Zachary Faria, "The NBA flaunts its social justice hypocrisy with games in the UAE," *Washington Examiner*, May 11, 2022, accessed on December 4, 2023, https://www.washingtonexaminer.com/opinion/the-nba-flaunts-its-social-justice-hypocrisy-with-games-in-the-uae.

113. Rick Maese and Matt Bonesteel, "PGA Tour agrees to merge with Saudi-backed LIV Golf," *Washington Post*, June 6, 2023, accessed on June 6, 2023, https://www.washingtonpost.com/sports/2023/06/06/liv-golf-pga-tour-merger/.

114. Mike Vorkunov, "Adam Silver discusses Saudi investment in sports and potential impact on NBA: 'It's a 2-edged sword,'" *The Athletic*, June 8, 2023, accessed on June 9, 2023, https://theathletic.com/4595053/2023/06/08/adam-silver-saudi-investment-nba/.

115. Stephen Whyno, "Qatar sovereign wealth fund buys stake in Washington's NBA, NHL, and WNBA teams, AP source says," *Associated Press*, June 22, 2023, accessed on June 22, 2023, https://apnews.com/article/qatar-investment-authority-buys-wizards-capitals-9e2d9e6246f79b5265e9891b29cae690.

116. David Aldridge, interviewed by Joshua K. Wright, January 5, 2024.
117. Ibid.
118. David Schuman, "At Timberwolves game, Israeli basketball team honors hostages taken by Hamas," *CBS News*, October 17, 2023, accessed on November 7, 2023, https://www.cbsnews.com/minnesota/news/israeli-basketball-team-honors-hostages-taken-by-hamas-at-game-against-timberwolves/.
119. Zainab Iqbal, "Israel-Palestine war: U.S. sports stars ignore Palestinians in pro-Israel posts, face fan backlash," *Middle East Eye*, October 12, 2023, accessed on November 7, 2023, https://www.middleeasteye.net/news/israel-palestine-war-us-sports-stars-ignore-palestinians-pro-israel-backlash.

Chapter 6

1. Seerat Sohi, "Toronto Raptors' GM Masai Ujiri on inspiring kids, the growth of basketball in Africa and what comes next," *SB Nation*, August 4, 2018, accessed on June 1, 2023, https://www.sbnation.com/2018/8/4/17649430/masai-ujiri-africa-nba-game-interview-raptors.
2. Bam Adebayo was born in Newark, New Jersey, and raised by his American mother in North Carolina. His father is from Nigeria and identifies as Yoruba.
3. Samantha Bresnahan, "'This is a dream': Burna Boy, Afrobeats stars take center stage at the NBA All-Star game," *CNN World*, February 21, 2023, accessed on June 2, 2023, https://www.cnn.com/2023/02/21/africa/afrobeats-burna-boy-tems-rema-nba-all-star-halftime-spc-intl/index.html.
4. Zach Baron, "Why Giannis Antetokounmpo Chose the Path of Most Resistant," *GQ*, November 16, 2021, accessed on June 2, 2023, https://www.gq.com/story/giannis-antetokounmpo-athlete-of-the-year-2021.
5. Skyler Caruso, "All About Giannis Antetokounmpo's Siblings, Including His NBA All-Star Brothers," *People*, February 17, 2023, accessed on June 5, 2023, https://people.com/sports/all-about-giannis-antetokounmpos-brothers/.
6. Helena Smith, "Neo-fascist Greek party takes third place in wave of voter fury," *The Guardian*, September 20, 2015, accessed on February 24, 2024, https://www.theguardian.com/world/2015/sep/21/neo-fascist-greek-party-election-golden-dawn-third-place.
7. *Giannis: The Marvelous Journey*, written and directed by Kristen Lappas, aired February 19, 2024, Amazon Prime.
8. Lee Jenkins, "Freak Unleashed: Greek Freak," *Time*, February 8, 2017, accessed on June 3, 2023, https://time.com/collection/american-voices-2017/4624632/giannis-antetokounmpo-american-voices/.
9. Giannis Antekounmpo, interviewed by Steve Kroft, March 25, 2018, on *60 Minutes*.
10. *Finding Giannis*, directed by Ross Hockrow, aired February 16, 2019, TNT.
11. Ibid.
12. *Giannis: The Marvelous Journey*.
13. *Finding Giannis*.
14. Bleacher Report, Twitter post, July 21, 2021, 11:39 a.m.
15. Lori Nickel, "Feeling the stress, Giannis almost quit the NBA. Now he wants to help as many people as possible with the foundation," *Milwaukee Journal Sentinel*, April 11, 2023, accessed on February 25, 2024, https://www.jsonline.com/story/sports/nba/bucks/2023/04/11/giannis-foundation-provides-many-different-types-of-support/70091667007/.
16. *Rewind with Ahmad Rashad*, NBA TV, July 2023.
17. Ruben Boumtje-Boumtje is the first native Cameroonian in the NBA. He played three years (2001–2004) with the Portland Trailblazers after attending Georgetown University.
18. Romona Shelburne, "Ex-NBA forward Mbah a Moute to focus on Africa as agent," *ESPN*, February 15, 2023, accessed on June 6, 2023, https://www.espn.com/nba/story/_/id/35666105/luc-richard-mbah-moute-joins-caa-player-agent.
19. Max Rappaport, "The Definitive History of 'Trust the Process,'" *Bleacher Report*, August 23, 2017, accessed on June 6, 2023, https://bleacherreport.com/articles/2729018-the-definitive-history-of-trust-the-process.
20. Andrew Lawrence, "Joel Embiid: the star who toppled critics and implicit bias to win NBA MVP," *The Guardian*, May 3, 2023, accessed on June 6, 2023, https://www.theguardian.com/sport/

blog/2023/may/03/joel-embiid-mvp-wokeism-philadelphia-76ers.

21. ESPN college basketball analyst Dick Vitale gave Hakeem Olajuwon the nickname The Dream during his freshman year at the University of Houston.

22. *Clutch City*, directed by Zak Levitt and written by Aaron Cohen, aired June 8, 2015, on NBA TV.

23. The African Games, previously named the Pan African Games and All-African Games, are an athletic competition held every four years in Africa. The games are organized by the African Union (AU), the Association of National Olympic Committees of Africa (ANOCA), and the Association of African Sports Confederations (AASC). The first event was held in 1965.

24. Dave Anderson, "Basketball's New Force," *New York Times*, April 4, 1983, Section C, Page 4.

25. Mirin Fader interviewed on *NBA Weekend*, October 26, 2024 (NBA Radio Sirius Satellite Radio).

26. Ibid.

27. Ibid.

28. *Phi Slamma Jamma*, directed by Chip Rives, aired October 18, 2016, ESPN.

29. Malcolm Moran, "Georgetown, led by freshmen, wins title; Georgetown 84, Houston 75," *New York Times*, April 3, 1984, Section B, Page 7.

30. Jonathan Fiegen, "Keeping the Faith—Olajuwon's, Rockets' quiet confidence has roots in Mecca," *Houston Chronicle*, September 6, 1996, accessed on June 8, 2023.

31. John Reimold, "Hakeem Olajuwon Remembered: The Best Center of All Time," *Bleacher Report*, April 13, 2011, accessed on June 8, 2023, https://bleacherreport.com/articles/663761-remembering-hakeem-olajuwon-the-best-center-of-all-time.

32. Chris Ballard, "Post Play Is a Lost Art in the NBA. What Happens to Those Who Still Believe in It?" *Sports Illustrated*, January 18, 2023, accessed on January 8, 2023, https://www.si.com/nba/2023/01/18/nba-lost-art-of-post-play-daily-cover.

33. Dan Roche, "Joel Embiid appears to clap back at Olajuwon's comments," *NBC Sports Philadelphia*, January 20, 2023, accessed on June 8, 2023, https://www.nbcsportsphiladelphia.com/nba/joel-embiid-appears-to-clap-back-at-olajuwons-comments/267447/.

34. Dan Feldman, "Hakeem Olajuwon named NBA Ambassador to Africa," *NBC Sports*, May 21, 2014, accessed on June 8, 2023, https://nba.nbcsports.com/2014/05/21/hakeem-olajuwon-named-nba-ambassador-to-africa/.

35. Excerpts from Hakeem Olajuwon's induction speech into the Naismith Memorial Hall of Fame on September 6, 2008.

36. Chris Milholen, *Basketball Beyond Borders: The Globalization of the NBA* (Washington, D.C., Amazon Kindle Direct Publishing, 2019), 91.

37. Case Western University received a two-year probation from the NCAA for violating financial assistance rules to support Bol and two other African basketball players.

38. Milholen, 91.

39. Ibid., 91.

40. Charles Ross, "Manute Bol: A Freak Show in the NBA, a Hero in Sudan," *Medium*, December 16, 2015, accessed on June 8, 2023, https://medium.com/@cross0328/manute-bol-a-freak-show-in-the-nba-a-hero-in-sudan-59e821dd7e01.

41. George Mackenzie, "Remembering Manute Bol, the tallest man in NBA," *The Versed*, January 11, 2017, https://www.theversed.com/10258/remembering-manute-bol-tallest-man-nba-history/#.Y29xbbG9Hc.

42. Frank James, "Manute Bol Left Sudan But Really Didn't," *NPR*, June 21, 2010, accessed on June 8, 2023, https://www.npr.org/sections/thetwo-way/2010/06/21/127981788/manute-bol-left-sudan-but-really-didn-t.

43. Excerpts from Dikembe Mutombo's Naismith Memorial Basketball Hall of Fame induction speech.

44. "NBA star makes a giant impact in his African homeland," *Yale Medicine Magazine*, Spring 2006, accessed on June 9, 2023, https://medicine.yale.edu/news/yale-medicine-magazine/article/nba-star-makes-a-giant-impact-in-his/.

45. https://www.hoyabasketball.com/players/d_mutombo.htm.

46. Ann Sanner, "NBA star Mutombo honored for his deeds in native Congo," *San Diego Union-Tribune*, January 18, 2010, accessed on June 9, 2023, https://

www.sandiegouniontribune.com/sdut-nba-star-mutombo-honored-for-deeds-in-native-congo-2010jan18-story.html.

47. "Bloomberg School Awards Goodermote Humanitarian Award to Dikembe Mutombo," April 14, 2001, accessed on June 9, 2023, https://publichealth.jhu.edu/2011/goodermote-award-mutombo.

48. David K. Li, "Dikembe Mutombo, Basketball Hall of Famer and NBA global ambassador, dies at 58," NBC News, September 30, 2024, accessed on September 30, 2024, https://www.nbcnews.com/news/sports/dikembe-mutombo-dies-58-rcna173258.

49. "The Serge Ibaka Foundation Helps the Congo," *The Borgen Project*, accessed on June 9, 2023, https://borgenproject.org/serge-ibaka-foundation/.

50. "NBA champ Pascal Siakam visits SOS Village in Cameroon," *SOS Children's Villages*, August 9, 2019, accessed on June 9, 2023, https://www.sos-childrensvillages.org/news/nba-champ-pascal-siakam-visits-sos-cameroon.

51. Marc J. Spears, "'My dad was everything to me': Bismack Biyombo is still healing in his NBA return," *Andscape*, February 11, 2022, accessed on June 9, 2023, https://andscape.com/features/my-dad-was-everything-to-me-bismack-biyombo-is-still-healing-in-his-nba-return/.

52. Marc J. Spears, "Dikembe Mutombo helps grow the game in Africa," *Andscape*, August 2, 2017, accessed on June 10, 2023, https://andscape.com/features/dikembe-mutombo-nba-africa-basketball-without-borders/.

53. Steve Fainaru and Mark Fainaru-Wada, "ESPN investigation finds coaches at NBA China academies complained of player abuse, lack of schooling," *ESPN*, July 29, 2020, accessed on July 13, 2024, https://www.espn.com/nba/story/_/id/29553829/espn-investigation-finds-coaches-nba-china-academies-complained-player-abuse-lack-schooling.

54. Nicolas Kohlhuber, "NBA Academy Africa: Uncovering Africa's top basketball prospects," *Olympics.com*, April 28, 2023, accessed on June 11, 2023, https://olympics.com/en/news/nba-academy-africa-discovering-africa-biggest-prospects.

55. Marc J. Spears, "Source: J. Cole finishes Basketball Africa League stint," *ESPN*, May 26, 2021, accessed on June 17, 2023, https://www.espn.com/nba/story/_/id/31515194/source-j-cole-finishes-africa-league-stint.

56. Timothy Rapp, "Report: Dwyane Wade's Son Zaire Agrees to Contract with BAL's Cape Town Tigers," *Bleacher Report*, February 3, 2023, accessed on June 18, 2023, https://bleacherreport.com/articles/10064103-report-dwyane-wades-son-zaire-agrees-to-contract-with-bals-cape-town-tigers.

57. "NBA Africa and Hennessy to Host League's First NBA Crossover Lifestyle Event on the Continent," *African Press Organisation* (January 26, 2022), distributed by Press Releases Related to Africa.

58. "Dambisa Moyo and Forest Whitaker Join Group of Strategic Investors in NBA Africa," *African Press Organisation* (December 23, 2021), distributed by Press Releases Related to Africa.

59. "Former President Barack Obama Joins NBA Africa as Strategic Partner," *African Press Organisation* (July 27, 2021), distributed by Press Releases Related to Africa.

60. Leonard Solms, "Toronto Raptors boss Masai Ujiri -BAL can produce NBA-level talent, but will need time to grow," *ESPN*, September 2, 2022, accessed on June 12, 2023, https://www.espn.com/espn/story/_/id/34506331/toronto-raptors-boss-masai-ujiri-bal-produce-nba-level-talent-need-grow.

61. *The Air Up There*, directed by Paul Michael Glaser (Buena Vista Pictures, 1994), 1hr., 47 min.

62. Rotten Tomatoes is a website that aggregates reviews for American films and television series.

63. Keli Goff, "Can 'Belle' End Hollywood's Obsession with the White Savior?" *Daily Beast*, March 4, 2014, accessed on June 13, 2023, https://www.thedailybeast.com/can-belle-end-hollywoods-obsession-with-the-white-savior.

64. The United States, United Kingdom, France, Germany, Austria, Belgium, Denmark, Spain, Italy, the Netherlands, Portugal, Russia, Sweden-Norway, and Turkey (Ottoman Empire) had representatives at the Berlin Conference.

65. Imperialism is the practice of achieving control of foreign nations using economic and military power (hard

power) and subtle diplomacy (soft power). New imperialism refers to the colonial expansion of Europe, Japan, and the United States between the late 19th and early 20th centuries.

66. Walter Rodney, *How Europe Underdeveloped Africa* (Brooklyn, New York: Verso, 2018).

67. Paul Hofmann, "Bunche says '60 is year of Africa," *New York Times*, February 16, 1960, 15.

68. https://www.britannica.com/topic/neocolonialism.

69. Wade Shepard, "What China Is Really Up To In Africa," *Forbes*, October 3, 2019, accessed on June 14, 2023, https://www.forbes.com/sites/wadeshepard/2019/10/03/what-china-is-really-up-to-in-africa/?sh=6210acc59304.

70. Sunday Adedini, "Nigeria's cities are growing fast: family planning must be part of urban development plans," *The Conversation*, March 12, 2023, accessed on June 14, 2023, https://theconversation.com/nigerias-cities-are-growing-fast-family-planning-must-be-part-of-urban-development-plans-199325.

71. Robin Fall, "The Myth of the Chinese 'Debt Trap' in Africa," *Bloomberg*, March 17, 2022, accessed on June 14, 2023, https://www.bloomberg.com/news/articles/2022-03-17/the-myth-of-chinese-debt-trap-diplomacy-in-africa#xj4y7vzkg.

72. Shepard.

73. BBC video, https://www.youtube.com/watch?v=MrVzFSXqn3w.

74. Fall.

75. David Aldridge, interviewed by Joshua K. Wright, January 5, 2024.

76. Christian Mulumba, "Basketball Africa League: Linking African teams to the NBA," *Africa Renewal*, October 19, 2022, accessed on June 16, 2023, https://www.un.org/africarenewal/magazine/november-2022/basketball-africa-league-linking-african-teams-nba.

77. "NBA Africa and Basketball Africa League Join 16 Days of Activism Against Gender-Based Violence," *African Press Organisation* (November 25, 2021), distributed by Press Releases Related to Africa.

78. "Former President Barack Obama Joins NBA Africa as Strategic Partner," *African Press Organisation* (July 27, 2021), distributed by Press Releases Related to Africa.

79. *Real Sports*, season 25, episode 10, first broadcast on October 22, 2019, by HBO.

80. An excerpt is borrowed from the 1951 poem "Harlem" (also known as a "Dream Deferred") by the African American poet Langston Hughes.

81. *Real Sports*.

82. *Ibid*.

83. *Ibid*.

84. *Ibid*.

Chapter 7

1. Sean Gregory and Karl Vick, "Shohei Ohtani Is What Baseball Needs," *Time*, April 7, 2022, accessed on July 7, 2023, https://time.com/6165003/shohei-ohtani-baseball/.

2. Juan Toribio, "Unanimous yet again: Ohtani wins third career MVP Award," *MLB.com*, November 21, 2024, https://www.mlb.com/news/shohei-ohtani-2024-nl-mvp.

3. Data provided by SportsUnfold.com.

4. Bobby Burack, "Stephen A. Smith has no idea MLB is more popular than the NBA," *Outkick*, March 2, 2022, accessed on July 7, 2023, https://www.outkick.com/stephen-a-smith-has-no-idea-mlb-is-more-popular-than-nba/.

5. "NBA Finals ratings down from 2022: but playoff viewership up," *ESPN*, June 13, 2023, accessed on July 7, 2023, https://www.espn.com/nba/story/_/id/37848871/nba-finals-ratings-2022-playoff-viewership-up.

6. Quinn Allen, "NBA reaches insane social media milestone, blowing NFL, MLB, NHL combined out of the water," *Clutch Sports*, August 12, 2022, accessed on July 7, 2023, https://clutchpoints.com/nba-reaches-insane-social-media-milestone-blowing-nfl-mlb-nhl-combined-out-of-the-water.

7. Anthony Castrovince, "Numerous indicators show youth MLB fandom is on the rise," *MLB*, October 3, 2022, accessed on July 7, 2023, https://www.mlb.com/news/number-of-young-mlb-fans-rising.

8. "Who Invented Baseball?" *History*, March 27, 2013, accessed on July 8, 2023, https://www.history.com/news/who-invented-baseball.

9. Information provided by the National

Baseball Hall of Fame, https://baseballhall.org/baseball-history-american-history-and-you.

10. Joon Lee, " 'This Is Our F-—king City': The Oral History," *Bleacher Report*, April 16, 2018, accessed on July 8, 2023, https://bleacherreport.com/articles/2768345-the-oral-history-of-this-is-our-f-king-city.

11. The Pentagon has signed 72 contracts with teams in the MLB, NFL, NHL, and MLS to have patriotic displays during their games. Eyder Peralta, "Pentagon Paid Sports Teams Millions for 'Paid Patriotism' Events," *NPR*, November 5, 2015, accessed on December 16, 2022, https://www.npr.org/sections/thetwo-way/2015/11/05/454834662/pentagon-paid-sports-teams-millions-for-paid-patriotism-events.

12. Manny Randhawa, "Opening Day rosters feature 269 players born internationally," *MLB*, March 31, 2023, accessed on July 4, 2023, https://www.mlb.com/news/international-players-on-2023-opening-day-rosters.

13. Oliver Clarke, "ESPN and MLB expand partnership with new rights agreement across Europe and Africa," *ESPN Press Room*, March 12, 2020, accessed on July 10, 2023, https://espnpressroom.com/espnuk/press-releases/2020/03/espn-and-mlb-expand-partnership-with-new-rights-agreement-across-europe-and-africa/.

14. An over-the-top (OTT) media service is offered directly to viewers via the internet. OTT bypasses cable, broadcast, and satellite television platforms.

15. Ed Dixon, "MLB and Tencent expand Chinese streaming deal to cover multiple Asian markets," *Sports Pro Media*, April 1, 2021, accessed on July 10, 2023, https://www.sportspromedia.com/news/mlb-tencent-china-streaming-deal-asia-wetv-oriental-pearl-media/?zephr_sso_ott=4G787z.

16. Minor league affiliates are often informally called "farm teams" in baseball.

17. "Opening Day rosters feature 275 internationally born players," *MLB*, April 8, 2022, accessed on July 11, 2023, https://www.mlb.com/news/opening-day-2022-international-representation.

18. Warren Turner, "World Baseball Classic: South Africa Shows Great Improvement," *Bleacher Report*, March 10, 2009, accessed on July 11, 2023, https://bleacherreport.com/articles/137024-impressions-of-the-wbc-south-africa-shows-great-improvement.

19. Joseph A. Reaves, *Taking in a Game: A History of Baseball in Asia* (Lincoln: University of Nebraska Press, 2002), 27.

20. *Ibid.*, 108.

21. *Ibid.*, 129.

22. Daniel Bloyce, "The Globalization of Baseball: A Figurational Analysis" (PhD diss., University of Leicester, 2004), 167.

23. *Ibid.*, 171.

24. "It's Not Just Baseball History," *Black Diamonds*, season three, podcast audio, July 27, 2023.

25. Tracy Ringolsby, "A half-century later, Murakami's legacy remains strong," *MLB*, March 21, 2014, accessed on July 15, 2023, https://www.mlb.com/news/tracy-ringolsby-a-half-century-later-masanori-murakamis-legacy-remains-strong/c-69771396.

26. *Ibid.*

27. The New York Mutuals existed from 1857 until 1876.

28. Bloyce, 140.

29. Christina Kahrl, "As MLB returns to Cuba, the legacy of Minnie Minoso—the Cuban Jackie Robinson—lives on," *ESPN*, March 19, 2016, accessed on September 19, 2023, https://www.espn.com/mlb/story/_/page/springtraining_minoso/as-mlb-heads-back-cuba-minnie-minoso-legacy-joy-lives-on.

30. Roberto Gonzalez Echevarria, *The Pride of Havana. A History of Cuban Baseball* (New York: Oxford University Press, 1999), 5.

31. Milton H. Jamail and Larry Dieker, *Full Count. Inside Cuban Baseball* (Carbondale: Southern Illinois University Press, 2000), 69.

32. *Ibid.*, 70.

33. Scott Edem, "No One Walks Off The Island," *ESPN The Magazine,* April 17, 2014, accessed on July 21, 2023, http://www.espn.com/espn/feature/story/_/id/10781144/no-one-walks-island-los-angeles-dodgers-yasiel-puig-journey-cuba.

34. Steve Dilbeck, "Yasiel Puig's incredible journey from Cuba to the U.S. told by LA Magazine," *Los Angeles Times,* April 14, 2014, accessed on July 20, 2023,

https://www.latimes.com/sports/dodgers/dodgersnow/la-sp-dn-dodgers-yasiel-puig-journey-20140413-story.html#ixzz2z60I2kfv.

35. Eden.

36. Marcus F. Cuellar, "Runners Left on Base: Cuban Baseball Defection Experience and a Reevaluation of Baseball Diplomacy" (Thesis, University of California Santa Barbara, 2014), 62.

37. Gregory Korte, "Obama brings baseball diplomacy to Havana," *USA Today*, March 22, 2016, accessed on July 19, 2023, https://www.usatoday.com/story/news/politics/2016/03/22/obama-goes-game-does-wave-castro/82126632/.

38. Brandon Brown and Gregg Bennett address reasons for the lack of Black baseball players in their 2014 article "Baseball is Whack!: Exploring the Lack of African American Baseball Consumption" in the *Journal of Sport and Social Issues*.

39. Mitchell S. Jackson, "Few Black Americans Play Baseball. MLB Doesn't Seem to Care," *Esquire*, February 22, 2023, accessed on July 21, 2023, https://www.esquire.com/sports/a43008619/mlb-black-baseball-players/.

40. Natalie Alonso, "60 years ago, the Alous formed the first all-brother outfield," *MLB.com*, September 19, 2023, https://www.mlb.com/news/featured/alou-brothers-formed-mlb-s-first-all-brother-outfield.

41. Sammy Sosa and Marcos Breton, *Sosa: An Autobiography* (New York: Grand Central Publishing, 2000).

42. Arturo J. Marcano and David P. Fidler, "The Globalization of Baseball: Major League Baseball and the Mistreatment of Latin American Baseball Talent," *Indiana Journal of Global Legal Studies* 6, no. 2 (1999): 511.

43. Lara D. Nielsen, "Exertions: Acts of Citizenship in the Globalization of Major League Beisbol" (PhD diss., New York University, 2002).

44. The Chicago Cubs earned the nickname "lovable losers" because they did not win a World Series from 1908 until 2016. They reached the World Series and lost seven times before 2016. Additionally, Chicago fans suffered through multiple losing seasons and unfathomable playoff losses, such as the 2003 National League Championship Series, which fans remember for the infamous Steven Bartman incident.

45. Zachary D. Rymer, "Remembering Mark McGwire, Sammy Sosa's Historic Summer of '98 Home Run Chase," *Bleacher Report*, April 13, 2020, accessed on July 27, 2023, https://bleacherreport.com/articles/2886003-remembering-mark-mcgwire-sammy-sosas-historic-summer-of-98-home-run-chase.

46. Ibid.

47. baseball-reference.com/players/s/sosasa01.shtml.

48. Gary Smith, "The Race Is On: With a Hot Bat and Little Fanfare, Sammy Sosa Served Notice That the Home Run Record Is Up for Grabs," *Sports Illustrated*, September 21, 1998, accessed on July 27, 2023, https://vault.si.com/vault/1998/09/21/the-race-is-on-with-a-hot-bat-and-little-fanfare-sammy-sosa-served-notice-that-the-home-run-record-is-up-for-grabs.

49. *Long Gone Summer*, directed by AJ Schnack, aired June 14, 2020, ESPN.

50. Nielson, 221.

51. M.L. Butterworth, "Race in 'the Race': Mark McGwire, Sammy Sosa, and heroic constructions of whiteness," *Critical Studies in Media Communication* 24, no. 3 (2007): 234.

52. "Major League Baseball Players Testify Before Congress About Steroid Use," *PBS News Hour*, March 17, 2005, accessed on July 27, 2023, https://www.pbs.org/newshour/show/major-league-baseball-players-testify-before-congress-about-steroid-use.

53. "Mark McGwire Admits Using Steroids," *CBS News*, January 11, 2010, accessed on February 3, 2024, https://www.cbsnews.com/news/mark-mcgwire-admits-using-steroids/.

54. Dan Bernstein, "Sammy Sosa then and now: Former MLB star explains why his skin color is lighter since retirement," *Sporting News*, June 15, 2020, accessed on February 2, 2024, https://www.sportingnews.com/us/mlb/news/sammy-sosa-skin-color-now/1aruhh5dunsn11lps943qzwlqk.

55. "Why So Many Baseball Players are Dominican," YouTube, July 11, 2023, educational video, 3:00–12:00, https://www.youtube.com/watch?v=40Je_0Jef_o.

56. Patrick C. Gentile, "MLB's Neocolonial Practices in the Dominican Republic

Academy System" (Thesis, University of North Carolina at Charlotte, 2018), 8.

57. Ibid., 8.

58. https://www.usaid.gov/dominican-republic.

59. Gentile, 9.

60. The Notorious B.I.G., "Things Done Change," *Ready to Die*, Bad Boy/Arista, 1994.

61. P. Ghosh, "Huge salaries and a poverty-stricken country: The economies of baseball in the Dominican Republic," *International Business Times*, January 14, 2014, accessed on August 21, 2023, http://www.ibtimes.com/huge-salaries-poverty-stricken-country-economicsbaseball-dominican-republic-1546993.

62. "Dominican Dreams: Chasing the Game," *YouTube*, October 6, 2019, educational video, 8:30–9:45, https://www.youtube.com/watch?v=hzbGQegKk4Y.

63. Gentile, 16.

64. Ibid., 24–25.

65. Alan Klein, *Dominican Baseball: New Pride, Old Prejudice* (Philadelphia: Temple University Press, 2014).

66. Dave Hannigan, "Likes of Fernando Tatis Jr take a loan in exchange for a percentage of future earnings," July 21, 2021, accessed on August 19, 2023, https://www.irishtimes.com/sport/other-sports/big-league-advance-is-a-major-league-scam-targeting-the-prodigious-and-vulnerable-1.4625721.

67. Segments of Michael Schwimer's interview with Soledad O'Brien were featured on HBO's *Real Sports* in June 2021.

68. The Jets-Colts championship game in 1969 is regarded as Super Bowl III despite being the first game to use that title.

69. Zach Koons, "NFL Had 82 of Top 100 U.S. TV Broadcasts in 2022," *Sports Illustrated*, January 6, 2023, accessed on August 4, 2023, https://www.si.com/extra-mustard/2023/01/06/nfl-82-top-100-american-television-broadcasts-2022-nielsen-ratings.

70. Julia Stoll, "TV viewership of the Super Bowl in the United States from 1990 to 2023," *Statista*, May 4, 2023, accessed on August 4, 2023, https://www.statista.com/statistics/216526/super-bowl-us-tv-viewership/.

71. Selome Hailu, "Super Bowl 2024 Was the Most-Watched Telecast of All Time, Reaching 123.7 Million Viewers," *Variety*, February 12, 2024, accessed on February 14, 2024, https://variety.com/2024/tv/news/super-bowl-2024-ratings-viewers-1235907666/.

72. Colin Salad, "The 20 Most Valuable Sports Teams," *TheStreet*, July 19, 2023, accessed on August 4, 2023, https://www.thestreet.com/sports/the-20-most-valuable-sports-teams.

73. Mike Ozanian, "World's Most Profitable Sports Teams: Cowboys Banked $1.2 Billion Over the Past Three Years," *Forbes*, June 2, 2023, accessed on August 8, 2023, https://www.forbes.com/sites/mikeozanian/2023/06/02/worlds-most-profitable-sports-teams-cowboys-banked-12-billion-over-the-past-three-years/?sh=5878939d6e44.

74. Derek Saul, "NFL's Roger Goodell Reportedly Makes $63 Million Per Year—Here's How That Compares To Other Top Execs and Sports Commissioners," *Forbes*, October 29, 2021, accessed on August 8, 2023, https://www.forbes.com/sites/dereksaul/2021/10/29/nfls-roger-goodell-reportedly-makes-63-million-per-year---heres-how-that-compares-to-other-top-execs-and-sports-commissioners/?sh=ae226a257029.

75. Andrew Jordan, "Globalization: The NFL's Future Depends on It," *Bleacher Report*, March 3, 2010, accessed on August 7, 2023, https://bleacherreport.com/articles/355662-globalization-the-one-word-that-nfl-fans-should-fear-the-most.

76. "2022 NFL International Player Pathway program: 13 athletes from nine countries selected," *NFL.com*, January 11, 2022, accessed on August 9, 2023, https://www.nfl.com/news/2022-international-player-pathway-program-13-athletes-nine-countries.

77. NFL radio on SiriusXM satellite radio aired an hourlong special on February 19, 2024, titled *NFL Africa*, documenting the NFL's relationship with Africa.

78. Christian Okoye and Greg Hanlon, *The Nigerian Nightmare: My Journey Out of Africa to the Kansas City Chiefs and Beyond* (Chicago, Illinois: Triumph Books, 2003).

79. Lamide Akintobi, "Former Super Bowl Champion Osi Umenyiora is creating a new path for African talent to make it to the NFL," *CNN*, July 12, 2022, accessed

on February 20, 2024, https://www.cnn.com/2022/07/12/sport/osi-umenyiora-nfl-africa-uprise-spc-spt/index.html.

80. Associated Press, "Vikings hire former Wall Street trader Kwesi Adofo-Mensah as GM," *New York Post*, January 26, 2022, accessed on February 20, 2024, https://nypost.com/2022/01/26/vikings-hire-ivy-league-educated-kwesi-adofo-mensah-as-gm/.

81. *NFL Africa*.

82. Howard Bryant, *Full Dissidence: Notes from an Uneven Playing Field* (Boston: Beacon Press, 2021).

83. Excerpt from Zach Thomas's Hall of Fame speech delivered in Canton, Ohio, on August 5, 2023.

84. Julia Chaffers, "[Opinion] The Hypocrisy of the NCAA's Amateurism Model," March 4, 2020, accessed on August 11, 2023, https://aas.princeton.edu/news/opinion-hypocrisy-ncaas-amateurism-model.

85. Caleb Nguyen, "USC Football: Caleb Williams Lands Among Top 5 NIL Earners," *Sports Illustrated*, October 23, 2023, accessed on February 4, 2024, https://www.si.com/college/usc/football/usc-football-caleb-williams-lands-among-top-5-nil-earners-cn2002.

Epilogue

1. Sam Quinn, "Adam Silver hints at eventual United States vs. World format for All-Star game," *CBS Sports*, November 7, 2023, https://www.cbssports.com/nba/news/adam-silver-hints-at-eventual-united-states-vs-world-format-for-all-star-game/.

2. NBA.com staff, "2023-24 NBA Awards: Full list of winners," May 23, 2024, https://www.nba.com/news/nba-names-2023-24-award-finalist.

3. Tom Dierberger, "Victor Wembanyama, NBA World React to France Dominating the 2024 NBA Draft," *Sports Illustrated*, June 26, 2024, https://www.si.com/nba/victor-wembanyama-nba-world-react-france-dominating-2024-nba-draft.

4. Fran Franschilla interviewed on *NBA Weekend* on June 29, 2024 (SiriusXM NBA Radio).

5. "U.S. women's basketball team beats France by 1 point to get 8th straight gold medal," *CBS News*, August 11, 2024, https://www.cbsnews.com/news/us-womens-basketball-france-olympics-gold-medal/.

6. Stephen A. Smith co-hosting ESPN's coverage of the 2024 NBA draft.

7. Ben Pickman, "Why the WNBA isn't always top choice for international women's basketball players," *The Athletic*, February 23, 2023. Accessed on July 6, 2024. https://www.nytimes.com/athletic/4242629/2023/02/23/wnba-euroleague-alina-iagupova/.

Bibliography

Adedini, Sunday. "Nigeria's cities are growing fast: family planning must be part of urban development plans." *The Conversation*. March 12, 2023. Accessed on June 14, 2023. https://theconversation.com/nigerias-cities-are-growing-fast-family-planning-must-be-part-of-urban-development-plans-199325.

Afseth, Grant. "'Why Not Give James Harden His Love?' Jamal Crawford Claims Luka Doncic Hypocrisy." *Sports Illustrated*. February 1, 2023. Accessed on April 8, 2023. https://www.si.com/nba/mavericks/news/dallas-mavs-luka-doncic-james-harden-houston-rockets-jamal-crawford-claims-hypocrisy.

Akintobi, Lamide. "Former Super Bowl Champion Osi Umenyiora is creating a new path for African talent to make it to the NFL." *CNN*. July 12, 2022. Accessed on February 20, 2024. https://www.cnn.com/2022/07/12/sport/osi-umenyiora-nfl-africa-uprise-spc-spt/index.html.

"Albright makes historic visit to North Korea." *The Guardian*. October 23, 2000. Accessed on May 6, 2023. https://www.theguardian.com/world/2000/oct/23/northkorea.

Alex, Rachel. "A Musician Who Can Jam." *Washington Post*. December 16, 1999. Accessed on January 13, 2023. https://www.washingtonpost.com/archive/sports/1999/12/16/a-musician-who-can-jam/56568bdf-4671-4ad3-8eac-e3aa7b78f75f/.

Alexander, Robert, director. *Shaq*, "The Fall." Aired December 7, 2022, on HBO Max.

Allen, Jonathan. "Dennis Rodman says he's going to Russia to seek release of Brittney Griner." *NBC News*. August 21, 2022. Accessed on May 17, 2023. https://www.nbcnews.com/news/dennis-rodman-says-going-russia-seek-release-brittney-griner-rcna44106.

Allen, Quinn. "NBA reaches insane social media milestone, blowing NFL, MLB, NHL combined out of the water." *Clutch Sports*. August 12, 2022. Accessed on July 7, 2023. https://clutchpoints.com/nba-reaches-insane-social-media-milestone-blowing-nfl-mlb-nhl-combined-out-of-the-water.

Alonso, Natalie. "60 years ago, the Alous formed the first all-brother outfield." *MLB.com*. September 19, 2023. https://www.mlb.com/news/featured/alou-brothers-formed-mlb-s-first-all-brother-outfield.

Anastacio, Nicolas, and Mark Murray. "The Iraq War—by the numbers." *NBC News*. March 20, 2023. https://www.nbcnews.com/meet-the-press/meetthepressblog/iraq-war-numbers-rcna75762.

Anderson, Dave. "Basketball's New Force." *New York Times*. April 4, 1983, Section C, Page 4.

Andrews, Evan. "How Ping-Pong Diplomacy Thawed the Cold War." *History*. April 8, 2016. Accessed on May 5, 2023. https://www.history.com/news/ping-pong-diplomacy.

Andrews-Dyer, Helena. "A brief guide to Dennis Rodman's long, weird history with North Korea." *Washington Post*. June 12, 2018. Accessed on May 9, 2023. https://www.washingtonpost.com/news/reliable-source/wp/2018/06/12/a-brief-guide-to-dennis-rodmans-long-weird-history-with-north-korea/.

Araton, Harvey. "Petrovic Carried Torch for European Players." *New York Times*. June 10, 1993. p. B15.

As We Rise: 25 Years of the WNBA. Aired May 14, 2022, on NBA TV.

Aschburner, Steve. "How a trio of pioneers gave rise to racial integration in the NBA." *NBA.com*. March 31, 2022. Accessed on March 15, 2023. https://www.nba.com/news/how-chuck-cooper-nat-clifton-earl-lloyd-changed-nba-racial-integration.

Baatai, Neamen. "How a former NBA Superstar is making a unique impact in STEM." *Jaro4me*. September 26, 2021. Accessed on January 20, 2023. https://jaro4me.com/technology/how-a-former-nba-superstar-is-making-a-unique-impact-in-stem/.

Babcock, Matt. "ABCD Camp: The mecca of high school basketball circa 2001." *Basketballnews.com*. May 12, 2022. Accessed on December 17, 2022. https://www.basketballnews.com/stories/abcd-camp-the-mecca-of-high-school-basketball-circa-2001.

Badenhausen, Kurt. "Kobe Bryant's Sponsorship Will Rebound." *Forbes*. September 3, 2004. December 20, 2022. https://www.forbes.com/2004/09/03/cz_kb_0903kobe.html?sh=666f208827c6.

Baer, Jack. "Luka Dončić scores 73 points vs. Hawks, tied for fourth-most in NBA history." *Yahoo Sports*. January 26, 2024. Accessed on January 27, 2024. https://sports.yahoo.com/luka-doncic-scores-73-points-vs-hawks-tied-for-fourth-most-in-nba-history-023607554.html.

Bailey, Andy. "Why Can't NBA Awards Voters See the Obvious MVP Front-runner?" *Bleacher Report*. December 19, 2022. Accessed on April 11, 2023. https://bleacherreport.com/articles/10059103-why-cant-nba-awards-voters-see-the-obvious-mvp-front-runner.

Bairner, Alen. "Globalization and Sport: The Nation Strikes Back." *Phi Kappa Phi Forum*. 83, no. 4. (Fall 2003): 34–37.

Baker, William J. *Sports in the Western World*. Champaign: University of Illinois Press, 1988.

Ballard, Chris. "Post Play Is a Lost Art in the NBA. What Happens to Those Who Still Believe in It?" *Sports Illustrated*. January 18, 2023. Accessed on January 8, 2023. https://www.si.com/nba/2023/01/18/nba-lost-art-of-post-play-daily-cover.

Bamiro, Yemi, director. *One Man and His Shoes*. Initial release May 25, 2020. London, England: Break Em Films.

Banks, John. "Who Invented Hockey?" *History.com*. April 22, 2022. Accessed on January 3, 2023. https://www.history.com/news/who-invented-hockey-origins-canada.

Baron, Zach. "Why Giannis Antetokounmpo Chose the Path of Most Resistant." *GQ*. November 16, 2021. Accessed on June 2, 2023. https://www.gq.com/story/giannis-antetokounmpo-athlete-of-the-year-2021.

Beamish, Mike. "NBA Grizzlies, 10 years later: Still in hibernation." *Vancouver Sun*. February 19, 2011. Accessed on September 16, 2023. https://vancouversun.com/news/nba-grizzlies-10-years-later-still-in-hibernation.

Beller, Thomas. "The Jokić Files: My quest to understand the oddest player in the NBA." *Slate*. November 14, 2022. Accessed on April 8, 2023. https://slate.com/culture/2022/11/nikola-jokic-denver-nuggets-history-profile-record.html.

Bembry, Jerry. "Francis gets boot to Houston; In an 11-player deal, Grizzlies part with disgruntled top pick; Trade NBA's largest ever; at last moment, Orlando joins mix." *Baltimore Sun*. August 28, 1999. Accessed on January 4, 2023. https://www.baltimoresun.com/news/bs-xpm-1999-08-28-9908280022-story.html.

Benedict, Jeff. *LeBron*. Chestertown, Maryland: Avid Reader Press, 2023.

Berkes, Howard. "Nazi Olympics Tangled Politics and Sport." *NPR*. June 7, 2008. Accessed on November 10, 2022. https://www.npr.org/2008/06/07/91246674/nazi-olympics-tangled-politics-and-sport.

Bernstein, Dan. "Sammy Sosa then and now: Former MLB star explains why his skin color is lighter since retirement." *Sporting News*. June 15, 2020. Accessed on February 2, 2024. https://www.sportingnews.com/us/mlb/news/sammy-sosa-skin-color-now/1aruhh5dunsn1llps943qzwlqk.

Biography. "The Harlem Globetrotters: America's Court Jesters." New York: A&E Television Networks, 1999, DVD.

"Bird Says League Needs More White Superstars." *Buffalo News*. June 10, 2004. Accessed on March 24, 2023. https://buffalonews.com/news/bird-says-league-needs-more-white-super

stars/article_f6ac08e5-b07b-538b-a501-5789992cdf7a.html.
Blackistone, Kevin B. "Washington Football is using the military as a deodorant, and the whole thing stinks." *Washington Post*. February 2, 2022. Accessed on August 10, 2023. https://www.washingtonpost.com/sports/2022/02/02/military-washington-commanders/.
Bleacher Report. Twitter post. July 21, 2021, 11:39 a.m.
"Bloomberg School Awards Goodermote Humanitarian Award to Dikembe Mutombo." April 14, 2001. Accessed on June 9, 2023. https://publichealth.jhu.edu/2011/goodermote-award-mutombo.
Bloyce, Daniel. "The Globalization of Baseball: A Figurational Analysis." PhD diss., University of Leicester, 2004.
Boesenberg, Eva. "Who's Afraid of Shaq Attaq? Constructions of Black Masculinity and the NBA." *Engendering Manhood* 43, no. 4 (1998): 681–691.
Borden, Sam. "For Frederic Weis, Knicks' Infamous Pick, Boos Began a Greater Struggle." *New York Times*. July 14, 2015. Accessed on January 9, 2023. https://www.nytimes.com/2015/07/15/sports/basketball/for-frederic-weis-knicks-99-draft-choice-boos-marked-start-of-a-greater-struggle.html.
Bosh, Chris. *Letters to a Young Athlete*. New York: Penguin Press, 2021.
Boyd, Todd. *Young, Black, Rich, and Famous: The Rise of the NBA, The Hip Hop Invasion, and the Transformation of American Culture*. Lincoln, Nebraska: Bison Books, 2008.
"Boys to Men." *The Dream Team Tapes*. Season 1, episode 2. Podcast audio, May 18, 2020.
Brainard, Lael. "Globalization in the Aftermath: Target, Casualty, Callous Bystander?" *Brookings*. November 28, 2001. Accessed on October 13, 2022. https://www.brookings.edu/research/globalization-in-the-aftermath-target-casualty-callous-bystander/.
Brenner, Marie. "American Nightmare: The Ballad of Richard Jewell." *Vanity Fair*. February 1997. Accessed on December 11, 2022. https://archive.vanityfair.com/article/share/1fd2d7ae-10d8-474b-9bf1-d1558af697be.
Bresnahan, Samantha. "'This is a dream': Burna Boy, Afrobeats stars take center stage at the NBA All-Star game." *CNN World*. February 21, 2023. Accessed on June 2, 2023. https://www.cnn.com/2023/02/21/africa/afrobeats-burna-boy-tems-rema-nba-all-star-halftime-spc-intl/index.html.
Briley, Ron. "Basketball's Great White Hope and Ronald Reagan's America: *Hoosiers* (1986)." *Film & History: An Interdisciplinary Journal of Film and Television Studies* 35, no.1 (Fall 2005): 12.
Brokhin, Yuri. *The Big Red Machine: The Rise and Fall of Soviet Olympic Champions*. New York: Random House, 1978.
Brown, Clifton. "1995 N.B.A. Playoffs; Anthony Could Go in the Expansion Draft." *New York Times*. June 14, 1995. Accessed on January 2, 2023. https://www.nytimes.com/1995/06/14/sports/1995-nba-playoffs-anthony-could-go-in-the-expansion-draft.html.
Bryant, Howard. *Full Dissidence: Notes from an Uneven Playing Field*. Boston, Massachusetts: Beacon Press, 2021.
Buckland, Jason. "Rise of Vinsanity: The story of the 2000 dunk contest." *ESPN*. June 25, 2020. January 15, 2023. https://www.espn.com/nba/allstar2014/story/_/page/dunk-2000/oral-history-2000-nba-slam-dunk-contest.
Burack, Bobby. "Stephen A. Smith has no idea MLB is more popular than the NBA." *Outkick*. March 2, 2022. Accessed on July 7, 2023. https://www.outkick.com/stephen-a-smith-has-no-idea-mlb-is-more-popular-than-nba/.
Burgess, Jessica. *The Rich and Shameless*. Episode 8, "Stolen Millions." Aired May 7, 2023, on TNT.
Burnett III, Zaron. "Why did the NCAA Ban the Slam Dunk for Nine Years?" *Mel*. Accessed on January 23, 2023. https://melmagazine.com/en-us/story/why-was-the-slam-dunk-banned.
Bush, George. *A World Transformed*. New York: Knopf, 1998.
Butterworth, M.L. "Race in 'the Race': Mark McGwire, Sammy Sosa, and Heroic Constructions of Whiteness." *Critical Studies in Media Communication* 24, no. 3 (2007): 228–244.
Cacciola, Scott, and Alan Blinder. "N.B.A. to Move All-Star Game From North Carolina." *New York Times*. July 21, 2016. Accessed on December 3, 2023. https://www.nytimes.com/2016/07/22/sports/

basketball/nba-all-star-game-moves-charlotte-transgender-bathroom-law.html.

Carroll, Rory. "NBA-China's NBA viewership approaching pre-ban levels—source." *Reuters.* December 8, 2022. Accessed on May 22, 2023. https://www.reuters.com/lifestyle/sports/nba-chinas-nba-viewership-approaching-pre-ban-levels-source-2022-12-08/.

"Carter criticized after loss." *CBC.* May 21, 2001. January 16, 2023. https://www.cbc.ca/sports/basketball/carter-criticized-after-loss-1.284617.

Caruso, Skyler. "All About Giannis Antetokounmpo's Siblings Including His NBA All-Star Brothers." *People.* February 17, 2023. Accessed on June 5, 2023. https://people.com/sports/all-about-giannis-antetokounmpos-brothers/.

Castrovince, Anthony. "Numerous indicators show youth MLB fandom is on the rise." *MLB.* October 3, 2022. Accessed on July 7, 2023. https://www.mlb.com/news/number-of-young-mlb-fans-rising.

Chaffers, Julia. "[Opinion] The Hypocrisy of the NCAA's Amateurism Model." March 4, 2020. Accessed on August 11, 2023. https://aas.princeton.edu/news/opinion-hypocrisy-ncaas-amateurism-model.

Chan, Melissa. "Read LeBron James and Carmelo Anthony's Powerful Speech on Race at the ESPYs Awards." *Time.* July 14, 2016. Accessed on May 24, 2023. https://time.com/4406289/lebron-james-carmelo-anthony-espy-awards-transcript/.

Chopra, Gotham, director. *Kobe Bryant's Muse.* February 21, 2015; Newport Beach, CA: Granity Studios.

Chotiner, Isaac. "Bomani Jones on the NBA, Analytics, and Race." *The New Yorker.* June 17, 2019. Accessed on April 11, 2023. https://www.newyorker.com/news/q-and-a/bomani-jones-on-the-nba-analytics-and-race.

Claiborne, William. "Bullets Pilgrims in Jerusalem." *Washington Post.* September 7, 1978: G1.

Clarke, Oliver. "ESPN and MLB expand partnership with new rights agreement across Europe and Africa." *ESPN Press Room.* March 12, 2020. Accessed on July 10, 2023. https://espnpressroom.com/espnuk/press-releases/2020/03/espn-and-mlb-expand-partnership-with-new-rights-agreement-across-europe-and-africa/.

"Clinton won't travel to North Korea." *CNN.* December 29, 2000. Accessed on May 6, 2023. https://www.cnn.com/2000/ASIANOW/east/12/28/clinton.nkorea/index.html.

"Coach K's Ways." *The Dream Team Tapes.* Season 2, episode 4. Podcast audio, March 16, 2021.

Cobey, Cam. "Looking back at the history of NBA Mexico Games." *NBA.com.* https://www.nba.com/news/looking-back-at-the-history-of-nba-mexico-games.

Cohen, Aaron, writer. *Clutch City.* Directed by Zak Levitt. Aired June 8, 2015, on NBA TV.

Collins, Hattie. "How Did Drake Become the World's Biggest Pop Star?" *British Vogue.* May 15, 2020. Accessed On January 24, 2023. https://www.vogue.co.uk/arts-and-lifestyle/article/drake-worlds-biggest-pop-star.

"The Cool Kids Don't Include Isiah." *The Dream Team Tapes.* Season 1, episode 3. Podcast audio, May 25, 2020.

Criblez, Adam J. "White Men Playing a Black Man's Game: Basketball's Great White Hopes of the 1970s." *Journal of Sports History* 42 (2015): 371–382.

Cronin, Mike. "The Globalisation of Sport." *History Today* 53, no. 7 (July 2003): 26.

Cuellar, Marcus F. "Runners Left on Base: Cuban Baseball Defection Experience and a Reevaluation of Baseball Diplomacy." Thesis, University of California Santa Barbara, 2014.

Cunningham, Carson. "American Hoops: The History of United States Basketball from Berlin to Barcelona." Thesis, Purdue University, 2006.

Dafor, James. "The NBA logo's complicated history, explained." *SB Nation.* February 25, 2021. Accessed on March 17, 2023. https://www.sbnation.com/nba/22300942/nba-logo-history-jerry-west-kobe-bryant.

"Dambisa Moyo and Forest Whitaker Join Group of Strategic Investors in NBA Africa." *African Press Organisation.* (December 23, 2021.) Distributed by Press Releases Related to Africa.

Davenport, Lisa. *Jazz Diplomacy: Promoting America in the Cold War Era.* Jackson: University Press of Mississippi, 2013.

Bibliography

Deb, Sopan. "How Kobe Bryant Helped the N.B.A. Conquer the World." *New York Times*. January 28, 2020. Accessed on December 23, 2022. https://www.nytimes.com/2020/01/28/sports/basketball/kobe-NBA-global.html.

Deboree, Dexton, writer and director. *UnBanned: The Legend of the AJ1*. Aired February 14, 2019 on Hulu.

DeCamp, Scott. "NCAA tournament final ratings up, but still a far cry from Magic-Bird in 1979." *MLive.com*. April 6, 2017. December 24, 2022. https://www.mlive.com/spartans/2017/04/ncaa_tournament_final_ratings.html.

Diamond, Jeremy, and Kevin Liptak. "Biden's North Korea strategy is a long way from Trump's showy diplomacy." *CNN*. May 16, 2022. Accessed May 21, 2022. https://www.cnn.com/2022/05/21/politics/joe-biden-north-korea-south-korea/index.html.

Dilbeck, Steve. "Yasiel Puig's incredible journey from Cuba to the US told by LA Magazine." *Los Angeles Times*. April 14, 2014. Accessed on July 20, 2023. https://www.latimes.com/sports/dodgers/dodgersnow/la-sp-dn-dodgers-yasiel-puig-journey-20140413-story.html#ixzz2z60I2kfv.

Dixon, Ed. "MLB and Tencent expand Chinese streaming deal to cover multiple Asian markets." *Sports Pro Media*. April 1, 2021. Accessed on July 10, 2023. https://www.sportspromedia.com/news/mlb-tencent-china-streaming-deal-asia-wetv-oriental-pearl-media/?zephr_sso_ott=4G787z.

"Drake the ultimate team fanboy." *Bay of Plenty Times*. Tauranga, New Zealand. May 30, 2019.

The Draymond Green Show. Season 2. Podcast audio, March 2, 2023.

"Drazen Petrovic and Basketball's Cold War." *Death at the Wing*. Season 1, episode 6. Podcast audio, June 10, 2022.

Dulka, Michael. "Dennis Rodman Joins Group of Harlem Globetrotters to Film Show in North Korea." *Bleacher Report*. February 26, 2013. Accessed on May 6, 2023. https://bleacherreport.com/articles/1544461-dennis-rodman-joins-group-of-harlem-globetrotters-to-film-tv-show-in-north-korea.

"Dwyane Wade Signs Lifetime Deal with Li-Ning Way of Wade." *Bleacher Report*. July 19, 2018. Accessed on December 22, 2022. https://bleacherreport.com/articles/2786663-dwyane-wade-signs-lifetime-deal-with-li-ning-way-of-wade.

Dye, Natasha. "Former UN Ambassador Bill Richardson Meeting with Russian Leadership to Discuss Brittney Griner." *People*. September 15, 2022. Accessed on May 17, 2023. https://people.com/sports/bill-richardson-former-un-ambassador-in-moscow-to-discuss-brittney-griner/.

Dyell, Stephen. "Oh Canada: The Next NBA Destination?" *Bleacher Report*. August 26, 2009. Accessed on January 4, 2023. https://bleacherreport.com/articles/243151-oh-canada-the-next-nba-destination.

Edelman, Ezra, director. *Magic & Bird: A Courtship of Rivals*. Aired March 10, 2010, on HBO.

Edem, Scott. "No One Walks Off The Island." *ESPN The Magazine*. April 17, 2014. Accessed on July 21, 2023. http://www.espn.com/espn/feature/story/_/id/10781144/no-one-walks-island-los-angeles-dodgers-yasiel-puig-journey-cuba.

Eschnar, Kat. "The YMCA First Opened Gyms to Train Stronger Christians." *Smithsonian Magazine*. December 29, 2017. Accessed on December 30, 2022. https://www.smithsonianmag.com/smart-news/ymca-first-opened-gyms-train-stronger-christians-180967665/.

Fader, Miran. *Dream: The Life and Legacy of Hakeem Olajuwon*. New York: Hachette, 2024.

Fader, Miran. *Giannis: The Improbable Rise of an NBA MVP*. New York: Hachette, 2021.

Fainaru, Steve, and Mark Fainaru-Wada. "ESPN investigation finds coaches at NBA China academies complained of player abuse, lack of schooling." *ESPN*. July 29, 2020. Accessed on July 13, 2024. https://www.espn.com/nba/story/_/id/29553829/espn-investigation-finds-coaches-nba-china-academies-complained-player-abuse-lack-schooling.

Fall, Robin. "The Myth of the Chinese 'Debt Trap' in Africa." *Bloomberg*. March 17, 2022. Accessed on June 14, 2023. https://www.bloomberg.com/news/articles/2022-03-17/the-myth-of-

chinese-debt-trap-diplomacy-in-africa#xj4y7vzkg.
Famuyiwa, Rick, writer and director. *They Call Me Magic*. "Junebug." Aired April 22, 2022, on Apple TV+.
Faria, Zachary. "The NBA flaunts its social justice hypocrisy with games in the UAE." *Washington Examiner*. May 11, 2022. Accessed on December 4, 2023. https://www.washingtonexaminer.com/opinion/the-nba-flaunts-its-social-justice-hypocrisy-with-games-in-the-uae.
Felt, Hunter. "Is Dirk Nowitzki the most important European player ever?" *The Guardian*. March 21, 2019. Accessed on February 10, 2024. https://www.theguardian.com/sport/2019/mar/21/is-dirk-nowitzki-the-most-important-european-player-ever.
Ferguson, Trixia Carungcong. "Trump-Kim Summit: US willing to offer North Korea 'unique' security guarantees in exchange for denuclearization, says Pompeo." *Straits Times*. June 12, 2018. Accessed on May 16, 2023. https://www.straitstimes.com/singapore/complete-verifiable-denuclearisation-is-only-outcome-us-will-accept-at-trump-kim-summit.
Fifield, Anna. "The secret life of Kim Jong Un's aunt, who has lived in the US since 1998." *Washington Post*. May 27, 2016. Accessed on May 16, 2023. https://www.washingtonpost.com/world/asia_pacific/the-secret-life-of-kim-jong-uns-aunt-who-has-lived-in-the-us-since-1998/2016/05/26/522e4ec8-12d7-11e6-a9b5-bf703a5a7191_story.html.
"First basketball game played." *History.com*. November 8, 2021. Accessed on December 29, 2022. https://www.history.com/this-day-in-history/basketball-invention-james-naismith.
First Take. Season 17. Aired March 7, 2023, on ESPN.
Flock, Elizabeth. "War in Iraq ends today." *Washington Post*. December 15, 2011. Accessed on December 13, 2022. https://www.washingtonpost.com/blogs/blogpost/post/iraq-war-ends-today/2011/12/15/gIQAAcksvO_blog.html.
"Former President Barack Obama Joins NBA Africa as Strategic Partner." *African Press Organisation*. July 27, 2021. Distributed by Press Releases Related to Africa.

Francis, Adam. "Toronto Raptors." *Canadian Encyclopedia*. June 14, 2019. Accessed on January 7, 2023. https://www.thecanadianencyclopedia.ca/en/article/toronto-raptors.
Francis, Steve. "I Got a Story to Tell." *Players' Tribune*. March 8, 2018. Accessed on January 4, 2023. https://www.theplayerstribune.com/articles/steve-francis-i-got-a-story-to-tell.
Fuqua, Antoine, writer and director. *Legacy: The True Story of the LA Lakers*. "Episode 1." Aired April 15, 2022, on Hulu.
"The Future King and the Greek Tragedy." *The Dream Team Tapes*. Season 1, episode 3. Podcast audio, May 25, 2020.
Game Theory with Bomani Jones. Season 2, episode 7. Aired March 10, 2023, on HBO.
Garcia IV, Bob. "Kim Jong-il Once Built a Michael Jordan Shrine Next to a Crocodile Handbag from Fidel Castro." *Sportscasting*. December 29, 2020. May 16, 2023. https://www.sportscasting.com/kim-jong-ii-once-built-a-michael-jordan-shrine-next-to-a-crocodile-handbag-from-fidel-castro/.
Gentile, Patrick C. "MLB's Neocolonial Practices in the Dominican Republic Academy System." Thesis, University of North Carolina at Charlotte, 2018.
Ghosh, P. "Huge salaries and a poverty-stricken country: The economies of baseball in the Dominican Republic." *International Business Times*. January 14, 2014. Accessed on August 21, 2023. http://www.ibtimes.com/huge-salaries-poverty-stricken-country-economicsbaseball-dominican-republic-1546993.
Glaser, Paul Michael, director. *The Air Up There*. Initial release January 7, 1994. Burbank, CA: Buena Vista Pictures.
"The Godfather." *The Dream Team Tapes*. Season 2, episode 4. Podcast audio, March 9, 2021.
Goff, Keli. "Can 'Belle' End Hollywood's Obsession with the White Savior?" *The Daily Beast*. March 4, 2014. Accessed on June 13, 2023. https://www.thedailybeast.com/can-belle-end-hollywoods-obsession-with-the-white-savior.
Goldstein, Richard. "Dave Gavitt, Founding Force of the Big East Conference, Dies at 73." *New York Times*. September 17, 2011. Accessed on November 16, 2022. https://www.nytimes.com/2011/09/18/

sports/ncaabasketball/dave-gavitt-the-big-easts-founder-dies-at-73.html.

Golliver, Ben. "With Olympic gold on the line, Steph Curry, LeBron James deliver for U.S." *The Washington Post.* August 10, 2024. https://www.washingtonpost.com/sports/olympics/2024/08/10/usa-france-olympic-basketball-gold-medal-steph-curry/.

Gonzalez, Alden. "Shohei Ohtani joining Dodgers on 10-year, $700M contract." ESPN. December 9, 2003. Accessed on December 9, 2023. https://www.espn.com/mlb/story/_/id/39076745/shohei-ohtani-join-dodgers-10-year-700m-deal.

Gonzalez, John. "An Oral History of the Shot That Changed Toronto and Kawhi Leonard Forever." *The Ringer.* December 10, 2019. Accessed on October 18, 2023. https://www.theringer.com/nba/2019/12/10/21003385/oral-history-the-shot-kawhi-leonard-toronto-raptors-philadelphia-sixers.

Graham, Tim. "LBJ and NFL: A fantasy based in reality." *ESPN.* July 7, 2010. Accessed on December 17, 2022. https://www.espn.com/nfl/news/story?id=5360552.

Grant, Laurens, writer and director. *The Nineties.* "New World Order." Aired July 30, 2017, on CNN.

Gregory, Sean, and Karl Vick. "Shohei Ohtani Is What Baseball Needs." *Time.* April 7, 2022. Accessed on July 7, 2023. https://time.com/6165003/shohei-ohtani-baseball/.

Haggard, Stephen, and Marcus Noland. *Famine in North Korea: Markets, Aid, and Reform.* New York: Columbia University Press, 2007.

Hailu, Selome. "Super Bowl 2024 Was the Most-Watched Telecast of All Time, Reaching 123.7 Million Viewers." February 12, 2024. Accessed on February 14, 2024. https://variety.com/2024/tv/news/super-bowl-2024-ratings-viewers-1235907660/.

Halberstam, David. *Playing for Keeps: Michael Jordan and the World He Made.* New York: Crown, 1991.

Hannigan, Dave. "Likes of Fernando Tatis Jr take a loan in exchange for a percentage of future earnings." July 21, 2021. Accessed on August 19, 2023. https://www.irishtimes.com/sport/other-sports/big-league-advance-is-a-major-league-scam-targeting-the-prodigious-and-vulnerable-1.4625721.

Haozhou, Pu. "From 'Ping-Pong Diplomacy' to 'Hoop Diplomacy': Yao Ming, Globalization, and the Cultural Politics of U.S.-China Relations." Master thesis, Florida State University, 2012.

Harris, Kenneth A., and Tim Povtak. "Barkley Throws Man Through Bar Window." *Orlando Sentinel.* October 27, 1997. Accessed on December 7, 2022. https://www.sun-sentinel.com/news/fl-xpm-1997-10-27-9710270306-story.html.

Harriston, Keith, and Sally Jenkins. "Maryland Basketball Star Len Bias is Dead at 22." *Washington Post.* June 20, 1986. Accessed on March 21, 2023. https://www.washingtonpost.com/archive/politics/1986/06/20/maryland-basketball-star-len-bias-is-dead-at-22/73426480-62f2-4f1e-912e-660b5c7d3c2e/.

Hehir, Jason, writer and director. *The Last Dance.* "Episode I." Aired April 19, 2020, on ESPN/Netflix.

———. *The Last Dance.* "Episode IV." Aired April 26, 2020, on ESPN/Netflix.

———. *The Last Dance.* "Episode V." Aired May 3, 202, on ESPN/Netflix.

Helin, Kurt. "Canada beats USA in overtime to win bronze medal behind 39 from Dillon Brooks." *NBC Sports.* September 10, 2023. Accessed on October 11, 2023. https://www.nbcsports.com/nba/news/canada-beats-usa-in-overtime-to-win-bronze-medal-behind-39-from-dillon-brooks.

Herbert, James. "The Dirk Nowitzki Stories: An oral history of the Dallas Mavericks legend." *CBS Sports.* April 9, 2019. Accessed on October 18, 2023. https://www.cbssports.com/nba/news/the-dirk-nowitzki-stories-an-oral-history-of-the-dallas-mavericks-legend/.

Hockrow Ross, director. *Finding Giannis.* Aired February 16, 2019, on TNT.

Hofmann, Paul. "Bunche says, '60 is year of Africa." *New York Times.* February 16, 1960, 15.

Holako, Sam. "A Look Back at the 96 Draft—Raptors Take Marcus Camby with the 2nd Pick." *Raptors Republic.* May 17, 2022. Accessed on January 7, 2023. https://www.raptorsrepublic.com/2022/05/17/a-look-back-at-the-96-draft-raptors-take-marcus-camby-with-the-2nd-pick/.

Hollander, David. *How Basketball Can Save the World: 13 Guiding Principles for Reimagining What's Possible*. New York: Harmony, 2023.

"Hong Kong Protests Explained." *Amnesty International*. September 2019. Accessed on May 19, 2023. https://www.amnesty.org/en/latest/news/2019/09/hong-kong-protests-explained/.

Howard, Adam. "Kareem Abdul-Jabbar: Michael Jordan chose 'commerce over conscience.'" *MSNBC*. November 5, 2015. Accessed on December 9, 2022. https://www.msnbc.com/msnbc/kareem-abdul-jabbar-michael-jordan-chose-commerce-over-conscience-msna717846.

Ignatiev, Noel. *How the Irish Became White*. New York: Routledge, 1995.

"The Invisible Revolution." *Death at the Wing*. Season 1, episode 1. Podcast audio, March 21, 2021.

Iqbal, Zainab. "Israel-Palestine war: US sports stars ignore Palestinians in pro-Israel posts, face fan backlash." *Middle East Eye*. October 12, 2023. Accessed On November 7, 2023. https://www.middleeasteye.net/news/israel-palestine-war-us-sports-stars-ignore-palestinians-pro-israel-backlash.

"It's Not Just Baseball History." *Black Diamonds*. Season 3. Podcast audio, July 27, 2023.

Iyengar, Rishi. "Dennis Rodman Says He Helped Secure Kenneth Bae's Release from North Korea." *Time*. November 9, 2014. Accessed on May 14, 2023. https://time.com/3575237/dennis-rodman-north-korea-prisoner-kenneth-bae-kim-jong-un/.

Jackson, Mitchell S. "Few Black Americans Play Baseball. MLB Doesn't Seem to Care." *Esquire*. February 22, 2023. Accessed on July 21, 2023. https://www.esquire.com/sports/a43008619/mlb-black-baseball-players/.

Jackson, Phil. *The Last Season: A Team in Search of Its Soul*. New York: Penguin Books, 2005.

Jamail, Milton H., and Larry Dieker. *Full Count. Inside Cuban Baseball*. Carbondale: Southern Illinois University Press, 2000.

James, Frank. "Manute Bol Left Sudan But Really Didn't." *NPR*. June 21, 2010. Accessed on June 8, 2023. https://www.npr.org/sections/thetwo-way/2010/06/21/127981788/manute-bol-left-sudan-but-really-didn-t.

James, LeBron. Twitter post. October 14, 2019. 10:35 p.m.

Jasner, Phil. "Will Barkley listen, or play Ugly American role?" *Baltimore Sun*. July 27, 1992. Accessed on August 16, 2023. https://www.baltimoresun.com/news/bs-xpm-1992-07-27-1992209182-story.html.

Jenkins, Lee. "Freak Unleashed: Greek Freak." *Time*. February 8, 2017. Accessed on June 3, 2023. https://time.com/collection/american-voices-2017/4624632/giannis-antetokounmpo-american-voices/.

Johnson, Claude. *Black Fives: The Alpha Physical Culture Club's Pioneering African American Basketball Team, 1904–1923*. Volume one. Greenwich, Connecticut: Black Fives Publishing, 2012.

Johnson, Earvin "Magic," and William Novak. *My Life*. New York: Random House, 1992.

Johnson, Roy S. "Thomas Explains Comments on Bird." *New York Times*. June 5, 1987. Accessed on November 25, 2022. https://www.nytimes.com/1987/06/05/sports/thomas-explains-comments-on-bird.html..

Jones, Bomani. Twitter post. March 7, 2023, 10:00 a.m.

Jordan, Andrew. "Globalization: The NFL's Future Depends on It." *Bleacher Report*. March 3, 2010. Accessed On August 7, 2023. https://bleacherreport.com/articles/355662-globalization-the-one-word-that-nfl-fans-should-fear-the-most.

"Joseph Tsai to buy rest of Nets from Mikhail Prokhorov." *NBA.com*. April 16, 2019. Accessed on October 11, 2022. https://www.nba.com/news/report-joseph-tsai-buy-nets-23-billion.

Juergensmeyer, Mark. *Thinking Globally: A Global Studies Reader*. Berkeley: University of California Press, 2014.

Kahrl, Christina. "As MLB returns to Cuba, the legacy of Minnie Minoso—the Cuban Jackie Robinson—lives on." *ESPN*. March 19, 2016. Accessed on September 19, 2023. https://www.espn.com/mlb/story/_/page/springtraining_minoso/as-mlb-heads-back-cuba-minnie-minoso-legacy-joy-lives-on.

Kalbrosky, Bryan. "With Nikola Jokic, NBA analytics aren't bad just because you don't understand them." *USA Today*. April 12, 2022. https://ftw.usatoday.com/2022/04/nba-mvp-nikola-jokic-advanced-analytics-stats-joel-embiid.

Kapostasy, Todd, director. *Rodman: For Better or Worse*. Aired September 10, 2019, on ESPN.

Karpf, Rory, director. *I Hate Christian Laettner*. Aired March 15, 2015, on ESPN.

Kaskey-Blomain, Michael. "Adam Silver on NBA using 'Governor' in place of 'owner' title: 'We moved away from that term years ago.'" *CBS Sports*. June 24, 2019. Accessed on October 11, 2022. https://www.cbssports.com/nba/news/adam-silver-on-nba-using-governor-in-place-of-owner-title-we-moved-away-from-that-term-years-ago/.

Killalea, Debra. "North Korea's Kim Yo-jong makes her debut on the world stage by blowing up a liaison office." *Australian Broadcasting Corporation*. June 17, 2020. Accessed on May 16, 2023. https://www.abc.net.au/news/2020-06-18/north-korea-blows-up-building-as-kim-yo-jongs-power-grows/12363650.

Kitwana, Bakari. *The Hip-Hop Generation*. New York: Civitas Books, 2002.

Klein, Alan. *Dominican Baseball: New Pride, Old Prejudice*. Philadelphia: Temple University Press, 2014.

Kohlhuber, Nicolas. "NBA Academy Africa: Uncovering Africa's top basketball prospects." *Olympics.com*. April 28, 2023. Accessed on June 11, 2023. https://olympics.com/en/news/nba-academy-africa-discovering-africa-biggest-prospects.

Koons, Zach. "NFL Had 82 of Top 100 US TV Broadcasts in 2022." *Sports Illustrated*. January 6, 2023. Accessed on August 4, 2023. https://www.si.com/extra-mustard/2023/01/06/nfl-82-top-100-american-television-broadcasts-2022-nielsen-ratings.

Korte, Gregory. "Obama brings baseball diplomacy to Havana." *USA Today*. March 22, 2016. Accessed on July 19, 2023. https://www.usatoday.com/story/news/politics/2016/03/22/obama-goes-game-does-wave-castro/82126632/.

Krawczynski, Jon. "Sam Mitchell reflects on Kobe's 81: 'I don't think too many were volunteering to guard him that night.'" *The Athletic*. December 18, 2017. Accessed on December 29, 2022. https://theathletic.com/188438/2017/12/18/sam-mitchell-kobe-bryant-81-point-game-i-dont-think-too-many-were-volunteering-to-guard-him-that-night/.

"La Busqueda Para El Oro." *The Dream Team Tapes*. Season 2, episode 10. Podcast audio, April 20, 2021.

La Roche Pietre, Natalie. "Al Horford's Celtics win kindles Dominican pride locally." *Boston Globe*. June 18, 2024. https://www.bostonglobe.com/2024/06/18/sports/al-horford-first-dominican-champion/.

LaFeber, Walter. *Michael Jordan and the New Global Capitalism*. New York: W.W. Norton & Company, 2002.

Lappas, Kristen, director. *Dream On*. Aired June 15, 2022, on ESPN.

Lappas, Kristen, writer and director. *Giannis: The Marvelous Journey*. Aired February 19, 2024, on Amazon Prime.

Large, David Clay. *Munich 1972: Tragedy, Terror, and Triumph at the Olympic Games*. Washington, D.C.: Rowman & Littlefield Publishers, 2012.

Lawrence, Andrew. "Joel Embiid: the star who toppled critics and implicit bias to win NBA MVP." *The Guardian*. May 3, 2023. Accessed on June 6, 2023. https://www.theguardian.com/sport/blog/2023/may/03/joel-embiid-mvp-wokeism-philadelphia-76ers.

Lazenby, Roland. *Michael Jordan: The Life*. New York: Back Bay Books, 2015.

Li, David K. "Dikembe Mutombo, basketball Hall of Famer and NBA global ambassador, dies at 58." NBC News. September 30, 2024. Accessed on September 30, 2024. https://www.nbcnews.com/news/sports/dikembe-mutombo-dies-58-rcna173258.

"LeBron James: 'Luka Doncic reminds me of the way I play the game.'" *MARCA*. February 19, 2022. Accessed on July 28, 2023. https://www.marca.com/en/basketball/nba/2022/02/20/6211d00146163f836a8b45e3.html.

Lee, Joon. "'This Is Our F--king City': The Oral History." *Bleacher Report*. April 16, 2018. Accessed on July 8, 2023. https://bleacherreport.com/articles/2768345-the-oral-history-of-this-is-our-f-king-city.

Let's Go. Podcast audio, November 21, 2022.

Leung, Christy. "Extradition bill not made to measure to mainland China and won't be abandoned, Hong Kong leader Carrie Lam says." *South China Morning Post.* April 1, 2019. Accessed on May 19, 2023. https://www.scmp.com/news/hong-kong/politics/aicle/3004067/extradition-bill-not-made-measure-mainland-china-and-wont.

Levitt, Zak, director. *Bad Boys.* Aired April 17, 2014, on ESPN.

———. *The Dream Team.* Aired June 13, 2012, on NBA TV.

Lindsay, Andrew John. "Has the Great White Hope left the building? White attitudes and Black opportunity in American heavyweight boxing, 1949–1983." PhD diss., University of Toledo, 2002.

Linn, Joey. "LeBron James Talking with Steph Curry and Kevin Durant About Teaming Up for Olympics." *Sports Illustrated.* September 11, 2023. Accessed on October 11, 2023. https://www.si.com/nba/warriors/news/lebron-james-talking-with-steph-curry-and-kevin-durant-about-teaming-up-for-olympics.

Lombardo, Ben. "The Harlem Globetrotters and the Perpetuation of the Black Stereotype." *Physical Educator* 35, no. 2 (1978): 60.

"Luka Dončić's 60-point, 21-rebound triple-double stuns NBA Twitter." *ESPN.com.* December 27, 2022. Accessed on April 6, 2023. https://www.espn.com/nba/story/_/id/35332269/luka-doncic-60-point-triple-double-stuns-nba-twitter.

Mackenzie, George. "Remembering Manute Bol, the tallest man in NBA." *The Versed.* January 11, 2017. https://www.theversed.com/10258/remembering-manute-bol-tallest-man-nba-history/#.Y29xbbG9Hc.

MacMahon, Tim. "How the NBL's Adelaide made their mark during a historic NBA preseason voyage." *ESPN.* October 6, 2022. Accessed on October 8, 2022. https://www.cbssports.com/nba/news/phoenix-suns-stunned-by-australian-club-adelaide-36ers-in-preseason-loss/.

MacMullan, Jackie, Rafe Bartholomew, and Dan Klores. *Basketball: A Love Story.* New York: Broadway Books, 2019.

———. *When the Game Was Ours.* Boston: Mariner Books, 2010.

Maese, Rick, and Matt Bonesteel. "PGA Tour agrees to merge with Saudi-backed LIV Golf." *Washington Post.* June 6, 2023. Accessed on June 6, 2023. https://www.washingtonpost.com/sports/2023/06/06/liv-golf-pga-tour-merger/.

"Major League Baseball Players Testify Before Congress About Steroid Use." *PBS NewsHour.* March 17, 2005. Accessed on July 27, 2023. https://www.pbs.org/newshour/show/major-league-baseball-players-testify-before-congress-about-steroid-use.

Maloney, Jack. "George Floyd Death: Celtics' Jaylen Brown drove 15 hours from Boston to Atlanta to lead peaceful protest." *CBS Sports.* June 1, 2020. Accessed on December 4, 2023. https://www.cbssports.com/nba/news/george-floyd-death-celtics-jaylen-brown-drove-15-hours-from-boston-to-atlanta-to-lead-peaceful-protest/.

Marcano, Arturo J., and David P. Fidler. "The Globalization of Baseball: Major League Baseball and the Mistreatment of Latin American Baseball Talent." *Indiana Journal of Global Legal Studies* 6, no. 2 (1999).

"Mark McGwire Admits Using Steroids." *CBS News.* January 11, 2010. Accessed on February 3, 2024. https://www.cbsnews.com/news/mark-mcgwire-admits-using-steroids/.

Markazi, Arash. "Oral History: Night Kobe scored 81 points." *ESPN.com.* January 21, 2016. Accessed on December 29, 2022. https://www.espn.com/espn/feature/story/_/id/14609380/how-los-angeles-lakers-kobe-bryant-made-history-81-point-game.

Marks, Dan, and Jon Weinbach, directors. *Sole Man.* Aired April 16, 2015, on ESPN.

McCallum, Jack. *The Dream Team: How Michael, Larry, Charles, and the Greatest Team of All Time Conquered the World and Changed the Game of Basketball Forever.* New York: Ballantine Books, 2013.

McCalmont, Lucy. "Rodman yells at CNN's Cuomo." *Politico.* January 7, 2014. Accessed on May 13, 2023. https://www.politico.com/story/2014/01/dennis-rodman-north-korea-basketball-101825.

McCurry, Justin. "North Korea holds funeral for Kim Jong-il." *The Guardian.* December 27, 2011. Accessed on May 15, 2023. https://www.theguardian.com/world/2011/dec/28/kim-jong-il-funeral-north-korea.

McDonald, Mary Genevieve. "Clean Air": Representing Michael Jordan in the Reagan-Bush Era." PhD diss., University of Iowa, 1995.

McKenna, Henry. "Jay Williams calls out Montrezl Harrell over exchange with Luka Doncic." *USA Today.* August 23, 2020. Accessed on April 6, 2023. https://ftw.usatoday.com/2020/08/jay-williams-ripsmontrezl-harrell-luka-doncic-white-boy.

McTague, Tom. "The Qatar World Cup Exposes Soccer's Shame." *The Atlantic.* November 19, 2022. Accessed on June 6, 2023. https://www.theatlantic.com/international/archive/2022/11/qatar-hosting-fifa-world-cup-soccer/672171/.

Melady, John. *Breakthrough! Canada's Greatest Inventions and Innovations.* Toronto: Dundurn, 2013.

Menard, Sean, director. *The Carter Effect.* Initial release September 9, 2917. Akron, Ohio: Uninterrupted, 2017.

Milholen, Chris. *Basketball Beyond Borders: The Globalization of the NBA.* Middletown, DE: Amazon Kindle Direct Publishing, 2019.

Moore, Matt. "Efficiency vs. production: The layered tale of Kobe Bryant's statistical legacy." *CBS Sports.* April 7, 2016. Accessed on April 10, 2023. https://www.cbssports.com/nba/news/efficiency-vs-production-the-layered-tale-of-kobe-bryants-statistical-legacy/.

Moran, Malcolm. "Georgetown, led by freshmen, wins title; Georgetown 84, Houston 75." *New York Times.* April 3, 1984, Section B, Page 7.

Morey, Daryl. Twitter post. October 4, 2019, 9:41 p.m.

———. Twitter post. October 7, 2019.

Morgan, Joe. "Brittney Griner sentencing: How the WNBA star's salary compares to her Russian earnings." *Fox Business.* August 4, 2022. Accessed on May 17, 2023. https://www.foxbusiness.com/sports/brittney-griner-sentencing-how-the-wnba-stars-salary-compares-to-her-russian-earnings.

Mullen, Jethro, and Paul Armstrong. "North Korea carries out controversial rocket launch." *CNN.* December 12, 2012. Accessed on May 6, 2023. https://www.cnn.com/2012/12/11/world/asia/north-korea-rocket-launch/index.html.

Mulumba, Christian. "Basketball Africa League: Linking African teams to the NBA." *Africa Renewal.* October 19, 2022. Accessed on June 16, 2023. https://www.un.org/africarenewal/magazine/november-2022/basketball-africa-league-linking-african-teams-nba.

Nakamura, David. "Wilder Releases VA. Prep Star Iverson from Jail." *Washington Post.* December 31, 1993. Accessed on December 14, 2022. https://www.washingtonpost.com/archive/sports/1993/12/31/wilder-releases-va-prep-star-iverson-from-jail/bb62aa7e-5138-4482-b7f0-41f49ffd0107/.

Narciso, Gerald. "Here Today, Gone Forever? Whatever to Bryant 'Big Country' Reeves?" *Bleacher Report.* September 26, 2018. Accessed on January 3, 2023. https://bleacherreport.com/articles/2796045-here-today-gone-forever-whatever-happened-to-bryant-big-country-reeves.

"NBA Africa and Basketball Africa League Join 16 Days of Activism Against Gender-Based Violence." *African Press Organisation.* November 25, 2021. Distributed by Press Releases Related to Africa.

"NBA Africa and Hennessy to Host League's First NBA Crossover Lifestyle Event on the Continent." *African Press Organisation.* January 26, 2022. Distributed by Press Releases Related to Africa.

"NBA champ Pascal Siakam visits SOS Village in Cameroon." *SOS Children's Villages.* August 9, 2019. Accessed on June 9, 2023. https://www.sos-childrensvillages.org/news/nba-champ-pascal-siakam-visits-sos-cameroon.

"NBA Finals ratings down from 2022: but playoff viewership up." *ESPN.* June 13, 2023. Accessed on July 7, 2023. https://www.espn.com/nba/story/_/id/37848871/nba-finals-ratings-2022-playoff-viewership-up.

"NBA star makes a giant impact in his African homeland." *Yale Medicine Magazine.* Spring 2006. Accessed on June 9, 2023. https://medicine.yale.edu/news/yale-medicine-magazine/article/nba-star-makes-a-giant-impact-in-his/.

Neuman, Scott. "North Korean Leader's Slain Brother Was Reportedly Working with the CIA." *NPR.* June 11, 2019. Accessed On May 16, 2023. https://www.

npr.org/2019/06/11/731539543/north-korean-leaders-slain-brother-was-reportedly-working-with-the-cia.

Newsham, Gavin. "How growing up in Italy for 7 years turned Kobe Bryant into a star." January 8, 2022. Accessed on December 19, 2022. https://nypost.com/2022/01/08/how-kobe-bryants-childhood-in-italy-turned-him-into-a-star/.

Nguyen, Caleb. "USC Football: Caleb Williams Lands Among Top 5 NIL Earners." *Sports Illustrated*. October 23, 2023. Accessed on February 4, 2024. https://www.si.com/college/usc/football/usc-football-caleb-williams-lands-among-top-5-nil-earners-cn2002.

Nickel, Lori. "Feeling the stress, Giannis almost quit the NBA. Now he wants to help as many people as possible with foundation." *Milwaukee Journal Sentinel*. April 11, 2023. Accessed on February 25, 2024. https://www.jsonline.com/story/sports/nba/bucks/2023/04/11/giannis-foundation-provides-many-different-types-of-support/70091667007/.

Nielsen, Lara D. "Exertions: Acts of Citizenship in the Globalization of Major League Beisbol." PhD diss., New York University, 2002.

Nizinski, John. "Drazen Petrovic: Remembering the Star That Didn't Get to Shine." *Bleacher Report*. January 17, 2012. Accessed on April 2, 2023. https://bleacherreport.com/articles/1020997-drazen-petrovic-remembering-the-star-that-didnt-get-to-shine.

"North Korea conducts nuclear test." *BBC*. May 25, 2009. Accessed on May 14, 2023. http://news.bbc.co.uk/2/hi/asia-pacific/8066615.stm.

O'Connor, Ian. *Coach K: The Rise and Reign of Mike Krzyzewski*. Boston: Mariner Books, 2022.

O'Deven, Ed. "Raptors and Rockets reflect on Tuesday's NBA Japan Games opener." *Japan Times*. October 9, 2019. Accessed on May 18, 2023. https://www.japantimes.co.jp/sports/2019/10/09/basketball/nba/raptors-rockets-reflect-tuesdays-nba-japan-games-opener/.

O'Grady, Siobhan, Ruby Mellen, and Miriam Berger. "What's happening in Hong Kong? Some key questions, answered." *Washington Post*. November 14, 2019. Accessed on May 19, 2023. https://www.washingtonpost.com/world/2019/08/09/airport-sit-ins-citywide-strikes-street-protests-whats-happening-hong-kong/.

Okoye, Christian, and Greg Hanlon. *The Nigerian Nightmare: My Journey Out of Africa to the Kansas City Chiefs and Beyond*. Chicago: Triumph Books, 2003.

"On Top of the World." *The Dream Team Tapes*. Season 2, episode 1. Podcast audio, February 23, 2021.

"The Once and Future King." *The Dream Team Tapes*. Season 1, episode 5. Podcast audio, June 8, 2020.

Onyalla, Father Don Bosco. "African Clergy, Religious, Laity Pay Tribute to Basketball Superstar Kobe Bryant." *ACI Africa*. January 28, 2020. Accessed on December 22, 2022. https://www.aciafrica.org/news/730/african-clergy-religious-laity-pay-tribute-to-basketball-superstar-kobe-bryant.

"Opening Day rosters feature 275 internationally born players." *MLB*. April 8, 2022. Accessed on July 11, 2023. https://www.mlb.com/news/opening-day-2022-international-representation.

O'Rourke, Beto. Twitter post. October 6, 2019. 11:22 p.m.

Ostler, Scott. "Ex-Laker Haywood Tells of Plan He Had to Kill Westhead." *Los Angeles Times*. June 5, 1988. Accessed on March 21, 2023. https://www.latimes.com/archives/la-xpm-1988-06-05-sp-6828-story.html.

Ozah, Chike, and Coodie Simmons, directors. *A Kid from Coney Island*. Aired April 6, 2020, on Netflix.

Ozanian, Mike. "World's Most Profitable Sports Teams: Cowboys Banked $1.2 Billion Over the Past Three Years." *Forbes*. June 2, 2023. Accessed on August 8, 2023. https://www.forbes.com/sites/mikeozanian/2023/06/02/worlds-most-profitable-sports-teams-cowboys-banked-12-billion-over-the-past-three-years/?sh=5878939d6e44.

Packer, George. "We Are All Realists Now." *The Atlantic*. February 16, 2022. Accessed on May 24, 2023. https://www.theatlantic.com/ideas/archive/2022/02/who-cares-human-rights-enes-kanter-freedom/622812/.

Parker, Josh. "This Day in History: First NBA Team Plays in China." *thatsmags.com*. August 24, 2018. Accessed on October 9, 2022. http://www.thatsmags.com/

beijing/post/20352/this-day-in-history-washington-bullets-visit-china.
Patton, Tracey Owens, and Julie Snyder-Yuly. "Any Four Black Men Will Do: Rape, Race, and the Ultimate Scapegoat." *Journal of Black Studies* 37, no. 6 (July 2007): 859–895.
Peralta, Eyder. "Pentagon Paid Sports Teams Millions for 'Paid Patriotism' Events." *NPR*. November 5, 2015. Accessed on December 16, 2022. https://www.npr.org/sections/thetwo-way/2015/11/05/454834662/pentagon-paid-sports-teams-millions-for-paid-patriotism-events.
Peszko, Paul. "Kobe Bryant: A Gold Medal More Important Than NBA Title." *Bleacher Report*. July 24, 2008. Accessed on December 10, 2022. https://bleacherreport.com/articles/40683-kobe-bryant-a-gold-medal-more-important-than-nba-title.
Peterson-Withorn, Chase. "LeBron James Is Officially A Billionaire." *Forbes*. June 2, 2022. Accessed on December 22, 2022. https://www.forbes.com/sites/chasewithorn/2022/06/02/lebron-james-is-officially-a-billionaire/?sh=5e4981b3453e.
Pickman, Ben. "Why the WNBA isn't always top choice for international women's basketball players." *The Athletic*. February 23, 2023. Accessed on July 6, 2024. https://www.nytimes.com/athletic/4242629/2023/02/23/wnba-euroleague-alina-iagupova/.
Pincus, Arthur. "Butch Lee's Road Winds to the Pros." *New York Times*. March 11, 1978. Accessed on January 10, 2024. https://www.nytimes.com/1978/03/11/archives/butch-lees-road-winds-to-the-pros-al-rode-him-pretty-hard-ncaa.html.
Pippen, Scottie. *Unguarded*. New York: Atria Books, 2021.
Pluto, Terry, and Brian Windhorst. *LeBron James: The Making of an MVP*. Cleveland, Ohio: Gray & Company, Publishers, 2009.
Pollard, Sam, writer and director. *Bill Russell: Legend*. Aired February 8, 2023, on Netflix.
Poole, Monte. "Race in America: A Candid Conversation." *NBC Sports*. September 11, 2020. Accessed on October 11, 2022. https://www.nbcsports.com/bayarea/kings/kings-vivek-ranadive-recalls-prevalence-racism-fear-after-911.
Popper, Steve. "BASKETBALL: ROUNDUP; Last 5 Players Named to U.S. Olympic Team." July 9, 2004. Accessed on December 14, 2022. https://www.nytimes.com/2004/07/09/sports/basketball-roundup-last-5-players-named-to-us-olympic-team.html.
Prewitt, Alex. "She Won Athletes' Hearts. And Robbed Them Blind." *Sports Illustrated*. September 19, 2019. Accessed on May 12, 2023. https://www.si.com/nba/2019/09/19/athete-financial-advisor-embezzlement-fraud-scandal-peggy-ann-fulford.
Pu, Brigitte. "Ex-NBA star Dwight Howard sparks anger in China by calling Taiwan a 'country.'" *NBC News*. May 12, 2023. Accessed on May 23, 2023. https://www.nbcnews.com/news/world/ex-nba-star-dwight-howard-sparks-anger-china-calling-taiwan-country-rcna84097.
Pucin, Diane. "Ship of Dream Teams." *Los Angeles Times*. August 26, 2004. Accessed on December 14, 2022. https://www.latimes.com/archives/la-xpm-2004-aug-26-sp-olyluxury26-story.html.
Quinn, Sam. "Adam Silver hints at eventual United States vs. World format for All-Star game." *CBS Sports*. November 7, 2023. https://www.cbssports.com/nba/news/adam-silver-hints-at-eventual-united-states-vs-world-format-for-all-star-game/.
Ramzy, Austin. "Dennis Rodman, Frequent Visitor to North Korea, Is Back." *New York Times*. June 13, 2017. Accessed on May 16, 2023. https://www.nytimes.com/2017/06/13/world/asia/dennis-rodman-north-korea.html.
Randhawa, Manny. "Opening Day rosters feature 269 players born internationally." *MLB*. March 31, 2023. Accessed on July 4, 2023. https://www.mlb.com/news/international-players-on-2023-opening-day-rosters.
Rapp, Timothy. "Report: Dwyane Wade's Son Zaire Agrees to Contract with BAL's Cape Town Tigers." *Bleacher Report*. February 3, 2023. Accessed on June 18, 2023. https://bleacherreport.com/articles/10064103-report-dwyane-wades-son-zaire-agrees-to-contract-with-bals-cape-town-tigers.
Rappaport, Max. "The Definitive History of 'Trust the Process.'" *Bleacher Report*.

August 23, 2017. Accessed on June 6, 2023. https://bleacherreport.com/articles/2729018-the-definitive-history-of-trust-the-process.

"Raptors superfan Nav Bhatia to miss first-ever home game Friday." *Sportsnet*. December 21, 2021. Accessed on January 24, 2023. https://www.sportsnet.ca/nba/article/raptors-superfan-nav-bhatia-miss-first-ever-home-game-friday/.

Real Sports. Season 25, episode 10. First broadcast October 22, 2019, on HBO.

Reaves, Joseph A. *Taking in a Game: A History of Baseball in Asia*. Lincoln: University of Nebraska Press, 2002.

Reimold, John. "Hakeem Olajuwon Remembered: The Best Center of All Time." *Bleacher Report*. April 13, 2011. Accessed on June 8, 2023. https://bleacherreport.com/articles/663761-remembering-hakeem-olajuwon-the-best-center-of-all-time.

"Remarks by President Biden on the Release of Brittney Griner." December 8, 2022. Accessed on May 17, 2023. https://www.whitehouse.gov/briefing-room/speeches-remarks/2022/12/08/remarks-by-president-biden-on-the-release-of-brittney-griner/.

Rhoden, William C. "LSU's Angel Reese, Iowa's Caitlin Clark and the double standards of race in sports." *Andscape*. April 3, 2003. Accessed on April 17, 2023. https://andscape.com/features/lsus-angel-reese-iowas-caitlin-clark-and-the-double-standards-of-race-in-sports/.

Rice, Nicholas. "Britney Spears Says Her Reaction to Victor Wembanyama Security Scuffle Was a 'Cry Out on All Levels.'" *People*. July 8, 2023. Accessed on July 9, 2023. https://people.com/britney-spears-on-her-reaction-to-victor-wembanyama-security-scuffle-7558276.

Richardson, Shandel. "Dwyane Wade's Son Get His First Signature Shoe." *Sports Illustrated*. February 13, 2023. Accessed on May 23, 2023. https://www.si.com/nba/heat/miami-news/dwyane-wades-son-gets-his-first-signature-shoe.

Ringolsby, Tracy. "A half-century later, Murakami's legacy remains strong." *MLB*. March 21, 2014. Accessed on July 15, 2023. https://www.mlb.com/news/tracy-ringolsby-a-half-century-later-masanori-murakamis-legacy-remains-strong/c-69771396.

Rivera, Paul, writer. *The Shop: Uninterrupted*. "Episode 18." Directed by Robert Alexander. Aired July 15, 2022, on HBO.

Rives, Chip, director. *Phi Slamma Jamma*. Aired October 18, 2016, on ESPN.

Rivoli, Pietra. *The Travels of a T-Shirt in the Global Economy: An Economist Examines the Markets, Power, and Politics of World Trade*. Hoboken, New Jersey: Wiley, 2014.

Roche, Dan. "Joel Embiid appears to clap back at Olajuwon's comments." *NBC Sports Philadelphia*. January 20, 2023. Accessed on June 8, 2023. https://www.nbcsportsphiladelphia.com/nba/joel-embiid-appears-to-clap-back-at-olajuwons-comments/267447/.

Rodman, Dennis, and Tim Keown. *Bad As I Wanna Be*. New York: Delacorte Press, 1996.

Rodney, Walter. *How Europe Underdeveloped Africa*. Brooklyn, New York: Verso, 2018.

Ross, Charles. "Manute Bol: A Freak Show in the NBA, a Hero in Sudan." *Medium*. December 16, 2015. Accessed on June 8, 2023. https://medium.com/@cross0328/manute-bol-a-freak-show-in-the-nba-a-hero-in-sudan-59e821dd7e01.

Runstedtler, Theresa. *Black Ball: Kareem Abdul-Jabbar, Spencer Haywood, and the Generation that Saved the Soul of the NBA*. New York: Bold Type Books, 2003.

_____. *Jack Johnson, Rebel Sojourner: Boxing in the Shadow of the Global Color Line*. Berkeley: University of California Press, 2013.

Russ, Floyd, director. *Untold: Malice at the Palace*. Aired August 10, 2021, on Netflix.

Russell, William F. *Second Wind: The Memoirs of an Opinionated Man*. New York: Random House, 1979.

Rymer, Zachary D. "Remembering Mark McGwire, Sammy Sosa's Historic Summer of '98 Home Run Chase." *Bleacher Report*. April 13, 2020. Accessed on July 27, 2023. https://bleacherreport.com/articles/2886003-remembering-mark-mcgwire-sammy-sosas-historic-summer-of-98-home-run-chase.

Salad, Colin. "The 20 Most Valuable Sports Teams." *TheStreet*. July 19, 2023. Accessed on August 4, 2023. https://

www.thestreet.com/sports/the-20-most-valuable-sports-teams.

Sanner, Ann. "NBA star Mutombo honored for his deeds in native Congo." *San Diego Union-Tribune*. January 18, 2010. Accessed on June 9, 2023. https://www.sandiegouniontribune.com/sdut-nba-star-mutombo-honored-for-deeds-in-native-congo-2010jan18-story.html.

Saul, Derek. "NFL's Roger Goodell Reportedly Makes $63 Million Per Year—Here's How That Compares To Other Top Execs and Sports Commissioners." *Forbes*. October 29, 2021. Accessed on August 8, 2023. https://www.forbes.com/sites/dereksaul/2021/10/29/nfls-roger-goodell-reportedly-makes-639-million-per-year---heres-how-that-compares-to-other-top-execs-and-sports-commissioners/?sh=ae226a257029.

Scheitrum, Kevin. "History of the NBA Global Games." *NBA.com*. n.d. Accessed on October 9, 2022. https://www.na.com/global/games2013/all-time-international-game-list.html.

Schnack, AJ, director. *Long Gone Summer*. Aired June 14, 2020, on ESPN.

Schumacher, Michael. *Mr. Basketball: George Mikan, the Minneapolis Lakers, and the Birth of the NBA*. Minneapolis: University of Minnesota Press, 2008.

Schuman, David. "At Timberwolves game, Israeli basketball team honors hostages taken by Hamas." *CBS News*. October 17, 2023. Accessed on November 7, 2023. https://www.cbsnews.com/minnesota/news/israeli-basketball-team-honors-hostages-taken-by-hamas-at-game-against-timberwolves/.

Schuman, Rebecca. "Kerri Strug Shouldn't Have Been Force to Do That Vault." *Slate*. July 31, 2021. Accessed on December 10, 2022. https://slate.com/culture/2021/07/kerri-strug-simone-biles-vault-atlanta-legacy-injuries.html.

Scott, Jelani. "Biden Administration Responds to Rodman's Brittney Griner Plan." *Sports Illustrated*. August 22, 2022. Accessed on May 17, 2023. https://www.si.com/wnba/2022/08/22/biden-administration-responds-dennis-rodman-brittney-griner.

Secular, Steven. *The Digital NBA: How the World's Savviest League Brings the Court to Our Couch*. Champaign: University of Illinois Press, 2023.

Semmelhack, Elizabeth. *Out of the Box: The Rise of Sneaker Culture*. New York: Rizzoli Electa, 2015.

"The Serge Ibaka Foundation Helps the Congo." *The Borgen Project*. October 16, 2021. Accessed on June 9, 2023. https://borgenproject.org/serge-ibaka-foundation/.

Shear, Michael D., and Baker, Peter. "Inside the Prisoner Swap That Freed Brittney Griner." *New York Times*. December 9, 2022. Accessed on May 17, 2023. https://www.nytimes.com/2022/12/09/us/politics/brittney-griner-prisoner-swap.html.

Shelburne, Ramona. "Ex-NBA forward Mbah a Moute to focus on Africa as agent." *ESPN*. February 15, 2023. Accessed on June 6, 2023. https://www.espn.com/nba/story/_/id/35666105/luc-richard-mbah-moute-joins-caa-player-agent.

———. "When the Donald Sterling saga rocked the NBA—and changed it forever." *ESPN*. August 20, 2019. Accessed on May 23, 2023. https://www.espn.com/nba/story/_/id/27474482/when-donald-sterling-saga-rocked-nba-changed-forever.

Shepard, Wade. "What China Is Really Up To In Africa." *Forbes*. October 3, 2019. Accessed on June 14, 2023. https://www.forbes.com/sites/wadeshepard/2019/10/03/what-china-is-really-up-to-in-africa/?sh=6210acc59304.

Sherman, Gabriel. *The Loudest Voice in the Room: How the Brilliant, Bombastic Roger Ailes Built Fox News—and Divided a Country*. New York: Random House, 2014.

Sherrill, Martha. "The Olympic Lip." *Washington Post*. July 29, 1992. Accessed on August 16, 2023. https://www.washingtonpost.com/archive/lifestyle/1992/07/29/the-olympic-lip/d6fb3fae-e48c-4b7a-a72c-60c31223777b/.

Sielski, Mike. *The Rise: Kobe Bryant and the Pursuit of Immortality*. New York: St. Martin's Press, 2022.

Silver, Michael. "Rodman unchained. The Spurs' no-holds-barred forward gives new meaning to the running game." *Sports Illustrated*. May 29, 1995. Accessed on May 10, 2023. https://vault.si.com/vault/1995/05/29/rodman-unchained-the-spurs-no-holds-barred-forward-gives-new-meaning-to-the-running-game.

Silverman, Drew. "Jerry Colangelo, Long-Time Architect of USA Basketball, Reflects on a Golden Career." July 29, 2021. *USAB.com*. Accessed on December 15, 2022. https://www.usab.com/news/2021/07/jerry-colangelo-feature.

Singer, Mike. *Why So Serious? The Untold Story of NBA Champion Nikola Jokić*. New York: Harper, 2024.

Smith, David. "'Michael Jordan changed the world': the true story behind Nike movie Air." *The Guardian*. April 5, 2023. Accessed on October 9, 2023. https://www.theguardian.com/film/2023/apr/05/michael-jordan-changed-the-world-the-true-story-behind-nike-movie-air.

Smith, Doug. "Raptors crowned NBA champions for first time in team history." *Toronto Star*. June 13, 2019. Accessed on September 16, 2023. https://www.thestar.com/sports/raptors/raptors-crowned-nba-champions-for-first-time-in-team-history/article_e90bdfa3-4381-5607-a5ba-a532916ebb39.html.

_____. *We The North: 25 Years of the Toronto Raptors*. New York: Viking Press, 2020.

Smith, Frank. "Reports of people 'starving as N Korea Struggles to feed itself." *Al Jazeera*. July 1, 2021. Accessed May 7, 2023. https://www.aljazeera.com/news/2021/7/1/humanitarian-disaster-looms-in-north-korea.

Smith, Gary. "A Few Pieces of Silver." *Sports Illustrated*. June 15, 1992. Accessed on November 8, 2022. https://vault.si.com/vault/1992/06/15/robbed-of-gold-medals-in-munich-the-72-us-olympic-basketball-team-will-not-betray-its-principles-for-a-few-pieces-of-silver.

_____. "The Race is On: With a Hot Bat and Little Fanfare, Sammy Sosa Served Notice That the Home Run Record Is Up for Grabs." *Sports Illustrated*. September 21, 1998. Accessed on July 27, 2023. https://vault.si.com/vault/1998/09/21/the-race-is-on-with-a-hot-bat-and-little-fanfare-sammy-sosa-served-notice-that-the-home-run-record-is-up-for-grabs.

Smith, Helen. "Neo-fascist Greek party takes third place in wave of voter fury." *The Guardian*. September 20, 2015. Accessed on February 24, 2024. https://www.theguardian.com/world/2015/sep/21/neo-fascist-greek-party-election-golden-dawn-third-place.

Sohi, Seerat. "Toronto Raptors' GM Masai Ujiri on inspiring kids, the growth of basketball in Africa and what comes next." *SB Nation*. August 4, 2018. Accessed on June 1, 2023. https://www.sbnation.com/2018/8/4/17649430/masai-ujiri-africa-nba-game-interview-raptors.

Solms, Leonard. "Toronto Raptors boss Masai Ujiri -BAL can produce NBA-level talent, but will need time to grow." *ESPN*. September 2, 2022. Accessed on June 12, 2023. https://www.espn.com/espn/story/_/id/34506331/toronto-raptors-boss-masai-ujiri-bal-produce-nba-level-talent-need-grow.

Songco, Paolo. "The biggest Kobe Bryant mural in Europe was just completed." *Clutch Points*. June 5, 2020. Accessed on December 22, 2022. https://clutchpoints.com/lakers-news-the-biggest-kobe-bryant-mural-europe-was-just-completed.

Sosa, Sammy, and Marcos Breton. *Sosa: An Autobiography*. New York: Grand Central Publishing, 2000.

Spears, Marc J. "Dikembe Mutombo helps grow the game in Africa." *Andscape*. August 2, 2017. Accessed on June 10, 2023. https://andscape.com/features/dikembe-mutombo-nba-africa-basketball-without-borders/.

_____. "'My dad was everything to me': Bismack Biyombo is still healing in his NBA return." *Andscape*. February 11, 2022. Accessed on June 9, 2023. https://andscape.com/features/my-dad-was-everything-to-me-bismack-biyombo-is-still-healing-in-his-nba-return/.

_____. "Source: J. Cole finishes Basketball Africa League stint." *ESPN*. May 26, 2021. Accessed on June 17, 2023. https://www.espn.com/nba/story/_/id/31515194/source-j-cole-finishes-africa-league-stint.

Spehr, Todd. *The Mozart of Basketball: The Remarkable Life and Legacy of Dražen Petrović*. Champaign, Illinois: Sports Publishing, 2016.

"The Spy Who Signed Me." *30 for 30*. Season 6, episode 1. Podcast audio, September 6, 2022.

"Stephen Curry about Wembanyama: 'He's like the NBA 2K create-a-player'" *Basketball News*. October 7, 2022. Access on October 10, 2022. https://basketnews.

com/news-178960-stephen-curry-about-wembanyama-hes-like-the-nba-2k-create-a-player.html.

Stern, Marlow. "Kobe Bryant's Disturbing Rape Case: The DNA Evidence, the Accuser's Story, and the Half-Confession." *The Daily Beast.* April 11, 2016. Accessed on December 20, 2022. https://www.thedailybeast.com/kobe-bryants-disturbing-rape-case-the-dna-evidence-the-accusers-story-and-the-half-confession?ref=scroll.

Stoll, Julia. "TV viewership of the Super Bowl in the United States from 1990 to 2023." May 4, 2023. Accessed on August 4, 2023. *Statista.* https://www.statista.com/statistics/216526/super-bowl-us-tv-viewership/.

Sutcliffe, Richard. "How NBA's new tournament takes inspiration from soccer's oldest cup competition." *The Athletic.* November 1, 2023. Accessed on December 7, 2023. https://theathletic.com/5016386/2023/11/02/nba-in-play-tournament-fa-cup/.

Szoldra, Paul, and Veronika Bondarenko. "How North Korean leader Kim Jong-Un, became one of the world's scariest dictators." *The Independent.* June 15, 2018. Accessed on May 15, 2023. https://www.independent.co.uk/news/world/asia/how-north-korean-leader-kim-jong-un-became-one-of-the-worlds-scariest-dictators-a7887916.html.

Taylor, Alan. "20 Years Since the Bosnian War." *The Atlantic.* April 13, 2012. Accessed on April 1, 2023. https://www.theatlantic.com/photo/2012/04/20-years-since-the-bosnian-war/100278/.

Telander, Rick. "Senseless. In America's cities, kids are killing kids over sneakers and other sports apparel favored by drug dealers. Who's to blame?" *Sports Illustrated.* May 14, 1990. Accessed on December 9, 2022. https://vault.si.com/vault/1990/05/14/senseless-in-americas-cities-kids-are-killing-kids-over-sneakers-and-other-sports-apparel-favored-by-drug-dealers-whos-to-blame.

"Terry Furlow and the Crash After the Party." *Death at the Wing.* Season 1, episode 2. Podcast audio, June 7, 2022.

"Text of President Bush's 2002 State of the Union Address." *Washington Post.* January 29, 2002. Accessed on May 6, 2023. https://www.washingtonpost.com/wp-srv/onpolitics/transcripts/sou012902.htm.

Thomas, Damion. "Around the World: Problematizing the Harlem Globetrotters as Cold War Warriors." *Cultures, Commerce, Media, Politics* 14, no. 6 (September 2011): 778–791.

Timlin, Mabel F. "Canada's Immigration Policy, 1896–1910." *Canadian Journal of Economics and Political Science* 26, no. 4 (November 1960): 517–532.

Tinsley, Justin. "The players' anthem: when Marvin Gaye sang 'The Star-Spangled Banner' at the 1983 All-Star Game." *Andscape.* February 13, 2008. Accessed on December 22, 2022. https://andscape.com/features/marvin-gaye-the-star-spangled-banner-1983-nba-all-star-game-players-anthem/.

Tong, Xingda. "The Impact of the NBA-Tencent Exclusive Streaming Agreement on Chinese Basketball Viewers." Master's thesis, Drexel University 2018.

Toribio, Juan. "Unanimous yet again: Ohtani wins third career MVP Award." *MLB.com.* November 21, 2024. https://www.mlb.com/news/shohei-ohtani-2024-nl-mvp.

"Toronto awarded WNBA's 1st Team outside U.S., to play in '26." *ESPN.* May 23, 2024. https://www.espn.com/wnba/story/_/id/40202150/toronto-awarded-wnba-1st-team-us-play-26.

"Toronto's Big Bang." *Dunkumentaries.* Season 1, episode 4. Podcast audio, April 4, 2016.

"The Triangulation of Phil Jackson." *Shattered: Hope, Heartbreak, and the New York Knicks.* Season 1, episode 6. Podcast audio, March 18, 2021.

Tumin, Remy. "NCAA Women's Tournament Shatters Ratings Record in Final." *New York Times.* April 3, 2023. Accessed on April 13, 2023. https://www.nytimes.com/2023/04/03/sports/ncaabasketball/lsu-iowa-womens-tournament-ratings-record.html.

Turner, Warren. "World Baseball Classic: South Africa Shows Great Improvement." *Bleacher Report.* March 10, 2009. Accessed on July 11, 2023. https://bleacherreport.com/articles/137024-impressions-of-the-wbc-south-africa-shows-great-improvement.

"2022 NFL International Player Pathway program: 13 athletes from nine countries selected." *NFL.com*. January 11, 2022. Accessed on August 9, 2023. https://www.nfl.com/news/2022-international-player-pathway-program-13-athletes-nine-countries.

Uggetti, Paolo. "Klay Thompson Is Having the Time of His Life in China." *The Ringer*. June 30, 2017. Accessed on May 23, 2023. https://www.theringer.com/2017/6/30/16044484/nba-klay-thompson-having-fun-in-china-golden-state-warriors-fdf2c4408f2d.

Vice. Episode 10, "Basketball Diplomacy." Aired June 14, 2013, on HBO.

Victor, Daniel. "Hong Kong Protests Put N.B.A. on Edge in China." *New York Times*. October 7, 2019. Accessed on May 18, 2023. https://www.nytimes.com/2019/10/07/sports/basketball/nba-china-hong-kong.html.

"Vikings hire former Wall Street trader Kwesi Adofo-Mensah as GM." *New York Post*. January 26, 2022. Accessed on February 20, 2024. https://nypost.com/2022/01/26/vikings-hire-ivy-league-educated-kwesi-adofo-mensah-as-gm/.

"Vive Barcelona." *The Dream Team Tapes*. Season 1, episode 7. Podcast audio, June 27, 2020.

Vorkunov, Mike. "Adam Silver discusses Saudi investment in sports and potential impact on NBA: 'It's a 2-edged sword.'" *The Athletic*. June 8, 2023. Accessed on June 9, 2023. https://theathletic.com/4595053/2023/06/08/adam-silver-saudi-investment-nba/.

Wacker, Brian. "Adam Silver issues tanking warning for teen phenom Victor Wembanyama." *New York Post*. October 6, 2022. Accessed on October 10, 2022. https://nypost.com/2022/10/06/adam-silver-warns-nba-teams-tanking-for-victor-wembanyama/.

Wahl, Grant. "Ahead of his class." *Sports Illustrated*. February 18, 2002. Accessed on December 18, 2022. https://vault.si.com/vault/2002/02/18/ahead-of-his-class-ohio-high-school-junior-lebron-james-is-so-good-that-hes-already-being-mentioned-as-the-heir-to-air-jordan.

Walsh, Erin. "Woj: Victor Wembanyama, Could Add $500m in Value to a Franchise, Says Team President." *Bleacher Report*. October 6, 2022. Accessed October 10, 2022. https://bleacherreport.com/articles/10051541-woj-victor-wem-banyama-could-add-500m-in-value-to-a-franchise-says-team-president.

Ward, Geoffrey C. *Unforgivable Blackness: The Rise and Fall of Jack Johnson*. New York: Vintage, 2006.

Washington, Booker T. *Up from Slavery*. Garden City, New Jersey: Dover Publications, 1995.

Watts, Jonathan. "North Korea 'using food as a weapon.'" *The Guardian*. January 20, 2004. Accessed on May 15, 2023. https://www.theguardian.com/world/2004/jan/21/northkorea.

Weinbach, Jon, director. *The Redeem Team*. Aired October 7, 2022, on Netflix.

West, Jerry. *West by West: My Charmed, Tormented Life*. Boston: Back Bay Books, 2012.

White, Jonathan. "Dennis Rodman's North Korea trips brought scorn and ridicule, but he deserves credit." *South China Morning Post*. May 12, 2020. Accessed on May 16, 2023. https://www.scmp.com/sport/basketball/article/3083842/dennis-rodmans-north-korea-trips-brought-scorn-and-ridicule-he.

"Who Invented Baseball?" *History*. March 27, 2013. Accessed on July 8, 2023. https://www.history.com/news/who-invented-baseball.

"Why So Many Baseball Players are Dominican." YouTube. July 11, 2023. Educational video, 3:00–12:00, https://www.youtube.com/watch?v=40Je_0Jef_o.

Whyno, Stephen. "Qatar sovereign wealth fund buys stake in Washington's NBA, NHL, and WNBA teams, AP source says." *Associated Press*. June 22, 2023. Accessed on June 22, 2023. https://apnews.com/article/qatar-investment-authority-buys-wizards-capitals-9e2d9e6246f-79b5265e9891b29cae690.

Williams, Madison. "Steph Curry Leads Powerful Message About Brittney Griner at the ESPYs." *Sports Illustrated*. July 20, 2022. Accessed on May 17, 2023. https://www.si.com/wnba/2022/07/21/steph-curry-leads-powerful-message-about-brittney-griner-at-the-espys-video.

Winkie, Luke. "The Dukeman Cometh." *Slate*. October 31, 2023. Accessed on November 2, 2023. https://slate.com/culture/2023/10/cooper-flagg-duke-basketball-race-oh-no.html.

Wright, Joshua K. "Coach John Thompson, Jr., in Retrospect." *Diverse*. September

8, 2020. Accessed November 11, 2022. https://www.diverseeducation.com/sports/article/15107716/coach-john-thompson-jr-in-retrospect.

———. *Wake Up, Mr. West: Kanye West and the Double Consciousness of Black Celebrity*. Jefferson, NC: McFarland, 2022.

Wright, Michael C. "What to know as Nets, Cavs meet in NBA Paris Game 2024." *NBA.com*. January 11, 2024. Accessed on January 11, 2024. https://www.nba.com/news/nets-cavs-nba-paris-game-2024.

Yang, Avery. "Black History Month: The Harlem Globetrotters' 1948 Win Over the Lakers Changed Basketball." *Sports Illustrated*. February 19, 2020. Accessed on May 5, 2023. https://www.si.com/nba/2020/02/19/black-history-month-harlem-globetrotters-lakers.

"A Young Man in Lower Merion." *I Am Kobe*. Season 1, episode 3. Podcast audio, November 23, 2021.

Yurdakul, Afsin. "He told Bush that 'America is under attack.'" *NBC News*. September 10, 2009. Accessed on December 12, 2022. https://www.nbcnews.com/id/wbna32782623.

Zibler, Ariel. "Nets owner Joe Tsai reportedly tried to get Daryl Morey fired over tweet." *New York Post*. April 15, 2022. Accessed on May 18, 2023. https://nypost.com/2022/04/15/nets-owner-joe-tsai-reportedly-tried-to-get-daryl-morey-fired/.

Zillgitt, Jeff. "How 1992 Dream Team shaped Dirk Nowitzki, Pau Gasol and Tony Parker on way to Hall of Fame." *USA Today*. August 10, 2023. Accessed on August 11, 2023. https://www.usatoday.com/story/sports/nba/2023/08/10/dirk-nowitzki-pau-gasol-tony-parker-basketball-hall-of-fame/70546505007/.

Zirin, Dave. Twitter post. March 8, 2023, 9:30 p.m.

———, and Frank Guridy. "Bill Walton Was Once a Trailblazing Radical." *The Nation*. September 6, 2023. Accessed on October 18, 2023. https://www.thenation.com/article/society/bill-walton-activism/.

———. *What's My Name, Fool? Sports and Resistance in the United States*. Chicago: Haymarket Books, 2005.

Zucchino, David. "The U.S. War in Afghanistan: How It Started, and How It Ended." *The New York Times*. October 7, 2021. Accessed on December 13, 2022. https://www.nytimes.com/article/afghanistan-war-us.html.

Index

AAU 127; *see also* Amateur Athletic Union
ABA *see* American Basketball Association
Abdul-Jabbar, Kareem 10, 28, 31, 43, 69, 108–109, 168
Abdur-Rahim, Shareef 79
ACB Spanish League 119
Aces *see* Las Vegas Aces
Adande, J.A. 54, 56, 69
Adebayo, Edrice Femi "Bam" 160
Adidas 24, 40–41, 62, 64, 85, 153
Adofo-Mensah, Kwesi 207
Afghanistan 51–52, 59
Africa 3, 6–7, 11, 17, 49, 106, 155, 159–184, 212
African Press Organization 1
Agresti, Travis 90
A.I. *see* Iverson, Allen
The Air Up There (film) 177–179
Albright, Madeleine 134
Alcindor, Lew *see* Abdul-Jabbar, Kareem
Aldridge, David 3, 129, 156, 181
Alexander, Shai Gilgeous 89
Ali, Muhammad 44–45, 154, 171
All-Star *see* NBA All-Stars
Allen, Forest "Phog" 76
Allen, Ray 79
al-Qaeda 51, 156
Amateur Athletic Union *see* AAU
Amazon Prime 204
American Basketball Association (ABA) 86, 108–109, 159
American exceptionalism 4, 20
American Football League 203; *see also* NFL
Anderson, Kenny 120
Anderson, Morten 206
Andre 3000 105
Andrews, Malika 147

Angola 19, 37, 53, 67
Anta 153
Antetokounmpo, Giannis 2, 7, 11, 71, 124–125, 127, 160–165, 169, 210
Anthony, Carmelo 52 -54, 62, 67–69, 154
Anthony, Greg 78
Araton, Harvey 120
Arenas, Gilbert 125–126, 169
Argentina 36, 53–54, 67–68
Arroyo, Carlos 53
Aruba 188
Ashe, Arthur 154
Asia 3, 7, 17, 148, 189, 190
Athens, Greece 50, 52, 54, 56, 68
The Athletic 3
Atlanta, Georgia 47
Atlanta Dream 128
Atlanta Hawks 10, 16, 49, 90, 110, 117, 150, 165, 172
Auerbach, Arnold Jacob "Red" 104
Augmon, Stacey 23
Australia 3, 13, 17, 23, 48–49, 51, 67, 76, 82, 106, 165, 175, 188

BAA *see* Basketball Association of America
Bad Boys *see* Detroit Pistons
Bahamas 17, 188
Bailey, Andy 126
Baker, Johnnie B. "Dusty," Jr. 195
Baker, William J. 22
BAL *see* Basketball Africa League
Baltimore Orioles 194
Barcelona, Spain 4, 18–20, 25, 27, 29, 31, 33–34, 36–38, 44–45, 47–50, 57, 68, 120, 132, 152, 210
Barkley, Charles 7, 19–20, 23, 27, 29–31, 35–39, 46, 49, 56, 68, 110, 117, 166, 169
Barrett, R.J. 174
Barry, Rick 108
baseball 106, 185–203, 208

263

Index

Basketball Africa League 3, 7, 152, 161, 174, 176–177, 181–184
Basketball Association of America (BAA) 17, 76, 108
Basketball Beyond Borders: Globalization of the NBA 1
basketball diplomacy 131–158
Basketball Without Borders 17, 164, 174–175, 211
Bayless, Skip 100
Beijing, China 5, 47, 60–61, 67, 93, 154
Belgium 94
Bellan, Esteban 192
Belov, Sergei 20–21
Bennett, Anthony 89
Berlin, Germany 22
Bhatia, Nav 96–98
Bias, Len 110
Biasatti, Hank 17, 116–117
Bickley, Dan 138–139
Biden, Joseph 147–148
Big East 24
Big League Advance (BLA) 202
Biles, Simone 48
Bin Laden, Osama 51
Bird, Larry 6, 28–30, 36–37, 39, 41, 46, 49, 100, 103, 112–117, 119, 124–125, 128, 197
Bird, Sue 146
Biyombo, Bismack 171, 173–174
Bjarkman, Peter 194
Black Ball: Kareem Abdul-Jabbar, Spencer Haywood and the Generation That Saved the Soul of the NBA 111, 154
Black Diamonds (podcast) 191
The Black Fives Era 103–104
Black Lives Matter 69, 154–155, 211
Black Mamba *see* Bryant, Kobe
Blue Ribbon Sports *see* Nike
Boeheim, Jim 181
Bogues, Tyrone "Mugsy" 170
Bol, Manute 7, 170–172, 182
Booker, Devin 70
Boozer, Carlos 52–53, 67, 152
Bosh, Chris 59, 67, 69, 74, 92–93, 98, 123
Bosnia 70, 126
Boston Americans 187
Boston Celtics 6, 26, 29, 42, 93, 101, 103–105, 110, 112–114, 116, 118–119, 124, 132, 147, 152–153, 155, 164–165, 168, 187
Boston Globe 104
Boston Red Sox 185, 188
boxing 106
Boyd, Todd 108, 110, 131
Bradley, Bill 105–108, 111, 124, 128
Brady, Tim 30
Brazil 36, 38, 48–50, 76, 117, 188

Breen, Mike 53
British Basketball League 95
Brokaw, Gary 94
Brooklyn Dodgers 188
Brooklyn Nets 11, 94, 148
Brown, Col. Bob 59
Brown, Dee 86
Brown, Hubie 16
Brown, Jaylen 155
Brown, Jim 154
Brown, Juan Ignacio Sanchez *see* Sanchez, Pepe
Brown, Larry 52, 55–57
Brown, Walter 104
Bryant, Howard 59–60, 207
Bryant, Joe "Jellybean" 63, 117
Bryant, Kobe 5, 46–47, 49, 52, 63–71, 73–74, 79, 81, 83, 85, 86, 102, 105, 117–118, 124–126, 152–154, 156, 164–165, 169, 172
Bucks *see* Milwaukee Bucks
Bullets *see* Baltimore Bullets
Bulls *see* Chicago Bulls
Burna Boy 160
Burns, Tommy 106–107
Bush, George H.W. 34, 38, 50
Bush, George W. 50–52, 135, 187
buscones 200
Buss, Dr. Jerry 28
Butler, Ernie 122
Butterworth, M.L. 198
BWB *see* Basketball Without Borders

cable television 1, 210
Camby, Marcus 81
Cameroon 11, 95, 160, 164, 173–174
Campo Las Palmas 200
Canada 2, 3, 5, 11–12, 17, 36, 49, 72, 74–99, 102, 116, 188
capitalism 4, 20, 44, 58
The Caribbean 3, 76, 91, 188, 195, 198–201, 213
Carter, Butch 87, 89
Carter, Jimmy 34
Carter, Vince 5, 49, 52, 73–74, 82–93, 97–98, 101, 116, 124
The Carter Effect 97
Casey, Dwane 95
Casiano, Eddie 53
Cavaliers *see* Cleveland Cavaliers
CBS 112
CCTV 148, 151
Celtics *see* Boston Celtics
Chamberlain, Wilt 74, 105, 108, 125
Charlotte Hornets 65, 118, 174
Chevrolet 32
Chicago American Gears 108

Index

Chicago Bulls 6, 14–16, 26, 30–31, 33, 37–38, 42, 45, 57, 79, 83, 98, 108, 118, 133, 140, 144, 150, 166, 210
Chicago Sky (WNBA) 69
China 5–6, 16–17, 67, 70–71, 76, 123, 134, 148–157, 161, 175, 180, 190, 212
Chinese Basketball Association 150
Chinese National Team 16, 150, 152
Chomche, Ulrich 211
Civil Rights Movement 6, 27, 104, 154
Clark, Caitlin 127–128
class 3
Clemens, Roger 196
Clemente, Roberto 188
Cleveland Cavaliers 26, 62, 69, 89, 93, 95, 155
Clifton, Nat "Sweetwater" 103
Clinton, Bill 134, 197–198
Clinton, Hillary 198
Clippers *see* Los Angeles Clippers; San Diego Clippers
Clooney, George 155
Coach K *see* Krzyzewski, Mike
Coimbra, Herlander 19, 37
Colangelo, Bryan 74, 93, 84
Colangelo, Jerry 56, 71, 93
The Cold War 2, 4, 39, 51, 117, 133–134
Cole, J. (Jermaine Lamarr Cole) 176
Collins, Doug 20–21, 53, 67, 69
Colombia 188
Contact Spaces of American Culture: Globalizing Local Phenomena 2
Converse 40–41
Cooper, Chuck 103–104
Cooper, Cynthia 87
Costas, Bob 115
Cousy, Bob 101, 104, 110, 111, 127
Cowens, Dave 127
Cowherd, Colin 100, 127
Crawford, Jamal 124
Creed (film) 112
Criblez, Adam J. 106
Croatia 16, 38, 108, 118, 120–121
Cruz, Ted 148
Cuba 36, 188
Cuban, Mark 121
Cuban Revolution 192
Cuellar, Marcus F. 194
cultural imperialism 178–179
Curacao 188
Curry, Stephen 10, 72, 90, 96, 101, 147, 210

Dallas Cowboys 204
Dallas Mavericks 11, 17, 73, 90, 115–116, 121–124, 141, 150, 152
Daly, Chuck 26, 35–36, 49, 57, 139–140

Daniels, Antonio 125, 127
Darfur, Sudan 155–156, 171
Darrell, Clipper (Darrell Bailey) 97
Davis, Anthony 70, 130
Dear Basketball 70
De Coubertin, Baron Pierre 14
Delfino, Carlos 53
Democratic Republic of the Congo 95, 172–174
Deng, Luol 175–176
Denver Nuggets 9, 53, 89, 94, 101, 102, 109, 115, 125–126, 130, 141, 166, 171–172, 182, 187
DeRozan, DeMar 93, 97, 99
Detroit Pistons 26–27, 30–31, 52, 57, 60, 62, 65, 81, 106, 113–115, 120, 139–140
The Digital NBA: How the World's Savviest League Brings the Court to Our Couch 1
DiMaggio, Joe 187
diplomacy 6, 131–137, 153, 194
Divac, Vlade 16, 65, 105, 118, 120
Do the Right Thing 113
Dolans, Jimmy 181
Dominican Republic 7, 188, 195, 199–203
Dominion Republic Academy System 201–202
Donaghy, Tim 118
Dončić, Luka 11, 16, 23, 71, 124, 126, 128–129, 209–210
Drake 5, 73–74, 90, 97–98, 159
The Dream Team 4–5, 18–20, 23, 25, 28–31, 33–38, 44, 46–50, 52–53, 57, 71, 77, 103, 112, 114, 120, 168, 210
Dream Team (book) 2
The Dream Team Tapes (podcast) 2, 49, 54, 69
Dream Team III 49
Dream: The Life and Legacy of Hakeem Olajuwon 2, 167
Drexler, Clyde 30, 35, 38, 168
Duffy, Ryan 135–137
Duncan, Tim 17, 46, 49, 52–54, 62–63
Durant, Kevin 10, 72, 96, 105, 116

E-40 97
Earth, Wind & Fire 159
Eastern Conference 30, 62, 89, 93, 95, 96, 120, 125, 140, 164–165
Edeshko, Ivan 21
Edwards, Aaliyah 212
Edwards, Theodore "Blue" 78
8 Mile (film) 114
Embiid, Joel 7, 11, 14, 96, 124–125, 127, 161, 164–166, 169, 173–174, 177
Eminem 114
Emirates NBA Cup 18

England 93–94
Erving, Julius "Dr. J" 63, 86, 87, 88, 109, 114
ESPN 1, 3–4, 7, 10, 14, 24, 29, 100, 154, 161, 176, 204
Europe 3, 6, 11, 70, 76, 103, 106
Ewing, Patrick 24, 29, 35–37, 168–169, 172

Facebook 187
Fader, Miran 2, 167
Falk, David 40
Fantasy football 204
Fernandez, Rudy 68
Fertitta, Tilman 148
FIBA 3, 7, 14–15, 21, 24, 60–61, 63, 67, 76–77, 174–175, 212
FIBA AmeriCup 36
FIBA Basketball World Cup 14, 71–72, 117, 146
FIBA EuroCup 95, 119
FIBA World Championships 49, 60, 119, 150
FIFA World Cup 14
Fifield, Anna 144
Finch, Chris 157
First Take 4, 100
football 186, 203–208
Forty Million Dollar Slaves 44, 103
France 9, 14, 17, 49, 76, 82, 174, 188, 211; see also Paris
Francis, Steve 79, 87, 88
Fraschilla, Fran 1, 116, 211
Frazier, Walt "Clyde" 105–106
Freedom, Enes Kanter 155
Friedman, Thomas 13
Full Dissidence: Notes from an Uneven Playing Field 59
Furphy, Johnny 211

G League Ignite 9
Gaines, Clarence "Big House" 116
Gaines, Clarence, Jr. 116
Game Theory with Bomani Jones 102
Garnett, Kevin 52, 64, 82
Gasol, Marc 46, 68, 95, 96
Gasol, Pau 17, 46, 68, 70, 95, 121, 129–130
Gaston, Cito 189
Gatorade 32
Gavitt, David 23–24, 38
Gaye, Marvin 159
gender equality 181–182
Gentile, Patrick 201
geopolitics 3, 120, 134, 156, 203, 205
Georgetown University Hoyas 23, 168, 172
Germany 16, 17, 20, 38, 67, 72, 94, 102, 115, 121, 123, 132, 188

Gervin, George "Iceman" 86
Geschwindner, Holger 121
Giannis: The Improbable Rise of an NBA Champion 2
Giddey, Josh 3, 174
Gilgeous-Alexander, Shai 129, 174, 210
Ginobili, Manu 17, 46, 53, 68, 130
Givony, Jonathan 163
globalization 2–4, 6–7, 13, 51, 71, 99, 102, 103, 112, 114, 129, 134, 156, 161, 169, 179, 186, 188–189, 203–205, 207–213
The Globetrotters *see* Harlem Globetrotters
Gobert, Rudy 14, 116, 210
Golden State Warriors 5, 17, 29, 74, 84, 86, 89, 96, 105, 123, 125, 152, 155, 168, 171, 187, 204
Goldstein, Jimmy 97
Good Morning America (TV) 10
Goodell, Roger 204
goodwill ambassadors 133, 138
governor 11, 46, 56, 77, 80, 90, 119, 121, 126, 148, 154
Graf, Steffi 123
Graham, Aubrey Drake *see* Drake
Granick, Russ 30, 48, 56
Gray, Jim 30, 66, 115
Great Britain 52
The Great Nowitzki: Basketball and the Meaning of Life 2, 122
Great White Hope 6, 103, 106–107, 111–113, 128
Greece 11, 14–15, 56, 60–61, 67, 94, 161–164
Green, Draymond 125–126
Griffey, Kenneth "Ken," Jr. 196
Griffiths, Arthur 78
Griner, Brittney 6, 133, 146–148, 156, 211
The Grizzlies *see* Memphis Grizzlies; Vancouver Grizzlies
Gulick, Luther 75
Gumbel, Bryant 29
Gumbrecht, Hans Ulrich 123

Hakeem Olajuwon Defensive Player of the Year Award 210
Halberstam, David 34
Halem, Mona 91
Hall, Arsenio 113
Hall of Fame *see* Naismith Basketball Hall of Fame
Hanes 32
Haozhou, Pu 51
Hardaway, Anfernee "Penny" 35, 49, 79
Harden, James 124, 131, 148, 165–166
The Harlem Globetrotters 6, 104, 131
Hasselhoff, David 122

Hawks *see* Atlanta Hawks
Hayes, Elvin 168
Haynes, Marques 104, 131
He Got Game (film) 54
Heat *see* Miami Heat
Heisley, Michael 80
Henderson, Edwin 104
Hennessy 176, 181
Hernández, Liván 193
Hernangomez, Juancho 115
Herrmann, Walter 53
Herzegovina 70
Hill, Brian 79
Hill, Grant 21, 35, 49, 54, 71–72, 176, 182
Hill, Jemele 41
hip-hop 5, 13, 43, 54–55, 60, 62, 70, 74, 91, 97, 108, 114, 115, 160, 176, 209
Hitler, Adolf 22
Hodges, Craig 31
Hollander, David 1
Holmgren, Chet 128, 210
Honduras 188
Hong Kong 148–150, 154, 156, 212
Hoop Dreams 200
hoops diplomacy *see* basketball diplomacy
Hoosiers 107
Hornets *see* Charlotte Hornets
horse racing 106
"the Houdini of the Hardwood" 104
Houston, Roland 213
Houston, Whitney 34, 40, 159
Houston Rockets 11, 16, 63, 79, 93, 148, 150–151, 166, 168–170, 172
How Basketball Can Save the World 1
Howard, Dwight 67, 152–153
human rights 6, 148, 155–156, 212
Huskies *see* Toronto Huskies
Hussein, Saddam 39–40, 52
Hustle (film) 115
hypermasculinity 114

Iba, Hank 21
Ibaka, Serge 95, 171, 173, 182
Ignatiev, Noel 116
Il Sung, Kim 142
immigration 74, 76, 92, 162, 211
India 11, 175
Indiana Fever 128
Indiana Pacers 18, 60, 109, 114, 118
Indiana State Sycamores 26, 111
Inside the NBA 19
Instagram 187, 204
Intercontinental Football League 205
International Basketball Federation *see* FIBA

International Olympic Committee 47
International Player Pathway program (NFL) 206, 212
Iran 52, 135
Iraq 39, 52, 59, 135
Irving, Kyrie 70, 101, 153
Ishbia, Matt 126
Israel 16, 157–158
Israel-Hamas War 157
Italy 16–17, 22–23, 63, 71, 116–117
Iverson, Allen 49, 52–56, 70, 79, 90, 124, 150, 163, 172

Jackson, Phil 33, 57, 65–66, 73, 108, 116, 140
Jackson, Stu 78–79
Jamaica 37, 168
James, LeBron 5, 10, 17, 46–47, 52, 61–63, 66–72, 93, 97, 115, 123–125, 130, 148, 154–158, 165, 169, 210
Japan 60, 185, 188, 190–192
Jefferson, Richard 52
Jeffries, Jack 106
Jeffries, Jim 106–107
Jeter, Derek 188
Jian, Ma 150
Jim Crow 132
"Jockey Syndrome" 103
Johnson, Earvin "Magic" 5, 27–29, 31, 33, 35–39, 41, 46, 49, 54–55, 60, 62, 100, 102, 103, 110, 112, 197
Johnson, Ernie 19
Johnson, Jack 106–107
Johnson, Jakob 206
Johnson, Jason 126
Johnson, Michael 47
Johnson, Robert L. 32
Joker *see* Jokić, Nikola
Jokić, Nikola 3, 6, 9, 11, 23, 71–72, 89, 101, 102, 123–139, 161, 164, 166, 169, 209, 210
Jones, Bomani 42, 102, 126
Jones, R. William 21
Jong-il, Kim 134
Jong-un, Kim 133–138, 142–146
Jordan, Michael 4, 7, 14–16, 20–21, 25, 27, 29–46, 48–50, 54–58, 60, 62, 65, 68, 70, 83, 86–89, 100, 103, 110, 117, 125, 134, 139–140, 144, 152, 166, 168–169, 198, 210
Jordan brand 7, 69, 152, 161, 176, 181
Joseph, Cory 88–89
Juergensmeyer, Mark 13
Jurassic Park 80

Kalbrosky, Bryan 126
Kamla, Rick 125, 127
Kennedy, John F. 193, 195

Kenon, Larry "Special K" 86
Kentucky Colonels 109
Kentucky Derby 103
Kenya 12, 38, 123, 177–178, 180, 182
Kern, Louis J. 2
Kerr, Steve 155
Kerry, John 163
Kidd, Jason 52, 67–68
Kings *see* Sacramento Kings
Knicks *see* New York Knickerbockers
Knight, Phil 40–41, 43, 46
Knight, Robert Montgomery "Bobby" 26, 58, 112
Kohl, Herbert 163
Kondrashin, Vladimir 21
Korea 22
Kornheiser, Tony 100
Krause, Jerry 38
Krzyzewski, Mike 5, 26, 35, 47, 57–60, 66–69, 71, 156, 212
Kukoc, Toni 16, 38–39, 68, 118, 120, 130
Kuwait 39
Kuzma, Kyle 12

Laettner, Christian 30, 37, 52, 114
LaFeber, Walter 43
Laimbeer, Bill 26
Lakers *see* Los Angeles Lakers; Minneapolis Lakers
Las Vegas Aces 98
Las Vegas Summer League tournament 98
The Last Dance (docuseries) 3, 14, 30, 44, 110, 140
Latin America 3, 7, 17, 70, 76, 106, 175, 186, 188–190, 192–203
Latvia 116
Lawrence, Andrew 166
Lebanon 11
LeBron *see* James, LeBron
LeBron, Inc.: The Making of a Billion Dollar Athlete 61
Lee, Alfred "Butch," Jr. 3
Lee, Jean H. 144
Lee, Spike 54, 97, 113
Leonard, Kawhi 95, 96, 99, 165
Lepenies, Wolf 123
Leslie, Lisa 48
Let's Go (podcast) 30
Lieberman, Joseph 171
Lin, Jeremy 95, 150
Li-Ning 69, 152
Lithuania 16–17, 38, 49, 53–54, 108, 117
Lloyd, Earl 103
Lobo, Rebecca 48
London 22, 132

Los Angeles, California 22
Los Angeles Clippers 84, 99, 150, 154, 166
Los Angeles Dodgers 186
Los Angeles Lakers 16, 18, 26, 28, 29, 37, 52, 57, 64–65, 68–70, 73–74, 90, 93–95, 102, 105, 108–109, 118, 125, 130, 141, 164, 168, 172, 204
Lowry, Kyle 93, 97
Lucas, Jerry 22, 107–108

Maccabi Tel Aviv 16
Magic *see* Orlando Magic
Magnificent Seven 47
Mahorn, Rick 26
Mailata, Jordan 206
Major League Baseball 1, 3–4, 7, 60, 71, 185–195, 198–203, 208, 212
Malcolm X 116, 157
Malone, Karl 29, 31, 35, 37, 49
Malone, Mike 9
Malone, Moses 168
Maloof Family 11
Manfred, Rob 204
Manila, Philippines 70–71
Maple Leaf Sports and Entertainment 12
Maravich, "Pistol" Pete 108
Marbury, Stephon 52–55, 153
March Madness 18
Marčiulionis, Raimondas Šarūnas 17
Maris, Roger 196
Martinez, Pedro 199
Mavericks *see* Dallas Mavericks
Maxwell, Cedric "Cornbread" 114
Mbah a Moute, Luc *see* Moute, Luc Mbah a
McCain, John 60
McCallum, Jack 2, 23, 36, 49, 54
McCloskey, Jack "Trader Jack" 26
McClung, Mac 159
McDonald's 32
McDonald's All-American team 33, 64, 84
McDonald's Open 15–16, 45, 119
McGrady, Tracy 52, 85, 87–89, 98
McGwire, Mark 196
McHale, Kevin 115
McNutt, Monica 10
Memphis 6
Memphis Grizzlies 68, 80, 90, 93, 95, 211
Mercury *see* Phoenix Mercury
Mexico 14, 17, 31, 36, 77, 175, 188
Miami Heat 9, 17, 57, 69, 93, 115, 123, 130, 154, 164, 171, 187
Michael Jordan and the New Global Capitalism 43
Michael Jordan Trophy 127

Index

Michigan State University Spartans 28, 111
Middle East 133
Midwest Basketball Conference (MBC) 76
Mikan, George 108, 131
Milholen, Chris 1
Miller, Cheryl 87, 88
Miller, Reggie 49
Milwaukee Bucks 10–11, 55, 83–84, 96, 109, 122, 125, 163–165
Ming, Yao 16, 46, 71, 79, 150, 152–153, 169, 172, 186
Minneapolis Lakers 76, 108, 131
Minnesota Timberwolves 55, 64, 78, 157
Miñoso, Orestes "Minnie" 192
minstrelsy 132
Mitchell, Sam 74, 127
MJ see Jordan, Michael
MLB see Major League Baseball
MLS (Major League Soccer) 60
Monae, Janelle 159
Moneyball 126
Monroe, Earl "the Pearl" 17, 105, 153
Monte Carlo, Monaco 36–37
Montreal Expos 189
Moore, Matt 126
Morant, Temetrius Jamel "Ja" 80, 101
Morey, Daryl 148, 150, 154
Most Valuable Player see MVP
Mourning, Alonzo 90, 172
Moute, Luc Mbah a 164
Moyo, Dambisa 176
The Mozart of Basketball 2
Mullin, Chris 24, 29, 37
Munich, Germany 20
Murakami, Masanori 191
Muresan, Gheorghe 170
Murphy, Isaac 103
Murray, Jamal 9, 89, 174
Muscular Christianity 75
Mutombo, Dikembe 7, 171–173, 175–176, 182
MVP 7, 11, 16, 29–30, 32, 49, 54–55, 66, 71, 80, 89, 101, 102, 105, 113, 122–123, 125–130, 148, 161, 164, 166, 169, 174–175
Myung-hun, Ri 135

Naismith, Dr. James 17, 75–76, 80
Naismith Basketball Hall of Fame 3, 17, 32, 46, 56, 69, 70, 76, 85, 89, 93, 97, 116–118, 122, 141, 150, 166, 168–169, 172
Naismith Cup 78
Nash, Steve 46, 79, 81, 102, 121, 123, 126
The Nation 108
National Basketball Association see NBA

National Basketball League (NBL) 16–17, 76, 108
National Football League see NFL
NBA (National Basketball Association) 17, 76, 147–148
NBA Academy 174–175, 177, 211–212
NBA Africa 175–176
NBA All-Stars 17, 42, 67, 114, 125, 128, 146, 154, 159, 163, 165–166, 172
NBA app 3, 4, 10
NBA Entertainment 48
NBA exhibition games 144
NBA Fan see "superfan"
NBA Finals 12, 37, 52, 55, 62, 65, 69, 71, 73–74, 90, 93, 96, 105, 110, 123, 130, 164
NBA home videos 34
NBA Inside Stuff 35
NBA Radio 3, 127, 181
NBA scouts 163
NBA TV 3, 7, 29, 161, 176
NBA Weekend 127
NCAA 18, 24, 29, 86, 146, 163, 168, 178, 185
Neal, Frederick "Curly" 104
Negro Leagues 191–192
Nelson, Don 16, 27
neocolonialism 3, 7, 179, 180, 199, 201, 202
Netflix 14
The Netherlands 189
Nets see New Jersey Nets; New York Nets
New Jersey Nets 16, 90, 117, 120
New World Order 39, 44
New York Knickerbockers 17, 55, 57, 76–77, 81–82, 89, 95, 103, 105, 107, 116, 124, 150, 153, 164, 169
New York Nets 109
New York Times 120
New York Yankees 185, 188
The New Yorker 126
New Zealand 132
Newble, Ira 155
NFL 3–4, 7, 14, 59–60, 71, 186–187, 203–208
NFL Africa 207
NFL Game Pass 204
NFL Network 204
NHL (National Hockey League) 60, 78, 187, 212
Nicaragua 188
Nicholson, Jack 97
Nickelodeon 204
Nigeria 5, 12, 49, 93–94, 160–162, 164, 167, 174, 176, 182
Nike 4, 7, 20, 24, 29, 40–46, 58, 62, 66, 86, 89, 97, 128, 152–153, 155–156, 161, 163, 181, 196, 210–211
1984 NBA draft 117

No Bull: The Unauthorized Biography of Dennis Rodman 138
Noah, Joakim 176
Nocioni, Andres 53
North Korea 6, 52, 133–138, 141–146, 156
Northern Ireland 133
Nostrand, George 77
Nowitzki, Dirk 2, 17, 46, 88, 102, 115, 121–124, 129–130
Nuggets *see* Denver Nuggets
Nurkic, Jusuf 126
Nurse, Nick 95, 98

Obada, Efe 206
Obama, Barack 69, 145, 173, 176, 182, 194
Ogulu, Damini Ebunoluwa *see* Burna Boy
Ogwumike, Nneka 147
Ohtani, Shohei 185, 212
OKK Beograd 24
Oklahoma City Thunder 16, 95, 98, 118, 128, 174
Okoye, Christian 206
Olajuwon, Hakeem 6–7, 49, 117, 164, 166–170, 172
Olimpia Basket Pistoia 71
Olowokandi, Michael 84
Olympiacos Piraeus 15
Olympics 2, 4–5, 14, 19, 21–22, 24–25, 27, 31, 34, 36–38, 40, 47–49, 52–55, 60, 62, 66–72, 77, 82, 93, 95, 114, 117, 120, 128, 133, 137, 146, 152, 181, 210, 212
O'Neal, Shaquille 19, 30, 49, 52, 54, 65–66, 70, 79, 87, 102, 108, 118, 124, 126, 150, 165–166, 169, 172
Ontario 17
Orlando Magic 65, 79, 89, 90, 94, 96, 118, 169
O'Rourke, Beto 148
Ortiz, David 188, 199
Owens, Jesse 22

Pacers *see* Indiana Pacers
Palestine 157–158
Pallacanestro Cantu 24
Panama 36
Panou, Georgios 162–163
Paralympics 24
Paris 10, 15, 18, 45, 57, 72, 128, 132, 144; *see also* France
Parker, Tony 17, 46, 211
Paschke, Bill 66
patriotism 5, 44, 47, 57–60, 69, 71, 187–188, 207, 212
Paul, Chris 67, 69, 154, 175
Payton, Gary 49, 88

PeacePlayers 133
Peacock 204
Perkins, Kendrick 101, 102, 130, 166
Persian Gulf War 40, 52
Peterson, Morris 74
Petit, Bob 127
Petrović, Dražen 2, 16, 118–121, 130
PGA 156, 212
Phelps, Michael 68
Philadelphia 76ers 20, 26, 28, 55–56, 63, 89, 90, 96, 114, 115, 159, 164–166, 171–172
Philadelphia Warriors 76
Philippines 190
Phoenix Mercury 56, 146
Phoenix Suns 56, 74, 90, 123, 125 -126, 130, 150, 164, 171
Pierce, Paul 49, 95
Pippen, Scottie 26, 29, 31, 33, 36–38, 49, 57, 68, 140, 169
Pistons *see* Detroit Pistons
Pitt, Brad 126
Pittsburgh Pirates 187–188
Pletzinger, Thomas 122
Popovich, Gregg 57, 71, 155
Portela, Eduardo 119
Portland Trailblazers 28, 78, 81, 117–119
Porziņģis, Kristaps 116
Prince, Tayshaun 67
Pro Football Hall of Fame 206
Prokhorov, Mikhail 11
propaganda 22, 135, 142–143, 146, 155, 193
PTI (Pardon the Interruption) 100
Puerto Rico 3, 17, 36, 38, 53, 150, 188
Puig, Yasiel 193
Puma 40, 85
Pyongyang, North Korea 144

Qatar 156–157

race 3
racial profiling 69
Radja, Dino 16, 118, 120
Rajaković, Darko 12
Ranadivé, Vivek Yeshwant 11
The Raptors *see* Toronto Raptors
Rautins, Leo 81
Reagan, Ronald 34, 39, 110
Real Madrid 16, 119
Real Sports 183
Reaves, Joseph A. 190
Redd, Michael 67
The Redeem Team 5, 47, 66–72, 93, 152–153, 159, 212
Redick, JJ 101, 102, 166
Reebok 41, 44, 58, 86, 211
Reed, Willis 105

Index

Reeves, Eric 155
Rema 160
Reyes, Sammie 206
Rhoden, William 44, 103
Rhodes scholarship 105
Richardson, Bill 147
Rihanna 159
Riley, Pat 27–28, 57
The Ringer 2, 96
Risacher, Zaccharie 210
Rise (Antetokounmpo biopic) 161
The Rise: Kobe Bryant and the Pursuit of Immortality 64
Rivers, Glenn "Doc" 94
Rivoli, Pietra 12
Roberts, Randy 86
Roberts, Robin 10
Robertson, Oscar 22
Robertson, Roland 13
Robinson, David 23, 29, 35, 37, 46, 49, 169
Robinson, Ermer 131
Robinson, Jackie 154, 188
Rock, Chris 148
Rockets *see* Houston Rockets
Rocky (film) 111, 137
Rodman, Dennis 6, 26, 30, 113–114, 133–142, 145–148, 212
Rodney, Walter 179
Romania 170
Rome 132
Rookie of the Year 7, 62, 112, 128, 210
Rose, Jalen 74, 90
Rubio, Ricky 68
Runstedtler, Theresa 106, 111, 154
Rupp, Adolph 76
Russell, Bill 31, 104, 108, 125, 159
Russia 6, 11, 16, 20–21, 23, 49, 51, 53, 67, 117, 133, 142–143, 146, 156, 193
Russo-Ukrainian War 147
Ruth, George Herman "Babe" 185, 199
Ryan, Bob 104

Sabonis, Arvydas 117–118, 130
Sabonis, Domantas 118, 210
Sacramento Kings 11, 90, 118, 174
Salley, John 27
Salters, Lisa 130
Sampson, Ralph 168
San Antonio Spurs 10, 16, 54, 57, 62, 68, 78, 83, 95, 109, 116, 140, 155
San Diego Clippers 63, 170
Sanchez, Pepe 53–54
Sandler, Adam 115
Saperstein, Abraham 131
Saratsis, Alex 162–164
Sarr, Alex 210

Saturday Night Live 3, 128, 144
Saudi Arabia 39, 51, 156, 211
Savoy Big Five *see* Harlem Globetrotters
Schmeling, Max 123
Schmidt, Oscar 50, 116–117, 130, 166
Scola, Luis 53
Scott, Byron 78
Scott, Rick 157
Seattle Supersonics 16, 98, 172–173
Sebastiani Rieti 63
Secular, Steven 1
selfless service 59
Senegal 174–175
Sengun, Alperen 11
Serbia 9, 12, 23–24, 65, 120
76ers *see* Philadelphia 76ers
Sharpe, Shannon 100
Shaw, Brian 73, 119
Siakam, Pascal 95, 160, 165, 171, 173–174, 177
Sibenka 119
Siberia 48
Sielski, Mike 64
Silver, Adam 10, 12, 44, 71, 98, 147, 154–156, 159, 175, 177, 183, 209
Simmons, Ben 3, 165–166
Simons, Raf 12
Sims, Calvin 142
Singapore 145
Singer, Mike 2,
Slaight, Allan 80
Slam (magazine) 62, 97
Slovenia 11, 119
Smelt Olimpija 119
Smiley, Capt. Scott 59
Smith, Dean 26, 57, 76, 84
Smith, Doug 2, 82
Smith, Kenny 19, 87, 88
Smith, Shane 134
Smith, Stephen A. 66, 88, 100–101, 116, 185–187, 211
soccer 5, 14, 17, 151, 167, 170
social justice 154–156
Soho 151
Sonics *see* Seattle Supersonics
Sosa, Sammy 195–199
South Africa 133, 189
South Korea 142, 188, 190
Soviet National Team 16
Soviet Union *see* Russia
Sovran, Gino 17
Spain 17, 24, 38, 46, 53, 67–68 115–117; *see also* Barcelona
Spears, Britney 11
Spehr, Todd 2
Spirits of St. Louis 109

Sports Illustrated 2, 25, 61–62, 100, 140
SportsCenter 85, 116
sportswashing 155–157, 212
Spurs *see* San Antonio Spurs
Stackhouse, Jerry 87
Staley, Dawn 48
Stalin, Joseph 143
Stallone, Sylvester 111
Stanković, Borislav "Bora" 15, 23–24, 210
"stat padding" 101
Stauskas, Nik 89
Steger, Manfred 13
Sterling, Donald 154
Stern, David 12, 15, 24, 29–30, 38, 44, 48, 55–56, 58, 77, 81, 87, 98, 116, 119, 121, 151, 155, 161, 169, 172, 181, 210–211
Stockton, John 29, 49, 117, 139, 166
Stoudamire, Damon "Mighty Mouse" 81
Strug, Kerri 48
Sudan 72, 170–171, 175
Suns *see* Phoenix Suns
Super Bowl 204
"superfan" 96–97
Supersonics *see* Seattle Supersonics
"Sweet Georgia Brown" 132
Switzerland 16, 143
Swoopes, Sheryl 48
Sydney *see* Australia

Tagliabue, Paul 205
Taiwan 11, 149, 153, 157, 188
Taliban 51–52
Tampa Bay Rays 194
Tannenbaum, Larry 12
Tao, Song 150
Tarkanian, Jerry 26
Tatum, Jason 70
Tatum, Reese "Goose" 132
Taurasi, Diana 146
Team Africa 175
Team USA 53–54, 56–58, 66–68, 82
Team World 175
Tems 160
Tencent 151, 176
Termine, Justin 104
Thomas, Isiah 26, 30–31, 81, 87, 96, 113–114, 124
Thomas, Zach 207
Thompson, John, Jr. 22–23, 55, 57, 172
Thompson, Klay 152
Thompson, Tristan 89
Thorn, Rod 25, 27–28, 30, 87
Thunder *see* Oklahoma City Thunder
TikTok 187, 204
Timberwolves *see* Minnesota Timberwolves

TNT 19–20
Tokyo 148
Toronto, Canada 49, 70, 90–99
Toronto Blue Jays 189
Toronto Huskies 17, 76–77, 89
Toronto Raptors 2, 5, 6, 11, 73–74, 77–78, 80–85, 87–90, 92–95, 97–99, 102, 116, 148, 160, 165, 169, 173, 177, 182
Trailblazers *see* Portland Trailblazers
The Travels of a T-Shirt in the Global Economy (book) 12–13
Trombone Shorty 160
Trudeau, Justin 98
Trump, Donald 133, 141, 145, 150, 155, 180
Tsai, Joseph 11, 148
Turkey 11
Twitter 187, 204

Ujiri, Masai 5, 12, 74, 93–95, 98–99, 159, 182–184, 207
Umenyiora, Ositadimma "Osi" 206–207
Un, Kim Jong 6
United Arab Emirates 156
United Nations 1
United States 14
Uprise 206
Uruguay 14, 36
USA Basketball 24, 47, 53, 56, 72
USSR *see* Soviet Union
Utah Jazz 14, 29, 45, 53, 65, 69, 116, 159

Vaccaro, Sonny 40, 62, 64, 85
Vancouver Grizzlies 2, 5, 74, 77–78, 80, 98
VanDerveer, Tara 48
Van Exel, Nick 122
Van Pelt, Scott 14
Venezuela 36, 188
Vice 134–135, 142
Vietnam 12, 191
Virgin Islands 17, 54
Virginia Interscholastic Association 103
Vitale, Dick 84

Wade, Dwyane 17, 52, 54, 59, 68–69, 93, 123, 152, 154
Wade, Zaire 176
Walter, Fritz 123
Walton, Bill 108, 111, 127
Warriors *see* Golden State Warriors; Philadelphia Warriors
Washington, Booker T. 32, 44
Washington, Denzel 116
Washington Bullets 16, 170
Washington Capitals 103
Washington Mystics 156, 212
Washington Wizards 46, 89, 95, 156

We the North 2, 82
Weis, Frederic 82–83, 116
Wembanyama, Victor 7, 9, 10, 11, 23, 71, 82, 127–128, 185, 200, 209, 210, 211
Wemby *see* Wembanyama
Wesley, William "Worldwide Wes" 62
West, Jerry Alan 22, 57, 64–65, 105, 111
West, Kanye 159
Westbrook, Russell 101, 127
Western Conference 118, 123, 125, 130, 168
Whelan, Paul 147
Whitaker, Forest 176, 182
white nationalism 69
white privilege 114
Why So Serious? The Untold Story of NBA Champion Nikola Jokic 2
Wiggins, Andrew 89, 165
Wilbon, Michael 38–39, 100
Wilder, Douglas 55
Wilkens, Lenny 16, 49
Wilkins, Dominique "The Human Highlight Film" 86, 87, 101
Windhorst, Brian 10, 61
Winning Time 113
Winters, Brian 78–79
WNBA (Women's National Basketball Association) 6, 48, 99, 128, 146–148, 212
Wojnarowski, Adrian 10

Women's National Basketball Association *see* WNBA
World Baseball Classic (WBC) 185
World Basketball Day 1
World Championships 4, 48, 66
World Football League 205
World League of American Football 205

xenophobia 120
Xu, Han 212

YMCA 75, 101, 151
Yo-Jong, Kim 146
Young, Trae 124, 165
Young Men's Christian Association *see* YMCA
YouTube 3, 4, 134, 187
Yugoslavia 14, 22–23, 49, 118

Zaire *see* Democratic Republic of the Congo
Zalgiris 117–118
Zamalek 177
Zedong, Mao 143, 151
Zhiyuan, Yao 16
ZhiZhi, Wang 150
Zirin, Dave 44, 56, 108

www.ingramcontent.com/pod-product-compliance
Lightning Source LLC
Chambersburg PA
CBHW032034300426
44117CB00009B/1051